This book reconsiders the existence of an early Stuart Puritan movement, and examines the way in which Puritan clergymen encouraged greater sociability with their like-minded colleagues, both in theory and in practice, to such an extent that they came to define themselves as 'a peculiar people', a community distinct from their less faithful rivals.

These voluntary communal rituals encouraged a view of the world divided between 'us' and 'them'. This provides a context for a renewed examination of the thinking behind debates on ceremonial nonconformity and reactions to the Laudian changes of the 1630s. From this a new perspective is developed on arguments about emigration and church government, arguments that proved crucial to Parliamentarian unity during the English Civil War.

Cambridge Studies in Early Modern British History

GODLY CLERGY IN EARLY STUART ENGLAND

Cambridge Studies in Early Modern British History

Series editors

ANTHONY FLETCHER
Professor of History, University of Essex

JOHN GUY
Professor of Modern History, University of St Andrews

and JOHN MORRILL
Reader in Early Modern History, University of Cambridge, and Vice-Master of Selwyn College

This is a series of monographs and studies covering many aspects of the history of the British Isles between the late fifteenth century and the early eighteenth century. It includes the work of established scholars and pioneering work by a new generation of scholars. It includes both reviews and revisions of major topics and books, which open up new historical terrain or which reveal startling new perspectives on familiar subjects. All the volumes set detailed research into our broader perspectives and the books are intended for the use of students as well as of their teachers.

For a list of titles in the series, see end of book

GODLY CLERGY IN EARLY STUART ENGLAND
The Caroline Puritan Movement
c.1620–1643

TOM WEBSTER

University of Edinburgh

CAMBRIDGE
UNIVERSITY PRESS

PUBLISHED BY THE PRESS SYNDICATE OF THE UNIVERSITY OF CAMBRIDGE
The Pitt Building, Trumpington Street, Cambridge CB2 1RP, United Kingdom

CAMBRIDGE UNIVERSITY PRESS
The Edinburgh Building, Cambridge CB2 2RU, United Kingdom
40 West 20th Street, New York, NY 10011–4211, USA
10 Stamford Road, Oakleigh, Melbourne 3166, Australia

First published 1997

Printed in the United Kingdom at the University Press, Cambridge

Typeset in Sabon 10/13 pt.

A catalogue record for this book is available from the British Library

Library of Congress cataloging in publication data
Webster, Tom.
Godly clergy in early Stuart England: the Caroline Puritan movement,
c. 1620–1643 / Tom Webster.
p. cm. – (Cambridge studies in early modern British history)
Includes bibliographical references.
ISBN 0 521 46170 7 (hardback)
1. Puritans – England – Clergy – History – 17th century.
2. Church of England – Clergy – History – 17th century.
3. England – Church history – 17th century.
I. Title. II. Series.
BX9334.2.W43 1997
285′.9′0942 – dc21 96–51848 CIP

ISBN 0 521 46170 7 hardback

CE

Singularity is cast upon Gods servants as their disgrace, but certainly it is their glory; they are singular, and their waies are singular, it is true, and they avouch it, they rejoyce in it, and blesse God for it; it is impossible but that it should bee so, for they are of another spirit, a peculiar people, separated from the world, set apart for God, their separation is a wonderful separation, *Exod*.33.16.

Jeremiah Burroughes, *A Gracious Spirit a Choyce and Pretious Spirit* (1638) p. 151

CONTENTS

ACKNOWLEDGMENTS

As a student working on sociability, I am aware of the emotional and intellectual aid given by my own friends and colleagues. It is, therefore, a pleasure to have the opportunity to acknowledge the benefits I have gained from the insight and encouragement I have received. My initial interest in this period was stimulated as an undergraduate and later enhanced during my transition into post-graduate work, first and foremost by Robert Ashton. The late Alan Carter offered supportive friendship which opened up the possibilities of religious history to me and gave me a pleasure in ecclesiastical architecture that will always be with me. My study was aided considerably by John Morrill, first as a supervisor and then as a friend. His patience, diligence and good humour have been invaluable sources of help in the past eight years. As anyone who has worked on early modern Essex will agree, John Walter is an indispensable guide with contagious enthusiasm. The importance I have accorded to sociability was encouraged by Frank Bremer, obviously as a writer but especially as a friend. I have gained a great deal from the following in both formal and semi-formal circumstances, not least from their tolerance of one more conversation dragged towards the subject of religion: Mary Baker, Tom Betteridge, Patrick Collinson, Richard Conner, John Craig, Mark Dever, Patrick Finney, Tom Freeman, Susan Hardman Moore, Christine Lalumia, Anthony Milton, Mike Norris, Sue Pitt, Jason Savage, John Scally, Roger Staff, Roger Thompson and Nicholas Tyacke. Two friends in particular have provided a variety of forms of support: my work would not be the same without the influence of Bob Eaglestone and Seán Matthews. Various parts of this work were presented as papers to the Early Modern British History seminar in Cambridge, to the Early Modern British History seminar in London, the History research seminar and the Inter-disciplinary group in Lampeter, the Gender and Religion colloquium at the University of East Anglia, the mid-Atlantic conference in Washington, DC and the conference on Politics and Beliefs in early modern England in Twickenham. On each occasion my thoughts were taken in new directions by the responses to each paper. I have met with unfailing efficiency and helpfulness at the various archives and libraries which I have explored. My particular thanks should be recorded to Michael Leslie of the Hartlib Papers Project in Sheffield, the staff of the Special Collections at Belfast, the archivists and staff at the Record Offices of Essex and Northamptonshire, the Rare Books Room at the Cambridge University Library and the staff of the Doctor Williams's Library and the Dean and Chapter Library at Norwich Cathedral. For parts of the research for this work I was funded by grants from the Lightfoot Fund, by the Archbishop Cranmer Fund and, above all, by the British Academy, both as a post-graduate and as a post-doctoral fellow. Easily the most influential individual in my experience has been Janice Allan. Without her, innumerable questions would not have occurred to me, innumerable possibilities would not have been explored, and innumerable problems would not have been overcome. As an inadequate expression of gratitude, this book is devoted to her and to the memory of Alan Carter.

ABBREVIATIONS

AFR	*Archiv für Reformationsgeschichte*
AHR	*American Historical Review*
AL	*American Literature*
ATR	*Anglican Theological Review*
BIHR	*Bulletin of the Institute of Historical Research*
BL	British Library
BodL	Bodleian Library, Oxford
BQ	*The Baptist Quarterly*
BRO	Berkshire Record Office
CH	*Church History*
Clarke (1662)	Samuel Clarke, *A Collection of the Lives of Ten Eminent Divines and some Other Christians* (1662)
Clarke (1677)	Samuel Clarke, *Lives of Sundry Modern Divines* appended to *A General Martyrologie* (1677)
Clarke (1683)	Samuel Clarke, *The Lives of Sundry Eminent Persons in this Later Age* (1683)
CO	Public Record Office, State Papers Colonial
CQR	*Church Quarterly Review*
CUA	Cambridge University Archives
CUL	Cambridge University Library
DNB	*Dictionary of National Biography* (ed. Sir L. Stephen and Sir. S. Lee) (London, 1908–09)
DWL	Doctor Williams's Library
EAL	*Early American Literature*
ECA	Emmanuel College, Cambridge Archives
EHR	*English Historical Review*
ER	*Essex Review*
ERO	Essex Record Office
GL	Guildhall Library, London
GLRO	Greater London Record Office
HJ	*Historical Journal*

HLB	*Harvard Library Bulletin*
HMC	*Historical Manuscripts Commission*
HRO	Hampshire Record Office
H&T	*History and Theory*
HT	*History Today*
HTM	*History Teachers' Miscellany*
HTR	*Harvard Theological Review*
JAS	*Journal of American Studies*
JBS	*Journal of British Studies*
JEH	*Journal of Ecclesiastical History*
JHI	*Journal of the History of Ideas*
JMH	*Journal of Modern History*
JMRS	*Journal of Medieval and Renaissance Studies*
JPHS	*Journal of the Presbyterian Historical Society*
JRH	*Journal of Religious History*
LP	Lambeth Palace Library
LRO	Leicestershire Record Office
Mather	Cotton Mather, *Magnalia Christi Americana* (1704)
MHSC	*Massachusetts Historical Society Collections*
MHSP	*Massachusetts Historical Society Proceedings*
NCO	New College, Oxford
NEHGR	*New England Historical and Genealogical Register*
NEQ	*New England Quarterly*
NorRo	Norfolk Record Office
NPP	*Northamptonshire Past and Present*
NRO	Northamptonshire Record Office
PAPS	*Proceedings of the American Philosophical Society*
PCSM	*Publications of the Colonial Society of Massachusetts*
PH	*Parliamentary History*
PP	*Past and Present*
PRO	Public Record Office
QUB	Queen's University, Belfast
RSCHS	*Records of the Scottish Church History Society*
SC	*The Seventeenth Century*
SCH	*Studies in Church History*
SCJ	*Sixteenth Century Journal*
SHR	*Scottish Historical Review*
SL	*Studia Liturgica*
SP	Public Record Office, State Papers Domestic
STC	A. W. Pollard and G. R. Redgrave (eds.), *Short Title Catalogue of English Books, 1475–1640* (London, 1976, 1986)

SU	Sheffield University
TB	*Tyndale Bulletin*
TBHS	*Transactions of the Baptist History Society*
TEAS	*Transactions of the Essex Archaeological Society*
TRHS	*Transactions of the Royal Historical Society*
VCH	*Victoria County History*
Venn	J. A. Venn and J. Venn, *Alumni Cantabrigienses* (Cambridge, 1922–54)
WMQ	*William and Mary Quarterly*

Introduction

'All thought', wrote Fernand Braudel, 'draws life from contacts and exchanges'.[1] In a sense, this may serve as an epigram for all that follows. I have been concerned to trace a clerical community, or rather a series of overlapping and interlocking communities, to examine forms of contact and exchange, and to root these forms in a piety that encouraged a sociability beyond the stimuli of professional identity and the duties of kinship ties. The godly clergy who are the subject of this study took their relationships with their like-minded colleagues well beyond these 'natural' needs, and it is this heightened sense of community that needs to be explained. We should not assume that the very notion of 'community' is a trans-historical phenomenon, simply a matter of 'friends getting together for a chat'. The communities that I deal with are not forms of the pre-modern, face-to-face, 'natural' communities of Ferdinand Tönnies' *Gemeinschaft* but the 'imagined communities' of a complex, pluralist society.[2] 'Community' here is not the organic solidarity of homogeneous individuals, not an integrative device as in Durkheim, but a way of thinking that aggregates and often serves to deny heterogeneities, particularly at the boundaries of community. As Arthur Hildersham pleaded: 'Though we differ in iudgement in these things, yet should we endeavour, that the people may discerne no difference, nor disagreements amongst us.'[3]

The communities that are the subject of this study defined themselves through a variety of voluntary religious practices which blurred our boundaries of religious, social and administrative activities. The intellectual

---

[1] F. Braudel, *Civilization and Capitalism from the Fifteenth to the Eighteenth Century, vol. I. The Structures of Everyday Life: the Limits of the Possible* (London, 1981), p. 401.

[2] F. Tönnies, *Community and Society* (trans. C. P. Loomis) (London, 1955), originally published as *Gemeinschaft und Gesellschaft* (Darmstadt, 1887); B. Anderson, *Imagined Communities* (London, 1991); A. P. Cohen, *The Symbolic Construction of Community* (Chichester, 1993). Anderson's concern is largely with national communities, but the point applies here.

[3] Cohen, *Symbolic Construction of Community*, pp. 20, 74; Arthur Hildersham, *CVIII Lectures upon the Fourth of John* (1632) p. 301.

and spiritual demands of the hotter sort of Protestantism challenged alternative allegiances and placed godly ministers in a network of like-minded brethren. This network in turn reinforced and sustained a particular style of piety. In conditions that made members of the godly clerical community feel under threat, even under a campaign of persecution, the protection of that community could come first, even at the expense of other loyalties.

To a large degree, the first half of this study can be seen as an extended meditation on the familiar theme from Durkheim that it is 'through common action that society becomes conscious of and affirms itself; society is above all an active cooperation. Even collective ideas and feelings are possible only through the overt movements that symbolize them. Thus it is action that dominates religious life, for the very reason that society is its source.'[4] My interest in the relationships between collective consciousness and religion may be a symptom of a current shift the former conditions of society and faith that preoccupied Durkheim and his tutor Fustel de Coulanges[5] have undergone, moving to an outlook where the primary focus of religion is on the relationship between a deity and the individual.[6] If my interests are a response to my historical context, I have also taken Durkheim's terms of religion and society in their place in seventeenth-century discourse. Professor Bossy has alerted us to the archaeology of these crucial terms: in particular, I have taken 'society' as the Northamptonshire divine Robert Cawdrey defined it, as a fellowship rather than as a commonwealth,[7] as a combination of individuals in a society rather than the modern (and usually capitalised) sense of an overarching society combining all within a nation. 'Religion' had a primary meaning of 'attitude of worship' or 'way of being pious' with an emergent abstract sense of *a* religion, of religions of differential veracity in a new condition of pluralism. This second sense, shorn of truth claims, is so powerfully our sense of the word that I have tended to employ the rather ugly term 'religiosity' in preference. The period in question was exactly that moment when, in both cases, the second sense was rising but the first still primary. In the strain between these two meanings, particular and general, I would

---

[4] E. Durkheim, *The Elementary Forms of Religious Life* (trans. and intro. K. E. Fields) (New York, 1995) p. 421.

[5] N. D. Fustel de Coulanges, *The Ancient City: a Study on the Religion, Laws and Institutions of Greece and Rome* (trans. W. Small) (Boston, Mass., 1900).

[6] L. Revell, 'The Return of the Sacred', in S. Wolton (ed.), *Marxism, Mysticism and Modern Theory* (London, 1996) pp. 111–34.

[7] J. Bossy, 'Some Elementary Forms of Durkheim', *PP* 95 (1982) pp. 3–18; Robert Cawdrey, *A Table Alphabeticall, Conteyning and Teaching the True Writing and Understanding of Hard Usuall English Words . . .* (1604), s.v.

suggest, lies the problem of Puritanism, both for contemporaries and for historians.[8]

Having established some patterns of association and contact, rooted in clerical piety and practice, I have drawn out a series of exchanges conditioned by the changed ecclesiastical environment of the 1620s and 1630s which disrupted the settled patterns of voluntary religion. Through these years, new, and renewed, questions were raised which created and deepened fissures and faultlines within godly society. These debates can best be understood by placing them in the context of the relationship with the ecclesiastical establishment, not least in the episcopal visitations. The social context of the first part of this study provides a context for the debates which led, through a series of mutations and transformations, to what I have called the 'diaspora' of the godly ministers, the fragmentation of clerical society. Before the emergent divisions of the 1640s, the godly community can be seen in action, considering questions of flight or suffering, and of support for the ecumenical efforts of John Dury. This context also serves to illuminate the content of some of these debates, particularly on ecclesiological issues.

I have generally followed recent practice in preferring terms like 'the godly' and 'the professors' to the dangerously nominalistic category of 'Puritan'. The name was, of course, coined as a term of opprobrium, and many students of the period would add a hearty 'Amen' to John Yates' wish, 'that this offensive name of a Puritan, wandring at large, might have some Statute passe upon it, both to define it, & punish it: for certainly Satan gains much by the free use of it'.[9] It may be true that Satan (or at least a considerable historiographical sub-discipline) has benefited from an over-enthusiastic employment of the term, but, as Ian Breward has pointed out, if contemporaries like Baxter had not used the term, historians would have had to invent it.[10] Where I have used the word it is intended to denote an anti-formalist search for 'heart religion', for truly valid religious experience that found it difficult to endure any stumbling block to that search. Among the obstacles so perceived were, for some, the controverted Prayer Book ceremonies. Non-conformity is not the definition of a Puritan, merely the symptom of an unwillingness to compromise what is seen as a scripturally given form. Moreover, it will become clear that a considerable part of that world-view overlapped with that which has been called 'mere' Protestant and also that the dangers of the term are never more apparent than when it is assumed to have a single, static and essential referent. The

[8] Bossy, pp. 3–5; R. Williams, *Keywords: a Vocabulary of Culture and Society* (London, 1983 edn) pp. 291–5.

[9] John Yates, *Ibis ad Caesarem* (1626) pt. III p. 40.

[10] I. Breward, 'The Abolition of Puritanism', *JRH* 7 (1972) p. 32.

communities that form the heart of this study proved to be extraordinarily heterogeneous, but their members could all be called godly and most could fairly uncontroversially carry the name Puritan. In addition, it has become clear that the dangers of labelling a practice or a doctrine 'Puritan' spring in part from an insensitivity to social contexts and usages, but that the term, having the authority of contemporary currency, is admissible if used in ways that allow for fluidity and variety within the English Church.[11] I hope I have used it in these ways, having paid particular attention to the social patterns and connections that marked those referred to as Puritans as, in Petrine terms, 'a peculiar people'.

However, it is part of my contention that it is not necessary to adhere strictly to this rubric. The term 'godly' is useful because it has the *imprimatur* of self-application, because 'the godly' referred to themselves as such. This is certainly a valuable addition to our vocabulary in describing and understanding the behaviour of these people. We should not, however, adopt the self-image of a group as uncritically as scholars once accepted the terms used by others to describe them. Self-descriptions are as polemically loaded as labels applied by others. An 'objective' *via media* is not available, so we have to examine the dialectic between competing contemporary descriptions, each of which is positioned in seventeenth-century discourse. Accordingly, my usage varies somewhat, depending on the point of view refracted through a third perspective, my own, positioned in relation to these debates and those of modern historiography.

At this point, it may not be premature to offer some preliminary auto-critique, less to disarm potential critics than to make explicit the limits of the claims this study makes. What follows is far from a comprehensive account of a Stuart 'Puritan movement', if such a creature existed. Here, I want to draw attention to some of the more glaring deficiencies and suggest reasons beyond the usual limitations of space and talent.

The most serious criticism is perhaps that this is a study that discusses Puritanism in exclusively clerical terms. I must make it clear that the account given of clerical Puritanism is not in any way intended to stand metonymically for Puritanism as a whole. Puritanism was not exclusively, or even predominantly, a clerical phenomenon. The restriction is taken precisely because this was not so: it is too easy in attempting an integrated account to allow the voluble, visible clergy to speak for groups less well represented in documentary traces. We have a growing body of literature on the laity, divided in terms of social status and gender, the noble professors, men and women, and the middling sorts, and important work on the particular inflections that these positions bring to religious experi-

---

[11] P. Collinson, 'A Comment: Concerning the Name Puritan', *JEH* 31 (1980) pp. 483–8.

ence and activity.[12] For women (though not yet for men) we are slowly learning how concepts of gender and piety interact in a dialectic, each being modified by the other.[13] It should prove possible to consider gender inflection for masculine piety, too, once we stop regarding it as the norm which is modified in feminine piety. For instance, bridal imagery drawn from Canticles is often seen as a particular resource sustaining a female piety. We might consider how this imagery, applied by male clergy to themselves, subverts normative gender categories.[14] Similarly, we might consider how the piety of an exclusively male clergy interacts with gender assumptions. To give just one example, the common depiction of the preaching clergy as 'breasts' to their congregations, drawn from scriptural examples, might be seen to modify clerical masculinities.[15]

To some, a more glaring omission will be the relative neglect of clerical relations with these other groups – the clergy depicted here are an inward-looking group, rarely interacting with the laity, with the noble professors or with humbler saints. While this dimension is not wholly neglected, it should be stressed that the emphasis on clerical collegiality has perhaps overstated the autonomy of the clergy. Stephen Foster, for instance, has pressed a compelling case for changes in clerical ideas being driven by changes in relations with an increasingly confident and vociferous laity.[16] One does not have to accept his argument uncritically to acknowledge the role of such relations in changes within godly culture.[17]

---

[12] J. T. Cliffe, *The Puritan Gentry: the Great Puritan Families of Early Stuart England* (London, 1984); P. Seaver, *Wallington's World: a Puritan Artisan in Seventeenth Century London* (London, 1985); D. Willen, 'Godly Women in Early Modern England: Puritanism and Gender', *JEH* 43 (1992) pp. 561–80; P. Lake, 'Feminine Piety and Personal Potency: the "Emancipation" of Mrs Jane Radcliffe', *SC* 2 (1987) pp. 143–65.

[13] P. Crawford, *Women and Religion in England 1500–1720* (London, 1993); A. Patterson, 'Women's Attraction to Puritanism', *CH* 60 (1991) pp. 196–209; A. Patterson, *Female Piety in New England: the Emergence of Religious Humanism* (New York, 1992) esp. ch. 2; M. P. Hannay (ed.), *Silent but for the Word: Tudor Women as Patrons, Translators, and Writers of Religious Works* (Kent, Ohio, 1985); E. Hobby, *Virtue of Necessity: English Women's Writing 1649–88* (London, 1988) ch. 2.

[14] See Willen, 'Godly Women', p. 568; C. W. Bynum, *Holy Feast and Holy Fast: the Religious Significance of Food to Medieval Women* (Berkeley, Calif., 1987) pp. 28, 290–1; L. Pollock, *With Faith and Physic: the Life of a Tudor Gentlewoman Lady Grace Mildmay 1552–1620* (London, 1993) pp. 50, 75; for clerical adoption of this imagery, Robert Bolton, *Directions for a Comfortable Walk with God* (1636) p. 93; QUB Percy Ms 7 ff. 62, 174, 218, 313, 319, 334. For a stimulating discussion of German masculinity in the early modern period, see L. Roper, *Oedipus and the Devil: Witchcraft, Sexuality and Religion in Early Modern Europe* (London, 1994) pp. 107–24.

[15] For examples, D. Leverenz, *The Language of Puritan Feeling: an Exploration in Literature, Psychology and Social History* (New Brunswick, N.J., 1980) pp. 29, 143–4, 216. See below, pp. 101–5, 126–8.

[16] S. Foster, *The Long Argument: English Puritanism and the Shaping of New England Culture, 1570–1700* (Chapel Hill, N.C., 1991).

[17] I have attempted a case study in *Stephen Marshall and Finchingfield* (Chelmsford, 1994).

A second set of criticisms might arise from the geographical focus of this study. If it is read as a comprehensive account of clerical professors in the reign of Charles I, it will justifiably be slighted as a story overly dominated by Cambridge University, by Emmanuel College and by the south-east of England. Here, it must be made clear that this is a regional study, drawing upon East Anglia and the east Midlands, with all the advantages and disadvantages of the genre: detail, particularism, contextual depth and a very real temptation to generalise to regions less well known. Other regions may well show different patterns of sociability, may encourage other routes to different ecclesiologies, particularly when those other areas are less densely colonised by the godly. The dynamics identified here, for instance, bear little relationship to the experience of the youthful Richard Baxter.[18]

As the reader will become aware, I have found godly biographies a useful source, especially those in Cotton Mather's *Magnalia Christi Americana* and in the collections of Samuel Clarke. Historians have, quite justly, been warned against taking these works as entirely trustworthy accounts, so it seems necessary to take a little time to contextualise them. We have been provided with an account of the genealogy of Clarke's works by Patrick Collinson, drawing attention to classical roots, the influence of John Foxe and to the emergence of godly hagiography, particularly in funeral sermons and 'lean-to' lives. For our purposes, it is most important to note the topos of 'moderation', both in spiritual and in ecclesiological terms, that Clarke's subjects were said to possess.[19] Of course, it was a common trait in early modern religious rhetoric, advocates of the Church of England presenting themselves as followers of a *via media* between Catholicism and Sectarianism, Congregationalists of the 1640s as the occupants of a *via media* between authoritarian Presbyterians and chaotic Separatists. As Clarke's collections were aimed at an audience of the post-Restoration world, we may not be surprised to find that part of his polemic was to show the godly of the first part of the century to be loyal members of the Church of England, doing battle with Separatists on the one side and Romanists on the other. I have, I hope, been appropriately cautious in trusting Clarke in his accounts of pastoral practice and lifestyle, being more inclined to accept his encomia of godly ministers as Boanerges, the son of thunder, a panegyric applied by contemporaries, than as Barnabus, the son of reconciliation, absent from earlier accounts.[20] As with my use of Mather, I have tested his biographies against the evidence of earlier sources. The first part of the *Magnalia*, the biographies of the four Johns, Cotton, Norton,

---

[18] J. M. Lloyd Thomas (ed.), *The Autobiography of Richard Baxter* (London, 1931) pp. 3–4, 6.

[19] P. Collinson, '"A Magazine of Religious Patterns": an Erasmian Topic Transposed in English Protestantism', in *Godly People: Essays on English Protestantism and Puritanism* (London, 1983) pp. 499–525.

[20] See below, p. 101.

Davenport and Wilson, with an appendix devoted to Thomas Hooker, had been published in 1695 as *Johannes in Eremo*, with two goals in mind. As has been shown, the idea was to make it clear to William III that New England's rebellion against James II had not been an expression of latent Separatism in the colonies and a defence of the Mathers against the 'presbyterianising' tendencies of Solomon Stoddard in Massachusetts. These biographies were included, with significant changes in the *Magnalia*, the changes intended to serve an English dissenting audience in an attempt to give some historical flesh to the union of Presbyterians and Congregationalists supported by Mather's father, Increase Mather.[21] Stylistically, attention has been drawn to Cotton Mather's constant attention to suffering and persecution experienced by his subjects, caused both by bishops and by ill-health, as a spiritual exercise revealing the convictions, patience and steadfastness of the godly.[22] While it would be a sign of foolishness to look to a godly biographer for a wholly detached account of the clerical experiences of the 1630s, special care must be taken with Mather not to be seduced by what amount to sensationalist stories of suffering, ecclesiastical or physical, that characterised his mixture of epic and jeremiad. As the work was completed shortly before 1700, it fits into a similar polemic context as *Johannes in Eremo*.[23] Mather is concerned to portray a relative Jacobean consensus, disrupted by Romanising changes under Laud, coincidently fitting into a framework surprisingly similar to the present historiographical context. Despite these reservations, *Magnalia Christi Americana* can be taken seriously as a source, evinced both by his voluminous correspondence,[24] and by the frequency with which his accounts find support in other sources, both godly and otherwise. Accordingly, I have used these sources, I hope constantly, with a reasonable amount of caution and borne in mind their limitations and dangers, relying upon their veracity only in areas where they are supported by other sources.

These criticisms, and I am sure there are many others, could be subsumed under a general heading. This book is not the answer to all the questions we have about Caroline religiosity among the godly. It is a contribution to an ongoing conversation, conducted in many different places, between many different people. That conversation shows no signs of abating, with or without my contribution. If I provide any new dimensions to that conversation, then this contribution will have been worthwhile.

[21] P. H. Smith, 'Politics and Sainthood: Biography by Cotton Mather', *WMQ* 3rd ser. 20 (1963) pp. 186–206.

[22] K. Halttunen, 'Cotton Mather and the Meaning of Suffering in the *Magnalia Christi Americana*', *JAS* 12 (1978) pp. 311–29.

[23] K. Silverman, *The Life and Times of Cotton Mather* (New York, 1984) pp. 156–66.

[24] See K. Silverman, 'Cotton Mather's Foreign Correspondence', *EAL* 3 (1968–9) pp. 172–85.

Part I

SOCIETY, CLERICAL CONFERENCE AND THE CHURCH OF ENGLAND

From 28 to 30 December 1625, a fast was held at Hatfield Broad Oak in Essex, the home of the Barrington family. Sermons were delivered to the gathering of ministers and laity by John Preston, the master of Emmanuel College, Cambridge, and by James Ussher, recently promoted to the archbishopric of Armagh.[1] It may be dangerous to speculate about the issues raised and discussed at this fast, but the timing is suggestive. As James Harrison, the Barrington chaplain, observed six months later, a fast is called 'when great things are undertaken . . . , when any judgement is imminent . . . , when the church is in danger and when affliction is upon the church'.[2] Preston preached on the first day on 1 Sam. 12.20.

And Samuel said unto the people, Fear not: ye have done all this wickedness: yet turn not from following the LORD, but serve the LORD with all your heart.

Preston stressed that this exhortation applied to his audience, whom God had chosen for His people, and stressed the dangers of the time, calling for renewed zeal in serving the Lord. On the following day, Ussher reminded them that 'it is the goodnesse of God though he hath his remnant here, yet he can have more close; wherefore it stands us in hand to labour to keep in God'. He called upon his audience to 'desire God to give uss peace, to build upp the walls'.[3] While renewal of zeal and watchfulness are common themes of godly preaching, it is difficult to believe that those present at the fast did not discuss the forthcoming York House Conference. The conference, which signalled the Duke of Buckingham's commitment to the Arminian cause, met between 11 and 17 February 1626.[4] Essex was likely

---

[1] ERO D/DBa F5/1.
[2] Ibid.; cf. Robert Bolton, *A Threefold Treatise* (1634) pp. 38, 62 (3rd pagination).
[3] ERO D/DBa F5/1. Can Preston's auditors have been unaware that the evil referred to was very specific? The previous verse reads: 'And all the people said to Samuel, "Pray for your servants to the Lord your God, that we may not die: for we have added to all our sins this evil, to ask for ourselves a King." '
[4] N. Tyacke, *Anti-Calvinists: the Rise of English Arminianism c. 1590–1640* (Oxford, 1987) ch. 7; B. Donegan, 'The York House Conference Revisited: Laymen, Calvinism and Arminianism', *BIHR* 64 (1991) pp. 312–30.

to be a focus of concern among Calvinists, for Richard Montague, whose writings have been traced as an index of the rise of Arminianism, was an Essex minister, and two ministers with close connections with the Essex godly, Nathaniel Ward, beneficed a mile from Montague, and John Yates, were prominent in the parliamentary attacks on his work.[5]

It cannot be entirely coincidental that informal meetings of London clergy were formalised on 15 February 1626, with the support of London merchants and lawyers, into the Feoffees for Impropriations, an organisation dedicated to buying the rights of presentation to benefices and using them to establish godly preachers in prominent pulpits. Within months, similar organisations can be traced in Leicester, Reading and Norwich, coordinated by central direction. Peter Heylin, who knew as much as any hostile informant, noted that the Feoffees began 'when Preston governed the affairs of the Puritans'.[6]

Here, however, we are more interested in a less noted event, one which provides an entry into godly preoccupations at once more mundane and of greater long-term consequence. At the Hatfield Broad Oak fast it seems likely that discussions were held regarding the settlement of Thomas Hooker in a preaching post in Essex.[7] Hooker had been unsettled for some years. In 1619, Preston had written to Ussher asking:

> What say you to Mr Hookers; his employment is too narrow here, and not adequate to his parts. He was in primis for scholarship while he was in Cambridge.[8]

Hooker had left Cambridge for his home county of Leicestershire, possibly residing with Arthur Hildersham, who had dominated his parish of Ashby-de-la-Zouch since the 1580s. In 1619, Hooker was detected preaching at Blaby and East Shilton, and in 1620 at Stoke Golding, Birstall and Whetstone.[9] His sermons proved popular with the godly of south Leicestershire: prosecutions followed for individuals following his progress and neglecting preachers in their own parishes.[10] He next appeared in Surrey, at Esher, where he was one of a number of divines ministering to

---

[5] Tyacke, ch. 6 esp. p. 148; cf. S. Lambert, 'Richard Montague, Arminianism and Censorship', *PP* 124 (1989) pp. 36–58.

[6] I. M. Calder, 'A Seventeenth Century Attempt to Purify the Anglican Church', *AHR* 53 (1948) pp. 760–75; Calder (ed.), *Activities of the Puritan Faction of the Church of England* (London, 1957); PRO SP 16/538/13; 531/134; J. M. Guilding (ed.), *Reading Records* (London, 1895) vol. II p. 266; Cotton Mather, *Magnalia Christi Americana* (1704) Book III, p. 73 (cited henceforth as Mather); Heylin, quoted in I. Morgan, *Prince Charles's Puritan Chaplain* (London, 1957) p. 180; see below, pp. 81–6.

[7] This is argued at greater length in T. Webster, 'The Godly of Goshen Scattered: an Essex Clerical Conference in the 1620s and its Diaspora', Cambridge PhD, 1993, pp. 68–77.

[8] C. R. Edrington (ed.), *Usher's Whole Works* (Dublin, 1847–64) vol. XVI p. 37.

[9] LRO 1D 43/13/50 ff. 48, 49, 175; 53 f. 43.

[10] LRO 1D 43/13 53 f. 43.

Joan Drake. After Drake moved to Amersham, in Hampshire, he followed her, and it was here he married her maidservant, on 3 April 1621.[11] According to an admirer, Hooker, 'being a Non-conformitan in judgement, not willing to trouble himselfe with Presentative Livings', was persuaded to accept the curacy by John Dod, a post from which Hooker was removed during 1622, possibly for preaching against the Spanish Match, and from this time he seems to have been seeking alternative employment.[12] Mather states that at this time, 'he did more publickly and frequently preach about London', and indeed he has been shown to have been available to give advice in the capital, for he helped to settle a dispute within the Plymouth Company in early 1625.[13] In 1624, Hooker was licensed to teach in the diocese of London without a parish being specified, which was very unusual: he seems to have been unsettled in this period.[14] He probably felt disinclined to take a new post while his patron's spiritual troubles continued. He was present at her deathbed on 18 of April 1625, and was probably there when John Preston preached her funeral sermon. He probably continued to preach in and around London and visited his friends in Essex; he was frustrated in his efforts to take a post at Colchester to be near his friend John Rogers of Dedham.[15]

If one of the tasks of the Hatfield Broad Oak fast was to place Hooker in a post where he might most effectively advance the godly cause, they seem to have met with some success. Shortly after, he was established as lecturer

---

[11] G. H. Williams, N. Pettit, W. Herget and S. Bush (eds.), *Thomas Hooker: Writings in England and Holland 1625–1633*, Harvard Theological Studies 28 (Cambridge, Mass., 1975) p. 5.

[12] Jasper Heartwell, *Trodden Down Strength* (1647) p. 117; (the title page of the tract attributes it to 'Hart On-Hi': for the attribution to Heartwell, see G. H. Williams, 'Called by thy Name, Leave us not: the Case of Mrs Joan Drake, a Formative Episode in the Pastoral Career of Thomas Hooker in England', *HLB* 16 (1968) pp. 278–90; John Browning's letter to Laud (see below pp. 152–3), mentioning Hooker's earlier trouble, suggests that his removal was on the explicit orders of King James, which would be consistent with Hooker's offence lying in preaching on this topic. He was certainly willing to pass judgement on Charles' eventual choice of wife: SP 16/151/12; Mather, III p. 60; HRO B/1A 28–9 (unfol., 1 June 1620 and 6 June 1622); part of the charge of Richard Churchman for gadding to Blaby to hear Hooker noted that 'the said mr Hooker being a silenced minister as yet is suspended', LRO 1D 41/13/50 f. 48; T. Cogswell, 'England and the Spanish Match', in R. Cust and A. Hughes (eds.), *Conflict in Early Stuart England* (London, 1989) pp. 134–67.

[13] Mather, III p. 59; F. Shuffleton, *Thomas Hooker 1586–1647* (Princeton, N.J., 1977) p. 72. It is interesting to note this early willingness to keep society with Separatists.

[14] GLRO DL/C 342 f. 44v.

[15] Mather, III p. 59. Mather seems to have an account separate from the published version of Joan Drake's life, which gave him accurate information for this part of Hooker's life. Susanna Hooker has been suggested as a source for Mather's account of the Esher period; she or John Eliot could have given information about his time in Essex. Eliot certainly furnished Mather with information about Hooker's seminary, see Williams *et al.*, *Thomas Hooker*, p. 6.

in Chelmsford, where he seems to have applied the lessons preached by Preston and Ussher. Cotton Mather tells us that:

The Godly Ministers round the Country would have recourse unto him to be directed in their difficult cases; and it was by his means that those Godly Ministers held their Monthly Meetings, for fasting and Prayer and Profitable Conferences. 'Twas the Effect of his consultations, also, that such Godly Ministers came to be here and there settled in several parts of the Country; and many others came to be better established in some great points of Christianity by being in his Neighbourhood and Acquaintance.[16]

Hooker's activities among the godly ministers were held, in some quarters, to be a wholly disruptive influence. By 1629, Samuel Collins, the vicar of Braintree, was convinced that his 'private conference . . . hath already impeached the peace of our church more than his public ministry . . . our people's pallets grow so out of taste that no food contents them but of Mr Hookers dressing'.[17] A more positive assessment was offered by John Fuller, the 'hot young fellow' who was lecturer of Great Waltham, when he recalled his friendship with John Beadle, the former rector of Little Leighs, the seat of the Earl of Warwick:

We often breathed out our souls together in Prayer, Fasting and conferences . . . at which time he had the happiness of a younger Elisha . . . to be watered by the droppings of the great Elijah, that renowned man of God in his generation, Mr Thomas Hooker.[18]

Mather's account gives four areas of activity requiring examination: firstly, fasting and prayer; secondly, 'profitable conferences'; thirdly, the settlement of godly ministers; and fourthly, the further education of ministers. These various functions were exercised in a monthly meeting of ministers who clearly identified, and recognised each other, as 'godly ministers'. This section will use Hooker's work to contextualise these activities. The contrasting perceptions of Collins and Fuller will be shown to correspond to tensions within the meetings of the godly in the context of the evolving church.

Hooker's early career may have been unusually unstable, but it was not markedly untypical of a generation of godly ministers emerging from Cambridge at this time. His appointment as Dixie fellow meant that he was a few years older than some of his associates, with perhaps a little more authority than most, but it is useful to place him in the context of a group of like-minded men in the Cambridge circle of John Preston who were leaving the university in the 1620s or who had left somewhat earlier. Many of those ministers would have been at Hatfield Broad Oak. We can identify

---

[16] Mather III pp. 59–60.   [17] SP 16/142/113.
[18] Ep. Ded. to John Beadle, *The Journal or Diary of a Thankful Christian* (1656).

those closest to Preston through the will he made in 1618. He made a bequest of a piece of plate to John Dod and provided for a number of friends to choose a book from his library. These friends included Richard Sibbes, John Cotton, Robert Bolton, William Price, the mentor of Thomas Goodwin, Peter Bulkeley and Thomas Hooker. Martin Holbeach, the schoolmaster of Felsted in Essex, who owed his job to Preston, witnessed the will.[19] The presence of John Dod reminds us that Preston was equally intimately connected with clerical leaders of the previous generation. Arthur Hildersham consulted Preston before publishing his lectures on John in 1615; Laurence Chaderton remained one of Preston's closest advisers after the older man had retired from the mastership of Emmanuel; John Rogers, the elderly lecturer of Dedham, exchanged pupils with him, and Richard Sibbes survived to edit some of his lectures with the assistance of John Davenport and Thomas Goodwin. In the 1620s, Preston was at the hub of a clerical community, receiving neophyte ministers into the world of Cambridge, guiding them through their education and on into the over-lapping communities of godly ministers in the provinces.[20]

In taking this social approach to the world of the godly cleric, we can trace something of a life-cycle, from college to preaching post, which is far from uniform but which allows an entry into a complex social world. Starting with the university, we can follow young clergymen into the country, to household seminaries and to meetings for further education, and then on into the mature ministry, examining the impulses that brought ministers together, forged and defined community.

In considering the occasions that ministers, godly or otherwise, came together for various purposes, a considerable fluidity of expression quickly becomes evident. Moreover, these activities easily combine and conflate: there is rarely a distinction between spiritual, administrative and educational spheres. Further taxonomical difficulties arise in the use, for instance, of 'conference' or, in hostile contexts, 'conventicle' for voluntary religious exercises involving clergy and laity, and also for exclusively clerical meetings. In the Wirrel, for example, 'besides these publick ordinances, we had once in three weeks ordinarily a day of Conference, unto which repaired all the Professors, both men and women, out of all the Countrey'.[21] Here my

[19] PRO PROB 11/154.
[20] For details, see ch. 1 below. The only modern biography of Preston is disappointing: I. Morgan, *Prince Charles's Puritan Chaplain*; the best introduction is the biography by his pupil, Thomas Ball: E. W. Harcourt (ed.), *The Life of The Renowned Doctor Preston* (Oxford, 1885) and *DNB*.
[21] Samuel Clarke, *The Lives of Sundry Eminent Persons in this Later Age* (1683) p. 4. Cited hereafter as Clarke (1683). For the elasticity of the term 'conventicle' as an index of voluntary religious activism see P. Collinson, 'The English Conventicle', *SCH* 23 (1986) pp. 223–61.

interests are principally with meetings attended exclusively by ministers or those intending to enter the ministry. The problems of nomenclature are not to be ignored: when activities which appear to us to be separate are self-evidently related for past actors, we can gain insights into their meanings. However, for the purposes of analysis, some distinctions can be made, and prove to be useful in mapping the structures of association among the godly ministry.

By inverting the order of the activities listed by Mather, we are given a framework for considering the social context of the typical career followed by students and young ministers in these regions, a career that integrated them into a godly clerical community. The following chapters examine this path from voluntary association in the University, through a period of further education to settlement in a preaching position. For those ministers settled in the areas densely populated with godly ministers there were, in addition, a number of circumstances that continued to bring ministers together, maintaining the godly community and defining its boundaries.

1

Clerical education and the household seminary

We can profitably begin a sketch of the life-cycle of the godly ministry at Cambridge. In what follows, I have focused on Emmanuel College, where John Preston was Master from 1622 to 1628, not because it was the only college to produce godly ministers but because it was the college which became identified with such ministers more than any other and because it was pre-eminent in the areas under study. I have paid little attention to the traditional areas of university histories, institutional details, social background and the structures of the curriculum, not least because we are ably served by other works.[1] Here, I am principally concerned with extra-curricular activities, ways in which students and prospective ministers were drawn into the social world of the godly ministry.

I

At the foundation of Emmanuel College in 1584, Walter Mildmay made quite clear the purpose he intended. He stressed that,

in establishing this College we have set before us this one aim of rendering as many persons as possible fit for the sacred ministry of the Word and the Sacraments; so that from this seminary the Church of England might have men who it may call forth to instruct the people and undertake the duty of pastors ... Be it known therefore to any Fellows or Scholars who intrude themselves into the College for

---

[1] J. Morgan, *Godly Learning: Puritan Attitudes towards Reason, Learning and Education, 1560–1640* (Cambridge, 1986); J. Twigg, *The University of Cambridge and the English Revolution, 1625–1688* (Cambridge, 1990); V. Morgan, 'Court, Country and Cambridge University, 1558–1640: a Study in the Evolution of a Political Culture', University of East Anglia PhD (1984); W. T. Costello, *The Scholastic Curriculum at Early Seventeenth Century Cambridge* (Cambridge, Mass., 1958); M. H. Curtis, *Oxford and Cambridge in Transition, 1558–1642* (Oxford, 1959). Frank Bremer addresses questions of voluntary association at Cambridge in his *Congregational Communion: Clerical Friendship in the Anglo-American Puritan Community 1610–1692* (Boston, Mass., 1994) pp. 17–40. I am grateful to him for discussions of these issues.

any purpose other than to devote themselves to sacred Theology and in due time to labour in preaching the Word, that they render our hope vain.[2]

Significantly for our purposes, Mildmay followed common practice in establishing a geographical preference for the college: the counties thus favoured were Northamptonshire, where Mildmay had his seat in Parliament, and Essex, where he was born.[3] In order to maximise the output of preachers, scholars were to proceed to take degrees as quickly as university statutes allowed: no one was to remain a scholar for more than a year after becoming eligible for the MA. Similarly, in 1587/8, Mildmay added a clause, *de mora sociorum*, which required fellows to resign within a year of graduating as a doctor, whether they were provided for or not. In mitigation, fellows were to be considered for any vacant benefices to which Emmanuel held the right of appointment.[4] The question of advowsons was thus a live one for the college, and might be expected to affect both the effectiveness of Emmanuel's influence in the parishes and the geographical impact of that influence. Curiously, the college does not seem to have actively pursued rights of presentment, although Mildmay made a gift of three advowsons when he enacted the new statute.[5] A total of eleven benefices were acquired from benefactors between the foundation and the last gift of two parishes in Suffolk from Robert Ryece, the chorographer. One chapelry in Somerset was given and quickly lost, and the college was given the right of the next presentment to West Whickham in Kent.[6] The

[2] F. H. Stubbings (ed.), *Statutes of Sir Walter Mildmay for Emmanuel College* (Cambridge, 1983) 'Preface'; for Emmanuel in general see E. S. Shuckburgh, *Emmanuel College* (Cambridge, 1904); R. S. Rolph, 'Emmanuel College, Cambridge, and the Puritan movements of old and New England', University of Southern California PhD (1979); R. Tyler, '"The Children of Disobedience": the social composition of Emmanuel College, Cambridge, 1596–1645', Berkeley, University of California PhD (1976); J. Schenk Ibish, 'Emmanuel College: the Founding Generation, with a Biographical Register of the Members of the College 1584–1604', Harvard University PhD (1985). I am grateful to Dr F. Stubbings for drawing this last thesis to my attention.

[3] Stubbings, *Statutes*, ch. 17; J. B. Mullinger, *The University of Cambridge* (Cambridge, 1884–1911) vol. II p. 312; for this custom and its effects, see V. Morgan, 'Cambridge University and "the Country" 1560–1640', in L. Stone (ed.), *The University in Society* (Princeton, N.J., 1974) vol. I pp. 183–245.

[4] Rolph, 'Emmanuel College', pp. 298–305; this clause caused a great deal of consternation in the 1620s. In 1627 King Charles overturned the *de mora* regulation against the opposition of John Preston and Laurence Chaderton, on condition that Henry Mildmay provided six benefices for Emmanuel fellows. The statute was reintroduced by Parliament in 1641. Shuckburgh, pp. 62–5, 66; CUL Baker MS 27.4 ff.67–68, 69–71; 30.25 ff. 415–16.

[5] Stubbings, *Statutes*, p. 29; there is some account of college benefices in Shuckburgh, *Emmanuel College*, pp. 227–30.

[6] ECA Col. 8.1; 9.2; 9.7; *VCH Rutland* II pp. 199, 203; Samuel Clarke, *Lives of Sundry Modern Divines*, appended to *A General Martyrologie* (1677) p. 146. Cited hereafter as Clarke (1677).

Earl of Huntingdon gave a total of four, three in the West Country and one in Leicestershire, but this hardly amounts to a campaign to maximise the ability of the college to place graduating fellows. Henry Mildmay seems to have failed in his promise to provide six benefices in the 1620s.[7] Part of the explanation might lie in the fact that advowsons are a fairly ineffective form of patronage, given the unpredictable nature of their vacancy, but there seems to be an element of religious scruple, too. When Richard Dawson, the vicar of Pinchbeck, in Lincolnshire, tried to give money to the college in his declining years to purchase the impropriation for his benefice, Laurence Chaderton, Emmanuel's first master, was less than encouraging:

we have no affection to impropriations, as we have oft times written to you, yet if we might be secured that there were a sufficient competency to maintain a Vicar in Liberal manner, we would advise of it, the rather because all our fellows and scholars being by our Statutes assigned to Divinity, might with better conscience participate with these kinds of Church living.[8]

There seems to be a certain squeamishness about the possession of church property that makes for a striking contrast with the Feoffees for Impropriations, so associated with Chaderton's successor, John Preston. One of the consequences was that Emmanuel had to work harder in building networks of contact and advice in order to place its graduates.[9]

In addition to their regular studies, the college adopted orders, probably from a model drafted by Chaderton, for an extra-curricular exercise for divinity students. The model, dating from the mid-1580s, is entitled 'An order to be used for the trayning upp and exercising of Students in Divinitye whereby they may be made fitte and meete to discharge the dewties belonging to that profession'. It divides the means of attaining the gifts necessary for a successful ministry into two: firstly, 'mutual conference' on passages of Scripture, and secondly, disputation. As actually adopted at Emmanuel, the order includes an exposition of the correct form for such exercises, based very firmly on the Pauline models, particularly on 1 Corinthians 14.29, which thus makes explicit the common roots of the

---

[7] For Huntingdon, C. Cross, *The Puritan Earl: the Life of Henry Hastings, Third Earl of Huntingdon, 1535–1595* (London, 1966) pp. 99, 122, and sources cited here in note 8; on benefactions generally, there is a very thorough analysis in J. Schenk Ibish, 'Emmanuel College', pp. 50–189.

[8] ECA Col. 9.1, Bennet's Register 1, 81, 1 June 1616.

[9] Compare the conclusions of Ibish, 'Emmanuel College', pp. 21–2 and P. Lake, *Moderate Puritans and the Elizabethan Church* (Cambridge, 1982) pp. 38–40. On scruples regarding impropriations, C. Hill, *Economic Problems of the Church from Archbishop Whitgift to the Long Parliament* (London, 1971 edn) pp. 150–2.

Emmanuel order and the Elizabethan Prophesyings.[10] The conference was to meet regularly, in secret, and was to proceed as follows:

1. That two or three at one meeting should speak.
2. That the rest of the prophets present, should judge of that which was spoken, and whether it was sound and agreeable to the Word or no: to the end that if it were sound, they might give the doctrine their allowance: if not, that the speaker might brotherly be admonished of it, and the church take no hurt thereby.
3. If anything were revealed to him that sat by, the first should hold his peace.
4. That Every of the Prophets should in his course be permitted to speak, as order and the Churches good would permit. Lastly, that such as had spoken, would willingly submit themselves, and doctrine, to the judgment and censure of the whole company of Prophets and be content to be advised or reformed (if need were) by their discreet and brotherly censure.

The conference was to begin and end with prayer. It was expected that the whole Bible would be handled over two years, and the mixture of study and prayerful revelation would enable prospective ministers 'to grow daily into a greater ripeness and perfection in that honourable calling wherein they serve the Lord'.[11] These exercises were still held in the opening decades of the seventeenth century, when Thomas Shepard benefited from 'times of Holy Conference', and Samuel Rogers enjoyed similar exercises while he was at Emmanuel in the early 1630s.[12] The conference that Thomas Hooker established in Essex seems to have been the extra-mural application of these principles; the practice was similarly exported to Ireland by William Bedell, to Herefordshire by Thomas Pierson, and to Northamptonshire by the many Emmanuel graduates settled there, among whom Thomas Ball was the most prominent.[13]

Practice does not seem to have been wholly static, however. The

---

[10] DWL Morrice Ms A f.191, partially transcribed in A. Peel (ed.), *The Second Parte of a Register* (Cambridge, 1915) vol. I pp. 133–4. The adopted order is in Emmanuel College MSS Col. 14.1, the College Order Book ff. 3–8, entitled, 'A mutuall conference or communication of giftes among students of divinity confirmed by the Canonical Scriptures'. For a justification of the Elizabethan Prophesyings in Essex using many of the same texts, BL Add. Mss 29546 ff. 48–50.

[11] ECA Col. 14.1 ff. 4, 5.

[12] M. McGiffert (ed.), *God's Plot: the Paradoxes of Puritan Piety Being the Autobiography and Journal of Thomas Shepard* (Amherst, Mass., 1972) p. 74; QUB Percy MS 7 f. 15.

[13] G. Rupp, *William Bedell 1571–1642, A Commemorative Lecture Given in the Old Library, Emmanuel College 1st December, 1971* (Cambridge, 1971) p. 8; BL Harl MS 7517 ff. 21v–23; W. J. Sheils, *The Puritans in the Diocese of Peterborough 1558–1610, Publications of the Northamptonshire Record Society* 30 (1979) pp. 99–101; J. Fielding, 'Conformists, Puritans, and the Church Courts: the Diocese of Peterborough, 1603–1642,' University of Birmingham PhD (1989) ch. 4; John Howe, *Real Comforts: a Sermon Preached at the Funeral of Thomas Ball* (1660).

opportunities for dissension and ill-will in such conferences were consider-able, and in 1595 the master was forced to ask twelve students to sign an order binding them to refrain from contention in the exercise. The students included Thomas Pickering, who became one of William Perkins' editors while he was vicar of Finchingfield, Joseph Hall, one of only two Emma-nuel men of this period to take English bishoprics, and Ralph Cudworth. Perhaps more noteworthy is the presence of Samuel Ward, not at this time a member of the college, suggesting that the exercise was open to selected visitors from other colleges.[14] This sort of incident seems to have encour-aged the godly to make their meetings more a matter of selective co-option as time went on. Samuel Rogers' meetings seem to have been more of a voluntary society than the compulsory exercises imagined by the founders. It may be that such voluntary conferences were developed from the form imported by Martin Bucer in the reign of Edward VI.[15]

The possibility of visitors from other colleges is strengthened in the only record we have of such an exercise in Emmanuel. At some point between 1606 and 1612, John Cotton provided the key address in a conference on the topic of the beginning of the Sabbath. He proposed that there were Scriptural reasons for beginning Sabbath observance on Saturday night, his own practice, rather than on Sunday morning, the consensus position. Rather more important in this context than the details of his argument is the high tone of reverential seriousness taken by the parties to the discus-sion. Cotton's opening deserves to be quoted at length:

Christian friends & beloved Brethren in our blessed saviour, I had much rather keepe silence than shew mine opinion in this question, the reverence I beare to many holy and blessed servants of god who have delivered their judgements that the rest of the Lords day is to begin the morning, maketh me afraid to conceive much more to utter this contrary apprehension that this rest should rather begin at the eveninge. It is a palsey distemper that carryeth a member to a notion different from the inclination of the rest of the bodye & I am apte to suffer that spirit that breaketh a private notion discrepant from the common consent of the body of christ & yet because the notion is not private which hath his motion from the voyce of the holy ghost speaking in the Scripture & and for that we are commanded to try all things & as we beleave so to speake when god offereth seasonal occasion I have therefore upon your reverend requests imparted to you the grounds & reasons of my opinion & practice in observing the reste of the Lords day from the evening to the intent

[14] ECA Col. 14.1.
[15] P. Collinson, *Archbishop Grindal* (London, 1979) p. 50; cf. B. Hall, 'Martin Bucer in England', in D. F. Wright (ed.), *Martin Bucer: Reforming Church and Community* (Cam-bridge, 1994) pp. 144–60; Martin Bucer, *De Regno Christi* in W. Pauck (ed. and trans.), *Melancthon and Bucer, Library of Christian Classics* vol. XIX (London, 1969) pp. 271–3 where the ideal college Bucer describes closely resembles Emmanuel. *De Regno Christi* was written in 1550 and first published in 1577.

that if you find them builte upon the worde you may believe and practice with me but otherwise if they shall appeare as hay & stubble in the cleare day light of my brethrens judgements they shall be burned but I saved, yea even now saved from a way of error.

On this occasion Cotton was answered at length by William Whately, apparently invited from his post in Banbury for the purpose. Equally significant is the fact that the conference appears to have been inconclusive; if Cotton was judged to have Scripture on his side, his practice did not prevail as the norm, and he does not appear to have changed his ways even if Whately was deemed to be more persuasive.[16]

Such practices within Cambridge helped to encourage the sort of extra-curricular study that we will encounter elsewhere. While he was a student at Clare Hall, John Carter met every week with Laurence Chaderton, Lancelot Andrewes, Ezekiel Culverwell, John Knewstub and others. When the young John Dod was invited to join Chaderton's group, he also met William Whitaker and William Fulke.

At their meetings they had constant exercises; first, they began with prayer, & then applied themselves to the Study of the Scriptures; one was for the Originall Languages, anothers task was for the Grammaticall Interpretation; anothers for the Logicall Analysis; anothers for the true sense, and meaning of the Text, another gathered the Doctrines.[17]

In the next generation, John Preston introduced Samuel Fairclough into a similar group, including John Davenant and Arthur Hildersham. This meeting seems to have been focused on Queens' College, but the meetings of the godly were not necessarily restricted in this way. After a conversion prompted by the writings of Richard Rogers, John Wilson took advice

---

16 ECA MS 181, viii. For Cotton's practice see Samuel Clarke, *A Collection of the Lives of Ten Eminent Divines and some other Eminent Christians* (1662) p. 63, hereafter cited as Clarke (1662); Mather, III p. 27. According to Increase Mather, only John Dod and Arthur Hildersham among the mainstream held the same position as Cotton before the migration to New England, although one of the charges against Charles Chauncy in his High Commission trial of 1630 was that he had preached that the Sabbath began at sundown on Saturday evening: Increase Mather, 'To the Reader', in Cotton Mather, *A Good Evening for the Best of Dayes* (Cambridge, Mass., 1708); SP 16/164/40. Cotton's position prevailed in New England; it was already practised in Plymouth colony: W. U. Solberg, *Redeem the Time: the Puritan Sabbath in Early America* (Cambridge, Mass., 1977) pp. 111–13. Solberg has published Cotton's contribution to the debate but not Whately's in 'John Cotton's Treatise on the Duration of the Lord's Day', *PCSM: Collections, Sibley's Heir 59* (1982) pp. 505–22. He gives a date of 1611 without convincing reasons; my date is influenced by the tenure of Cotton as a fellow: if anything, the manuscript context suggests a later date – the argument follows a tract by John Preston which makes possible a date in the 1620s.

17 Clarke (1677) pp. 2–3; DWL Morrice MS J, 1626 (6), 1645 (4); John Carter [Jr], *The Tombstone* (1653) p. 3; cf. M. M. Knappen, 'The Early Puritanism of Lancelot Andrewes', *CH* 11 (1939) pp. 95–104.

from William Ames and 'associated himself with a Pious Company in the University' who met for 'Prayer, Fasting, Holy Conference, and the Exercises of True Devotion'. In this way he came into the company of Preston, Chaderton, Richard Sibbes, William Gouge, Thomas Taylor, John Cotton (who had converted Preston) and John Norton.[18] Godly tutors could be very active in bringing their more pious charges into contact with like-minded students and in promoting voluntary religious society. Herbert Palmer, a fellow of Queens' College under John Preston, was said to have been 'more than ordinarily carefull' with his students and was known for

keeping them to their studies, and the performance of disputations and other exercises of learning, privately in his chamber, beside the more publique exercises required of them by the Colledge, to the great benefit of those that were his pupils.[19]

In 1634, Samuel Rogers noted that 'a companye of us have ioined together to meet often to pray together, and discourse' under the supervision of his tutor, Mr Frost. He drew a great deal of benefit from the company of Peter Sterry and others.[20] It is difficult to be sure, but it seems that private, voluntary religious exercises, at least within Emmanuel, were becoming more important. Given the 'laicization' of the college charted by Dr Tyler, this may not be surprising.[21] Students could be as active in the shaping of godly society as tutors. Thomas Cawton, who studied at Queens' College under John Goodwin and John Preston, limited his company to the godly. He drew new arrivals into such circles:

when any young youths came to the University either from his own Country, or else where, such as he knew, or was informed, were well educated under godly Parents, or a godly Ministry, he would be sure to get acquaintance with them . . . before they were ingaged, intangled, or infected with bad company, and would bring them into the society of some pious Schollars.[22]

These exercises formed an entrance into a network of advancement and recognition of the godly in the university and beyond, and put at the disposal of the young cleric a resource of professional and religious advice that we will examine more fully below. It became axiomatic that a minister could return to Cambridge to take advantage of this resource. Thomas Ball asked for a meeting of 'divers Reverend Ministers, his worthy friends, who were occasionally met at Cambridge, by reason of the Commencement', to

---

[18] Clarke (1683) p. 157; Mather, III pp. 42, 47. Thomas Pierson seems to have had similar experience, although his biographer mentions only William Perkins as an associate: BL Harl MS 7517 f. 3.
[19] Clarke (1677) p. 185.   [20] QUB Percy MS 7 ff. 15, 22.
[21] R. C. Tyler, 'Children of Disobedience', *passim.* and esp. pp. 147, 162–3, 199, 332.
[22] Anon., *Life and Death of the Reverend and Holy Man of God Mr Thomas Cawton* (1662) pp. 9–10.

settle his scruples regarding a move to Northampton.[23] In July 1629, Isaac Johnson wrote to another Emmanuel graduate, Emmanuel Downing:

> It would have been an excellent Tyme for Mr Winthrop to have been this commencement at Cambridge, where I heare are many Reverend Divines, to consider of Mr Whites call.[24]

Similarly, in the 1630s, Daniel Rogers returned to Cambridge for the Commencement with family and friends from Essex; it was the practice of Charles Chauncy and Henry Jessey to return for the Commencement each year. Puritan conferences at the July Commencement were an established Elizabethan practice, which continued down to the 1630s,[25] but prospective ministers were introduced to the county networks in the other direction, too. Essex, and the Stour valley in particular, were ideally placed for divinity students to visit painful preachers outside the university. Such gadding could be on the initiative of an individual, as when John Wilson made a pilgrimage to Richard Rogers at Wethersfield, or on organised visits, as when John Shaw was moved by a sermon preached by Thomas Weld to an audience at Haverhill that included a group of Cambridge students.[26] Thomas Goodwin, Jeremiah Burroughes and William Bridge 'travelled from Cambridge into Essex, on purpose to observe the Ministers in that County' and were very impressed with John Wilson's lectures at Sudbury. These trips took students as far afield as Dedham, where Goodwin was strongly affected by John Rogers' preaching. He had been unimpressed with plain-style preaching, 'and I often thought thus with myself, they talk of their Puritan powerful Preaching, and of Mr Rogers of Dedham, and such others, but I would gladly see the man that could trouble my Conscience'. However, having travelled to see Rogers, he witnessed a dramatic Jeremiad on the neglect of Scripture which

> put all the congregation into so strange a posture, that he never saw any congregation in all his life; the place was a mere Bochim, the people generally (as it were) deluged with their own tears, and he told them that he himself, when he got out and

23 John Howe, *Real Comforts*, p. 40.
24 *Winthrop Papers* (Boston, Mass., 1929–43) II p. 178.
25 QUB Percy MS 7 f. 267; Edward Whiston, *The Life and Death of Mr Henry Jessey* (1671) p. 5; C. R. Elrington (ed.), *Usher's Whole Works* (Dublin, 1847–64) vol. XV p. 341; P. Collinson, *The Elizabethan Puritan Movement* (London, 1967) pp. 219, 305, 320. John Ball returned to Oxford each year for the Act, a journey 'made profitable unto his Christian friends . . . by conference, his assistance in private Fasts and other exercises of Religion': Clarke (1677) p. 150.
26 Mather, III p. 42; C. Jackson (ed.), 'Life of Master John Shaw', in *Yorkshire Diaries and Autobiographies of the Seventeenth and Eighteenth Centuries, Surtees Soc 65* (1875) p. 124.

was to take horse again to be gone, he was fain to hang a quarter of an hour upon the neck of his horse weeping, before he had power to mount.[27]

Such inspirational preaching proved a magnet for young ministers: Henry Jessey was not the only minister encouraged to settle in the area 'in regard that he had sometime been there and heard famous Preachers, and found many precious Christians'.[28]

Similarly, for godly students at a later stage of development, such connections afforded early opportunities to preach, as students and tutors provided villages around Cambridge and further afield with regular sermons. Thomas Gataker and William Bedell both benefited from such opportunities, and Abdias Ashton and Thomas Hill were among those promoting these exercises.[29] Tutors and friends within the University were active in turning these sorts of contacts into regular positions upon the completion of a student's time in college. John Preston probably encouraged Thomas Shepard to settle in Terling with Thomas Weld after he graduated, and Stephen Marshall apparently owed his first preaching post at Wethersfield to his tutor at Emmanuel, John Garnons.[30] These practices eased the transition from an academic training to a pastoral, preaching ministry, a process that came to be an increasing concern among the godly as Elizabethan preoccupations changed from a need to fill as many pulpits as quickly as possible to a feeling that an academic degree was insufficient qualification for a truly reformed ministry.

II

Education was not completed with graduation. The formal requirements for a degree, even supplemented with voluntary exercises that might furnish a graduate with something like a vocational training, scarcely guaranteed a supply of godly preachers. The conviction that the ministry was best improved by 'on-the-job' training was one of the impulses behind the Prophesying movement of the 1570s. After the suppression of the

---

[27] Mather, III p. 46; Thomas Goodwin, 'Life of Dr Goodwin', in *The Works of Thomas Goodwin* (1704) vol. V p. 6; J. Hunt (ed.), *The Whole Works of Rev. John Howe* (London, 1814) vol. VI pp. 493–4.

[28] Whiston, *Life and Death of Henry Jessey*, p. 6; cf. the experience of John Wilson: Richard Rogers became his mentor and gave Wilson a death-bed blessing 'among his children'. Among the ministers Jessey knew in the Stour valley were John Wilson, Thomas Weld and George Philips. His letters suggest that he also knew John Rogers, Stephen Marshall, Nathaniel Ward, Samuel Wharton and Edmund Brewer: *Winthrop Papers*, III pp. 57–60, 128.

[29] Clarke (1662) pp. 92, 132.

[30] McGiffert (ed.), *God's Plot*, pp. 41, 45, 73; Anon., *The Godly Mans Legacy* (1681) pp. 3, 26; cf. P. Lake, *Moderate Puritans and the Elizabethan Church* (Cambridge, 1982) pp. 38–40; Morgan, *Godly Learning*, pp. 290–2.

Prophesyings, godly ministers felt that the responsibility had, to some extent, fallen to them. The 1584 the Dedham conference resolved that

the ministers which are able to bear the charges of it shall entertain a student of Divinity being well grounded on other knowledge of Arts and Tongues whom directing in those studies, by his own example and all good means he shall make fit to serve the church in the ministry of the Gospel and that such as are not able should yet (the charges being otherwise born) perform the like duty and care that there may be always sufficient and able men in the Church for that calling.[31]

Although there are Elizabethan examples of such parochial tutelage, this was a practice that characterises the Jacobean godly ministry more than that of their predecessors. Richard Greenham and Bernard Gilpin will serve as exemplars for the earlier period.[32] For the later period a little more detail may be given, in order to open a discussion of the nature of the phenomenon. One of the most famous parochial tutors was John Cotton, minister at Boston between 1612 and 1633. He boarded students in his own house, which became a model godly household: every morning and evening the company met for readings and prayers, while Cotton expounded doctrine and corrected the errors of the group by the application of Scripture. Observation of the Sabbath began on Saturday night, and time away from public duties was spent in catechising, sermon repetition, study and psalm-singing. He taught graduates from Holland and Germany, but most of his students came from Cambridge: 'For Dr Preston would still advise his near fledg'd Pupils, to go live with Mr Cotton, that they might be fitted for Publick service; insomuch that it was grown almost a Proverb, That Mr Cotton was Dr Preston's seasoning vessell.' Among the continental divines trained under Cotton was John Rulice, who benefited from the tutelage of Preston, Cotton and John White of Dorchester before he ministered to the Dutch congregation in London. Cotton's English students came mainly from Queens' College, Preston's first home, and Emmanuel, Cotton's college. He taught Anthony Tuckney, Thomas Hill and John Angier, a protégé of John Rogers.[33]

The case of another of Preston's pupils, Samuel Winter, gives a rare

[31] R. G. Usher (ed.), *The Presbyterian Movement in the Reign of Queen Elizabeth as Illustrated by the Minute Book of the Dedham Classis 1582–89* Camden Soc. 3rd ser. 8 (1905) p. 93.
[32] P. Collinson, *The Religion of Protestants: the Church in English Society 1559–1625* (Oxford, 1982) p. 118; Clarke (1667) pp. 14–15.
[33] Clarke (1662) pp. 63, 86; Mather, III pp. 17–18; Anthony Tuckney, *Death Disarmed* (1654) p. 47; for Rulice, J. Crossley (ed.), *Diary and Correspondence of John Worthington, Chetham Soc.* 33 (1855) pp. 58–60; D. Underdown, *Fire from Heaven: Life in an English Town in the Seventeenth Century* (London, 1992) pp. 93–4; for his later career, O. P. Grell, *Dutch Calvinists in Early Stuart England: the Dutch Church in Austin Friars* (Brill, 1989) pp. 15, 181, 106–9. H. Hajzyk, 'The Church in Lincolnshire c.1590–1640', University of Cambridge PhD (1980) notes a brisk turnover of curates and schoolmasters at Boston

insight into the motives of these students. At Queens' he attained 'a great measure of knowledge, both in the Tongues and Arts, and also Divinity'. However, even after receiving his MA, Winter was 'as yet unwilling to enter upon that great and dreadful work of the Ministry' and so was referred to Cotton.[34] Such misgivings would be much less likely, and perhaps considered indulgent, in an Elizabethan context, but by the second decade of the seventeenth century a period of vocational training under the direction of a godly minister was almost requisite.

Although such seminaries are often difficult to trace, chance remarks in funeral sermons and biographies often reveal godly ministers providing such tutelage. Thomas Gataker taught Joseph Symonds, John Grayle, Thomas Young and Hugh Peter while he was at Rotherhithe.[35] Thomas Taylor seems to have provided preaching opportunities and possibly tuition for young ministers during his years at St Mary Aldermanbury in London. John Davenport was quite probably one of his protégés and Robert Saxby recorded many 'stranger' preachers at his church.[36] Taylor certainly ran a graduate school when he moved to Reading.[37] John Ball, perhaps the most important ecclesiological scholar of his generation, tutored students at Whitmore in Staffordshire; John Dod kept students at Canons Ashby in Northamptonshire.[38] Arthur Hildersham, having been tutored under Richard Greenham, may well have tutored the young Thomas Hooker; he certainly boarded the exorcist John Darrell and John Brinsley, who later benefited from the learning of the prominent Leicestershire divine John Ireton at Kegworth where the younger man was schoolmaster. Hooker sent his pupil Simeon Ashe on to Hildersham after his time at Emmanuel.[39] Francis Higginson continued his work in Leicester, tutoring Lazarus Seaman, John Bryan, later curate at Woodhouse, Richard Richardson and Edward Howe, later curate at Braunston.[40] Jeremiah Whitaker developed a

---

during Cotton's incumbency, including Banks Anderson, George Perkins, Edward Spinkes, Edward Wright (curates), Jeremy Vasin and William Watson (schoolmasters), pp. 178–9.

[34] Clarke (1683) p. 95.

[35] Simeon Ashe, *Gray Hayres Crowned with Grace* (1654) p. 54; Clarke (1662) pp. 145–6. Clarke also names a 'Mr Goodal', whom I have not been able to identify with any certainty. John Grayle went on to become master of Guildford school. My account of household seminaries is clearly indebted to the examples provided by K. W. Shipps, 'Lay Patronage of East Anglian Puritan Clerics in Pre-Revolutionary England', Yale University PhD (1971) appendix II, pp. 351–6.

[36] GLRO DL/C 314 f. 124v; DL/C 316 f. 107v; CUL Add MS 3117 *passim.*

[37] 'Life' by Joseph Caryl in Thomas Taylor, *Works* (1653) sig. b2.

[38] Samuel Bold, *Man's Great Duty* (1693) preface; A. G. Matthews, *Calamy Revised* (Oxford, 1934) pp. 397–8.

[39] John Darrell, *A Detection of that Sinful Shameful Lying and Ridiculous Discourse of Sam. Harsnet* (1600) pp. 73, 77; LRO Misc Cor M/2 f. 38; John Brinsley, *A Consolation for our Grammar Schools* (1622) p. 28; Clarke (1667) p. 123.

[40] Mather, III p. 73.

close relationship with William Peachy in Oakham in Rutland. After four years acting as usher in the free school, Whitaker married Peachy's daughter, Chephtzibah, before taking a preaching post at Stretton, ten miles to the north-east.[41] Thomas Cawton felt the need for a training in theology when he took his MA and so joined the household of Herbert Palmer at Ashwell in Hertfordshire. Here, he 'studied Theological Truths with a Theological Heart', assisted Palmer in the pulpit and was drawn to the attention of his next patron, William Armin of Huntingdonshire, by Thomas Down, a minister visiting from Exeter.[42] Although it has not proved possible to identify any ministers who were tutored in a household seminary by Thomas Ball, it seems that some were. He told Samuel Hartlib that one of the best ways to export English practical divinity to the continent 'is to traine up young divines in our Country . . . and therfore I wil doe my endeavour that not only this yong Man, but many others of like quality may be maintained in Ministers-houses'.[43] One of the best documented seminaries, and perhaps the most institutionalised, was that presided over by Charles Offspring at St Antholin, Budge Row, in London. Three lecturers had been maintained since 1566; between 1621 and 1629 numbers rose to between four and six. We may assume that the young ministers contributing the St Antholin's lectures were among his pupils. As the lecturers were intitialy paid out of collections administered with the general parish funds until 1626 some identifications can be made. The parish enjoyed the services of Henry Gray, an Emmanuel graduate, Edward Spendlowe, who was unlicensed in 1628, Nicholas Profett, who graduated with an MA from Emmanuel College while he was at St Antholin's, a Mr Tuke, a Mr Holyday and a Mr Close.[44] We know a little more about John Archer, later placed by the Feoffees in Hertford, Thomas Foxley, a co-defendant in the trial of the Feoffees, and Zachery Symmes, who wrote the earliest biography of Richard Sibbes.[45] The lecturers provided by the seminary came to be placed under the control of the Feoffees for Impropriations in 1627. In the course of the trial, William Noy drew attention to what he saw as this subversive influence:

[41] Simeon Ashe, *Living Loves betwixt Christ and Dying Christians* (1654) pp. 50–1.

[42] Anon., *Life and Death of . . . Thomas Cawton*, pp. 12–14.

[43] SU Hartlib MS 29/3/55b.

[44] GL 1046/1 ff. 109v, 113r, 116v, 123r, 126v, 130r, 133r, 136r, 139r, 143r, 146r. After the dissolution of the Feoffees, the administration reverted to the parish but accounts were kept separately: the accounts are mentioned f. 164v, but have not survived for this period. For Spendlowe, GLRO DL/C 317 f. 13r. The churchwardens' accounts only give surnames and some identifications cannot be made. Mr Close may be the George Close who graduated with a BA from St John's College, Cambridge in 1625.

[45] I. M. Calder, 'The St Antholins Lectures', *CQR* 160 (1959) pp. 52–6.

And how they doe order their Lecturers, after six years they are to be sent abroad, and soe this shalbe a Seminary for other places.

He felt that the King should take over

the nominacion of the Lecturers of St Antholyns for theis are worse than the Advowsons And a greater breach of trust in them for their purchasing them, And to make seminaries and bringing up of youth as they please.[46]

Given this reaction, it is astounding that the practice was never, as far as we know, suppressed elsewhere. We may see this as a testament to the tightly knit communities of interest created, in part, by such seminaries.

Despite the continental tradition of the *Hausvater* literature and some Calvinist traditions of 'on-the-job' training, the household seminary seems to have been essentially an indigenous development.[47] As we have seen in the case of John Cotton, it was a scheme admired and sought out by continental divines. Walter Teelinck, 'the father of Dutch Pietism', left a vivid description of his time in William Whateley's seminary at Banbury. He recalled how he was accepted into the community at a day of fasting and prayer and entered into Banbury's devotional round. The day began with prayer and a passage of Scripture which was to be the set topic of conversation at the communal midday meal. The week was filled with attendance at sermons and sermon repetition, culminating in the Sabbath when two sermons were heard and repeated in the evening, when the group submitted themselves to discipline and received spiritual advice. The practice of the seminary was intended to dovetail with the spiritual life of the town,

in aid to the poor, in visiting the sick, in the consolation of the afflicted, in instruction of the ill-informed, in reprimanding the transgressor, in encouragement of the humble. Just as the public life of the town, especially on Sundays, showed the fruits of the spiritual life. For not only the magistrates but also the fathers of the town urged the strictest Sabbath, so uproar and noisy entertainment were neither seen nor heard anywhere.[48]

---

[46] I. M. Calder (ed.), *Activities of the Puritan of the Church of England 1625–1633* (London, 1957) pp. 79, 83.

[47] L. Roper, *Oedipus and the Devil: Witchcraft, Sexuality and Religion in Early Modern Europe* (London, 1994) p. 154; L. Roper, *The Holy Household: Women and Morals in Reformation Augsburg* (Oxford, 1989); cf. K. Maag, 'Education and Training for the Calvinist Ministry: the Academy of Geneva, 1559–1620', in A. Pettegree (ed.), *The Reformation of the Parishes: the Ministry and the Reformation in Town and Country* (Manchester, 1993) pp. 133–52.

[48] Teelinck's description is in the foreword to his *Hausbuch* (1618). I am grateful to my father and Mr G. D. Walker for translating this passage. The description of Teelinck is that of F. E. Stoeffler, see *The Rise of Evangelical Pietism* (Leiden, 1965) p. 117; it must be remembered that this account is somewhat idealised: cf. P. Collinson, *The Birthpangs of Protestant England* (London, 1988) pp. 137–9 for a different view of Banbury.

However important they became in the preparation of a godly minister, household seminaries depended heavily upon the central charismatic figure and rarely survived the death or departure of the central light. John Morgan attributes this to some sort of organisational immaturity, but, in the context of experimental Calvinism, the seminary was not an institution which could be separated from the piety and practical divinity of its head. A rare exception was the seminary associated with John Dod at Hanwell, not far from Whately's Banbury. When Dod was silenced, in 1604, he took refuge in Warwickshire and then Northamptonshire. In his former home, 'God was pleased to supply his want by the resort of sundry young students from Oxford' who were then tutored by Robert Harris, a former student of Dod's, with the assistance of Whately, Richard Capel, William Scudder and Dod's collaborator, Robert Cleaver. This continuity was rare and may relate to the community of clergy knit together by Dod before his troubles.[49] It seems that there was no group of ministers to take up the slack when Cotton departed for Massachusetts in 1633; it may not be irrelevant that Dr Hajzyk concluded that in Lincolnshire, 'the ecclesiastical authorities sought in vain for a clerical network'.[50]

However, it would be an injustice to suggest that vocational training was an exclusively Puritan preoccupation. Elizabethan schemes for the reformation of the ministry did not completely end with the suppression of the Prophesyings. The Queen's ban did not extend to the northern province, and individual bishops were active in grooming prospective ministers and providing in-service training. Kenneth Fincham's major reassessment of the Jacobean episcopal bench has provided later examples of the diocesan concern for vocational training.[51] However, most of these schemes were linked to the irregular machinery of visitations, and aimed at the lowest level of ministerial competence. Seminaries like Cotton's were intense courses of study for ministers with academic achievements that already surpassed many beneficed ministers. Moreover, some of the most successful episcopally sponsored projects depended upon the abilities and energy of parish ministers. In Herefordshire the exercises for the improvement of non-preaching clergy were adapted from Elizabethan models, and the

---

[49] Morgan, *Godly Learning*, p. 294; Clarke (1662) pp. 249, 252, 274–83. Robert Harris was able to recommend a former boarder of Dod's, John Poynter, for the Fishbourne lecture at Huntingdon, P. Seaver, *Puritan Lectureships: the Politics of Religious Dissent 1560–1662* (Stanford, Calif., 1970) pp. 176, 146–7. Dod was an active promoter of clerical society during his time at Fawsley: N. Tyacke, *The Fortunes of Puritanism, 1603–1640, Friends of Dr Williams's Library Lecture 1990* (London, 1991) pp. 18–19; see below, ch. 11.

[50] H. Hajzyk, 'The Church in Lincolnshire c.1595–1640', pp. 260–2.

[51] R. O'Day, *The English Clergy: the Emergence and Consolidation of a Profession 1558–1642* (Leicester, 1979) ch. 10; K. Fincham, *Prelate as Pastor: the Episcopate of James I* (Oxford, 1990) pp. 198–206.

practice of Emmanuel College on the initiative of Thomas Pierson, a nonconformist graduate of Emmanuel, although they benefited from the support of Bishop Bennet.[52] The same conditions prevailed in Yorkshire, where exercises for the improvement of the clergy survived into the archiepiscopate of Toby Matthew: they benefited from his indulgence, but were driven by nonconformist ministers like Ezekiel Rogers. Marchant describes 'voluntary association of ministers to promote preaching, stimulate study of the scriptures and improve the quality of the pastoral ministry,' which did not collapse at the death of Matthew, but prospered until the hand of Samuel Harsnett fell upon them.[53] It seems difficult to escape Rosemary O'Day's conclusion:

It is true to say that whereas in the earlier part of the period many bishops laid equal weight upon attempts to produce graduate clergy and upon experiments to improve the vocational performance of ministers, by the 1620s and 1630s there was an increasing tendency among the bishops to hide behind the success of the first policy and shirk responsibility for further improvement.[54]

In these conditions the peculiarity of those ministers who chose to devote further years to study after university can only have been more evident, both to themselves and to those who heard them preach.

III

In Essex, as elsewhere, it was the godly ministers who remained committed to the improvement of the ministry when the interest of the bishops waned. Here the household seminary reached its highest point of evolution; it is not known how far the Dedham conference acted upon their mandate,[55] but in the next reign the county was well served. In the south of the county, from at least 1607, Alexander Richardson, a graduate of Queens' College, Cambridge, who received his MA in 1587, ran a school in Barking which offered post-graduate instruction, usually in preparation for the MA in a range of subjects, but focusing on Ramist logic and rhetoric. He published nothing in his own lifetime, but manuscript notes from his lectures were

[52] BL Harl MS 7517 ff. 20v-23. Bennet's main contribution was to grant a licence for the exercises and lend authority when Pierson encountered resistance. He did pursue the same aims on visitation, as Fincham notes, p. 203, but I contend that such exercises attached to a triennial visitation could have, at best, limited effects.

[53] Mather, III p. 102; R. C. Marchant, *The Puritans and the Church Courts in the Diocese of York 1560–1642* (London, 1962) pp. 30–1, 40–5. For the nonconformity of Ezekiel Rogers, the brother of Daniel, see ibid. p. 274; H. F. Waters, *Genealogical Gleanings in England* (Boston, Mass., 1901) vol. II p. 227.

[54] O'Day, *English Clergy*, pp. 142–3.

[55] Dr Pennie is silent on this issue: A. R. Pennie, 'The Evolution of Puritan Mentality in an Essex Cloth Town', Sheffield University PhD (1989).

prized and circulated among students in Cambridge. The benefits of his tutelage were spiritual as well as simply educational, and Thomas Hooker, who attended Richardson's seminary, admired him 'for a man of transcendent Abilities and a most exalted Piety'.[56]

Richardson also taught William Ames, Charles Chauncy, who lectured in Greek at Trinity College, Cambridge, before he was forced to emigrate in 1637 after ceremonial struggles in Hertfordshire and Northamptonshire, and who crowned his career with the presidency of Harvard from 1654 to 1672, George Walker, who emerged as a staunch defender of Calvinist orthodoxy during his London ministry, Daniel Cawdrey, who went on to distinction in his Northamptonshire ministry and in the Westminster Assembly, and prospective ministers from Emmanuel and Christ's Colleges in Cambridge, such as John Greenham, and John Barlow, the painful preacher of Godalming in Surrey. Hooker and Ames are not the only students to have links to the Stour valley, for John Wilson was referred to Richardson, probably by his mentor at Cambridge, William Ames. In 1609, having been encouraged to leave Cambridge after voicing his doubts regarding the ceremonies, Wilson commuted from the Inner Temple to Barking, where he taught grammar and benefited from Richardson's knowledge of the arts, languages and divinity, until he graduated in 1613. Similarly, John Yates left Emmanuel to study with John Rogers in Dedham in 1611, when he took his MA, and then studied with Richardson before he became lecturer at St Andrews, Norwich and an early opponent of Richard Montague.[57]

The Stour valley connections provide a link with another active and successful seminary of this period. From around 1605 to 1628, Richard Blackerby, a former chaplain to the Jermyn and Lewknor families in

---

[56] GL 9537/10 f. 57v; Alexander Richardson, *The Logicians Schoolmaster: or, a Comment upon Ramus Logicke* (1629), 'To the Christian Reader'; Mather, III p. 60. Richardson's election as a fellow of Queens' in 1585 was quashed in response to court pressure: W. G. Searle, *The History of Queens' College of St Margaret and St Bernard in the University of Cambridge 1446–1662* (Cambridge, 1867) pp. 375–6; CUL Baker MS 4 ff. 184, 185.

[57] George Walker, *A True Relation* (1642) p. 6; Mather, III pp. 60, 42; Wilson also numbered Nathaniel Rogers, Thomas Shepard, John Preston and Henry Jessey among his friends in England, ibid. pp. 47, 49; *Winthrop Papers* III p. 128; McGiffert (ed.), *God's Plot*, p. 63; for his time at Barking, GLRO DL/C 339 f. 75. For Cawdrey, GLRO DL/C 340 f. 210 and *DNB*; for Yates, see Walker, *True Relation*, p. 6; C. A. Jones, *History of Dedham* (Colchester, 1907) p. 124. It is not entirely clear whether Yates was at Barking before or after his time with Rogers. The fullest treatment of Yates' early career is K. L. Sprunger, 'John Yates of Norfolk: the Radical Puritan Preacher as Ramist Philosopher', *JHI* 37 (1976) pp. 697–706, but Sprunger seems unaware of his time at Dedham. For his later career see Tyacke, *Anti-Calvinists*, pp. 40, 47, 147–8 and J. Eales, *Puritans and Roundheads: the Harleys of Brampton Bryan and the Outbreak of the English Civil War* (Cambridge, 1990) pp. 56, 59–60, 145, 152, which corrects the account in R. L. Greaves and R. Zaller (eds.), *Biographical Dictionary of British Radicals in the Seventeenth Century* (Brighton, 1982–4).

Suffolk and an irregular preacher at Feltwell in Norfolk, hired a house in Ashen, on the border between Suffolk and Essex. He spent most of his time teaching young boarders, 'the sons of Pious Gentry, Tradesmen and Yeomen'. He also tutored prospective ministers. Clarke tells us that

Divers young Students (after they came from the University) betook themselves to him to prepare them for the ministry, whom he taught the Hebrew tongue, to whom he opened the Scriptures, and read Divinity, and gave them excellent advice for Learning, Doctrine and Life.[58]

Here again, his reputation for learning had to be matched by his piety. John Rogers, with hardly a peer in his own reputation for godliness, could never enter Blackerby's presence 'without some kind of trembling upon him; because of the Divine Majesty and Holiness' which seemed to shine within him.[59] Like Cotton, he took students from continental backgrounds, including Jonas Proost, later minister to Dutch congregations in Colchester and London. He tutored Nicholas Bernard, whom he recommended to James Ussher, a great friend, and set upon a career as Dean of Kilmore and later Ardagh, and Christopher Burrell, who married Blackerby's daughter and became rector of Great Wrating in Suffolk. One of his most famous pupils was Samuel Fairclough, who was referred to Blackerby by Samuel Ward, the brother of Nathaniel, who was town preacher in Ipswich and former minister at Fairclough's birthplace, Haverhill, at the west end of the Stour valley. Fairclough expressed the same doubts as Samuel Winter:

. . . he did think himself not fully prepared and furnished for so great a work as that of taking the care of souls upon him; he therefore resolved to retire from a stated publick ministry again, and betake himself to his private studies for a year or two longer, desiring to enter into a family of some eminent noted Minister, where he might go through again and compleat a whole Cursus Theologicus, a whole course of Divinity-Studies, and by converse with some experienced minister, he might gain a more full knowledge of the nature of his work, and attain unto greater measures and degrees of Grace in his own heart.

With Blackerby he spent four days each week studying divinity, and two on humane learning. He was invited to preach in many of the pulpits that welcomed his tutor, including Colchester, Braintree, Thaxted and Belchamp Walter in Essex, and Hadleigh, Sudbury and Clare in Suffolk.[60]

Blackerby can be seen as a precursor of a more organised scheme promoted by Hooker after his arrival. There are personal connections with ministers who reappear in Hooker's circle. Blackerby tutored Samuel Stone, later associated with Hooker in Essex and New England, and Stephen Marshall lived in nearby Clare, possibly attending his seminary, during

---

[58] Clarke (1683) p. 58.   [59] Quoted in Collinson, *Religion*, p. 111.
[60] Clarke (1683) pp. 58, 153–61; J. Browne, *History of Congregationalism and Memorials of the Churches in Norfolk and Suffolk* (London, 1877) p. 117; ERO D/ABA 1 ff. 69, 73.

1618 and 1619. Blackerby was certainly an important figure in the intellectual life of the area; Clarke notes that Blackerby persuaded John Rogers, Stephen Marshall and others that it was God's intention to convert the Jews before the Millennium. Clarke's account suggests that Blackerby only achieved this after many discussions and conferences.[61] This sort of disputation, for the benefit of established ministers and young students, was central to the business of Hooker's activity in Essex. Samuel Collins, the vicar of Braintree, described Hooker's great popularity, particularly with the younger ministers, 'to whom he is their oracle in cases of conscience and points of divinity, and their principal library'.[62]

The number of ministers in Hooker's circle in the 1620s who were providing this sort of tutelage is striking. Thomas Shepard moved from Cambridge to reside with Thomas Weld at Terling on the advice of John Preston in late 1626. He felt he was in 'the best county in England' and 'in the midst of the best ministry in the country by whose monthly fasts and conferences I found much of God'.[63] After he left Weld's household he was replaced by another student, John Cullen, who was presented in 1631 for preaching and expounding Scripture at a prayer meeting in the house of the schoolmaster's widow.[64]

Hooker ran a seminary of his own, based at the school he organised at Little Baddows, a parish neighbour to Chelmsford, where he lectured. He taught John Beadle, who became chaplain to the Earl of Warwick and later rector of Barnston. John Fuller recalled the benefits of Hooker's tutelage in his introduction to a sermon of Beadle's. Fuller had already enjoyed a period living with John Rogers in 1612, after the departure of John Yates, and had since gone on to undermine the work of a conformist minister as lecturer at Great Waltham. He met Beadle, who became a close friend, at Hooker's conference.[65] Hooker also tutored Jeremiah Burroughes, who enjoyed visits to the Stour valley while he was at Emmanuel. Shepard remembered him as one of the ministers whose 'sweet society' he had enjoyed in Essex, and in fact there was an attempt to settle Burroughes in an Essex benefice in early 1626, although the post went

---

61 Clarke (1683) pp. 58, 63, 161; ERO D/DMs C2; Giles Firmin, *A Brief Vindication of Stephen Marshall* appended to *Questions between the Conformist and the Nonconformist* (1681) n.p.; T. Webster, *Stephen Marshall and Finchingfield* (Chelmsford, 1994) p. 2. It is suggestive, though not conclusive, proof of Blackerby's influence that so many ministers in the area, including John Eliot, Thomas Shepard and Henry Jessey, were committed to the conversion of the Jews. For details, see Webster, 'The Godly of Goshen Scattered: an Essex Clerical Conference in the 1620s and its Diaspora', University of Cambridge PhD (1993) p. 62.

62 SP 16/142/133.   63 McGiffert (ed.), *God's Plot*, p. 47.

64 ERO D/ACA 48 f. 29v.

65 John Beadle, *Journal or Diary of a Thankful Christian* (1656) ep. ded.; GL 9537/11 f. 27v; SP 16/218/43.

elsewhere.[66] Nathaniel Rogers, son of the Dedham lecturer, was another who benefited from Hooker's counsel; educated at Dedham and Emmanuel, he returned to a chaplaincy in Essex and then lectured at Bocking until the rector, Dr Barkham, encouraged him to leave his curacy there on the grounds of his nonconformity.[67] Hooker's assistant at the Little Baddows school was John Eliot, a graduate of Jesus College, Cambridge. He wrote an account of the seminary, which was available to Cotton Mather but does not seem to have survived. In his time studying under Hooker, he made a great deal of spiritual, as well as intellectual, progress.[68]

At Felsted, the vicar was Samuel Wharton, an appointee of the Earl of Warwick. He took up the mantle of his predecessor, Ezekiel Culverwell, who offered to accompany Joan Drake to Dedham, and, working with the schoolmaster, Martin Holbeach, Wharton kept Felsted a fruitful centre of godliness. William Gouge had been an early product of this environment, and after John Preston recommended his pupil, Holbeach, as schoolmaster, this tradition continued. Holbeach attracted pupils from a wide geographical area, including four sons of Oliver Cromwell. When Samuel Rogers attended the school he 'got more good in 2. yeares with the blessing of god, upon the diligent labours of my godly master Mr Holbeach then I got in many twoos before'.[69] As elsewhere, the usher's salary was used to fund the study of divinity students. After the Restoration, Holbeach was remembered as a tutor who 'scarcely bred any man that was loyall to his prince', and Wharton was troubled for his nonconformity long before the arrival of Bishop Laud.[70] Wharton certainly attended the conference, and Holbeach knew Shepard in Essex, and Hooker in Preston's circle in Cambridge,

---

[66] K. Shipps, 'Lay Patronage of East Anglian Clerics in Pre-revolutionary England', Yale University PhD, 1971, p. 175, citing a letter from the Davis MSS in the possession of the Massachusetts Historical Society, printed as Appendix XIII to his thesis; Mather, III p. 46; McGiffert (ed.), *God's Plot*, p. 74 (Burroughes lodged the Shepard family while they waited for a ship to New England, see ibid., pp. 34, 63); GLRO DL/C 193 ff. 166, 192–5.

[67] Rogers was eventually persuaded to emigrate 'by his respect unto Mr Hooker', Mather, III pp. 104–6; H. Smith, *The Ecclesiastical History of Essex under the Long Parliament and Commonwealth* (Colchester, 1933) pp. 30, 32. See below, pp. 170–2 for Rogers' troubles.

[68] Mather, III pp. 59, 173–211. Hooker was licensed as a schoolmaster at Great Baddows from 1628, GL 9537/13 f. 12, but this was probably in response to the prompting of the visitation of 1627, when he was presented for teaching without a licence, GLRO DL/C 344 f. 32v.

[69] QUB Percy MS 7 ff. 2–3.

[70] B. Donegan, 'Clerical Patronage of Robert Rich, Second Earl of Warwick', *PAPS* 120 (1976) p. 405; for Gouge and Culverwell, P. S. Seaver, *Puritan Lectureships*, p. 182; Morgan, *Prince Charles's Puritan Chaplain*, pp. 44, 151, 195; M. Craze, *A History of Felsted School* (Chelmsford, 1989) pp. 11–12; ERO D/Q 11/33/1; GL 9537/11 f. 139v; SP 16/175/104. Felsted also provided an education for the sons of Thomas Fairfax and the godly minsters Edmund Sparrowhawke, William Leigh, Giles Allen and Giles Firmin: F. S. Moller (ed.), *Alumni Felstedienses 1564–1691* (London, 1931).

where he attended Queens'.[71] It seems probable that, like the preceding examples, Wharton and Holbeach introduced aspiring ministers to Hooker's conference.

At the funeral of Samuel Collins, vicar of Braintree since 1614, Matthew Newcomen asked: 'Yea, how many have cause to bless God for the Ministers that were brought up in his family, under his Eye, Care and Tuition who have since proved eminent and worthy instruments in the Church of Christ.'[72] John Rogers of Dedham inspired students going to and coming from Cambridge; Richard Rogers trained students in his household; his son, Daniel, followed these examples. At Finchingfield, Stephen Marshall trained Hugh Glover, who eventually succeeded his tutor. While he was at Finchingfield, Glover assisted Marshall as curate and in the parish school, which he took over in 1631.[73] Essex may well have been the best provided county in England for household seminaries; this may well have been one of the factors that encouraged Thomas Hooker to settle there. It seems unreasonable to resist the conclusion that the coordination of the further education of godly ministers was a central task of his work in the county.

We may close this discussion with a brief assessment of the impact of the household seminary. On an institutional level, the impact was probably fairly slight. We have no way of assessing the proportion of the ministry that experienced the seminaries and if we could it seems likely that it would be a minority. It was by no means the only destination for a young minister fresh out of university: many spent time as chaplains in the households of gentle professors, others moved directly into benefices, lectureships or became schoolteachers. On an individual level, however, the impact of a seminary could be enormous. It provided a model household, fitting into the Reformation model of the 'spiritualised household',[74] and cannot have failed to make an impact on those parishes which provided a home for a seminary. For the students, the impact must have been greater still. Unlike

[71] McGiffert (ed.), *God's Plot*, pp. 51, 50, 74; Morgan, *Puritan Chaplain*, pp. 43–4. Holbeach later disagreed acrimoniously with his patron when he became a convinced Independent in the 1640s, and went on to become vicar of High Easter and a clerical assistant to the commissioners for the ejection of scandalous ministers in the 1650s: CUL Add MSS 33 unfol.; Smith, *Ecclesiastical History of Essex*, p. 337.

[72] Matthew Newcomen, *A Sermon Preached at the Funerals of the Reverend and Faithful Servant of Jesus Christ in the Work of the Gospel, Mr Samuel Collins* (1658) p. 50.

[73] For John Rogers: John Collinges, *A New Lesson for the Indoctus Doctor* (1654) pp. 8–10; E. Axon (ed.), *Oliver Heywood's Life of John Angier of Denton, Chetham Soc.* n.s. 97 (1937) pp. 50–1; for Richard Rogers, W. Haller, *The Rise of Puritanism* (New York, 1938) p. 35; for Daniel Rogers, QUB Percy MS 7 ff. 23, 26, 49, 352; for Marshall and Glover, ERO D/P 14/18/1A; D/P 14/25/3; GLRO DL/C 342 f. 59v (Marshall's licence to teach at Wethersfield, 1624); DL/C 343 f. 128v; GL 9537/15 f.30; 9537/14 f. 15v.

[74] See C. Hill, *Society and Puritanism in Pre-Revolutionary England* (Harmondsworth, 1969) ch. 13.

the other early career options, the seminary placed the young minister in a clerical environment. The lessons of the seminary were imbibed through constant intercourse with the clerical ideal, in the practice of the ministry, and in the ordering of the household and of the self. For many ministers, time in the seminary was a critical stage in their spiritual growth. Of his time with Thomas Hooker, John Eliot wrote,

the Lord said unto my dead Soul, Live; and through the Grace of Christ, I do live, and I shall live forever! When I came to this blessed Family, I then saw, and never before, the Power of Godliness, in its Lively Vigour, and Efficacy.[75]

The godly household integrated the young minister into godly society. As the idea of lineage was so central to the sense of self for early modern people, it is not surprising to find this integration expressed in these terms. Often, the cleric was drawn into a godly lineage literally; like Christopher Burrell and Thomas Shepard, many ministers married the daughters of their mentors. In a more spiritual sense, however, the same is true. We are familiar with the replication of biblical genealogies from godly biography:[76] residing in the family of an eminent preacher, many young clerics could inscribe themselves in a spiritual lineage which was as important, if not more so, than their biological one. The connection was made explicit by John Beadle. He advised his audience to

set down the time when, the place where and the person by whom he was converted . . . You keep an account of the day wherein you were born, and why not of the day wherein you were born again.[77]

The household seminaries were, then, a means of drawing the young godly minister ever more completely into godly society. As alternative bonds of loyalty were forged, sometimes threatening, sometimes reinforcing older ones, the godly minister was established within a community of like-minded clerics. The dual influences of piety and education were expressed in the language of family ties, an affective but also an authoritative bond. When Increase Mather dedicated the *Life* of his father, Richard, to his Dorchester congregation, he wrote of the 'Life of him that was to many of you a Spiritual (as to me a Natural) Father'; the former bond was seen to be at least as important as the latter.[78] As Thomas Foxley was said to remark of the people he converted: 'Behold, I and the children that God hath given me.'[79]

[75] Mather, III p. 59.   [76] Haller, *Rise of Puritanism*, pp. 65–6.
[77] Beadle, *Journal or Diary of a Thankful Christian*, p. 48.
[78] [Increase Mather] *Life and Death of Richard Mather* (1670), 'To the Church and Inhabitants of Dorchester in New England.'
[79] Thomas Fuller, *The Worthies of England* (ed. J. Freeman) (London, 1952) pp. 670–1.

2

Profitable conferences and the settlement of godly ministers

I

A period of tuition in the household of a godly minister was plainly intended to be a temporary arrangement. The task of the seminaries was to fit young ministers for service in the parishes. It comes as no surprise, therefore, to find that clerical networks existed to promote the settlement of such ministers in appropriate posts. The placement of godly ministers was an abiding concern, one which, naturally, was one of the functions identified by Mather in his account of Thomas Hooker's work in Essex.

We noted earlier the refusal of Emmanuel to pursue impropriations for its graduates and fellows; in such circumstances, social networks fostered by profitable conferences were of paramount importance. The effect of such contacts is the heavy weighting of the college's geographical influence. The statutory preference for Essex and Northampton was not over-whelming, and it is in the networks of patronage and advice that we find the explanation of the dominance of these counties in the careers of Emmanuel graduates. Once connections had been built, their continued employment would tend to strengthen geographical biases. As Joan Schenk Ibish has shown in detail, this dominance, especially pronounced in Essex, was well established before our main period of interest. The number of ministers moving to Essex outweighed the numbers of Essex natives attending the college, the main effect of the statute, by four to one.[1]

For a minister with a strong sense of pastoral calling, the translation from one post to another was not to be taken lightly: established channels of consultation reinforced concentrations of college men with every new generation. Moreover, as a minister gained a reputation more than one post might be offered to him.[2] While Samuel Fairclough was being tutored by

---

[1] J. Schenk Ibish, 'Emmanuel College: the Founding Generation, with a Biographical Register of the Members of the College, 1584–1604', Harvard University PhD (1985) pp. 282–8 and ch. 2 *passim*.

[2] These questions were considered sufficiently serious to merit inclusion among the cases of

Richard Blackerby in his seminary at Ashen, on the Essex side of the Stour, he preached every Sunday ' . . . and Providence so ordered it, that he was sent for, far and near, and especially by the Ministers and Congregations of Market Towns, and these in divers Counties. In Essex he was invited often to preach at Colchester, Braintree, Walden and Thackstead [and also Pentlow and Belchamp Walter]. In Suffolk, he preached at Hadleigh, Sudbury and Clare . . . .' In 1619, Kings Lynn was in need of a lecturer: they turned to Emmanuel College for advice, and Lawrence Chaderton, the master, recommended Thomas Hooker. When Hooker turned down the offer, the town turned to Fairclough and offered him the lectureship, unfortunately at the same time as the lectureship at Clare fell vacant; Clare was a poorer pulpit, but closer to Blackerby. 'Returning therefore to Mr Blackerby and advising with him, and with divers other friends they all persuaded him to go to Lynn . . . .' Unfortunately, he was not allowed to settle there and returned to Clare, forced out by the attentions of Bishop Harsnett. On his return, Nathaniel Barnardiston called him to preach at Barnardiston, in Suffolk. Others proposed that Thomas Weld, who had completed his studies and was without employment, could fill the vacancy and so a second conference was called to deal with the problem. In the event, Fairclough took the Barnardiston post, and Weld was probably promised a lectureship at Haverhill, further up the Stour valley, where he appears shortly after.[3]

These conferences were more than administrative; they were associated with forms of fasting and prayer which invested the decision taken with an element of divine sanction. For instance, John Wilson, drawn into the Stour valley by his reading of Richard Rogers' *Seven Treatises* while he was an undergraduate at King's College, Cambridge, preached at those same centres which welcomed Fairclough and Blackerby, at Steeple Bumpstead, Stoke-by-Clare, Clare and Candish. He was invited to settle at Sudbury, 'with which invitation he cheerfully complied, and the more cheerfully because of his opportunity to be near old Mr Richard Rogers . . . and yet he accepted not the Pastoral Charge of the Place, without a Solemn Day of Prayer and Fasting (wherein the Neighbouring Ministers assisted) at his election.'[4] This functional elision allowed a variety of interrelated interpretations: ministers could be seen to be offering practical and professional support and advice, to be calling for the candidate's ministry to be blessed,

conscience discussed by William Ames in *Conscience with the Power and Cases Thereof* (1639) Book IV pp. 64–71.

[3] Clarke (1683) pp. 160–1; ERO D/ABA 1 ff. 69, 73; K. Shipps, 'Lay Patronage of East Anglian Puritan Clerics in pre-Revolutionary England', Yale University PhD (1971) p. 305; C. Jackson (ed.), 'Life of Master John Shaw', in *Yorkshire Diaries and Autobiographies of the Seventeenth and Eighteenth Centuries*, Surtees Soc. 65 (1875) p. 124.

[4] Mather, III p. 43.

or formally to be inducting a minister into his pastoral charge. The practice had ecclesiological connotations, which seem to have been only rarely discussed before the controversies in the Westminster Assembly.[5]

The close-knit godly clergy of north Essex continued to call special conferences and fasts right up to the establishment of Hooker's conference. Such a meeting was called to deal with the doubts of Stephen Marshall regarding an offer from Finchingfield late in 1625. Upon the death of Thomas Pickering in September, William Kempe tried to persuade Marshall, who had succeeded Richard Rogers as lecturer at neighbouring Wethersfield, to accept the vacant benefice. However, Marshall had accepted a library worth fifty pounds from his Wethersfield auditors in return for a promise that he would stay with them. Moreover, there were other candidates for the vacancy, including Daniel Rogers and William Leigh, Kempe's grandson. A conference was called to discuss Marshall's scruples and, after some debate, it was determined that his recent marriage and the changed economic circumstances following from that allowed him to accept the more valuable living. It was further decided that Daniel Rogers should follow Marshall into the pulpit that Rogers' father had made famous.[6]

It was natural for this practice to become one of the functions of Hooker's conference. The best-documented example is the case of Thomas Shepard. He had left Emmanuel College for a period of pastoral training and preparation for his master's degree in the household of Thomas Weld, now vicar of Terling, on the advice of John Preston.[7] Shepard's account deserves quotation at some length, as it shows the intricate mixture of pragmatism and providential religiosity which informed the ministers' meetings and Shepard's understanding of them.

> But before I came there [i.e. Terling] I was very solicitous what would become of me when I became Master of Arts, for then my time and portion would be spent, but when I came thither and had been there some little season until I was ready to be Master of Arts, one Dr Wilson had purposed to set up a lecture and give thirty

[5] See R. S. Paul, *The Assembly of the Lord: Politics and Religion in the Westminster Assembly and the 'Grand Debate'* (Edinburgh, 1985) pp. 319–25. For concern expressed in the 1630s see a letter of Henry Jessey to John Winthrop in February 1635, *Winthrop Papers* III (Boston, Mass., 1929–43) p. 188.

[6] Anon., *Life and Death of Stephen Marshall* (1680) pp. 3–4; Giles Firmin, *A Briefe Vindication of Mr Stephen Marshall*, appended to *Questions between the Conformist and the Nonconformist* (1681) n.p. William Leigh was curate at Denston in Suffolk in 1625. He later became rector of Groton and a Presbyterian. John Winthrop held him to be 'a man of verye good partes but of a melacholicke disposition, yet as sociable, and full of good discourse as I have knowne'. *Winthrop Papers* I p. 339. For more details on this phase of Marshall's career, see T. Webster, *Stephen Marshall and Finchingfield* (Chelmsford, 1994).

[7] M. McGiffert (ed.), *God's Plot: the Paradoxes of Puritan Piety being the Autobiography and Journal of Thomas Shepard* (Amherst, Mass., 1972) pp. 41–2, 45, for Preston's influence.

pounds per annum to the maintenance of it, and when I was among those worthies in Essex where we had monthly fasts they did propound it to me to take the lecture and to set it up at a great town in Essex called Coggeshall, and so Mr Weld especially pressed me unto it and wished me to seek God about it, and after fasting and prayer the ministers in those parts of Essex had a day of humiliation and they did seek the Lord for direction where to place the lecture. And towards the evening of that day they began to consider whether I should go to Coggeshall or no; most of the minsters were for it because it was a great town, and they did not know any place did desire it but they. Mr Hooker only did object against my going thither for being but inexperienced, and there being an old yet sly and malicious minister in the town who did but seem to give way to it to have it there, did therefore say it was dangerous and uncomfortable for little birds to build under the nests of old ravens and kites. But while they were thus debating it, the town of Earle's Colne, being about three miles off from Essex [*sic*: from Coggeshall], hearing that there was such a lecture to be given freely and considering that the lecture might enrich that poor town, they did therefore just at this time of day come to the place where the ministers met, viz. at Terling in Essex, and desired that it might be settled there for three yeares ... And when they thus came for it the ministers with one joint consent advised me to accept of the people's call and to stay among them if I found upon my preaching a little season with them that they still continued in their desires for my continuance there.[8]

The terms of the endowment funded the lectures for three years: if any good had been achieved in that time it was felt that the town would gladly pay for the lecturer, and if no good had been done 'it were pity they should have it any longer'. Shepard's preaching met with some measure of success, for the town provided forty pounds per annum for him at the end of the three years. Thereafter, the conference resolved to use the endowment, with Dr Wilson's permission, to fund a lecturer at Towcester, in Northamptonshire, Shepard's birthplace, which he referred to as 'Egypt, that profane and wicked town' and 'that sink and Sodom', perhaps a rather harsh verdict on a town that had enjoyed Anthony King, the veteran of the Vestarian Controversy, as a lecturer in the 1570s. The new lecturer was to be Samuel Stone, who, on completion of his education at Emmanuel, had studied under Richard Blackerby at Ashen. After taking his Master's degree he had been curate at Stisted but was silenced shortly before Shepard's three-year tenure was over, and so became available to take the gospel to Shepard's home town. Robert Sibthorpe later complained to Sir John Lambe that Towcester men opposing Laudian changes had 'been infected by Stoner a lecturer'.[9]

[8] Ibid., pp. 46–7.
[9] Ibid., pp. 48, 72, 40; W. J. Sheils, *The Puritans in the Diocese of Peterborough 1558–1610*, Publications of the Northamptonshire Record Society 30 (Northampton, 1979) p. 26; Clarke (1683) p. 58; J. Cox (ed.), *The Records of the Borough of Northampton* (Northampton, 1898) vol. II p. 397. In 1640, a survivor of Hooker's conference, Samuel Wharton, vicar of Felsted, recommended Ralph Josselin for the Earls Colne lectureship: A. MacFarlane (ed.), *The Diary of Ralph Josselin 1616–1683, Records of Social and Economic History* n.s. III (London, 1976) p. 10.

The religious dimensions emerge more strongly in John Howe's account of Thomas Ball's removal to Northampton. Having followed John Preston from Queens' College, Cambridge to Emmanuel, 'he was not onely entreated, but zealously sollicited by the affectionate Letters of the neighbouring Ministers', to accept the lectureship at Northampton, but was unsure about relinquishing his fellowship.

> But yet, that he might not, like Jonas flee to Tarshish, when God give him a call to Nineve, he would not acquiesce in his own Judgement, but communicated the business to divers Reverend Ministers . . . These Reverend Ministers did appoint a time of meeting, and after the impartial ballancing of all arguments, they judged the arguments for his removal to be the most weighty, in the scales of the Sanctuary.[10]

Similarly, when Julines Herring was suspended and received a call to Amsterdam from John Rulice, he travelled to London and only accepted the call 'after much seeking of God, and serious consulting with godly Brethren', including John Ball, Thomas Pierson and Josias Nichols, at the home of Lady Bromley; Jeremiah Whitaker only moved from Stretton in Rutland to Mary Magdelen, Bermondsey when he had received 'the approbation of many godly Ministers, whom he consulted in the case'.[11] Thomas Wilson, preacher at Teddington, was offered a post at Otham, whereupon he 'asked the judgement of his Neighbour Ministers in the Country and some in the City of London' who granted him permission to accept the offer.[12]

There was nothing inherently subversive about activities like these: ministers were needed and it was natural that lay patrons and corporations should turn to the preachers they admired most, perhaps more readily than to an episcopal hierarchy which, *pace* Fincham, may sometimes have seemed a little remote. Conflict was most likely when a town turned repeatedly to the network of ministers, and patrons consistently selected ministers known to be out of sympathy with the hierarchy, nonconformists or unbeneficed lecturers. In Colchester, for instance, there was an ongoing struggle between bishop and corporation which ran from the early seventeenth century to beyond the Restoration. Thomas Ravis, Bishop of London between 1607 and 1609, tried to encourage the corporation to use local preachers, 'men of learning, integrity and honest conversation, and whose maintenance was very small'. He issued an order to reform the lecture and included a list of twenty-two ministers to supply the lecture as a combination, including Richard Harris, recently dismissed by a narrow majority in the corporation.[13] The bishop's efforts went unrewarded: the

---

[10] John Howe, *Real Comforts . . . a Sermon Preached at the Funeral of Thomas Ball* (1660) p. 40.

[11] Clarke (1677) p. 165; Simeon Ashe, *Living Loves*, p. 51.   [12] Clarke (1683) p. 20.

[13] P. Morant, *History and Antiquities of Essex* (1768) vol. I p. 100; H. Smith, *The Ecclesias-*

corporation's next choice was William Ames, newly forced out of Christ's College, Cambridge, East Anglian born and a close friend of Daniel Rogers and Thomas Hooker. As he was unlicensed, Ravis' successor, George Abbot, easily moved Ames on to begin his Dutch exile.[14] The next two lecturers, William Eyre to 1617 and Francis Liddell to 1628, were both Emmanuel trained. Eyre may have been a compromise or a disappointment, for a scurrilous anti-Laudian satire of the early 1630s claimed that 'if times of Popery would come, A dainty friar he would make'.[15] Francis Liddell, in contrast, prompted Robert Aylett, the bishop's commissary and a vigorous promoter of Laudian policy in the 1630s, to write to the corporation in 1623, denouncing Colchester's 'factious multitude who will allow no minister but of their own calling'.[16] From 1628 to 1631 the lecturer was a beneficed minister, Richard Maden of St Peter's, Colchester, but in 1631 Bishop Laud was presented with a new candidate.

> Colchester men would have had his admission of Mr Bridges of Emmanuel for their lecturer in Mr Maiden's stead. He was angry, and said, When you want one, you must go first to Dr Gouge and then to Dr Sibs, and then you come to me: I scorn to be so used; I'll never have him lecture in my diocesse, that will spew in the pulpit . . . [Bridge had evidently lectured on Rev. 3.15].

William Bridge was forced out and, after a period in Norwich, exiled to the Netherlands, returning as one of the authors of the *Apologeticall Narration*. Richard Maden was restored for three years, until in his turn he was replaced by John Knowles, who ministered to John Rogers on his deathbed and preached his friend's funeral sermon.[17]

In this context, the details of a struggle between ecclesiastical centre and localities are less important than the recognition, implicit in the complaints of Ravis and Aylett, and explicit in Laud's outburst, that there were alternative mechanisms of prestige and advancement in the church. The mechanisms translating ministers from college to a suitable benefice or lectureship were oiled by ministerial sociability, and reached a height of

tical History of Essex under the Long Parliament and the Commonwealth (Colchester, 1933) pp. 23–4; GLRO DL/C 339 f. 62v–63; ERO Morant MSS 41 f. 121. Ravis may have been responding to an appeal from within a divided corporation but, if so, his intervention was heavy handed, judging from the following unanimous appointment. Cf. O. U. Kalu, 'The Jacobean Church and Essex Puritans', University of Toronto PhD (1972) p. 417ff.

[14] S. A. Bondos-Greene, 'The End of an Era: Cambridge Puritanism and the Christ's College election of 1609', *HJ* 25 (1982) p. 201; K. L. Sprunger, *Learned Doctor William Ames* (Urbana, Ill., 1972) pp. 13, 17, 25. The Aldermen of Colchester paid Ames £5 'for his paines': ERO Morant MSS 45 f. 99.

[15] SP 16/229/123; Smith, pp. 63–7. Eyre signed the conformist petition against Hooker (on which see below, pp. 152–3), SP 16/152/4.

[16] ERO Morant MSS D/Y 2/7 f. 19.

[17] *MHSC* 3rd ser. I (1825) p. 236; Smith, pp. 23–4; T. W. Davids, *Annals of Evangelical Nonconformity in the county of Essex* (London, 1863) pp. 528, 547.

efficiency in conferences such as Hooker's. The perception of subversion in such activity was by no means necessary, but it was not seen by Laud in isolation. As *Mercurius Civicus* reported in the civil war years, 'if any man . . . had letters testimonial from Patriarch White of Dorchester, Mr Cotton of Boston, or the like . . . this man was a choyce plant, and fit for their soyle'.[18]

On occasions, however, the machinery worked in reverse: in 1628, for instance, the mastership of Emmanuel College fell vacant with the death of John Preston. It was vital that this post, crucial for the godly, was filled quickly and suitably. Experience had taught that if action was not swift and effective, a master would be imposed on the college, with disastrous consequences. Puritan control of Christ's College had been lost in 1609 with the election of Valentine Cary, and in 1622 Emmanuel had been very careful to avoid a similar fate. Laurence Chaderton's retirement had been carefully stage-managed in secret. William Bedell, writing from Bury St Edmunds, claimed:

> The news of Dr Chaderton's resigning and the election of Mr Preston to the Mastership of Emmanuel was altogether unexpected in these parts; whereof I doubt not there are secret motives and perhaps conditions more than the world knowes of.

Preston's rapid decline, and his death at the home of John Dod in Fawsley on 20 July, 1628, allowed no such luxury.[19] By the end of the month, Nathaniel Ward, who had graduated from Emmanuel in 1603, had written to William Sandcroft, beneficed at Stanford-le-Hope in Essex, urging him to accept the mastership. Sandcroft seems to have been hesitating and was probably reluctant to give up his living before the mastership was secure. Ward was concerned that delay would make a contested election more likely. He wrote,

> my earnest suite to yow is, that yow would lay downe all fleshly pleas, all private and personal respects, melancholy and such modest objections and make all haste to give way to their motions. The kingdome of Satan finds instruments inough and such as crowd fast inough for advantages agst Xt and the truth.

Ward had visited Sandcroft at his home in the company of Thomas Hooker, but Sandcroft had been away. Evidently, he had also declined to attend a meeting of the conference, possibly at Inworth, where he 'might have met with incouragement inough and arguments pro and con; I mean as full a discussion as London can afford yow'.[20]

---

[18] *Mercurius Civicus* in *Somers Tracts* IV pp. 534–84. Robert Harley turned to Stephen Marshall to check the credentials of a minister being considered for one of his Herefordshire benefices, BL Add MS 70106 f. 21.

[19] Bondos-Greene, 'End of an Era', pp. 197–208; BodL Tanner MSS 73 f. 129; E. S. Shuckburgh, *Emmanuel College* (London, 1904) pp. 54–6, 66.

[20] BL Harl MS 3783 f. 11.

At the same time, four of the fellows of Emmanuel were writing in similar terms communicating the 'desires of the colledge, Sir Henry Mildmay, Mr Cotton, with many others of your friends'. To make it clear that this was not the request of a faction, the whole body of the fellowship wrote the following week:

. . . we not only earnestly desire you, but in Christ chardge you to accept of this our call: if you fayle us the Colledge sinkes certainly, and way will be made for a mandat[e] to our undooinge.[21]

It is not clear whether Sandcroft had accepted Ward's arguments, or if he responded to his advice to consult with Laurence Chaderton, but by the first week in August Sandcroft had yielded and accepted the post. This must have come as a great relief to the godly. Ward had hoped that 'if it come to a contestation or if the King interpose,' he had 'some friends, powerful with his Majesty and the Duke [of Buckingham] that shall trye their strength faithfully and freely in the coll[ege's] behalf, but I pray prevent all hazzards with a speedy dispatch of the business'.[22]

The intensity of concern for the fate of Emmanuel is hardly surprising. It will be clear by now that the conference drew upon many former members of the college, including, among those already mentioned, Shepard, Marshall, Hooker, Ward and John Rogers. However, it was more than feelings of loyalty towards the *alma mater* that provoked such feverish consultation, which, according to Ward, extended throughout East Anglia, into London and Northamptonshire. It is clear that the wider community of godly ministers appreciated that Emmanuel College was an integral part of a system to provide godly ministers and integrate them in the clerical community. If the system was to work well, the college had to provide the candidates for the parishes and the parochial ministry to be careful for the future of the college.

II

Collegiality in the counties was not, of course, dependent upon such occasions. In addition to the further education and settlement of young ministers, Thomas Hooker was, according to Mather, engaged in the promotion of 'Profitable Conferences', establishing a monthly meeting of godly ministers in the county. Regarding these, it is possible, initially at least, to speak less equivocally in terms of Puritanism. A monthly conference of godly ministers immediately reminds us of the conferences of the 1580s, which rose after the suppression of the prophesyings. R. G. Usher wrote of the conferences baldly in terms of the Presbyterian movement and

---

[21] BodL Tanner MS 155 ff. 22, 21.   [22] BL Harl MS 3783 f. 11.

although Patrick Collinson, writing of the famous Dedham conference, suggested that 'to call it a Presbyterian *classis* would be to beg too many questions', his discussion was still very much in terms of the Elizabethan Puritan movement.[23]

This context has proved attractive to Hooker's biographers. Although none have treated his circle in Essex in depth, it has been the norm to refer to his monthly meeting with an assumption of ecclesiological significance. For G. H. Williams, Hooker 'became the spiritual leader of a large company of Essex ministers of nonconformist sympathies'; for Frank Shuffleton, the meeting was 'a sort of shadow synod'.[24] To a degree, this is not unreasonable. Thomas Cartwright had, after all, defined the business of a conference in his *Second Admonition*, of 1573, drawing on Scottish and continental practice, but naturally rooting the practice in Scripture:

A conference I call the meeting of some certain ministers and other brethren . . . at some certain place as it was at Corinth . . . to confer and exercise themselves in prophesying or in interpreting the scriptures . . . At which conferences . . . any of the brethren are to be at the order of the whole, to be employed upon some affaires of the Church . . . The demeanours also of the ministers may be examined and rebuked.[25]

The conferences of the 1580s differed from Cartwright's model in important respects: they ignored diocesan boundaries; allowed only one speaker in discussion, whereas Cartwright anticipated several; tended to be exclusively clerical meetings and adopted a secret and mobile meeting, whereas Cartwright expected a public and static institution. As Collinson concluded, the Elizabethan conferences 'adopted a pragmatic rather than a doctrinaire attitude to the realities of life under the Elizabethan settlement'.[26]

Although conferences were found in every county where there were Puritan ministers in any strength, the best documented of the meetings was focused on Dedham, where a group of reformers exiled from Norwich instituted a formal order of conference on 22 October 1582. In itself the

[23] R. G. Usher (ed.), *The Presbyterian Movement in the Reign of Queen Elizabeth as Illustrated by the Minute Book of the Dedham Classis, 1582–89*, Camden Society 3rd ser., 8 (1905); P. Collinson, *The Elizabethan Puritan Movement* (London, 1967) pp. 226, 208–21.

[24] G. H. Williams *et al.*, *Writings*, p. 12; F. Shuffleton, *Thomas Hooker, 1586–1647* (Princeton, N.J., 1977) p. 74; S. Bush, *The Writings of Thomas Hooker: Spiritual Adventures in Two Worlds* (London, 1980) does not devote much space to these aspects of Hooker's Essex career.

[25] W. H. Frere and C. E. Douglas (eds.), *Puritan Manifestos: a Study of the Origin of the Puritan Revolt* (London, 1954) pp. 107–8, citing 1 Cor. 14, Acts 8.14 and 13.2 and Galatians 2.14. For the contemporary models see Collinson, *Movement*, pp. 177–9, 296–7, 299–301.

[26] Ibid., p. 228.

surviving minute book of the Dedham conference is a crucial document of the Elizabethan Puritan movement, and for my present purposes it is an important part of the background to Stuart clerical association in Essex, and so deserves some attention.[27]

The Dedham conference held meetings up to the summer of 1589, when a scandal involving Richard Parker, the vicar of Dedham, seems to have struck at the heart of the formal meetings, although ministerial exercises continued on an ad hoc basis. The practice of the conference through these years was closely modelled on the Norwich order for prophesying of 1575. The proceedings followed a tripartite division of activity: firstly, a single sermon, on a pre-selected text; secondly, conference on the text, progressively examining a book of the Bible, as in the prophesyings, with the moderator, selected by rota, delivering the judgement of the assembly; thirdly, the conference taking an innovative administrative role, allotting time for questions about 'necessary matters' and 'profitable questions'.

In another important respect the conference departed from the practice of prophesying: there was less concern with the improvement of the abilities of non-graduate ministers, than with the needs of a very well educated godly elite. Those who accepted the benefits of the conference theoretically submitted themselves to the advice, if not the direction of their brethren and were not permitted to break fellowship voluntarily, although in practice the members tended to follow their own best judgements in matters regarding their own congregations.

Although the fame of the Dedham conference owes much to the caprices of documentary survival, the Stour valley developments were exceptional. It cannot be argued from this, and more shadowy conferences, that there was a formal *classis* structure dedicated to the subversion of the ecclesiastical *status quo*. Collinson concludes that the influence of the Norwich ministers, Edward Chapman and Richard Crick, the position of the group at the edge of the two dioceses, and the established Protestantism of the area combined to make the Dedham conference 'precocious and unusual' although they were rivalled by the *classes* in Northamptonshire. There were other conferences in the area but none approached the formality or cohesion of the Dedham group. John Knewstubb was at the centre of a west Suffolk nexus of ministers, and Richard Rogers was involved in a meeting to the west of the Dedham

---

[27] Ibid., pp. 222–39. For detailed discussion see P. Collinson, 'The Puritan Classical Movement in the Reign of Elizabeth I', University of London PhD (1957) pp. 357–60; and for a more recent and intense examination of Puritanism in the Stour valley see A. R. Pennie, 'The Evolution of Puritan Mentality in an Essex Cloth Town', Sheffield University PhD (1989). Dr Pennie confines his discussion of clerical association to the first half of this period.

conference.[28] Although Rogers regretted the 'small use' of the ministerial meetings, these two men were sufficiently active to act as correspondents for the godly ministers in their respective neighbourhoods. Clearly, the intercourse of East Anglian ministers was not wholly dependent upon formal organisation and so, while Collinson is undoubtedly correct when he argues that formal conferences 'may have ceased in almost all districts', the habit of association could not have been eradicated entirely by the efforts of Whitgift and Bancroft.[29]

Something like a disciplinary meeting seems to have survived in south Leicestershire under the influence of Arthur Hildersham, who was accounted 'the prime Ringleader of all schismaticall persons in that countrey, both of the Clergy and Laiety',[30] but for most areas we have to consider other forms of association. There were many circumstances that brought godly ministers together, many reasons for clerical sociability, and for most gatherings, even Richard Bancroft would have struggled to have found a Presbyterian plot. In the period following the Whitgiftian reaction, there are hints that association continued in the Stour valley. Richard Blackerby was perhaps the most active promoter of extra-parochial association in Jacobean East Anglia: 'if any such sin were committed in a neighbour town, or any judgement fell out in the vicinage, or in the nation he would be sure to get divers ministers and Christians together, and keep a day of fasting and prayer'.[31] Edward Chapman's successor as lecturer of Dedham, John Rogers, seems to have been another agent of clerical collegiality in the first quarter of the seventeenth century. A suggestive series of wills of the Dedham family of Edmund Anger, who married Rogers' daughter, Bridget, offers shadowy evidence of ministerial links in the neighbourhood. John Angier, the nephew of Edmund, lived with Rogers before his university career and his family left legacies to Rogers, Thomas Cottesford and Henry Gullson, vicar and schoolmaster of Dedham respectively, and also to a number of neighbouring ministers including John Carter, preacher at Belstead, near Ipswich, of whom Clarke observed: 'Many ministers that privately did converse with him, lighted their candles at his.' Another was Ezekiel Culverwell, the editor of Richard Rogers and former rector of Great Stambridge in the south of the county, who had a great respect for John Rogers' pastoral gifts; others were Edward Sparrowhawke, the fiery

[28] These two paragraphs draw upon Collinson, *Movement*, pp. 222–39 and *passim*, and Usher (ed.), *Presbyterian Movement, passim*.

[29] M. M. Knappen (ed.), *Two Elizabethan Puritan Diaries* (Chicago, Ill., 1933) p. 53; Collinson, *Movement*, p. 437.

[30] N. B. Shurtleff (ed.), *Records of the Governor and Company of Massachusetts Bay in New England* (Boston, Mass., 1853) vol. I p. 37; DWL Morrice MS J 1631 (14).

[31] Clarke (1683) p. 62; cf. John Ball of Whitmore in the same period, Clarke (1677) pp. 147–8.

preacher of Coggeshall, Francis Liddell, lecturer at Colchester, Edward Collins of Boxted, John Edes of Lawford and ministers in Mistley and Layer Breton.[32] Similar connections can be shown for early Stuart Suffolk. In 1604 Nicholas Chaplin, the minister of Capel St Mary left an instruction for his executor, his son-in-law, the preacher Thomas Chambers, to purchase ten pairs of winter gloves and to distribute them among his colleagues. Among these friends were Henry Sandes and John Knewstubb. If we turn to the wills of these two, written in the mid-1620s, we find the same pattern. Knewstubb gave five pounds to 'my anncient good freind' Henry Sandes, two pounds to Humphrey Munnings, Thomas Chambers and Mr Chamberlin of Hunston, one guinea to Ezekiel Culverwell, and smaller sums to about a dozen other ministers, including Robert Stansby, Samuel Ward, the Ipswich lecturer, Humphrey Morgan and John Wilson. When Sandes came to make his will two years later, six 'reverent true friends' were each to receive a silver spoon. Each of these friends had been recognised by Knewstubb or Chaplin or by both; they were Chambers, Wilson, Stansby, Morgan, John Harrison and Richard Peachy.[33]

Such slender evidence is bolstered by impressions of the peripatetic preaching of Rogers and others in the Stour valley in this period. Rogers preached at Kersey and Boxted in Suffolk in James' reign; Daniel Rogers appeared regularly in the Boxford pulpit before he held a preaching post of his own, as did John Knewstubb, a pastoral colleague of John Rogers, and William Ames and John Carter. Richard Blackerby delivered sermons at Castle Hedingham, Stoke-by-Clare, Hundon, Ashen, Polstead, Yeldham

[32] E. Axon (ed.), *Oliver Heywood's Life of John Angier of Denton, Chetham Soc.* n.s. 97 (1937) p. 2. John Angier, the subject of Heywood's biography, was the first of his family to spell his name this way. For his uncle's marriage to Bridget Rogers, see H. F. Waters, *Genealogical Gleanings in England* (Boston, Mass., 1901) vol. I p. 210. This source also suggests the sort of intermarriage between clerical families which Rosemary O'Day has identified as an important factor in clerical society: R. O'Day, *The English Clergy*, ch. 12. For Carter, Clarke (1662) p. 6–7; for Culverwell's respect for Rogers, Heartwell, *Trodden Down Strength*, p. 97; for Sparrowhawke, H. Smith, *Ecclesiastical History of Essex*, p. 55f and below, ch. 12; for Francis Liddell, ibid., p. 23. John Rogers also taught the son of Edward Collins, the minister of Boxted, John Collinges, *A New Lesson for the Indoctus Doctor* (1654) p. 8; John Edes, vicar of Lawford from 1615 to 1638, later signed a petition defending Thomas Hooker and survived to join the thirteenth classis of the Essex Presbytery and witness in the Essex witchcraft trials of the 1640s, T. W Davids, *Annals of Evangelical Nonconformity in the county of Essex* (London, 1863) pp. 156–7, *A True and Exact Relation of the Several Examinations and Confessions of the late witches arraigned and executed in Essex* (1645). Sparrowhawke may have had family in Dedham, G. Selement and B. Wooley (eds.), *Thomas Shepard's 'Confessions', PCSM: Collections* 58 (1981) p. 62. Three of these men, Liddell, Sparrowhawke and Rogers were *alumni* of Emmanuel College, where John Collinges and John Angier were also educated; all the other identifiable ministers were also educated at Cambridge.

[33] 'Bequest of Gloves to "Preachers"', *East Anglian* n.s. 11 (1905–6) p. 352; NorRo NCC Mittings f. 296; PRO PROB 11/143 f. 429. I am grateful to Frank Bremer for drawing the last two wills to my attention.

Parva and Belchamp Walter. Some of these occasions can be shown quite explicitly to have brought clergy together, as when Knewstubb preached Robert Welsh's funeral sermon at Little Waldingfield 'and he with other preachers carried his coffin on their shoulders'.[34] Unbeneficed men such as Daniel Rogers and Blackerby also made themselves available for nonconformist baptisms and communions.[35]

It would be quite incorrect to look for a sort of sub-Presbyterian *classis* in such links; there are a number of more fruitful approaches. On one level, they are better explained in terms of the natural sociability of members of a profession increasingly set apart from their neighbours by education and experience. Rosemary O'Day has considered clerical society in terms of group identity, and her impression is that such links were strongest in areas where natural sociability was supplemented by clerical activity of the types already discussed. She suggests that

> It would be precipitate to conclude that clerical associations only emerged within the context of such gatherings [i.e. fasts and conferences] or within the Puritan connection, but it is evident that in these gatherings a sense of professional cohesion and awareness was fostered and the tremendous enthusiasm for improved preaching and scriptural learning through communal effort was engendered.[36]

This enthusiasm for professional improvement is central to Jacobean clerical associations. Here we have to consider the impact on clerical collegiality of the combination lecture. The regularity and voluntarism of these lectures made them more significant occasions for clerical gatherings than episcopal visitations and synods, especially as the sermons were usually attended by other ministers in the combination, or panel of preachers, who supplied these lectures, and were frequently followed by conference among the ministers and dinner paid for by corporations or even by the preachers themselves. Professor Collinson has suggested that such meetings were more indicative of the 'settled life' of the church than of its 'tensions and divisions'.[37] While this is true, it does not necessarily follow that all

---

[34] *Winthrop Papers* I pp. 244, 217, 243, 96, 258, 98, 103–4, 90, 105. For Welsh's funeral, ibid., p. 89; on clerical funerals cf. Clarke (1662) p. 20, where he notes 'a great confluence' of ministers at the funeral of John Carter, when the sermon was preached by Samuel Ward, the son of Richard Rogers' first wife. Ward was town lecturer at Ipswich. For Blackerby, Clarke (1683) p. 58; ERO D/ABA 1 f. 69; D/ABA 8 f. 8; GLRO DL/C 314 f. 252v.

[35] *Winthrop Papers* vol. I p. 259; ERO D/ABA 1 f. 185. Our knowledge of such pulpit exchanges and 'guest appearances' would greatly be improved if the books in which churchwardens were required to record the names of visiting preachers had been better kept or had a better survival rate. As it is, only one such fragment survives for Essex and none for Suffolk. The Essex survival is a note among the parish records of Great Dunmow ERO D/P 11/1/2, recording eleven visitors between mid-1632 and mid-1635. I am grateful to John Craig for discussions on this point.

[36] O'Day, *The English Clergy*, pp. 169–70.

[37] P. Collinson, 'Lectures by Combination: Structures and Characteristics of Church Life in

combination lectures fostered the peace of the church. William Bradshaw cut his teeth in the Midlands exercises at Repton, Burton-on-Trent and Ashby-de-la-Zouch, where the form was as close to the forbidden prophesyings and a suspended minister such as Arthur Hildersham could (admittedly with the connivance of his diocesan) exercise an influence otherwise stifled.[38] Such influence can be seen more explicitly in the case of John Norton. While he was a young curate at Bishops Stortford, Norton came under the influence of Jeremiah Dyke, the painful preacher of Epping, during conferences after the combination lecture. Becoming convinced of the sinfulness of ceremonies, he emigrated in 1634.[39]

It is interesting that Dyke had to cross the county border to join a combination, for Essex appears to be one of the few English counties where the institution put down very shallow roots.[40] There had been an abortive attempt to establish such provision for Chelmsford before Thomas Hooker arrived, and a slightly more successful one after his removal, albeit an attempt that failed to inspire confidence in the neighbouring ministry, which expected 'small success' in following their 'much affected single lecturer'. Earlier attempts to persuade the authorities in Colchester to convert their stipendiary lecture into a combination were similarly unsuccessful.[41]

Northamptonshire was rather better served in this respect. The most famous combination lecture in the county was probably that at Kettering, where the young John Williams, a future Bishop of Lincoln, preached. The combination, dominated by Robert Bolton, Joseph Bentham and Nicholas Estwick, was suppressed in the middle of the 1630s, despite the relatively moderate stances taken by the ministers, and, although he denied any part in its suppression, Bishop Dee declined to take any part in resurrecting the exercise. 'Where any such are in my diocese, while they deport themselves peaceably and conformably, I rest contented', he told Lord Montague, with the implication that the Kettering lecturers had not done so.[42] Such lectures existed across the county, at Brackley, Daventry, Oundle, Oakham, Peter-

17th-century England', in *Godly People: Essays on English Protestantism and Puritanism* (London, 1983) p. 469; cf. the conclusions of Dr Hajzyk, 'The Church in Lincolnshire c.1590–1640', University of Cambridge PhD (1980) pp. 266–73.

[38] Clarke (1677) pp. 49, 52, 56, 117–18. It must be noted that Collinson is careful to qualify his conclusions, 'Lectures', p. 497.

[39] Mather, III pp. 32–3.

[40] Another Essex minister who travelled over the border to preach in the Stortford lecture was Edward Symmons of Rayne, a friend of Stephen Marshall: Edward Symmons, *Foure Sermons* (1642). The second and third sermons in this collection were delivered at 'the public lecture at Stortford' in 1637 and 1638. It is intriguing that Samuel Rogers never mentions the combination lecture in his diary, for he was a resident of the town in the mid-1630s.

[41] SP 16/142/113; 144/36; 151/45; 152/16; 160/66; 161/54. For Colchester, see pp. 40–1.

[42] Collinson, 'Lectures by Combination', p. 484; *HMC Buccleuch MSS (Montagu House)* (London) I p. 175.

borough and Northampton. These combinations ranged across the Protestant spectrum, with that in Peterborough served by allies of the bishop, while Northampton provided a pulpit for more Puritanical preachers. Thomas Ball, the minister of All Saints, contributed to the lectures on Thursdays, and he was assisted by John Bullivant, William Castle, Daniel Cawdrey, James Cranford and others, a mixture of local incumbents and men who served parishes twenty miles to the east or west of Northampton. The geographical origins of ministers who visited and preached on Sundays were even further from the town. Thomas Hill came south-west from Titchmarsh, Thomas Perkins and Archibald Symmer south from Naseby and Great Oakley respectively. Sunday sermons were also provided by ministers visiting from beyond the diocese: Thomas Case and William Rathband, for instance. Although we have fewer details on the Daventry lecture we can be confident that it provided a godly diet of sermons, as it was patronised by the Knightly family and so could draw upon the godly ministers associated with the sheltered living of Fawsley. The principal lecturer was Daniel Wight, supported by John Dod, Robert Cleaver and Sampson Sheffield.[43]

In this context, it is perhaps more important to note that such settled patterns of professional association can only take us so far in explaining clerical collegiality among the godly. If, as seems to be the case, godly ministers were more inclined to sociability, we have to identify needs beyond the professional characteristics which, by the seventeenth century, were the common property of the majority of ministers of all stripes.

III

What stimuli existed to supplement the professional sociability of the godly minsters in Essex, given the limited impact of the combination lecture? The regularity of private fasts will be discussed later, but one particular form of private fast evolved into another form of 'profitable conference'. Late in the reign of Elizabeth, the practice of exorcism became a source of controversy, partly on theological grounds, but also for political reasons. The protracted pamphlet war focused on the activities of John Darrell, but he was far from alone in his efforts, and the official response in the 1604 Canons was not to deny the efficacy of fasting and prayer in exorcism, but to forbid exorcisms that lacked public authority.[44]

---

[43] Collinson, 'Lectures', pp. 483–4, 496; J. Fielding, 'Conformists, Puritans and the Church Courts: the Diocese of Peterborough, 1603–42', University of Birmingham PhD (1989) pp. 146–61.

[44] For exorcisms, K. Thomas, *Religion and the Decline of Magic* (London, 1971) pp. 574–80; M. MacDonald, 'Religion, Social Change and Psychological Healing in England,

Without denying the reality of the theological issues involved, this was a political act to curtail further the voluntary association of Puritan ministers for religious exercises. The common form of exorcisms brought together a number of ministers to wear down the possessed patient by a predetermined rota of preaching and prayer. As Stephen Greenblatt points out, there is a theatricality involved, an exposition of the power of Protestant ministers, with the audience intended to be the Catholic priesthood and the Church of England hierarchy as well as the general public. These efforts resembled the public attempts to convert imprisoned Catholic priests in England and the, perhaps more dramatic, competitive exorcisms staged by Catholic and Protestant clerics in post-Reformation Germany.[45] The theatre of exorcism (or more generally, spiritual healing) cannot have been lost on those ministers who participated and helped to foster the self-image of the godly as the most efficacious and painful of the clergy.

Although licences do not seem to have been issued, exorcisms were not unknown after the end of the Darrell episode and Colchester was one of a number of centres of such activity early in the reign of James. As described in the account of Mary Glover, the practice encouraged clerical society as ministers seem commonly to have outnumbered the laity on these occasions, increasingly so as exorcisms became less public.[46] One of the side-effects of this minimalisation of publicity may have been to harden the divisions between those who participated and those who did not. In fact, such activity was difficult to legislate out of existence, for there was, in

1600–1800', in *The Church and Healing SCH* 19 (1982) pp. 101–25; D. P. Walker, *Unclean Spirits: Possession and Exorcism in France and England in the Late Sixteenth and Seventeenth Centuries* (London, 1981). For a more detailed treatment of the Darrell episode, Collinson, *Movement*, pp. 437–8 and R. C. Marchant, 'John Darrell – Exorcist', *Transactions of the Thoroton Soc.*, 64 (1960); for the official response, E. Cardwell, *Synodalia: a Colection of Articles, Canons and Proceedings of Convocation . . . from 1547 to 1717* (Oxford, 1842) vol. I pp. 287–8, Canon 72.

[45] S. Greenblatt, *Shakespearean Negotiations: the Circulation of Social Energy in Renaissance England* (Oxford, 1990) pp. 94–128; L. Roper, *Oedipus and the Devil: Witchcraft, Sexuality and Religion in Early Modern Europe* (London, 1994) pp. 171–98; L. Roper, 'Magic and the Theology of the Body: Exorcism in Sixteenth-century Augsburg', in C. Zika (ed.), *No Gods except me: Orthodoxy and Religious Practice in Early Modern Europe 1200–1600* (Melbourne, 1991) pp. 84–113. The theatrical elements of the relations between imprisoned Catholic priests and godly ministers are discussed in M. Questier and P. Lake, 'Agency, Appropriation and Rhetoric under the Gallows: Puritans, Romanists and the State in Early Modern England', *PP* 153 (1996) pp. 87–95 and *passim*. cf M. Questier, *Conversion, Politics and Religion in England, 1580–1625* (Cambridge, 1996) pp. 175–6, 193–200.

[46] For the form of exorcisms and the Colchester example, J. Swan, *A True and Briefe Report of Mary Glovers Vexation, and of Her deliverance by the Means of Fasting and Prayer* (1603) p. 70 and *passim*; for the continuing practice and the lack of official sanction, Thomas, *Religion and the Decline of Magic*, pp. 579–80. John Yates defended exorcism by fasting and prayer in his *Gods Arraignment of Hypocrites* (1615) 'To the Christian Reader'; cf. Robert Bolton, *A Threefold Treatise* (1634) p. 36.

practice, no clear division between exorcism and the more extreme cases that formed the normal pastoral calling of the Puritan ministry as spiritual physicians. One Essex example of this elision survives in the testimony of a young man, E. R., who said:

> my parents did send for Mr Newstubs and Minister in Edmondsbury, and one Mr Rogers another minister of Deddam, who took a great deal of paines with me, and asked mee whome I did beleeve in; and I told them that I did beleeve in God that he would damne me; and they asked me, if God woulde damne me because I did beleeve in him; I answered no, but it was for that sin committed against God, and my innocent sister; and they asked mee, whether I was not sorry for that act, and I told them yes, for I had cause enough to be sorry, for I must be damned for that sin.

The efforts of John Rogers and John Knewstubbs were, on this occasion, unsuccessful,[47] but from such 'difficult cases' (in Mather's phrase) it is possible to reconstruct networks of referral and consultation which were characteristic of pastoral practice. As the biographer of William Gouge noted:

> By reason of his ability and dexterity in resolving Cases of Conscience, he was much sought unto for his judgement in doubtful cases, and scruples of Consciences, and that not only by ordinary Christians, but by divers Ministers also both in the City and the Country sometimes by Word of Mouth, and other sometimes by writing.[48]

This was the case in the action of Robert Woodford and his friend Jason Reading, the son of his patron, who took their disagreements to Gouge and to John Stoughton, hoping for the divines to come to a godly conclusion, as 'we are weake & exceedinge shallow, & too too partiall in judging thinges that concerne our selves', a conclusion which was, in fact, delivered some two months later.[49]

Similarly, Mather wrote of Thomas Hooker, that the 'Godly Ministers round about the Country would have recourse unto him, to be directed and resolved in their difficult cases'.[50] Well-documented cases of spiritual healing, particularly with gentle or noble melancholics, reveal the ground where pastoral reputations were made and advanced. The case of Joan

---

[47] Henry Walker, *Spirituall Experiences of Sundry Beleevers* (1652) pp. 359–62. For a parallel case involving Arthur Hildersham and Mr Aberley, minister of Burton-on-Trent, and a mortalist, see Clarke (1677) p. 117.

[48] Clarke (1662) p. 114. The phrase 'cases of conscience' usually refers to questions of conformity and concerns of lifestyle and ethics, but the resource of advice and opinion is the same; cf. E. Rose, *Cases of Conscience: Alternatives Open to Recusants and Puritans under Elizabeth I and James I* (Cambridge, 1974); P. Collinson, *The Religion of Protestants: the Church in English Society 1559–1625* (Oxford, 1982) p. 246; K. Thomas, 'Cases of Conscience in Seventeenth Century England', in J. Morrill, P. Slack and D. Woolf (eds.), *Public Duty and Private Conscience in Seventeenth century England: Essays Presented to G. E. Aylmer* (Oxford, 1993) pp. 29–56.

[49] NCO MS 9502 13 February 1639, 26 April 1639 (pp. 327, 359).

[50] Mather, III p. 59.

Drake exposes the pastoral network, and also illustrates how close such treatment could be to exorcism. John Dod was called in to comfort the melancholic woman, but in his attempts to counsel her he found that 'the Devill's rhetoricke taught her against herself' and his reason failed to prevail. Her husband heard of Thomas Hooker's reputation and persuaded him to attend her.

> Mr Hooker being newly come from the University had a new answering methode . . . wherewith she was marvellously delighted.

Other ministers were called upon to make visits to Mrs Drake at Esher, including John Preston, James Ussher, Richard Sibbes and Ezekiel Culverwell, and when all these failed, a visit was planned to add the powers of John Rogers to her treatment.[51] Such cases fuelled godly clerical sociability and provided testing grounds for pastoral skills in front of colleagues and, given a successful cure, provided the spectacle of a triumphant return to the Christian community, a victory for the powers of the ministry no less than for the individual minister. Stephen Marshall's reputation was suitably enhanced when he returned his patron, William Kempe, to the parish church after an absence of seven years.[52] However, the Darrell episode and the subsequent canonical restrictions were not without effect. The theatre of the public cure or exorcism was diminished. A side-effect of this was to turn pastoral sociability inwards, to make it an affair of invitation and selection, and perhaps to make the sociability of the godly clergy in these circumstances more self-reflexive, to sharpen the boundaries between the spiritual physicians and their colleagues less devoted to these exercises. It would be easy to overstate the effects, but I think it would be foolish to ignore the possibility that the pastoral efforts of the seventeenth century tended to take on an aggregative function among the godly ministry.

At the same time, we should not ignore the public dimension to the formation of a godly clerical community. In tandem with weekday sermons where painful clerics could demonstrate their preaching prowess before a partly clerical audience, the spiritual cure established and consolidated clerical reputations. The Essex ministers whose occasions were formalised into Hooker's monthly conference importuned the newly promoted Archbishop Ussher 'to preach on the week dayes, because they could not come

[51] Jasper Heartwell, *Trodden Down Strength* (1647) pp. 22, 117 and *passim*; C. R. Elrington (ed.) *Usher's Whole Works* (Dublin, 1847–64) vol. XVI pp. 331–2, 338.

[52] Giles Firmin, *A Brief Vindication*, n.p. For other examples, see Henry Jessey, *The Exceeding Riches of Grace* (1652), which mentions Heartwell's tract; Robert Bolton, *The Last Visitation: Conflicts and Death of Mr Thomas Peacock B. D. Published by E[dward] B[agshaw] from the Copie of that Famous Divine Robert Bolton* (1662) published by Edmund Bagshawe from an MS account owned by Bolton; Clarke (1662) pp. 294–5 for the wife of Robert Harris and Clarke (1677) p. 149 for John Ball and Sarah Mainwaring.

to hear him on the Sabbath'.[53] These pastoral and preaching roles were, of course, complementary: John Angier recalled the following occasion from Dedham in the early 1630s.

> Mr Rogers being called to preach a marriage sermon, I think insisted on the Wedding Garment [Matt. 22.1–15]. God did so set in with the Word, that the Marriage Solemnity was turned into bitter mourning, so that all the ministers that were at the marriage were imployed in comforting or advising consciences awakened by that sermon.[54]

Such clerical society can be traced in many parts of England. John Ball, the Staffordshire preacher who was central, as we shall see, to the ecclesiological debates of the 1630s, maintained a monthly fast at Whitmore and promoted clerical collegiality through his 'helpfulnesse in holy Fasting and Prayer elsewhere', retreating with his ministerial colleagues to the household of Lady Bromley of Sheriff Hales 'when they durst not preach'. Ball met regularly with John Ford, an early influence, with John Taylor of Checkley, Thomas Langley of Middlewich in Cheshire, who lived with Ball when he was troubled for nonconformity, Simeon Ashe and George Crosse of Clifton, who attended Ball on his death bed. The retreat provided by Lady Bromley introduced Julines Herring, Thomas Pierson, Mr Masters and Mr Nicholls to the group. Samuel Crook, one of Emmanuel's first fellows, was an important promoter of such society: he provided a meal for ministers after his lecture and organised informal ministerial meetings to encourage learning among the Somerset clergy.[55] By contrast, Ralph Cudworth, writing in 1617 from the same county, complained that 'I am seated in a barren place, where my neighbour ministers either want skill and cannot, or have some skill and will not, confer together about matters of learning. If they chance to be questioned they think they are posed.'[56] Francis Higginson was more fortunate: he was active in the 'maintaining of profitable Conferences', although these were less rigidly clerical affairs.[57] To the south, a group clustered round John Dod and survived his departure for Fawsley in 1604: Richard Harris met with Robert Capel, William Scudder, William Whately, Robert Cleaver and

---

[53] Clarke (1662) p. 214. Ussher was an old friend of Richard Blackerby and Nathaniel Ward. He held Thomas Hooker in great esteem: Clarke (1683) p. 58; Giles Firmin, *The Real Christian* (1670) p. 51.

[54] Axon (ed.), *Life of John Angier*, p. 50.

[55] Clarke (1677) pp. 149, 147, 153, 155, 165; DWL Morrice MS J 1640 (4); B. Brook, *The Lives of the Puritans* (London, 1813) vol. II p. 441; Clarke (1662) p. 42. Arthur Hildersham may have also joined the group from time to time; while he was suspended, one of the places he visited was in the area: DWL Morrice MS J 1631 (14).

[56] Elrington (ed.), *Usher's Whole Works*, vol. XVI p. 347. Both these ministers had been placed in benefices to which Emmanuel College had been given the right of presentment.

[57] Mather III, p. 72; LRO 1D 41 4/1262; SP 16/88/13.

others.[58] Ann Hughes has documented in detail the circle of improving clergy centred on Warwick and the patronage of Lord Brooke. She has suggested that the protection of such a powerful lay patron and the division of Warwickshire between two dioceses encouraged 'an alternative church structure independent of the ecclesiastical hierarchy', which amounted to 'a quasi-Presbyterian clerical community'.[59] Traces of similar meetings survive from most areas where there were Puritan ministers in any numbers. The close-knit community of painful preachers in London deserves more attention than it has received: the circle of Thomas Gataker, Charles Offspring and William Gouge provided a focus for London ministers and for visitors to the capital. Gouge was 'accounted a father among the London Ministers'. Daniel Cawdrey was one minister who travelled from his Essex home to preach in Gouge's pulpit and enjoy his company; there must have been many others.[60] In Berkshire, a weekly fast brought together Thomas Parker, James Noyes and his brother Nicholas; William Sedgewick and the deprived minister George Hughes sponsored a meeting in Farnham in Hertfordshire; John Fielding has revealed a regular conference in Northamptonshire, linking divines by ties of blood and education.[61] As we have noted, in this county the society of Bentham, Bolton and Estwick fuelled one cluster of godly divines around Kettering. In Northampton itself, Thomas Ball could meet regularly with the primary godly ministers who were invited to preach in the town. In the period covered by the diary of Robert Woodford we can get some impression of the numbers and stature of these preachers. Normally, the townsfolk heard sermons given by Ball and his curate, Charles Newton, and, from April 1639, Newton's replacement, William Holmes.[62] They were often joined by visitors, by the town's schoolmaster Daniel Rogers, the son of the

[58] Clarke (1662) pp. 280–2, 313.

[59] A. Hughes, 'Thomas Dugard and his Circle in the 1630s – a "Parliamentary-Puritan" Connexion?' *HJ* 29 (1986) pp. 271–93; A. Hughes, *Politics, Society and Civil War in Warwickshire 1620–1660* (Cambridge, 1987) pp. 62–87, quotes p. 79.

[60] Clarke (1662) pp. 103–53; Daniel Cawdrey, *Humilitie, the Saints Liverie . . . as was Delivered (for Substance) in Two Sermons at Black Fryars in London, the one September 22 the Other October 6 1622* (1624); I. M. Calder, 'The St Antholin's Lectures', *CQR* 160 (1959) pp. 49–52ff; V. Pearl, *London and the Outbreak of the Puritan Revolution* (Oxford, 1961) pp. 160–9; William Jenkyn, *A Shock of Corn Coming in in its Season* (1654) p. 35. There is a great deal of relevant material to be found in P. Seaver, *The Puritan Lectureships: the Politics of Religious Dissent, 1560–1662* (Stanford, Calif., 1970).

[61] Mather, III p. 146; QUB Percy MS 7 ff. 179, 181, 195, 197–8, 204, 271; Fielding, 'Conformists, Puritans and the Church Courts', ch. 4.

[62] NCO Ms 9502 5 April 1639 (p. 462). For Woodford, see J. Fielding, 'Opposition to the Personal Rule of Charles I: the Diary of Robert Woodford, 1637–1641', *HJ* 31 (1988) pp. 769–88. The diary is unpaginated; Dr Fielding has given page numbers, a practice I have followed in parentheses, but, to aid reference checking, my primary notation is through dates. With some exceptions in the later parts of the diary and a few prayers transcribed in the last few pages, the diary follows a strict chronological pattern.

Wethersfield lecturer,[63] Thomas Hill of Titchmarsh,[64] Thomas Perkins of Naseby,[65] John Bullivant of Abingdon,[66] James Lewis of Durston,[67] William Castle of Courteenhall,[68] Frederick Schloer of Rushden,[69] James Cranford of Brockhall,[70] and by Daniel Cawdrey of Great Billing.[71] To list all the visitors would tax the patience; simply let it be noted that in these four years twenty five preachers appeared who did not hold livings in the town. Northampton may be an extreme example, but if we had such rich evidence for other towns it is hard to believe that it would stand out as far as it does with our present knowledge. The various meetings and contacts, resulting from a conflation of social, educational and religious impulses, provided a resource of support and advice for godly ministers in their professional and spiritual lives.

Such connections could be called upon to resolve disagreements among the godly. For instance, in the second decade of the seventeenth century, a doctrinal dispute between Anthony Wooton and George Walker was dealt with by these means. Walker had accused Wooton of advancing Arminian, or even Socinian, views in his lecture at Barking. After Walker denounced Wooton in a sermon at Blackfriars in London, the two men agreed to dispute 'in a Christian conference before eight learned and godly ministers'. The clerics chosen to adjudicate included George Downham, Thomas Gataker, William Gouge and Lewis Bayly, and, although they failed to bring the parties to agreement, the significant fact is that such a conference was accepted by all involved as preferable to a solution involving the ecclesiastical authorities.[72] Walker was resolved to send the relevant papers to Canterbury only if Wooton refused to submit to the authority of the conference. However, while the clerical parity and discipline might recall a Presbyterian *classis*, the presence of Lewis Bayly and George Downham,

---

[63] NCO MS 9502 5 April 1639, 5 August 1640 (pp. 351, 549).

[64] NCO MS 9502 17 September 1637 (p. 30).

[65] NCO MS 9502 15 October 1637, 30 September 1638, 27 December 1640 (pp. 40, 248, 525).

[66] NCO MS 9502 3 December 1637, 21 April 1639 (pp. 77, 357).

[67] NCO MS 9502 3 March 1639, 20 September 1640, 20 December 1640 (pp. 335, 501, 522).

[68] NCO MS 9502 25 April 1639 (p. 358).   [69] NCO MS 9502 4 April 1639 (p. 350).

[70] NCO MS 9502 20 March 1639 (p. 344).

[71] NCO MS 9502 13 March 1638, 13 December 1638, 22 December 1639 (pp. 142, 297, 443).

[72] George Walker, *A True Relation of the Chiefe Passages between Mr Anthony Wotton and Mr George Walker, in the Year of Our Lord 1611, and in the Yeares Next following to 1615* (1642); Thomas Gataker, *An Answere to Mr George Walkers Vindication* (1642); Wooton's *Defence against Mr George Walkers Charge* (1641) was published by Wooton's son, Samuel, with a preface and postscript by Gataker. The dispute flared up in the context of Walker's writings against the nascent Arminianism of John Goodwin. Concern spread to the West Country and beyond: C. R. Elrington (ed.), *Usher's Whole Works*, vol. XVI pp. 347–8.

future bishops of Bangor and Derry respectively, brings the ambiguity of such meetings into sharp relief.[73]

This ambiguity is captured in the definition of conference offered by Robert Cawdrey: 'communication, talking together'. Cawdrey's definitions are not to be taken at face value, but most uses of the term refer to little more than this, a common sociability in religious matters.[74] Like fasting and prayer, conference was a means of individual and social sanctification. Meetings to discuss and repeat sermons, to administer admonition, to pray and read Scripture were a settled and constant prescription in practical divinity, in Sibbes' terms, 'a sanctified means'.[75] As with private fasts, it is unusual to find detailed accounts of what actually happened at such conferences, but we have occasional hints. Formality varied and we should be wary of accounts that are as concerned to prescribe as to describe. William Bradshaw's biographer described the manner of clerical meetings at Ashby-de-la-Zouch, Repton and Burton-on-Trent: 'some one of them preached his hour on the Scripture propounded the meeting before, and the rest or a certain number of them spent afterward, each one in his halfe Hour or thereabout on some other portion of Scripture, one being appointed to moderate, by minding each that spake, if occasion were, of the time, and to close up all with some succint Rehearsal of what had been delivered, together with an Additament, if it seemed good, of his own'.[76] Clarke's own experience in the Wirral was of days of conference every three weeks, by means of which 'all the Professors, though living ten or twelve miles asunder, were as intimate and familiar, as if they had been of one household'.

In the morning when they first met, the Master of the family began with Prayer, then was the question to be conferred of read, and the younger Christians then gave in their answers, together with their proofs of Scripture for them; and then the more experienced Christians gathered up the other answers which were omitted by the former; and thus they continued till dinner time, when having good provision made for them by the Master of the Family, they dined together with much cheerfulness; after Dinner having sung a psalm, they returned to their Conference upon the other questions (which were three in all) till towards the Evening; at which time, as the Master of the Family began, so he concluded with Prayer, and I gave them three new questions against their next meeting.

Conferences to deal with specific issues and circumstances were part of

---

[73] Walker, *A True Relation*, pp. 8–21. Downham was a advocate of *iure divino* episcopacy: *A Sermon Defending the Honourable Function of Bishops* (1608).

[74] Robert Cawdrey, *A Table Alphabeticall, Conteyning and Teaching the True Writing and Understanding of Hard usuall English words* (1604) s.v. 'conference'; cf. 'association', 'combination', 'consociate'.

[75] Richard Sibbes, *The Complete Works* (ed. A. B. Grosart) (London, 1862–3) vol. 7 p. 170; Robert Bolton, *The Saints Sure and Perpetuall Guide* (1634) pp. 185–6, 227; Richard Rogers, *Seven Treatises* (1625) pp. 206–13, 364.

[76] Clarke (1677) pp. 51–2. This was on the evidence of Oliver Bowles.

the normal regulatory apparatus of the godly: not all, however, were as canonically innocent as this. Indeed, Clarke added that: 'Under the pretence of these Meetings, we enjoyed the opportunities, as occasion was offered of private fasts and days of Thanksgiving, which otherwise would quickly have been taken notice of, and suppressed.'[77] In a more clear-cut instance, shortly before their emigration in 1633, John Cotton and Thomas Hooker were persuaded to address a conference of prominent divines on issues relating to ceremonial nonconformity. Philip Nye, John Davenport, Thomas Goodwin and Henry Whitfield, the minister of Ockley, in Surrey, who hosted the conference, all broadly accepted adiaphorous defences of conformity and were all, apparently, persuaded by the arguments of the two ministers.[78]

Clerical society, similarly, was the first recourse of those ministers driven to consider emigration in the 1630s. Richard Mather framed a number of reasons for and against removal: 'These considerations were presented unto many Ministers and Christians of Lancashire at many Meetings.'[79] John Cotton and Thomas Hooker conferred with 'many able heads (amongst whom that holy man of God, Mr Dod . . .)'; Francis Higginson referred to his pastoral adviser, Arthur Hildersham, before he decided to emigrate; Thomas Parker, James Noyes 'and others that came over with them, Fasted and Prayed together many times before they undertook the voyage'.[80] In Essex, it was natural for John Sherman, a former pupil of John Rogers, to return from Emmanuel to consult with the circle of his mentor before taking the decision to emigrate.[81] Thomas Shepard and John Allin pointed out that the Lord 'knowes what prayers and teares have been poured out to God by many alone, and in dayes of fasting and prayer with Gods servants together, for his counsell, direction, assistance, blessing in this worke . . . Yea, how many serious consultations with one another, and with the faithfull Ministers, and other eminent servants of Christ, have been taken about this work.' On one such occasion, in March 1635, John Wilson, visiting England to promote the colonial venture and staying at Wethersfield with Daniel Rogers, finally convinced Shepard to leave England and encouraged Rogers' son, Samuel, to consider the possibility.[82]

---

[77] Clarke (1683) pp. 4–5.   [78] Mather, III pp. 20, 52–3, 218. See below, ch. 7.
[79] Mather, III p. 125. This was in 1635.
[80] Clarke (1662) p. 65; Mather, III pp. 74, 145.
[81] Mather, III p. 162. Sherman's father had been churchwarden at Dedham and made excuses for Rogers during the 1605 episcopal visitation: GLRO D/LC 305 f. 317; and below p. 200.
[82] John Allin and Thomas Shepard, *A Treatise of Liturgies* (1653) p. 6; QUB Percy MS 7 f. 26; McGiffert (ed.), *God's Plot*, pp. 55–63. Wilson also came close to recruiting John Stoughton in London: *Winthrop Papers*, vol. III pp. 88–9. For the content of some of these discussions, see below, ch. 14.

Such meetings, clearly in breach of Canon 73, were, however, exceptional. The normal business of a clerical conference was less often so clearly in conflict with the ecclesiastical *status quo*. The point is less to identify conferences as evidence of a continuation of the *classes* of the 1580s or as subversive ginger groups among the clergy, than to note that the reflexes of the godly ministers were sociable. It became natural for the ministers to look to their brethren for advice and support in moments of stress and doubt. Ecclesiological thought, no less than pastoral and professional practice, was informed by long experience of this resource.

3

Fasting and prayer

I

'Fasting and Prayer' has been a constant refrain in our examination of clerical sociability. We began with a fast at Hatfield Broad Oak and have noticed fasting in the context of the settlement of ministers and in other decision-making meetings. The ambiguities of clerical association are perhaps strongest in this field, and for this reason the practice deserves particular attention. Unlike the activities discussed earlier, fasting and prayer had a set place within the public worship of the church in addition to its place in voluntaristic religious life.

Fasting is also, to an extent greater than the rituals of sociability already discussed, an aspect of voluntary religion that is at least as likely to occur in mixed groups of laity and ministers as among strictly clerical groups. John Stalham was attracted to his Terling congregation in 1632 by 'that inviting support which was given of you that you were a fasting and praying people'. A letter from their former pastor, Thomas Weld, written upon his arrival in New England backs this up. After celebrating the Congregational government of the colony, the very next thing he celebrated was that 'Fast days & holy days & holy fest days and all such things by A[u]thority Commanded & performed according to the precise rule'.[1] Fasting had been an important part of pre-Tridentine Catholicism and remained a practice that characterised post-Tridentine English Catholicism.[2] It has been argued that enthusiastic Protestant fasting was partly a response to this continued example,[3]

---

[1] Weld went on to stress that the colonists fasted and prayed for the conditions of the colony and those of his former parishioners: K. Wrightson and D. Levine, *Poverty and Piety in an English Village: Terling 1525–1700* (London, 1979) p. 161; BL Sloane MS 922 ff. 90–3.

[2] J. Bossy, *The English Catholic Community 1570–1850* (London, 1975) pp. 210–16. The best treatment of medieval practice is C. W. Bynum, *Holy Fast and Holy Feast: the Religious Significance of Food to Medieval Women* (London, 1987).

[3] P. Collinson, *The Elizabethan Puritan Movement* (London, 1967) p. 214; Collinson, *The Religion of Protestants: the Church in English Society 1559–1625* (Oxford, 1982) pp. 260–1. These two works contain a good deal of information regarding fasting down to

and there may be an element of truth in this,[4] but the Protestant fast, with all its familiar features, had been described as early as the middle of the sixteenth century. Thomas Becon, the Edwardian reformer, contrasted 'the true and Christian fast' with the 'popish manner of fasting' in that the former was dedicated to 'all godly and spiritual exercises unto the glory of God, the comfort of our neighbour, and the health of our own souls', while the latter depended only on custom and superstition. A useful side product of such godly abstention was the provision of alms, which was to become a characteristic of Puritan fasts.[5]

In the church as established under Elizabeth and James, days of fasting occurred in three different, and notionally complementary, contexts. Firstly, there were fasts within the liturgical calendar: the twelve Ember days, three in each quarter, Ash Wednesday and Good Friday were all days associated with fasting which were inherited from the Roman church. Secondly, there were publicly ordained fast days within the commonwealth, appointed to deal with specific misfortunes, such as plagues, threats of invasion and the like.[6] Thirdly, these were supplemented by private fasts, with or without specific authority, usually within a single household, although the godly generally interpreted the notion of a single household fairly broadly. Although Becon was concerned largely with the second type, from the reign of Elizabeth Protestant writers generally concurred that the second and third forms were important: moderate Calvinist writers such as George Buddle could stress that 'a Fast of absolute command, whether private or publicke, is of the essence of mortification and is altogether

---

1625: cf. Collinson, *Movement*, pp. 214–19, 437–42; Collinson, *Religion*, pp. 167–8, 248, 260–3.

[4] See, for instance, the argument in William Perkins, *The Whole Treatise of the Cases of Conscience* (1606) pp. 433–8, contrasting Catholic and godly forms of fasting; cf. Robert Bolton, *The Saints Soule Exalting Humiliation* (1634) p. 39ff; Joseph Hall, *The Christian's Crucifixion with Christ*, in *Works* (ed. P. Wynter) (Oxford, 1837) vol. V p. 333.

[5] Thomas Becon, *A Fruitfull Treatise of fasting* (?1552), printed in *Works of Thomas Becon*, ed. J. Ayre, *Parker Society* (Cambridge, 1844); quotes from this edn. pp. 530, 533–4, 545. Becon sets the tone for most of the Protestant writing on fasting from Cartwright to Mason by leading his criticism of Roman practice with Matt. 6.16–18. For fasting and alms see Collinson, *Religion*, pp. 261–2; D. Underdown, *Fire from Heaven: Life in an English Town in the Seventeenth Century* (London, 1992) pp. 117, 125–8, and pp. 62–3 below. For an example in Leicestershire, SP 16/88/13.

[6] See C. J. Kitching, '"Prayer fit for the time": Fasting and Prayer in Response to National Crises in the Reign of Elizabeth I', in *SCH* 22 (1985) pp. 241–50. In addition to these publicly ordained religious fasts, there were also civil fasts, periods of abstinence from meat designed to encourage fishing, and so forth. Although some Protestants would attempt to widen the definition to include Lent and so deny the period any religious value, these lie largely outside the scope of this discussion. See Robert Bolton, *A Threefold Treatise* (1634) p. 47 (3rd pagination); Thomas Taylor, *Christ's Temptation*, in *Works* (1653) p. 50. The only godly people who observed the Ember day fasts that I have come across were the Harleys: T. T. Lewis (ed.), *Letters of the Lady Brilliana Harley*, *Camden Society* o.s. 58 (1854) p. 15.

unvariable and unomissable'.[7] Nicholas Bownde, in a series of sermons dedicated to Bishop Jegon and delivered at public fasts, stressed the necessity of private fasts:

And truely if we had that zeale in us to the glorie of God, and love to the salvation of our brethren that wee should, we might see, that besides this grievous plague that is . . . upon our neighbours & friends, which requireth publicke fasting, wee had many causes to have done it privately often & long before this.[8]

Bishop Laud, preaching at a parliamentary fast in the mid-1620s, was prepared to state that fasting and prayer were necessary and to suggest that part of the purpose of a public fast was to encourage private fasting: 'a powerful edict hath made that duty public which else perhaps would have been as much neglected in the private, as the time itself and the danger have been'.[9]

It is not quite accurate to see views on fasting as part of a Collinsonian consensus before the Laudians. Archbishop Parker voiced concerns about Grindal's form of Common Prayer for fasts in 1563, concerns that were echoed by Bishop Aylmer in 1593. More important is the point that public fasting was not exclusively a Puritan preoccupation; in 1661, for instance, an annual fast was established for 30 January, the anniversary of Charles I's execution; the custom did not depend on Puritanism in the early 1690s, when a programme of fasting and prayer was promoted along similar, public lines by Gilbert Burnett, with court approval.[10]

However, it is true that 'the hotter sort of Protestant' dominated the literature of fasting for much of the period. When Arthur Hildersham preached on the doctrine that

the chief use of a religious fast is to humble, and afflict the soul with sorrow, and grief, and a chief thing that makes our prayer effectual with God is the inward humiliation, and sorrow of our soules from whence they proceed . . .

and equated the practice of days of humiliation with fasting, prayer,

---

[7] George Buddle, *A Short and Plaine Discourse, Fully Containing the Whole Doctrine of Evangelical Fasts* (1609) p. 11. For Buddle's place on the ecclesiastical spectrum, see n. 15.

[8] Nicholas Bownde, *The Holy Exercise of Fasting Described* (1604) p. 231.

[9] William Laud, *A Sermon Preached before his Majestie on Wednesday 5 July* (1626) in *Works of William Laud* (ed. J. Bliss and W. Scott), Anglo-Catholic Library vol. I pp. 124–5.

[10] P. Slack, *The Impact of Plague in Tudor and Stuart England* (London, 1985) p. 229. Slack discusses other aspects of fasting from a different perspective, ch. 3, esp. pp. 237–8. B. S. Stewart, 'The Cult of the Royal Martyr', *CH* 38 (1969) pp. 175–87; T. Claydon, *William III and the Godly Revolution* (Cambridge, 1996) pp. 100–10. While considerable attention has been paid to parliamentary fasts in the 1640s, we must not forget that Royalist fast days were observed on the first Friday of every month: C. Durston, '"For the Better Humiliation of the People": Public Days of Fasting and Thanksgiving during the English Revolution', *SC* 7 (1992) pp. 133, 136, 139, 143.

psalm-singing, 'almsdeeds and censuring and reforming of grave sins',[11] he was reproducing sentiments that could be found in the works of Thomas Cartwright, Nicholas Bownde and William Perkins.[12] Much of this writing was concerned to take a sideswipe at Roman Catholic practice and tended to stress the voluntaristic nature of Protestant practice. Cartwright wrote, 'we may know, that there was never a Thread in the olde cloth of the Popish fast which was not thoroughly infested with the spiritual leprosie of disobedience unto the Lord'.[13]

However, in the works of Richard Hooker there arose a form of religiosity that was more likely to emphasise the set fasts of the Christian year to the disadvantage of private and voluntary fasts. Hooker allowed 'Prayers, fasting and Almsdeeds' the power of satisfaction for sin, and denied the rights of any other than bishops to proclaim extraordinary fasts.[14] In the first decade of the seventeenth century, writers following Hooker developed a conformist defence of fasting no less scornful of Roman practices, but stressing the improved efficacy of fasting within the church. George Buddle suggested that 'Private extraordinary penance doth little good, when the calamity and sin is publicke.'[15] John Mayo was able to quote approvingly from the works of William Perkins, King James and Richard Hooker. In his work, as in Buddle's, fasting is linked, once again, to the liturgical calendar.[16]

[11] Arthur Hildersham, *The Doctrine of Fasting and Prayer and Humiliation* (delivered at a publicly appointed fast in 1625) (1633) pp. 72, 51–3.

[12] Thomas Cartwright, *The Holy Exercise of a True Fast*, in *Cartwrightiana* (ed. A. Peel and C. Leland) *English Nonconformist Texts* (London, 1951) vol. I pp. 127–42; Nicholas Bownde, *Holy Exercise*; William Perkins, *A Reformed Catholick* (1597) pp. 220–9; cf. Henry Holland, *The Christian Exercise of Fasting, Private and Publicke* (1596), preaching on Matt. 6.16–18 and equating fasting and almsgiving. For the continuation of this tradition in New England, R. P. Gildrie, 'The Ceremonial Puritan: Days of Humiliation and Thanksgiving', *NEHGR* 136 (1982) pp. 3–16.

[13] Cartwright, *Holie Exercise*, p. 139; cf. Bolton, *A Threefold Treatise*, pp. 39–49.

[14] Richard Hooker, *Laws of Ecclesiastical Polity* bk VI, v, 6; VII, vi, 8; I, xvi, 7, in *Works* (ed. J. Keble) (Oxford, 1888). For Hooker and his churchmanship, see P. Lake, *Anglicans and Puritans? Presbyterian and English Conformist Thought from Whitgift to Hooker* (London, 1988) ch. 4.

[15] Buddle, *Short and Plaine Discourse*, p. 36. Buddle cited Hooker with approval and dedicated his work to Bishop Barlow, sig. A2v–3, ep. ded. Despite his Arminianism, Barlow was eclectic in his patronage, and it is perhaps best to describe Buddle as a credal Calvinist in his divinity and as Hookerian in his churchmanship. For Barlow, see K. Fincham, *Prelate as Pastor: the Episcopate of James I* (Oxford, 1990) p. 287. For Buddle see also H. Hajzyk, 'The Church in Lincolnshire c.1595–1640', Cambridge University PhD (1980), where he is described as a 'staunch conformist', pp. 454, 269–73.

[16] John Mayo, *A Sermon of Fasting, and of Lent, and of the Great Antiquitie, Dignitie and Great Necessitie Thereof* (1607) pp. 26, 33–4. Mayo was a conformist in the sense of Lake's definition, *Anglican and Puritan?*, p. 7. In the dedicatory epistle to his work, he berated those who are still 'muttering against princely proceedings in ecclesiastical government and against things that are in themselves indifferent, but by authority necessary'. For Buddle's approval of Lenten fasting, *Discourse*, p. 78.

These works anticipated the writings of Laudian churchmen on fasting. Laudian authors ridiculed Roman practices, but also stressed set times of fasting, rather than 'extraordinary fasts in cases of doubt and danger'. John Browning praised the observance of Lent and Ember days, in which he followed Henry Mason, who opposed the arguments of Cartwright and the practices of 'forraigne churches beyond the seas'. Fast days should be purged of Popish corruptions, but 'as it had been too much violence to pull down the Temple for the uncleaness' sake that was in it, so it is too much violence now to abolish all times of fasting and humiliation for the superstition that some men have placed in them'.[17]

The liturgical regularity of Mason's devotion stands in stark contrast to the voluntarism and implicit elitism of Thomas Hooker's view of fasting. In an exhortation delivered at a publicly ordained day of thanksgiving in 1626, Hooker noted:

> However wicked men will not be persuaded and humbled, yet if there be a competent number, if there be so many as will make an army of fasting and prayer to grapple with God, they may prevail with God for mercy for a kingdom.[18]

The fasts regularised by Hooker were not signposts in the rhythm of the liturgical year, but fervent responses to the prevailing conditions. The purpose of this part of godly practice is made explicit in Stephen Marshall's explanation of the use of a fast, delivered to the fasting Long Parliament:

> The one was to rent, and breake and teare every one of your hearts in the sens of your sins . . . The other was to provoke you to a strong resolution to leave the waies of sin . . . In which two things, humiliation and Reformation, stands the very life of an unfeigned repentence and the spiritual part of a religious fast; without which all our abstinence and sackcloth, and bodily exercise in watching and hearing etc. are mere abominations in the sight of God.[19]

---

[17] John Browning, *Concerning Publick Prayer and the Fasts of the Church* (1636) pp. 169, 173. Browning was rector of Rawreth in Essex, a former chaplain of Bishop Andrewes. For his anti-Calvinism, see N. Tyacke, *Anti-Calvinists: the Rise of Arminianism in England, c.1590–1640* (Oxford, 1987) p. 192. Henry Mason, *Christian Humiliation, or The Christians Fast* (1625) pp. 22, 56, 66–8, 159, 147. Contrast, for instance, Robert Bolton, *A Threefold Treatise*, p. 47, where he notes 'here I do condemne not the Lent fast among us, so it be observed only as a civill and politicke ordinance, and not as any religious fast or observation'. Mason ridiculed Roman practice in *The Epicure's Fast or a Short Discourse, Discovering the Licentiousness of the Romane Churches in her Religious Fasts* (1626); he cooperated with Samuel Hoard in producing the Arminian work, *God's Love to Mankind* (1633). I employ the term 'Laudian' here, bearing in mind the caveats expressed by P. Lake, 'The Laudian Style: Order, Uniformity and the Pursuit of the Beauty of Holiness in the 1630s', in K. Fincham (ed.), *The Early Stuart Church, 1603–42* (London, 1993) pp. 161–2. Lake's practice seems to me to be the best compromise in a difficult area of nomenclature.

[18] Thomas Hooker, *The Churches Deliverances* (1638) (delivered 1626), in G. H. Williams, N. Pettit, W. Herget and S. Bush, Jr (eds.), *Thomas Hooker: Writings in England and Holland 1625–1633, Harvard Theological Studies* 28 (1975) pp. 60–88, quoted at p. 84.

[19] Stephen Marshall, *Reformation and Desolation* (1642) pp. 17–18. The history of parlia-

This account, as it stands, is somewhat misleading. The practice of fasting was not contested equally between conformist and godly writers. It was, at most, a marginal concern for the former while for the latter it was a central practice that appears regularly among the 'means of spiritual advancement'.[20] From the 1580s, when Richard Rogers described this sort of spiritual exercise in detail because he felt it might be new to his readers,[21] it is a constant in practical divinity. Fasting is to be practised in public, in the household, and as part of the solitary practice of the godly person. For Thomas Taylor, 'religious fasting is the whetstone of prayer'; for Daniel Rogers, fasts were a 'Sabbath of reconciliation'. For Robert Bolton, it was 'a solemne exercise of religion and ordinance of God' required by the second and fourth commandments.[22] John Yates saw fasting as 'of the same nature that preaching and administring the sacraments': they 'work where and whensoever God pleaseth'.[23] Taylor recommended the saint annually to 'set apart a day of expiation, to make an atonement for himself, for his house, for all the people . . . a day of humiliation in serious fasting and prayer'.[24] When the layman Robert Saxby copied a recipe for the cure of a sick soul, he began with fasting and prayer.[25] By the late 1630s, John Brinsley could claim that God 'hath assured us by so long and so happy experience, that the innocent shall deliver the Iland: and hath shewed us that fasting and praying vanquisheth the very Divels, and therefore it will confound and bring to nothing the deepest and most hellish stratagems'.[26] Occasionally, a public fast was associated with the arrival of a godly minister in a parish. When John Wilson became Sudbury's new preacher the ministers from neighbouring parishes joined Wilson and his congregation in

mentary fasting in the tradition of Cartwright and Hildersham, is sketched in J. F. Wilson, *Pulpit in Parliament: Puritanism in the English Civil Wars 1640–48* (Princeton, N.J., 1969) ch. 2; C. Durston, '"For the better Humiliation . . ."', pp. 129–49.

[20] *Pace* the suggestion of J. Bossy, *Christianity in the West 1400–1700* (Oxford, 1987) p. 132.

[21] Richard Rogers, *Seven Treatises* (1625 edn) p. 383.

[22] Thomas Taylor, *The Pilgrims Profession* (1622); Daniel Rogers, *Two Treatises* (1640) III pp. 4, 108, 133–5, quoted at p. 134; Robert Bolton, *A Threefold Treatise*, p. 37; cf. Ezekiel Rogers, *The Chiefe Grounds of Christian Religion* (1642) n.p. (a catechism probably written for the Barrington family); John Preston, *The Golden Scepter* (1638) pp. 38–9; John Yates, *Gods Arraignment of Hypocrites* (1615) 'To the Christian Reader'; Robert Bolton, *Helpes to Humiliation* (1633) *passim*; William Ames, *Conscience with the Power and Cases Thereof* (1639) book IV pp. 46–8; Joseph Bentham, *The Christian Conflict* (1635) pp. 265–78; Arthur Hildersham, *CLII Lectures of Psalm LI* (1635) p. 311.

[23] John Yates, *Gods Arraignment of Hypocrites*, 'To the Christian Reader'.

[24] Thomas Taylor, *Christ Revealed: or the Old Testament Explained* (1635) pp. 149–50.

[25] CUL Add MS 3117 f. 53v, cf. ff. 62v–4v. His recipe began, 'First fast and pray, then take a quart of Repentance of Infirmity and put in two handfuls of faith in the blood of Christ'. He seems to have adapted his recipe from Michael Sparke, *Crumms of Comfort, the Valley of Teares, and the Hills of Joy* (1627) sig. A11–12v. Sparke came into conflict with the authorities over his role in the printing and distribution of Prynne's works.

[26] John Brinsley, *The True Watch and Rule of Life* (1637) 2nd pag., p. 54.

a day of fasting and prayer. This became the practice for ordinations in New England, and was discussed in the debate regarding ordination in the Westminster Assembly. It was not universally observed, though, for Lazarus Seamen objected that if fasting was seen to be a requisite for ordinations then their ordinations were incomplete. However, those who had this reservation were too few, and the proposal was passed.[27] The exercise of fasting was clearly established as part of the social vocabulary of the hotter sort of Protestants.[28]

Despite the wealth of prescriptive material in the literature of practical divinity, we have relatively little information on what actually went on in private fasts. Although John Dod abstained from food from the dinner of the day before a fast to the supper of the day after, physical abstinence seems to have been rather a low key element: disciplines of the body were much less central than disciplines of the soul, a point that lends credence to the idea of a Protestant fast as an implicit response to Roman practice. If, as Robert Bolton suggested, the godly marked themselves with a rejection of fine apparel, if one was expected to 'dress down' for a fast, then it is clear that a material distinction would be drawn between the godly and their neighbours.[29] Sermons seem to have been an expected part of the exercise, but the heart was probably extended *extempore* prayer on a topic, or more often topics, determined beforehand. On occasion these were the most public of concerns. John Dod joined with Ezekiel Culverwell and Samuel Ward to fast through the time of Prince Henry's funeral and Robert Bolton attributed the failure of the Spanish Match to the fervent fasting and prayer of the godly.[30] Simeon Ashe recalled that, in the period of Jeremiah Whitaker's last illness, three fast days were held by ministers in London, 'yea, in remote Countryes, besides the Ordinary prayers made for him, there were some Fasts kept, with speciall reference to his affliction'.[31] On occasion, an 'agenda' was drawn up. Two of these survive among the papers of Robert Harley, the godly Herefordshire gentleman. The subjects

---

[27] Mather, III p. 43; D. D. Hall, *The Faithful Shepherd: a History of the New England Ministry in the Seventeenth Century* (New York, 1974) p. 105; George Gillespie, *Works* (ed. W. H. Hetherington) (Edinburgh, 1843) pp. 45–7, 54.

[28] It was not until the works of Jeremy Taylor that voluntaristic fasting became part of 'Anglican' practice: see Taylor, *The Rules and Exercises of Holy Living and Dying* (London, 1838 edn) pp. 201–7, a decidedly defensive account.

[29] Clarke (1677) p. 171, a parallel to his Sabbath observation; Bolton, *A Threefold Treatise*, pp. 16–17; cf. Bentham, *Christian Conflict*, p. 270, where he enjoins abstinence from food and also from 'costly and curious apparell, Matrimoniall benevolence, or the marriage bed: part of our ordinary sleepe; all mirthe, musicke, pleasures and pastimes ... and all bodily workes of profit and pleasure'.

[30] C. R. Elrington (ed.), *Usher's Whole Works* (Dublin, 1847–64) vol. XVI p. 320; Bolton, *Threefold Treatise*, p. 36.

[31] Simeon Ashe, *Living Loves betwixt Christ and Dying Christians* (1654) p. 65.

to be covered during the fast are listed. Most are public: ministers being harassed by the ecclesiastical authorities, the Feoffees for Impropriations, the state of continental Protestantism, the prospect of a parliament, and the suppression of Popery and Arminianism at home. The godly at Brampton Bryan prayed for 'the prosperity of the Gospell at sanctification of the Sabbath', for greater and lesser magistrates, for the universities and for various godly families.[32] On other occasions, the central concern was more personal, as when the godly of Leicestershire, led by Simeon Ashe, fasted and prayed, 'by Sermons and supplications', during the last illness of Arthur Hildersham.[33] In the clerical attempts to rescue Joan Drake from her spiritual troubles, 'Divers fasts were kept for her in private', and in her later discomfort, medical doctors were called for, 'But all in vaine, *No physick could cure her but heavenly physick*: Therefore on the Saturday, Mr *Dod*, Dr *Preston*, and Mr *Hooker*, kept a private fast for her; the issue whereof was, in that forenoone she fell asleep, rested soundly five or six houres together, and then waked in a very milde gentle temper.'[34]

We will return to the spiritual significance of Protestant fasting later, but in our present context the potential of the practice as an agent of clerical collegiality is more important. Patrick Collinson suggested that the 'fasting movement' was near its peak in the 1580s,[35] and the special conditions preceding the elevation of Whitgift and the subsequent persecution may make voluntary exercises more visible in this period, but in a region such as East Anglia discretion was often all that was required to maintain such exercises. For the Jacobean period, we have already noted the influence of Richard Blackerby.[36] While godly writers, as we have seen, were generally lukewarm about set fasts,[37] the fallen nature of the world and their own pessimistic assessment of the human condition, as well as the genuinely precarious status of the Protestant cause encouraged members of the godly to find many occasions that required fasting. There were frequent fasts in Stephen Marshall's Finchingfield and John Rogers' Dedham and John White found enough causes of humiliation to institute a weekly fast in Dorchester.[38] John Dod promoted fasts at Hanwell and

---

[32] BL Add MS 70062 unfol. heads of prayer for fasts dated 22 February, 12 April 1633 and 24 January 1634.
[33] Clarke (1677) p. 123.
[34] Jasper Heartwell, *Trodden Down Strength* (1647) pp. 27, 160.
[35] Collinson, *Movement*, p. 216.   [36] Above, pp. 30–2, 46. Clarke (1683) p. 62.
[37] In 1603, one of the accusations levelled against practice at Emmanuel College, Cambridge, was that Friday fasts and Ember days were not observed: R. Tyler, '"The Children of Disobedience": the Social Composition of Emmanuel College, Cambridge 1596–1645', Berkeley, University of California PhD (1976) p. 3.
[38] ERO D/P 14/18/1A ff. 32, 44, 53, etc.; G. Selement and B. Woolley (eds.), *Thomas Shepard's Confessions, PCSM, Collections* 58 (1981) p. 63; Collinson, *Religion*, p. 262. Similarly regular fasts were held in New England: W. DeLoss Love, *The Fast and*

Banbury; as John Ball became acquainted with the godly of Staffordshire, 'he often associated with them, in keeping private daies of Fasting and Prayer', a practice he followed when he returned to the Oxford area each year.[39] For aspiring divinity students and young ministers, fasts gave early opportunities to exercise the ministerial function. John Swan was surprised to be asked to pray and preach at a day-long fast he was invited to in London in 1602. Similarly, Jeremy Walker, a Rutland schoolmaster and a graduate of Sidney Sussex College, Cambridge, made his reputation in private fasts in the adjacent counties 'whensoever he was called, and invited thereunto'.[40] Fasts represented one way in which voluntary religion aided the mutual recognition of the godly, one way in which communities could be formed and maintained among people divided by distance.

We should not be misled by the present emphasis on the communion of saints to assume that all fasting was sociable. Godly writers also assumed that the properly disciplined saint would fast on his or her own, in 'secret exercises'. Nicholas Estwick recalled that Robert Bolton, 'by his fasting, often and extraordinary prayers, often hath stood in the gap, and mightily wrastled with the Lord to keep away judgements'.[41] Richard Rogers followed his own advice to fast privately: he found that fasting, combined with solitary meditation and study, left his mind 'well-seasoned', an interesting metaphor in the context of abstinence! Samuel Ward may have fasted only occasionally, but at least he felt guilty when he failed to do so.[42] Samuel Rogers set aside full days for solitary fasting to seek a decision about moving to New England and when he received a call to preach for the first time, but also to 'get into the sweet communion with g[od] which I was wont to have'.[43] A more regular occasion for solitary fasting was in preparation for the sacrament. In August, 1638, Rogers recorded:

This day Fasting and prayer privately for preparat[ion] to sacram: I find the ld very gracious: hee makes my heart bleed for the times and inlarges mee yet to mourne

Thanksgiving Days of New England (Boston, Mass., 1895) pp. 79, 239–55. According to Hambrick-Stowe, this can be linked to a continuing dependence upon a traditional seasonal cycle: C. E. Hambrick-Stowe, *The Practice of Piety: Puritan Devotional Disciplines in Seventeenth-Century New England* (Chapel Hill, N. C., 1982) pp. 101–2.

39 Clarke (1677) pp. 169, 147, 149, 150.
40 John Swan, *A True and Briefe Report of Mary Glover's Vexation, and of her Deliverance by the Means of Fasting and Prayer* (1603) *passim*, esp. p. 34; Clarke (1662) pp. 160–4.
41 Nicholas Estwick, *A Learned and Godly Sermon Preached on the XIX day of December 1631* (1639) p. 63.
42 M. M. Knappen (ed.), *Two Elizabethan Puritan Diaries* (Chicago, Ill., 1933) pp. 89, 100, 110.
43 QUB Percy MS 7 ff. 217, 264.

and wrestle; and hath given some hints; and a sweete comfortable confidence in him that I am his, and shall be refreshed at his Feast.[44]

Paradoxically, we may note that such solitary fasting had a social dimension. There is a sense in which the secrecy of the practice made it less of a separation in terms of the public face of the godly, but, for the secluded saint, the isolation and discipline taken on voluntarily when others were about their worldly affairs must, if anything, been a particularly sharp process of identification and separation from the ungodly. In any case, the secrecy of 'secret' fasting may be an illusion. Although John Carter senior told only his wife when he fasted in private, 'yet all the Family knewe it, because at night hee supped not, but only had a Toste, and a draughte of ordinary Beer to sustaine nature'.[45] Joseph Bentham claimed that 'in this as in other Christian exercises we must not desire to be seene of men, onely to our Father in secret', but also encouraged his readers to give their dinner to the poor before fasting privately, surely something of a public act.[46]

With the consolidation of the Laudian hegemony into the 1630s, this process of identification became more acute as the attitudes expressed by Mason and Browning seemed to reflect the official line on fasting.[47] There were no publicly ordained fasts outside the time of parliamentary sessions until late in 1636, after a long spell of plague, a particularly offensive neglect, given the complex relationship in early modern discourses between sin and disease.[48] As early as 1630, Charles Chauncy was reported to have 'said that the Church hath power to appoint days for fasts and prayers but that they did not find the conscience but are indifferent'.[49] Perhaps even earlier, in a section excluded from his publication on fasting, Arthur Hildersham argued that 'Christians of sundry familyes may lawfully (even in these tymes and in such a church as ours is) in a private house join together in fasting and prayer'.[50] Robert Bolton included among his reasons for calling a private fast the negligence of the authorities in calling a public fast in times of danger.[51] In September 1636, the Suffolk

---

[44] QUB Percy MS 7 f. 341. This practice was also recommended by Joseph Bentham, *Christian Conflict*, p. 275.

[45] John Carter [junior], *The Tombstone* (1653) p. 20.

[46] Bentham, *Christian Conflict*, pp. 273, 278.

[47] Cf. E. S. Cope, *Politics without Parliament 1629–1640* (London, 1987) pp. 141–2.

[48] For the related perceptions of sin and disease, see M. Healy, 'Discourses of the Plague in Early Modern London', in J. A. I. Champion (ed.), *Epidemic Disease in London, Centre for Metropolitan History, Working Papers Series*, No. 1 (London, 1993) pp. 19–34, and below, p. 242. A proclamation of 28 September 1630 encouraged the observance of fish days, Ember Days and Lent, but this seems to have been a civil fast, a practical rather than a spiritual response to dearth: J. F. Larkin and P. L. Hughes (eds.), *Stuart Royal Proclamations* (Oxford, 1973) vol. I Proc.141; SP 16/175/44.

[49] SP 16/164/40.   [50] BL Add MS 4275 f. 281.

[51] Bolton, *Threefold Treatise*, p. 53.

chorographer Robert Ryece complained to John Winthrop that despite the rising death toll, the cancellation of the Stourbridge fair and other important provincial events, no fast had been proclaimed.

In all these calamities wee never went to God publickly, by fasting and prayer, which was deemed as hatefull as conventicles, the frute of vestry elders, there vestry doctrine & the disciplinarian faction.[52]

When a fast was finally proclaimed in the middle of October, there were restrictions that seriously devalued the fast in the eyes of the godly. In regions where the plague was worst, there were to be no sermons; in unaffected areas, sermons were not to exceed one hour.[53] William Prynne's response was predictably forceful: the sermon was 'the very life and soule of a faste, as being the only meanes to humble men for their synns, & bring them to repentance'. In terms of the godly, he was probably correct when he suggested that the fast was thus made distasteful and regarded as 'a dombe faste & a mocke fast'. He was not alone in his conviction that 'we can never hope to abate any of God's plagues or draw any of his blessings on us by such a faste and Fastebook as this, but augment his plagues and judgements'.[54] Daniel Rogers derided such affairs as 'those Popish dumbe Pageants', and James Harrison was censured for preaching above three hours at the fast at Hatfield Broad Oak.[55] Throughout the 1630s voluntaristic fasting remained an important part of godly practice, both in Essex and beyond.[56] In Leicestershire, as early as 1626, St John Burrows, the son of a famous preacher, was presented for holding an unauthorised public fast. Burrows admitted

that he of his owne authoritie did call a fast and cause sermons 2 or 3 of a day preached and he confessed that on wednesday the 14 of this month he did celebrate a fast in the church of Thornton at which there was a congregation and he himselfe did preach & 2 other ministers did preach 2 other sermons each of the said 3 almost 2 houres long. And further he saith he believeth it was lawful soe to doe for that the fast established by the Kings booke was not yet called in.[57]

The ecclesiastical authorities detected fasts in a number of places in the county during the 1620s. Burrows continued to promote fasts at Thornton and Burrow; John Bryan, Mr Coates and Mr Foxcroft conducted a fast at

[52] *MHSC* 4th series (1864) 7 p. 408.
[53] Larkin and Hughes (eds.), *Stuart Royal Proclamations*, vol. II Proc. 229. Public fasts had been proclaimed four times in the first five years of Charles' reign, ibid., Procs. 19, 47, 89, 107. The 1636 restrictions were not unprecedented: in 1625, the form of Common Prayer issued for the fast stated that it could be used in households to prevent the spread of plague (*STC* 16540), *Acts of the Privy Council 1625–6*, 125.
[54] William Prynne, *Newes from Ipswich* (1636) n.p.
[55] Daniel Rogers, *Two Treatises* (1640) III p. 134; SP 16/151/100.
[56] SP 16/127/101; 362/106.
[57] LRO 1D 41/13/58 f. 262. Burrows was suspended and excommunicated *ex officio*.

Woodhouse, and others were detected at Wigston, Leicester, Loughborough, Rotherby and Frowlesworth. Most of these ministers were products of Francis Higginson's seminary or associated with the godly of Leicester.[58] The contrast with former conditions was all the greater in that earlier fasts had received active encouragement from John Pregion, the bishop's registrar.[59] This continuity in the changed circumstances served to fuel the fears of the ecclesiastical authorities that such exercises were subversive, and also to make clearer the separation between the godly and their less active neighbours. It was sufficient for George Goodman, the rector of Croft, in Leicestershire, to be reputed 'a great fast maker' to attract the disapproval of the authorities.[60] In Northampton, Robert Sibthorpe's suspicions were aroused when a fast was called in June 1638 with Thomas Ball preaching in the morning and Charles Newton in the afternoon.[61] Immanuel Bourne was called into the High Commission for proclaiming a public fast day during the spell of plague.[62] Clarke noted of William Gouge: 'In the Bishop's times, when it was not permitted to keep Fasts in the publick congregations, he was one of those Ministers who frequently holp [*sic*] private Christians in their more retired Humiliations. In times of fears and dangers, he with divers others, had sometimes monthly, yea sometimes weekly Fasts, whereof many were kept in his own house, and others of them in his Vestry.'[63] Similarly, the biographer of Thomas Taylor recalled that he was noted for 'keeping fast among the godly of the place, which in those daies was something a dangerous practice'.[64] These conditions can only have served to foster the sense of community and self-identification of the godly against what they saw as the recidivist authorities. Fasts in Herefordshire, promoted by the Emmanuel graduate Thomas Pierson, included prayers for 'the continuation of our exercises' in Herefordshire, Shropshire, Cheshire, Lancashire and London.[65] Thomas Hooker's promotion of fasting and prayer in Essex, an exercise as characteristic of the Jacobean church as the combination lecture, came at exactly the moment when official attitudes were turning against such exercises with unprecedented vigour.

The meaning of fasting was, then, susceptible to change in different political circumstances. When we consider the meaning of rituals of sociability this is clearly one of the contexts we must take into account. However, the voluntary Protestant fast has more meanings than those

---

[58] LRO 1D 41/13/55–60 *passim*; SP 16/88/13.
[59] SP 16/88/13.　　[60] SP 16/535/26.
[61] J. Cox (ed.), *The Records of the Borough of Northampton* (Northampton, 1898) vol. I p. 396.
[62] R. O'Day, 'Immanuel Bourne: a Defence of the Ministerial Order', *JEH* 27 (1976) p. 103.
[63] Clarke (1662) p. 119.　　[64] Clarke (1677) p. 126.
[65] BL Add MS 70062 unfol. dated 12 April 1633.

generated by religio-political contexts. We have seen how Protestant fasting defined itself against Roman Catholic practice; the contrast is considerable indeed. Before the Reformation, fasting was embedded within a complex set of meanings relating to suffering as part of the *imitatio Christi*, to a theology of the body and to a way of thinking about food and nourishment that had profound Christological consequences. In particular, fasting was part of the late medieval efflorescence of female piety, a part that drew resonances from the idea of women's bodies as nurturing (linking with the lactating and bleeding Christ), and as providers and regulators of the provision of food in the domestic environment.[66] Although we will have cause to question some aspects of the sharp break that the Reformation represents in terms of religiosity, here the break seems clean. The gender resonances of fasting seem to disappear as the practice is purged of 'super-stitious' accretions. Fasting seems to be one of those rituals 'emptied out' or 'evacuated' by the Reformation, to use Stephen Greenblatt's description.[67] Food is no longer the issue; the body is no longer the site of the struggle for redemption; abstention is no longer the means of grace.[68] This is not to say, however, that the Protestant fast was wholly vacuous, impoverished, as it might appear next to its pre-Reformation counterpart. Fasting was asso-ciated, as we have seen, with 'days of humiliation', with a casting down. The practice provided a space for inversion that proved particularly important for godly clerics. The inversion is implicit in bodily abstinence, however moderate: fasting can only have meaning in a society of relative plenty. Although many writers praised fasting as of practical benefit during times of dearth,[69] the practice necessarily draws upon contrasts with the availability of food and a voluntary neglect of sustenance. The muting of this aspect of inversion was accompanied by a relative stress on others. The rejection of food was replaced by the rejection of spiritual power, a humiliation and powerlessness that, likewise, draws its greatest resonance by contrast with a normal position of spiritual authority. The inversion must have been most marked for the clergy, although the social standing of noble professors, placed in abeyance during fasts, is also significant. Samuel

---

[66] C. W. Bynum, *Holy Fast and Holy Feast*, provides a marvellous exposition of these matters. My summary necessarily does violence to the subtlety of her work. Reservations regarding the changes may be drawn from the material discussed in E. K. Hudson, 'English Protestants and the *imitatio Christi*, 1580–1620', *SCJ* 19 (1988) pp. 541–58 and J. Sears McGee, 'Conversion and the Imitation of Christ in Anglican and Puritan Writing', *JBS* 15 (1976) pp. 21–39.

[67] S. Greenblatt, *Shakespearean Negotiations: the Circulation of Social Energy in Renaissance England* (Oxford, 1990) pp. 119, 126–7.

[68] Those Protestant authors surveyed by R. L. Greaves, *Religion and Society in Elizabethan England* (Minneapolis, Minn., 1981) pp. 471–99, strike this reader, at least, as holding more in common than differing on attitudes to food and fasting.

[69] Ibid., pp. 491–6.

Rogers exemplifies this sort of inversion in his note on a fast held at Emmanuel College in December 1635:

This day we fasted &c. at Em: the Ld went out mightily in inlarging my heart; and though I cannot see so clearlye; yet the Ld hath made mee to lye at his feet; and there I will perish if I dye.[70]

This may lead us to qualify the statement that fasting lost its gender implications during the Reformation: perhaps the possibilities for this sort of inversion made the practice one with masculine inflections. After all, the renunciation of authority is rather less meaningful for women in this society. Joseph Bentham described one of the benefits of fasting, 'that wee may groane, and grieve, sigh and sorrow, mourne and lament under the intollerable and insupportable weight and burden [of sin]; yea this bewailing and bemoaning of our sins ought to be like the sorrowes of a woman in travaile'. Against this, we can set the martial language of Hooker, 'an army of fasting and prayer' and the 'wrestling' described by Samuel Rogers and Nicholas Estwick, both ways of thinking that provide the possibility of inversion for women. In fact, extraordinary fasting was a symptom of divine guidance taken up by two female Congregationalist prophets in the 1640s and 1650s, Sarah Wight and Martha Hatfield, the latter having the extra challenge of being a child. Not surprisingly, both called upon Psalms 8.2 and Matt.21.16 as sources of authority.[71]

However, this does not exhaust the meanings that can be attached to such rituals of sociability as fasting and prayer, godly conference and so forth. What we have gained from the Collinsonian perspective is what we might term the view of an 'experiential insider'. For the godly minister, the structures and opportunities of voluntary religion were an entirely innocent adjunct to public worship. In a sense, this view is disingenuous, for godly exercises were always exclusive; very rarely closed, but never comprehensive. In fact, their theoretical openness is an implicit criticism of those, the formal majority, who chose not to partake of godly society. In a complex and heterogeneous society, such fragmented sociability always implies

---

[70] QUB Percy MS 7 f. 77.
[71] Bentham, *Christian Conflict*, p. 276, but cf. pp. 265, 278; B. Ritter Dailey, 'The Visitation of Sarah Wight: Holy Carnival and the Revolution of the Saints in Civil War London', *CH* 55 (1986) pp. 438–55; N. Smith, 'A Child Prophet: Martha Hatfield as *The Wise Virgin*', in G. Avery and J. Briggs (eds.), *Children and their Books: a Celebration of the Work of Iona and Peter Opie* (Oxford, 1989) pp. 79–93; cf. N. Smith, *Perfection Proclaimed: Language and Literature in English Radical Religion 1640–1660* (Oxford, 1989) pp. 45–53. These points will be developed in greater detail later. Psalm 8.2: 'Out of the mouth of babes and sucklings hast thou ordained strength because of thine enemies, that thou mightest still the enemy and the avenger.' Matt. 21.16: 'And said unto him, Hearest thou what these say? And Jesus saith unto them Yea; have ye never read, Out of the mouths of babes and sucklings thou hast perfected praise?'

others, those who are absent.[72] Nathaniel Sparrowhawk, a layman of Dedham who became a deacon in Thomas Shepard's church in Massachusetts, fasted in solitary and found that 'I could walk up and down the room rejoicing in Him and hitting those out of the window that were otherwise employed'.[73] Indeed, the absent others are necessary for the identity of the godly. The neutral voluntarism of one strand of godly rhetoric is undercut by this Other, implied by the voluntary gatherings of the godly. The Other is, by definition, ungodly: even canonically innocent rituals of sociability are, in this sense, divisive.[74] John Brinsley made the failure of those who neglect fasting in times of danger clear: 'Whereas otherwise, if such a judgement come upon us, as hath been so often almost fully executed (which the Lord in mercy still save us from), we are every one accessary to it, who have not sought in time to turne it away: we are also accused with *Meroz*, because we came not to help the Lord against the mighty.'[75] The demarcations of 'us' and 'them' clearly fit into the consequences Durkheim associated with rituals of sociability:

> The only way to renew the collective representations that refer to sacred beings is to plunge them again into the very source of religious life: assembled groups. The emotions aroused by the periodic crises through which external things pass induce the men witnessing them to come together, so that they can see what it is best to do. But by the very fact of being assembled, they comfort one another; they find the remedy because they seek it together. The shared faith comes alive again quite naturally in the midst of reconstituted collectivity. It is reborn because it finds itself once again in the same conditions in which it was first born. Once it is restored, it easily overcomes all the private doubts that had managed to arise in individual minds.[76]

If one intended consequence of such collective piacular practices was a reconstituted collectivity, another, perhaps unintended, consequence was a sharper division between those willing to contribute to such spiritual work and those unwilling to make the effort. In this way, rituals of sociability are also rites of separation.

---

[72] G. Baumann, 'Ritual Implicates "Others": Rereading Durkheim in a Plural Society', in D. Coppett (ed.), *Understanding Ritual* (London, 1993) pp. 97–116; A. P. Cohen, *The Symbolic Construction of Community* (Chichester, 1993) ch. 2.

[73] Selement and Woolley (eds.), *Thomas Shepard's Confessions*, p. 63.

[74] This reading gains support from the habits of thought identified in S. Clark, 'Inversion, Misrule and the Meanings of Witchcraft', *PP* 87 (1980) pp. 98–127; P. Lake, 'Anti-Popery: the Structure of a Prejudice', in R. Cust and A. Hughes (eds.), *Conflict in Early Stuart England* (London, 1989) pp. 72–106 and P. Collinson, *From Iconoclasm to Iconophobia: the Cultural Impact of the Second English Reformation* (Reading, 1986) p. 6; cf. S. Lukes, 'Political Ritual and Social Integration', *Sociology* 9 (1975) pp. 289–308.

[75] John Brinsley, *The True Watch*, 2nd pag., p. 55.

[76] E. Durkheim, *The Elementary Forms of Religious Life* (trans. and introduced by K. E. Fields) (New York, 1995) p. 350, cf. pp. 392–417.

4

Clerical associations and the Church of England

We have suggested that the forms of clerical association discussed in the preceding chapters seem to have been given an extra degree of activism in the mid-1620s. At this point, this claim must be substantiated further and we must turn to the causes of this increased sociability. We must consider what the circumstances were that produced Thomas Hooker's conference in Essex and the Feoffees for Impropriations and, more importantly, what these activities mean. What is the relation of these rituals of sociability and the schemes they promoted to the Church of England in the early seventeenth century? Are we to see them as inherently subversive, as the product of a Puritan movement by definition at odds with the clerical establishment, or as activities merely adding to the public life of the church, a voluntarism which supplements without undermining?

I

Thomas Hooker's conference and the Feoffees for Impropriations represented a formalisation of ad hoc arrangements and practices present from early in the century, to go back no further. That formalisation took place early in 1626. In Essex and the south-east, the last months of 1625, indeed the time from Charles' accession to the throne in March, had been characterised by a heightened fear of Popish plots and concern among those best informed about church matters, regarding the inroads made by anti-Calvinists at the political centre. Francis Barrington, who played host to the fast in December, wrote to Lord Conway reporting 'a rumour in this County of the great Concourse of people to papests houses both hear & adiacent counties', hoping thereby to be a means by which 'the recusants and papists may be disarmed'.[1] The agitation surrounding the York House Conference, which met between 11 and 17 February 1626, increased the

---

[1] W. Hunt, *The Puritan Moment: the Coming of Revolution in an English County* (London, 1983) pp. 186–99; SP 16/6/41.

fears that the godly cause was under threat. Although the Feoffees[2] had been meeting in some form since 1613, they were formalised on 15 February. The provision of godly preachers was obviously the key role of the Feoffees; perhaps Hooker's conference may be considered as a parallel venture, concerned to provide properly trained ministers as the Feoffees ensured that pulpits were available for such ministers.

If one of the objects of extra activism was the provision of suitable education for young ministers, we must also look to Cambridge for the impulses behind the conference. It has been conjectured that one of the tendencies that encouraged a period of parochial tutelage was the challenge to reformed doctrine at the universities from the 1590s.[3] From the middle of this decade to the 1640s, Calvinism was no longer the unchallenged orthodoxy it had seemed to be in the early 1590s, and a period of cleansing under a securely orthodox minister was perhaps seen as newly necessary. Moreover, the university as a whole, and Emmanuel College especially, were undergoing a process of laicisation. In the 1620s, this process accelerated at Emmanuel College, encouraged by John Preston, and it may have been felt that the college no longer worked as a ministerial seminary in itself, and a period under a godly tutor would reinforce clerical vocation and remove candidates from ungodly influences.[4] Perhaps a related cause may have been a change perceived by the godly in the moral standards of Cambridge. When Robert Woodford, the godly steward of Northampton, visited Oxford in 1639 he noted that 'this place here is prodigiously profane I perceive for drunkennesse swearing & other debauched Course, stage players & Lord reforme these seminaryes if it be thy will for the Lords sake'.[5]

In the first half of 1626 such fears were intense among the godly, and help to explain the wish to make seminarial arrangements more secure. In February, there were attempts in Parliament to prevent corruption and outside manipulation of college elections. The worst fears of the godly were realised in June, when the Duke of Buckingham was elected as Chancellor in an election that split the Heads of Colleges broadly along religious lines. John Preston, perhaps still hoping to regain the patronage of the Duke, was one of only two Calvinist heads to abstain. Within two weeks of the

---

[2] In what follows, 'Feoffees' refers to the Feoffees for Impropriations and is capitalised to make this distinction.

[3] J. Morgan, *Godly Learning: Puritan Attitudes to Reason, Learning and Education, 1560–1640* (Cambridge, 1987) p. 293.

[4] N. Tyacke, *Anti-Calvinists: the Rise of English Arminianism, c.1590–1640* (Oxford, 1987) ch. 2; H. C. Porter, *Reformation and Reaction in Tudor Cambridge* (Cambridge, 1958) pp. 397–407; Tyler '"Children of Disobedience"', *passim*, and pp. 147, 162–3, 199, 332; for Preston, see I. Morgan, *Prince Charles's Puritan Chaplain* (London, 1957) pp. 28–34.

[5] NCO MS 9502 10 July 1639 (p. 392).

election, Calvinism was muzzled within the University and, as Bishop Neile, one of the Duke's supporters in the election, observed, the event 'in a sort purchase[d] His Majestie himself as our royall patron and Chancellor'. Buckingham's election probably post-dates the beginning of the new activism, but the drift of power had been evident to the godly at least since the publication of Montague's *Appello Caesarum* in 1625.[6]

The change in the ecclesiastical balance of power created a redistribution of priorities among the godly: the *laissez-faire* approach to ministerial post-graduate education, to the shaping of the doctrine and the placement of young godly ministers was no longer appropriate in the conditions that obtained after 1625. As John Preston observed elsewhere,

the Church of God hath times and seasons, and the Commonwealth hath some seasons and times when men should be set aworke to do more than at other times; and you all know this is such a season, wherein there should be a working of everyone in their severall places, more than ordinarily.[7]

For the godly ministers, the first half of 1626 was such a time, and such a season.

II

William Hunt, writing in an Essex context, noted that 'throughout England 1625 was a vintage year for popish plots, comparable to the legendary *vendages* of 1588 and 1605. Almost all of them were either imaginary or wildly exaggerated.' In a different context, and writing of a more violent age, Carlo Ginzburg observed that 'every phantasmic plot tends to generate a real one of an inverse nature'.[8] Is this how we are to understand the renewed activism of the mid-1620s? Was this activism the correlative of a perceived Popish fifth column and can King Charles and the Durham House clergy be said, in effect, to have recreated Puritanism? How far were conferences of godly ministers, and specifically the Essex conference, a threat to the ecclesiastical *status quo*; how far were they a subversive element in Caroline church life?

Our first approach to these questions is a legalistic one. The relationship of conferences to canon law was at best ambiguous, at worst precarious.

[6] C. H. Cooper, *Annals of Cambridge* (Cambridge, 1842–1908) vol. III pp. 184–9; J. Twigg, *The University of Cambridge and the English Revolution, 1625–1688* (Cambridge, 1990) pp. 12–16; Tyacke, ch. 2, Neile quoted at p. 49. The best, and most detailed, account of these events and of the atmosphere in Cambridge prior to the election is V. Morgan, 'Court, Country and Cambridge University, 1558–1640: a Study on the Evolution of a Political Culture', University of East Anglia PhD (1984) ch. 1.

[7] John Preston, *The Breastplate of Faith and Love* (2nd edn, 1630) p. 236.

[8] Hunt, *The Puritan Moment*, p. 189; C. Ginzburg, *Ecstasies: Deciphering the Witches' Sabbath* (London, 1990) p. 52.

Canon 72 of the 1604 Canons forbade 'public or private fasts or prophecies
... other than such as by law are, or by public authority shall be
appointed', but the canon arose specifically out of the anxieties of Bancroft,
Harsnett and others at the activities of John Darrell. Despite the practice of
fasting and the ambiguities of pastoral work, most meetings avoided the
main target of the canon, as no exorcism was practised and no sermon
publicly preached. Canon 73 held that 'all conventicles and secret meetings
of priests and ministers have been ever justly accounted hurtful to the State
of the Church', but prohibited such meetings only if they 'tend to the
impeaching and depraving of the doctrine of the Church of England, or of
the Book of Common Prayer, or of any part of the government or discipline
now established . . . '.[9]

However much Bancroft felt that any privately conducted meetings for
'extraordinary expositions of Scripture or conferences together' stood
condemned as 'schismaticall conventicles', a position that appealed to
William Laud, these questions of ecclesiology and conformity are the issues
that defined the legality of meetings. Dr Arthur Duck, Laud's Chancellor as
Bishop of London, allowed that meetings might be innocent if no seditious
opinions were allowed: 'we take it that the 73 Canon may give some
defence to ministers in such cases, if in such meetinges they preach nothing
against the doctrine of the Church'.[10]

Thomas Hooker was an active evangelist of nonconformity, persuading
Nathaniel Rogers and Francis Higginson among others of the unlawfulness
of certain ceremonies, but this was effected in private conversation, not in
conferences; while this was a distinction not always likely to seem germane
to the authorities, it means that his monthly conference was canonically
legal.[11] According to his autobiography, Thomas Shepard had attended the
conference for more than three years without dealing with issues of
conformity until Laud's agents accused him of nonconformity. Until 1630,
he 'was not resolved either way, but was dark in those things'.[12] We will
return to the apparently schizophrenic attitudes of moderate godly clerics
in the appropriate place. Here we may just note that there were plenty of
arguments by and cases of nonconforming ministers who declined to

[9] E. Cardwell, *Synodalia: a Collection of Articles, Canons and Proceedings of Convocation
from 1547 to 1717* (Oxford, 1842) vol. I pp. 287–8; J. R. Tanner, *Constitutional
Documents of James I 1603–1625* (Cambridge, 1930) p. 240.
[10] Bancroft quoted in P. Collinson, 'The English Conventicle', in *SCH* 23 (1986) p. 232; for
Laud's sympathy, ibid., pp. 223–4; Duck was defending John Vicars, a Lincolnshire
minister accused of holding conventicles in his parish. It should be noted that he lost the
case: S. R. Gardiner (ed.), *Reports of Cases in the Courts of Star Chamber and High
Commission, Camden Soc.* n.s., 39 (1886) pp. 218, 221.
[11] Mather, III pp. 106, 71.
[12] M. McGiffert (ed.), *God's Plot: the Paradoxes of Puritan Piety Being the Autobiography
and Journal of Thomas Shepard* (Amherst, Mass., 1972) p. 46. See below, pp. 169–70.

proselytise on the issue. In these circumstances, we should be careful before assuming, as Laud often did, that the influence of a nonconformist minister would necessarily produce nonconforming disciples.

Canon 73 refers to 'clandestina presbyterorum' and arises out of the Elizabethan conference movement.[13] While we have noted the qualifications that must be made to any account of the earlier conferences in terms of the pursuit of Presbyterian reform, the question must be put in this context: was Hooker's conference an enclave of Presbyterians, and indeed, was it subversive in a Presbyterian sense in itself? For the first question, it must be noted that the conference generated no uniform ecclesiological stance. For the second question, the same qualifications apply to Hooker's group as to the Dedham conference. The later association drew together ministers spread over a considerable area, with far from comprehensive coverage: in no sense can this be said to resemble a regional *classis*. Moreover, it must be noted that there was no attempt at discipline, no Presbyterian effort to claim jurisdiction over the parochial activities of members.

The position most ministers would take is that such conferences for edification were a profitable part of any scheme of church government: Ezekiel Rogers was able to use such meetings with the approval of a moderate episcopal regime;[14] John Eliot was in favour of 'frequent Synods' within the framework of the New England way, with 'a deep and due care to preserve the rights of particular churches';[15] Hooker himself thought that conferences of ministers could exist happily within any ecclesiological position. He felt that if

such meetings be attended only in way of consultation, as having no other power, nor meeting for any other end: Then they are lawfull, so the root of them lies in a most common principle which God and Providence hath appointed for human proceeding, and that is
He that harkens to counsel shall be safe [Prov.12.15]
In the multitude of counsellors there is safety [Prov.11.14]
Hence all conditions and callings, as they need, so they use a Combination of Counsel, for the carrying on of their occasions under their hand.[16]

Even on the Separatist wing, clerical association was not impossible. In the

---

[13] Cardwell, *Synodalia*, vol. I p. 206.
[14] Mather, III p. 102; R. C. Marchant, *Puritans and the Church Courts in the Diocese of York 1560–1640* (London, 1962) pp. 30–1, 40–5.
[15] Mather, III pp. 189–90. Eliot allowed that particular churches were 'accountable' to synods.
[16] Thomas Hooker, *A Survey of the Summe of Church Discipline* (1648) IV, p. 51. It might be noted that these were far from the traditional proof texts for local *classes*: W. Frere and C. E. Douglas (eds.), *Puritan Manifestoes: a Study of the Origin of the Puritan Revolt* (London, 1954) pp. 108–9. This whole question is much more complicated than has often been assumed, and will be discussed at length below, chs.15 to 17.

mid-1640s, Henry Jessey brought together ministers of all the Calvinist separate churches in London, including Jeremiah Burroughes, Thomas Goodwin, Sidrach Simpson, William Erbury and Praise God Barbon, for conferences dealing with paedo-baptism and other issues.[17] To show similar practices in a spectrum of ecclesiological circumstances is not to suggest that the practice was not ecclesiologically subversive, only that it was not *necessarily* subversive. As we will see, there were tensions raised by the practice among Congregationalist ministers, no less than within episcopacy.

III

We have seen that the settlement of ministers took place within a godly network that could be seen as subversive, and was perceived to be so by Bishop Laud.[18] Similarly, fasting and prayer, meetings for edification among ministers and for sermon repetition among lay people could be read as disruptive of the peace of the church, as nurseries of schism.[19] However, it may be that such activity becomes subversive only within a perception of the church predicated upon a conflict model; such was Laud's perception; such also were the perceptions of historians from Gardiner to the early Collinson. More recently, we have received a historiographically necessary corrective. As Professor Collinson reminds us:

> There flourished in Jacobean conditions, especially among the clergy dominating what might be called the middle heights of the ecclesiastical economy, in leading London pulpits and important country and market town livings, a phalanx of evangelical Calvinists whom it would not be very sensible to try to label as either Puritans or otherwise.[20]

This much accepted, the systems which brought these men to livings often involved, on a less organised level, the experiences already discussed: tutelage under a godly minister, and a resource of advice and opinion that enabled ministers whose scruples finally excluded them from the active ministry altogether to exercise an influence that must be seen as disruptive of the peace of the church. We have seen this in the case of Richard Blackerby among others, and the same holds for Thomas Hooker. Samuel Collins warned that if Hooker was to be suspended, 'it is the resolution of his friends and himself to settle his abode in Essex, and maintenance is

---

[17] Anon., 'The Debate on Infant Baptism', *TBHS* 1 (1908–9) pp. 243, 245; David Brown, *Two Conferences between some of those that are Called Separatists* (1650).

[18] See, p. 41.   [19] Collinson, 'The English Conventicle', *passim.*

[20] P. Collinson, *The Puritan Character: Polemics and Polarities in early Seventeenth Century English Culture* (Los Angeles, Calif., 1989) pp. 15–16.

promised for the fruition of his private conference. His genius will still haunt all the pulpits.'[21]

A scrupulous nonconformist could obtain a schoolmaster's licence with a clear conscience, as Canon 77 exempted them from the third clause of the second article in subscription, which avowed that the public liturgy 'and none other' should be followed in divine worship.[22] In these circumstances, even the educational aspects of a conference become suspect: when Laud cited Shepard, by now suspended from his lecture, to appear before him at Kelvedon, in 1631, according to Shepard,

> he asked me what I did in the place, and I told him I studied, he asked me what – I told him the fathers: he replied I might thank him for that, yet charged me to depart the place. I asked him whither I should go. To the University, said he.[23]

The issue here was less the subject of study, than the opportunity to regulate and control it. The influence of a tutor like Thomas Hooker was plainly not a neutral matter for a bishop like Laud. As Collins complained, Hooker was a dangerous presence among young ministers: to them he was 'an oracle, and their Principle library'. Even though his own preaching had been stopped, 'All mens ears are filled by the obstreperous clamours of his followers against my Lord of London, as a man endeavouring to suppress preaching and advance popery.'[24]

It is an interesting, but ultimately insoluble, question of whether such activities were subversive or not. We can only learn so much within this framework. What is more important is to note that the hermeneutics of historians correspond to contemporary interpretations; these activities are susceptible to multiple readings, readings that were made by the actors and those who observed them. This point may become clearer if we take a slightly closer look at the Feoffees for Impropriations. We need not spend too much time on the details of the enterprise; the main lines of the project have been ably drawn elsewhere.[25] Informal meetings began, as we have noted, around 1613 but the Feoffees, four ministers, four lawyers and four merchants, were not formally convened until 1626, under the eye of John

---

[21] SP 16/142/113.   [22] Cardwell, vol. I p. 292.

[23] McGiffert (ed.), *God's Plot*, p. 50. Laud had encouraged patristic studies in the Universities: J. Davies, *The Caroline Captivity of the Church: Charles I and the Remoulding of Anglicanism 1625–41* (Oxford, 1992) p. 51.

[24] SP 16/142/113.

[25] I. M. Calder, 'A Seventeenth Century Attempt to Purify the Anglican Church', *AHR* 53 (1948) pp. 760–75; Calder (ed.), *Activities of the Puritan Faction of the Church of England*; E. W. Kirby, 'The Lay Feoffees', *JMH* 14 (1942) pp. 1–25; C. Hill, *Economic Problems of the Church from Archbishop Whitgift to the Long Parliament* (London, 1971) pp. 245–74. Calder's accounts give a wealth of detail and most of the documentation. Hill's account sets the project in context and must be read alongside Calder's rather hermetically sealed discussion.

Preston. The scheme accepted gifts of impropriated tithes, not in order to restore them directly to the church, but to fund lecturers in market-town pulpits. We must note, in passing, that this seems to be a reversal, under Preston, of Chaderton's earlier attitude to the use of impropriations. Preston's influence is in the background: the four original clerical feoffees were Richard Stock, Richard Sibbes, John Davenport and Charles Offspring. Upon Stock's death in 1626, he was replaced by William Gouge. Thomas Foxley, one of the St Antholin's lecturers, was closely involved and cited as a co-defendant. We should not see this group as acting alone: we know that other groups appeared in Norwich (led by the clerics John Ward, John Yates, Robert Peck and Jeremy Benton), Reading and Leicester at least, collectives which related to the London group as 'proto-trustees', other clerics in London, such as Thomas Taylor and Hugh Peter, and beyond, such as John White, were involved, but the London ministers give us a core group.[26] The first lesson we may learn from the Feoffees is their capacity for organisation. This was a feature drawn to his congregation's attention by Peter Heylin in the sermon in which he denounced the project, noting those 'constant conferences which they hold, at all publicke meetinges, and assemblies; here [that is, in Oxford], at our sister universitie, at the great cittie, that their resorte from all the quarters of the land may be less suspected: what is the purpose of it! Doe they not therefore doe it, to receive intelligence, to communicate their counsailes, and confirme their partie!'[27] Between 1626 and 1633, the Feoffees collected £6,361. 6s. 1d. and funded some eighteen preachers in eleven counties. In 1633, Peter Heylin brought the scheme to hostile attention, and Laud took a great interest in the trial of the Feoffees in Exchequer court, noting with satisfaction in his diary when they were dissolved and their funds taken from their control.

Laud regarded the project as 'a cunning way, under a glorious pretence, to overthrow the church government by getting to their power more dependency of the clergy than the king and all the peers and all the bishops in all the kingdom had'. His judgement may have been tempered by historians, but in essentials remains. Kevin Sharpe concludes that 'on this occasion [Laud] did not react with excessive paranoia'; William Hunt regards the project to be evidence of 'a new radicalism'; Susan Doran and Christopher Durston describe the Feoffees as 'some of Laud's most

---

26 SP 16/531/134; *VCH Norfolk* vol. II pp. 281–2; J. M. Guilding (ed.), *Reading Records* (London, 1895) vol. II p. 266; SP 16/88/13. While the Feoffees were being dissolved, it appears that an attempt was being made to set up a similar group in York: C. Cross, 'Achieving the Millennium: the Church in York during the Commonwealth', in *SCH* 4 (1967) p. 124.

27 G. E. Gorman, 'A Laudian Attempt to "Tune the Pulpit": Peter Heylin and his Sermon against the Feoffees for the Purchase of Impropriations', *JRH* 8 (1974–5) p. 344.

committed Puritan opponents'; for Frank Bremer, the project was part of the 'fight to preserve the Calvinist basis of the Church of England', and for Leo Solt, they intended to 'maintain the Puritan ministry'.[28] The Feoffees were attempting to reform without 'tarrying for the magistrate'; the scheme was quintessentially Puritan and cannot be seen in anything but a subversive light.[29]

However, this cannot be a complete account. While many of the ministers appointed by the Feoffees were troubled at one time or another over ceremonial issues and not a few of them endorsed non-episcopal ecclesiologies in later life, the organisation was not condemned as a nest of schismatics.[30] Christopher Hill seems almost disappointed to note that they were convicted of functioning as a body corporate without ever being incorporated. 'Behind this technical point', he argues, 'is the fact that the Feoffees were taking upon themselves the political and economic reconstruction of the church not only without authorization from the government, but in a way which conflicted with its policy.'[31]

We might pay more attention to this 'technical point': the Feoffees were engaged in an act of voluntary religion, promoting preaching and advancing a learned ministry. As Patrick Collinson has observed, to favour such things was 'to be in favour of motherhood and apple pie'.[32] Throughout their trial the Feoffees represented their efforts as 'a pious work', 'for the mainteynance of worthie paynefull and conformable preachers'. They stressed that they had not 'to their knowledge presented or nominated any to any Church or place in their disposicion which hath not been conformable to the doctrine and discipline of the Church of England'. This became

---

[28] K. Sharpe, *The Personal Rule of Charles I* (London, 1992) p. 311; Hunt, *Puritan Moment*, p. 196; S. Doran and C. Durston, *Princes, Pastors and People: the Church and Religion in England 1529–1689* (London, 1991) p. 153; F. J. Bremer, *Congregational Communion: Clerical Friendship in the Anglo-American Puritan Community 1610–1692* (Boston, Mass., 1994) p. 75; L. F. Solt, *Church and State in Early Modern England 1509–1640* (Oxford, 1990) p. 179. A slightly more subtle (if brief) account can be found in N. Tyacke, *The Fortunes of Puritanism 1603–1640*, Friends of Doctor Williams's Library Lecture 1990 (London, 1991) p. 14.

[29] Mark Dever struggles to accommodate Sibbes' part in the project within his account of the minister's moderation and is forced into a series of qualifications. While his account is very helpful in many respects, I cannot accept his version of Sibbes as a 'conforming reformer'; later discussion of attitudes to conformity will, I hope, illuminate the position of such as Sibbes. M. E. Dever, 'Moderation and Deprivation: a Reappraisal of Richard Sibbes', *JEH* 43 (1992) pp. 409–10. I am grateful to Mark Dever for discussions of Sibbes and much else.

[30] Although the point will not be pursued in detail here, most of those appointees that came into conflict with the authorities were untroubled before the 1630s. This point will be substantiated elsewhere.

[31] Hill, *Economic Problems*, p. 262.

[32] P. Collinson, 'Puritans, Men of Business and Elizabethan Parliaments', *PH* 7 (1988) pp. 189–90.

a constant refrain in the defence.[33] Of course, it might be objected that this is exactly what the defendants would say: the informant regarding the Norwich feoffees claimed that their ministers were required to be 'Conformable', 'but this only to the eye of the worlde', and that it might be true that 'Conformity is put in, but its onely for a pretence'.[34] However, the nineteenth article of the orders adopted by the London Feoffees in February 1625 makes the same point:

[It is ordered] That they shall not present any Minister to be admitted and placed in any of their Church livings, but such as are conformable to the discipline and doctrine and government of the Church of England and an able and faithfull preacher of the word of God.

Given the intense concern for secrecy shown by the Feoffees (a concern that was used against them in the trial), there is no need to assume that this was purely a front for the authorities: the book was not a public document, if anything the opposite, so I think we can take this intention seriously.[35]

One case that became a bone of contention during the trial was that of John Archer, a former St Antholin's lecturer. The Feoffees appointed him as vicar of Hertford in May 1631. Noy was unhappy about the circumstances in which the Feoffees made the place available for Archer, and drew particular attention to the qualities of the candidate.

How fit a man he was to be presented, and how conformable I shall leave to your lordships to Consider, I shall loath to wrong any man, The Bishop of London his ordinary thought him worthy to be suspended for certaine strange opinions which he had delivered I have the sentence of the suspension in my hand Let it be read.

Noy returned to Archer's case repeatedly, using him to demonstrate that the stated practice of appointing conformable ministers was specious.[36] The defence made no effort to deny that Archer had been suspended but pointed out that he 'acknowledged his fault, and was restored to his ministery by his Ordinary'. Archer had indeed been suspended on 10 December 1630, during Laud's primary visitation as Bishop of London. He was closely questioned by his bishop in the four months of his suspension, but the issue was mainly with some injudicious expressions of hyper-Calvinism in his catechism which certainly seemed to be sailing close to the

---

[33] Calder (ed.), *Activities*, pp. 8, 16; cf. 17, 74, 75, 84, 85, 90, 91, 96, 97, 98, 92. What exactly is meant by 'conformable' should not be neglected and will be discussed below, pp. 157–67.

[34] SP 16/531/154.

[35] Calder (ed.), *Activities*, pp. 70, 78. The orders were read into the record. The books of the Feoffees were returned to the surviving Feoffees in the 1640s and do not seem to have survived.

[36] Ibid., pp. xx, 82, 100, quote p. 55. Francis Cottington drew attention to Archer's, in his opinion, 'blasphemy' p. 122.

winds of Antinomianism, and clearly breached the Declaration prefixed to the Thirty-nine Articles in 1628. The questions regarding ceremonial conformity were a peripheral issue in his examination before Laud and Arthur Duck. Archer debated the patristic authorities with his bishop, but once he admitted his fault in 'the most doubtful and ambiguous manner' of his soteriological expression, Laud relaxed his suspension.[37] The attempts of the prosecution to prove that the Feoffees promoted schismatics in doctrine, discipline or on ceremonial issues can hardly be judged to have been entirely successful. Neither could the prosecution put a convincing case to prove the seditious intent of the enterprise itself; even the most hostile judges had to concede that, in itself, the advancement of godly preaching was a laudable aim. Baron Trevor acknowledged that 'many godly men gave them money for good uses at least in intention', that 'we cannot be too Godly'. Baron Davenport could say no more than that 'the manner of doing this is not good though the use be good'.[38]

If we remove the perspective of Laud and Heylin, it becomes a distinct possibility that the Feoffees were not subversive, that they were merely more enthusiastic in their pursuit of objects universally recognized as desirable. The Feoffees seem to fit well into the Collinsonian framework: a consensual Protestantism disrupted only by the alien priorities of Laudianism.

If we turn to the central clerical figures, the ambiguities multiply. John Davenport was, at this point, a good distance from the radical ecclesiologist and ceremonial nonconformist he was to become.[39] The legend of the deprivations suffered by Richard Sibbes has finally been laid to rest by Mark Dever. William Gouge protested himself wholly in favour of conformity to Bishop Laud, admittedly in a context that should lead us to weigh his words carefully. He had not only subscribed under James but then and later had been used by the authorities as a consultant to persuade recalcitrant nonconformists to compromise.[40] Charles Offspring had never been troubled for nonconformity. The question of John Preston's commitment to 'Puritanism' is more often asserted than demonstrated. Thomas Foxley had been questioned during Laud's primary visitation as Bishop of London but indicated his willingness to conform.[41]

On the other hand, Sibbes clearly thought twice about subscribing,

---

[37] Ibid., p. 90; GL 9531/15 ff. 23–24r; SP 16/176/63; 187/17; LPL 942 no. 14. Peter White incorrectly states that he was deprived: P. White, *Predestination, Policy and Polemic: Conflict and Consensus in the English Church from the Reformation to the Civil War* (Cambridge, 1992) p. 301.

[38] Calder (ed.), pp. 111, 114, 118.   [39] See below, ch. 7.

[40] M. E. Dever, 'Moderation and Deprivation', pp. 396–413. For Gouge, SP 16/202/3; GLRO DL/C 310 f.142r; GL 9531/15 f. 23v.

[41] P. Seaver, *The Puritan Lectureships: the Politics of Religious Dissent 1560–1660* (Stanford, Calif., 1970) p. 251.

accepting the academic point that the cross in baptism was lawful while fearing to offend.[42] Preston had been brought before courts in Cambridge for preaching irregularly in St Botolph's, Cambridge, upon which he was required to add a condemnation of gadding and approval of set prayers.[43] Davenport's conformity and his support for episcopacy were, as we will see, strictly conditional. As early as 1615 he had been active as an agent trying to restore the liberty of Arthur Hildersham, reporting his efforts to the imprisoned minister. Gouge was a protégé of Hildersham and Ezekiel Culverwell who had been closely questioned over ceremonial conformity in 1611. In the 1630s, of course, he emerged as a major clerical opponent of Laudianism.[44] Foxley and Archer, as we will see, emerged as radicals later in the decade.[45]

The point here is not to propose a new interpretation of the episode as such: it seems more important and perhaps more fruitful to draw attention to the necessary ambiguity of the Feoffees and to clerical association and godly projects more generally. Every meeting and each category of activity is polysemic, that is, open to an infinite multiplicity of readings. Trying to identify a stable, inherent meaning in the Feoffees, in Hooker's conference and similar enterprises is futile: understandings are necessarily contextual, are positioned. It is no more true to say that Bishop Laud's reading of the Feoffees is more valid than that of the godly ministers who believed the project to be pious and beneficial to the church than to say the opposite. The same point can be made about the readings of historians who try to identify the 'essential' meaning of these rituals of sociability and their products: we can only identify and explore the clash of competing interpretations among contemporaries.

Similar remarks could be made about other godly projects advanced by rituals of sociability. In 1626, Davenport, Gouge, Taylor and Sibbes had circulated a letter soliciting aid for distressed preachers in the Palatine, having failed to rouse official interest in 1622. For this they were questioned in the Court of High Commission. However, they were released with a mild reprimand, and, as Patrick Collinson has made clear, their activities were part of a long tradition of Protestant internationalism, a tradition with strong roots in official soil.[46] If the group were driven by their

---

[42] CUA V-C Ct I 42 f. 202; Dever, pp. 405–6.

[43] CUA V-C Ct I 9 ff. 173–4; III Exhibita files 24, loose paper numbered 88, supplementing the account in Morgan, *Puritan Chaplain*, pp. 29, 47–9.

[44] DWL Morrice MS J 1631 (14); W. Haller, *The Rise of Puritanism* (New York, 1938) pp. 67–8; GLRO DL/C 309 136r, 308 f. 308v.

[45] SP 16/395/48; 418/99; 420/64; 422/126–7.

[46] SP 16/56/15; Seaver, *Puritan Lectureships*, p. 237; P. Collinson, 'England and International Calvinism 1558–1640', in M. Prestwich (ed.), *International Calvinism 1541–1715* (Oxford, 1985) pp. 197–223.

religious priorities to meddle in state affairs, their meddling was intended to advance a goal that the state had usually seen fit to advance in conjunction with private projects. The troubles of Davenport *et al.* contrast nicely with a list of ministers inserted into the ecclesiastical court records of Northamptonshire in the early 1620s, which appointed six ministers for each deanery to pursue such collections and was by no means dominated by Puritan clergymen.[47]

So, without trying to pin down the meaning of these practices too firmly, we may identify an element in the godly world view before the arrival of Laud and his new readings which is, if not actively and inherently subversive, then perhaps indifferent to the peace of the church. Some practices could be seen as a voluntarism merely supplementing the formal duties of religion, on one hand, or as seditious activities on the other, but co-exist uneasily in a state of tension, a tension regulated by the relative power accorded to different readings of the circumstances. Thus, in the mid-1620s, Henry Jessey spent some of his time in the Stour valley 'distributing godly practical books', a pastime described by Samuel Collins from a different viewpoint when he complained that the 'refractory ministers of the country' made his congregation ungovernable 'by leaving schismaticall books among them'.[48] By the end of the decade, this tension was drawn out by a new vigour on the part of the ecclesiastical authorities, and a heightened suspicion of voluntarism. When this happened the structures established for the promotion of what were perceived (by the godly) as merely pious works could promote more clearly disruptive purposes. By this time Jessey's godly practical books had been supplemented: in 1629, Stephen Marshall and John Borodale of Steeple Bumpstead were found to be involved in a network of divines distributing copies of Prynne's *Old Antithesis to the New Arminianism* from Cambridge into Essex; in 1636, Robert Ryece, a layman on the Suffolk side of the Stour, was using similar channels to publicise Prynne's *Newes from Ipswich*, and in the following year Jeremiah Burroughes and William Greenhill, who had preached at Dedham, were importing Bastwick's *Litany* into East Anglia.[49]

This process can be seen at work in the rituals of sociability: prayer and fasting, a characteristic of clerical voluntarism with an uneasy existence in canon law, could be forced to confirm a Laudian prophecy of subversion and even opposition. Samuel Harsnett, Bishop of Norwich from 1619 to 1628, had earned the disapproval of the godly, not least for his harassment

[47] NRO Misc. Dioc. Rec. 88.
[48] Edward Whiston, *Life and Death of Mr Henry Jessey* (1671) p. 6; SP 16/210/44.
[49] SP 16/141/17; 142/22; 144/10, 48; T. Webster, *Stephen Marshall and Finchingfield* (Chelmsford, 1994) pp. 11–12; *MHSC* 4th ser. 6 (1863) pp. 422–32; BodL Tanner 68 ff. 9, 10.

of Samuel Ward of Ipswich and John Wilson of Sudbury. After his elevation
to York, Harsnett was remembered by the godly, who feared his 'Designs of
Mischief against the Reforming Pastors and Christians' of the north. As he
returned to his manor of Southwell in Nottinghamshire from Bath in
March 1630, a meeting of ministers was set apart for 'solemn Fasting and
Prayer, to implore the Help of Heaven against those designs'.[50] This action
must not be underestimated as an act of opposition: as Thomas Hooker
noted, 'Prayer is of great force. It will bring punishment upon a man, and
he shall not know who hurt him.' Harsnett would have done well to have
followed Hooker's advice – 'Take heed therefore of wronging a Praying
Minister' – for, as Mather noted with satisfaction, 'on that very day, he was
taken with a Sore and an odd Fit which caused him to stop at a blind
House of Entertainment on the Road where he died suddenly'.[51]

IV

If we have come to a position emphasising ambiguity but recognising a
certain potential for subversion, we must also acknowledge that clerical
society could be turned to more clearly oppositional purposes. This was the
experience of Hooker's group. In the period leading up to and including the
1631 episcopal visitation, Laud had struck at, and shattered, the preaching
outlets of the conference. Hooker was silenced, as were John Rogers, albeit
temporarily, Thomas Shepard, Thomas Weld and Daniel Rogers.[52] These
were the depressing circumstances when Stephen Marshall, Thomas Weld,
Daniel Rogers, Nathaniel Ward, Thomas Shepard and Samuel Wharton
met two days before Laud was due to visit Dunmow and 'consulted
whether it was best to let such a swine to root up God's plants in Essex and
not give him some check. Whereupon in was agreed upon privately at
Braintree that some should speak to him and give him some check.' The
group attended the court at Dunmow and Weld remonstrated with Laud.
Shepard tried to add his voice and was forcibly dragged away by Martin
Holbeach, who collected their horses and hurried Shepard away.

This overt gesture of opposition, however futile, was understood by all

---

[50] DWL Morrice MS J 1630 (4); Mather, III p. 44. For Harsnett's career at Norwich, R. W.
Ketton-Cremer, *Norfolk in the Civil War* (Norwich, 1985) pp. 52–5; cf. P. Collinson,
'Lectures by Combination', in *Godly People: Essays on English Protestantism and
Puritanism* (London, 1983) pp. 488–9. Essex ministers may have had a particular animus
against Harsnett as he was an Essex man. He was buried at Chigwell, his first living.
Among those 'Reforming Pastors of the north' were Ezekiel Rogers and Samuel Winter,
both in Barrington livings in Yorkshire.

[51] Thomas Hooker, *Spiritual Munition* (1626), in G. H. Williams, N. Pettit, W. Herget and
S. Bush Jr (eds.), *Thomas Hooker: Writings in England and Holland, 1625–1633, Harvard
Theological Studies* 38 (Cambridge, Mass., 1975) p. 47; Mather, III p. 44.

[52] This episode will be dealt with in greater detail below, pp. 195–6.

involved to be an act directed against William Laud whether as a representative of the ecclesiastical authorities or in his own right. This does not require the conference *per se* to be subversive in any but the limited sense argued above, but it displays dramatically the process whereby latent tensions could be brought to the surface when the painful preaching ministry was seen to be under threat. This is not to describe a Walzerian revolutionary potential, but merely to reinstate Puritanism as a set of priorities that could dissolve restraints of authority and deference in circumstances that appeared to threaten the *sine qua non* of a true church: godly preaching.[53] This set of priorities could make an accommodation with a regime that exercised tolerance towards painful preachers,[54] but the tensions that characterised the occasional clashes with the pre-Laudian authorities remained sensitive to changes in the ecclesiastical atmosphere. As we will see, the resolution of these tensions in individuals did not necessarily lead to opposition, but the structures of association established to promote godly preaching also facilitated the active defence of a ministry conceived of in terms of the pure delivery of the Word through sermons.

Once again, the religio-political context does not exhaust the possibilities of our understanding of the rituals of sociability. If the demonstration of godly *angst* at Dunmow takes a theatrical form, perhaps we can apply this account more seriously to these rituals generally. If we follow Victor Turner and regard ritual as a form of 'social drama', we may gain further insights into the dynamics of these meetings. For Turner, there are four phases to the social drama. Firstly, there is 'a visible breach in one of the major expectable regularities of group living'; secondly, a 'crisis' in which sides must be taken, 'coalitions are formed, scapegoats pointed to, degrees of opposition – from harsh words to physical violence – mooted and/or resorted to'. Thirdly, in Turner's view the most interesting phase, is the attempt at redress or restoration of the social equilibrium, an attempt which may succeed or fail. The final phase is the outcome, either the reconstitution of the group, albeit necessarily altered in some way by the drama, or a recognition of an unbridgeable gap and some more far-reaching reconfiguration.[55]

---

[53] M. Walzer, 'Puritanism as a Revolutionary Ideology', *H&T* 3 (1964) pp. 59–90: cf. P. Lake 'Puritan Identities', *JEH* 35 (1984) pp. 112–23.

[54] This is implicit in K. Fincham and P. Lake, 'The Ecclesiastical Policy of James I', *JBS* 24 (1985) pp. 169–207; cf. K. Fincham, *Prelate as Pastor: the Episcopate of James I* (Oxford, 1990) ch. 7.

[55] V. Turner, 'Images of Anti-temporality: an Essay in the Anthropology of Experience', *HTR* 75 (1982) pp. 246–8. Carolyn Bynum makes some trenchant criticisms of Turner's account in 'Women's Stories, Women's Symbols: a Critique of Victor Turner's Theory of Liminality', in *Fragmentation and Redemption: Essays on Gender and the Human Body in Medieval*

What we might call 'normal' rituals of sociability among the godly follow this form. The original breach is, of course, the Fall, but the meeting may be in response to some local manifestation of the Fall, a judgement or affliction, plague or some advance of the Antichrist. In this form, the crisis is manageable: sides are taken and the means of redress, fasting and prayer, readily available. The outcome is usually a fairly successful reconstitution of the group through satisfaction internal to the meeting: a proper humiliation, the heartfelt expression of contrition and a right orienting to God. There is a striking correspondence between this account and the shape of the voluntary fast described by Joseph Bentham.[56]

Here, the third phase, the attempt at redress, is characterised by what Turner, following Van Gennep, calls 'liminality', a time when the old structure loses its hold and the new is not yet fully constituted. In this gap of 'anti-structure', potential roles and relationships are unlimited and for this reason taboos tend to proliferate around these transitions.[57] In godly society, this space attracts just such taboos: consider John Rogers' strictures on behaviour in private meetings, for instance. William Twisse felt that such occasions were so fraught with danger that written conference was to be preferred to verbal discussion.[58] This space is one of a number in which the group or any individual within the group may be re-oriented, either in terms of the society or of God. Samuel Rogers expresses both the anti-structural, anti-temporal nature of such occasions and also the importance of this space in social and spiritual terms when he writes, 'I have bin in

---

Religion (New York, 1991) pp. 27–51. Her main point, that Turner's model, in the context of western Christianity, is gendered and proves more illuminating for the experience of men than women, reinforces the successful 'fit' I find for the experiences of the clergy, an exclusively male group. The most sustained critique of Turner's work on ritual is B. C. Alexander, *Victor Turner Revisited: Ritual as Social Change* (Atlanta, Ga., 1991) pp. 1–66, although Alexander places rather too much emphasis on the transformational nature of ritual in Turner's account: one of the strengths, it seems to me, is the conditional, contextual stress upon the potentialities of ritual, a possibility of change or critique, against traditional structural-functionalist accounts that stress the ways in which ritual affirms the *status quo ante*, and progressive accounts that focus on the subversive effects of anti-structure. For Turner, ritual is always a dialectical process between structure and anti-structure.

56 Joseph Bentham, *The Christian Conflict* (1635) pp. 277–8. The use of 'satisfaction' here should not be taken in the theological sense of 'meriting grace'.

57 V. Turner, *Dramas, Fields and Metaphors: Symbolic Action in Human Society* (Ithaca, N. Y., 1974) pp. 13–14, 272–99; A. Van Gennep, *The Rites of Passage* (1908; London, 1980) p. 13. We should perhaps prefer the term Turner adopts for sectional rituals in complex societies, *liminoid*, that is, quasi-liminal: V. Turner, *From Ritual to Theatre: the Seriousness of Human Play* (New York, 1982) pp. 32, 52–5; Alexander, *Victor Turner Revisited*, pp. 20–6. I have preferred his earlier term because the rituals discussed here, while sectional, are clearly not secularised.

58 John Rogers, *A Godly and Fruitful Exposition upon the First Epistle of Peter* (1650) pp. 340f; cf. Arthur Hildersham, *CVIII Lectures of the Fourth of John* (1632) pp. 499–500; William Twisse, *The Riches of Gods Love* (1653) book II p. 21.

heaven a litle this evening'.[59] Robert Saxby was of the opinion that by 'religious fasting a man comes nearest the life of Angeles'.[60]

As we have observed, however, those outside the ritual can be implicated within the ritual rather more explicitly. In some conferences, under exceptional conditions, for instance, the meeting to pray *against* Bishop Harsnett, a slightly different drama unfolds. Here, the local manifestation of the breach leads to a resolution that straddles Turner's notion of alternative outcomes. The reconstitution of the group is successful, precisely at the expense of the cause of the breach. The group is turned further inward, joined by a starker definition against the external object. The breach is not healed, but is made, in a sense, more external.

Those rituals of sociability among the godly that often come to our attention through printed disputes are a third form of the social drama. Here the breach is internal to the group, a violation of one of the 'major expectable regularities' of shared doctrine, as in the Walker–Wooton dispute, in practice, as in the conference on conformity in Ockley, or in a matter of lifestyle or morality.[61] The liminal phase contains the potential for radical change in the society, for the reintegration of the dissenting parties or for a radical reconfiguration of the group, at its most extreme, the fission of the group and the emergence of new alignments, reaffirming society by expunging dissidents.

Each of these dynamics occurred within godly society, although the outcomes were rarely as tidy as this scheme suggests. Moreover, we should not be misled by the greater visibility of the last two forms: under 'normal' conditions, rituals of sociability were remarkably successful in defining and maintaining a society lacking in institutional frames. Part of this success, we might suggest, grows out of a further characteristic of liminality as identified by Turner. The anti-structural space of ritual, where status, hierarchy and precedence are placed in abeyance, is also a space of *communitas*, of social levelling and homogeneity, where authority moves from the high to the low, from the individual to the group.[62] Expression of *communitas* does not abolish status differentiation – it is reaffirmed outside the liminal phase – but it has a powerful aggregative action. One of the products of this process is godly society itself. Rituals of sociability do not

---

[59] QUB Percy MS 7 f. 92. Other such spaces would include private devotions and public worship as among the most likely situations for conversion.

[60] CUL Add MS 3117 f.62v.

[61] See above, pp. 56–7, and below, ch. 7. An example of the latter might be the meeting of the Dedham *classis* concerning the accusations against one of their members, the vicar of Dedham, Richard Parker: Collinson, *The Puritan Character*, p. 9.

[62] V. Turner, *The Ritual Process: Structure and Anti-Structure* (London, 1969) pp. 94–165; for a critique, M. J. Sallnow, 'Communitas Reconsidered: the Sociology of Andean Pilgrimage', *Man* 16 (1981) pp. 163–82.

merely define: they actively aggregate the saints. As Martin Buber put it in a similar context,

Community, growing community . . . is the being no longer side by side but *with* one another of a multitude of persons. And this multitude, though it moves also towards one goal, yet experiences everywhere a turning to, a dynamic facing of, the others, a flowing from *I* to *Thou.* Community is where community happens.[63]

In conclusion, we may discuss early Stuart clerical associations in terms of rising professionalism and continuing education, often enabling silenced ministers to influence the rising generation, but this discussion will only take us so far. We need to address the relationship of associations to the Church of England, but should pay more attention to the ambiguities expressive of the possibility of different readings. We can also trace the ways in which godly clerical society was created, defined and maintained through regular rituals of sociability. From the mid-1620s we may, I suggest, detect an added activism that led to conferences such as Hooker's and the London conference that formed the Feoffees for Impropriations. These organisations provided a framework for activities that were open to multiple readings, but which required a Laudian perspective to be labelled thoroughly subversive – the collections for the Palatinate, the collation of a body of practical divinity for John Dury, the promotion of the New England colonies or the Feoffees themselves[64] – but they also fostered a sense of identification, a community of discussion, opinion and piety that helped to crystallize pre-existing divisions. Laud did not recreate Puritanism, but he struck at the roots of the Jacobean compromise and unleashed forces held in dynamic tension since the early years of the century.

---

[63] M. Buber, *Between Man and Man* (trans. R. G. Smith) (London, 1961) p. 51. Italics in original.
[64] For more on these projects, see below, chs. 13 and 14.

Part II

THE GODLY MINISTRY: PIETY AND PRACTICE

We have spent some time exploring clerical sociability among the godly clergy. However, we have had relatively little to say about what it meant to be a godly minister. We have encountered strong opinions among these clerical communities but rather neglected the holistic context from which these opinions drew their force. It is the purpose of this section to redress this balance. In what follows, I want to approach the godly ministry phenomenologically, as it were. That is to say, I want to attempt to enter into the experience of being a godly minister. One obvious way of doing this is to consider what the ministers wrote about their role. This approach is followed, but I want to do something more. It is necessary to go beyond printed pieties about the clerical ideal in order to gain insights into the meanings that shaped the world of the godly clergy. Thus I will begin by looking at the self-image of the ministers, giving some space to the preoccupations of their work and then go on to see how they structured experience, to examine the ways in which the subjectivity of godliness was constructed. There is space here for theology but, it will emerge, theology and doctrine are not sufficient in themselves to give a rounded view of clerical experience. The emphasis so far has been on a particular social dynamic and it would be both a step backwards and a missed opportunity to abandon this approach: the social context reveals a great deal about the religiosity and vice versa.

These approaches have a number of side effects. We have an opportunity to consider what, if anything, makes this piety distinctive. What marks the godly clergy out from their colleagues? We need to address the possible existence of a 'Puritan' view of the ministry. Have all the elements that once seemed characteristically Puritan disappeared in the current view of a pre-Laudian consensus? We can try to situate the clerical experience in the wider context of the parish. How are these clergymen different from the godly men and women to whom they minister? Can we get any further with the question of why godly ministers exhibited this propensity to associate even without the stimulus of a commitment to classical discipline?

We have to ask whether there might be something in the godly experience that encouraged association to a degree greater than those characteristics which, by the 1620s, were increasingly shared by most ministers: a university education, a separation from their parishioners in the neglect of other occupations, and a consequent social distance from most of their lay neighbours. Finally, we have to explore the changing fortunes of the sets of priorities we identify through time. How did the clerical experience and practice of Puritans relate to wider views of the clergy in society as they developed in the early seventeenth century? Why was it that Laudianism represented such a threat to the godly?

5

The image of a godly minister

The Reformation was, potentially, a disaster for the clergy. Their central role, as mediators between God and humanity in the Mass, was, to a greater or lesser degree across Protestant Europe, removed in the theological changes of the sixteenth century. Indeed, as Andrew Pettegree has pointed out, it was by no means inevitable that a differentiated clergy should survive the Reformation.[1] However much we will have cause to question the postulated 'professionalisation' of the clergy, the sixteenth and seventeenth centuries undoubtedly saw a massive shift in clerical identities.[2] Some of the themes explored in this chapter are elements in that transformation, others may be more specific to the English godly clergy.[3] In a period when a status position is rising but not unquestioned, we should not be surprised to hear holders of that position making large claims for their function. We might ask if it was vocational insecurity that led John Rogers to claim that 'The Office and Calling of the Ministery is of all others the most needful and necessary . . . The souls of the people depend on the Ministery; and where the Prophesie faileth, the people perish.' In a more succinct phrase, he wrote, 'the calling of the Ministry is a very painful calling'.[4] It will emerge, as views of the calling are discussed, that the high

---

[1] A. Pettegree, 'The Clergy and the Reformation: from "Devilish Priesthood" to New Professional Elite', in A. Pettegree (ed.), *The Reformation of the Parishes: the Ministry and the Reformation in Town and Country* (Manchester, 1993) pp. 1–21.

[2] The 'professionalisation' thesis, which has certainly enhanced our knowledge of the early modern clergy, was the product of a brief dialogue between historians and sociologists. Unfortunately, as so often, that dialogue has not continued, with the result that historians have not always registered the disquiet with the concept that has been increasingly expressed by sociologists. See R. O'Day, *The English Clergy*, and M. Hawkins, 'Ambiguity and Contradiction in "the Rise of Professionalism": the English Clergy, 1570–1730', in A. L. Beier, D. Cannadine and J. M. Rosenheim (eds.), *The First Modern Society: Essays in Honour of Lawrence Stone* (Cambridge, 1989) pp. 241–69.

[3] On general issues, see E. Cameron, *The European Reformation* (Oxford, 1991) pp. 148–50, 390–6; I. Green, '"Reformed Pastors" and "Bons Curés": the Changing Role of the Parish Clergy in Early Modern Europe', in *SCH* 26 (1989) pp. 246–86.

[4] John Rogers, *A Godly and Fruitful Exposition upon the First Epistle of Peter* (1650) pp. 572, 615.

claims for the ministry and equally high expectations are linked, and related to responses to Laudianism.

It is a truism to suggest that the ministry as conceived of by the godly focused on the act of preaching almost to the exclusion of all else.[5] Daniel Rogers stressed that 'as the Lord hath planted such a light in the Sunne, as gives light to all inferiour planets, so hath he given to the Ministry of the Word an eminency above the rest', while Thomas Shepard advised,

if ever you would have the Spirit dispensed to you, wait upon the Ministry of the Gospel for it; neglect not private helps, books and meditations, &c. but know, if ever you have it dispensed, here it is chiefly to be had; buy at this shop.[6]

John Rogers could take this as given:

this we are sure, that there is no more weighty part of any Ministers duty, nor none like unto it, than to Preach the Word of God . . .[7]

'The preaching of the word is the greatest blessing that the Lord bestoweth upon any people', declared Thomas Taylor.[8] An emphasis on preaching, however, takes us a very little way towards an understanding of a distinctly godly view of the ministry or of the crisis that Laudianism represented to godly eyes. As we have seen, the perception that preaching was 'a good thing' was common to all English Protestants. According to Robert Sanderson, only 'loose persons and prophane ones' sneered at ministers.[9] A minister as moderate as Stephen Marshall's neighbour, Edward Symmons of Rayne, who was sufficiently conformable to survive the 1630s and suffer imprisonment in the 1640s, could still be found berating 'your nonpreaching Ministers, the belly-Gods of the Clergy, those idle Drones, those dumbe Dogges' and condemning 'Ecclesiasticall Courtiers, your Proctors, Apparitors, Registers and the rest . . . Fellow Commoners with the Devill' when he came to preach a visitation sermon at Halstead in 1632.[10] This was, perhaps, a more tempered assault than John Rogers' attack on those 'that are in the room of Ministers, but feed not, either cannot or will not Preach the Word; such are no feeders but starvers, blinde leaders of the blinde, Soul slayers, blood suckers, yea, worse than

---

[5] See, for instance, C. Hill, *Society and Puritanism in Pre-Revolutionary England* (London, 1964) ch. 2; P. Collinson, 'Shepherds, Sheepdogs, and Hirelings: the Pastoral Ministry in Post-Reformation England', in *SCH* 26 (1989) pp. 194–8.

[6] Daniel Rogers, *A Practicall Catechisme, 3rd Edition much Enlarged and Corrected* (1640) p. 108; Thomas Shepard, *The Parable of the Ten Virgins Opened and Applied* (1695 edn) part II p. 96; cf. Thomas Hooker, *The Soules Vocation* (1638) p. 63.

[7] Rogers, *Godly and Fruitful Exposition*, p. 632; cf. Rogers, *The Doctrine of Faith* (1636) pp. 54–58; Ezekiel Rogers, *The Chiefe Groundes of Christian Knowledge* (1642) n.p.

[8] Thomas Taylor, *A Commentarie upon the Epistle of S. Paul written to Titus* (1612) p. 49.

[9] Robert Sanderson, *Twelve Sermons* (1632) p. 33.

[10] Edward Symmons, *Foure Sermons* (1642) pp. 7, 21. For this sermon he was 'questioned and much menaced' and protected by his patron, Lord Capel: ibid., Ep. Ded.

Cannibals, as living of the blood of souls, whereas these live on mens flesh'.[11] None the less, the difference is of degree, not kind. The same is true of godly rejections of a reading ministry: for Robert Bolton, 'the Word preached is the ordinarie means to beget the unconverted to God'; John Rogers agreed.[12] Thomas Shepard might slight reading in favour of preaching, 'good books may be blessed, but there is not that spirit in them as in lively dispensations of the gospel by ministers themselves', and John Rogers concur in that 'Reading is like a fair carpet rolled up. Preaching is the same opened', but the same sentiments could be found in Bishop Downham's companion sermon to his defence of *iure divino* episcopacy, a work that Rogers was prepared to cite repeatedly.[13] These negative definitions can only take us so far.

There are some distinctive emphases in the priorities expected in the preaching of godly ministers: effectual delivery of the Word required much more than correct doctrine, as John Yates stressed: there 'is no preaching or meanes effectual but that is accompanied by the Spirit'.[14] This necessity was made more explicit by Thomas Hooker, who claimed that for a powerful ministry, 'an inward spiritual heat of heart and holy affection is required . . . Thus we speak from heart to heart and that is the best way to be in the bosome of the Hearer, and the only way to make our words take place and prevail.'[15] Similarly, John Rogers exhorted ministers 'so to preach, that it may appear to all, that its the Spirit of God which preacheth in them', and, in his characteristically pithy manner, called for them to 'Preach Christ Crucified in a Crucified Phrase'.[16] For Daniel Rogers, the effectual preacher was necessarily one 'bearing the privie mark of that wee preach'.[17]

In this, the minister was not the passive instrument that seems to be implied here. Thomas Shepard makes this clear when he asks his clerical audience to 'Preach convincing truth and Gospel-Truth, fetched from heaven, and bathed in tears'.[18] For this, assiduous preparation was necessary, as John Rogers stressed: 'to Preach painfully, what preparation is required hereto? What Reading, Meditation, Prayer, Labour of the minde &c?'[19] Thomas Taylor took the same position. To preach effectively, the minister 'must by Study, Prayer and Meditation store himself with things

[11] Rogers, *Exposition*, p. 619.
[12] Robert Bolton, *A Threefold Treatise* (1634) p. 59; John Rogers, *Exposition*, p. 694.
[13] Shepard, *Parable*, pt. II p. 97; Rogers, *Exposition*, p. 234; George Downham, *Of the Duty and Dignity of Ministers* (1608) p. 97; cf. Rogers, *Exposition*, pp. 32, 221, 615, 620, etc.
[14] John Yates, *The Saints Suffering and Saints Sorrows* (1631) p. 160.
[15] Thomas Hooker, *The Application of Redemption* (1657) p. 213.
[16] Rogers, *Exposition*, pp. 502, 236.
[17] Daniel Rogers, *Practicall Catechisme*, pt.I p. 69.
[18] Thomas Shepard, *Subjection to Christ in all his Ordinances* (1657) p. 106.
[19] Rogers, *Exposition*, p. 615; cf. Richard Baxter, *Gildas Silvanus: the Reformed Pastor* (1655) ch. 1, sect. 1.5.

new and old, for a vessel must receive in before powreth out'.[20] It is clear that Shepard took this advice: William Greenhill recalled that Shepard 'took great pains in his preparation for his publicke labours, accounting it a cursed thing to do the work of the Lord negligently; and therefore spending usually two or three whole dayes in preparing for the work of the Sabbath'. Greenhill went on to quote Shepard to the effect that 'God will curse that mans labours that lumbers up and down in the world all week, and then upon Saturday in the afternoon goes to his Study, when as God knows that time were little enough to pray and weep in, and to get his heart in frame'.[21] The complex discipline of study and meditation involved here will be discussed further below, but here it is perhaps more useful to consider the style of preaching that these priorities encouraged.

The stereotype of the Puritan plain style, 'avoiding the frothy tinkling of quaint and far-fetched phrases', is clearly part of this, but so too were the pastoral priorities that adjusted normal social restraints. Thomas Hooker suggests that plain speaking means more than clarity:

Plainness of Preaching appears also in the matter that is spoken: when sin and sinners are set out in their native and natural colours, and carry their proper names, whereby they may be owned suitable to the loathsomness that is in them, and the danger of those evils which are their undoubted reward: A Spade is a Spade, and a Drunkard is a Drunkard, &c. and if he will have his sins he must and shall have hell with them.[22]

This involved a general avoidance of flattery, as William Greenhill stressed:

The Messengers of God must deliver the mind of God, be it pleasing or provoking, be it matter of comfort or terrour ... they must denounce judgements to the wicked, as well as pardon to the penitent; threats to the stubborn, as well as promises to the fainting, they must not give out what pleases themselves, but what the Lord hints and commands them.[23]

This mandate allowed the minister to denounce not only sin from the pulpit, but also the sinner. If, as John Bossy has argued, the primary social task entrusted to the parochial clergy from the fourteenth to the seventeenth centuries was to settle conflicts, the ministry of reconciliation,[24] then the godly ministry of this account seems to be a notable exception. As Daniel Rogers urged,

---

[20] Thomas Taylor, *Works* (1653) p. 238.   [21] Shepard, *Subjection*, 'To the Reader'.

[22] Hooker, *Application of Redemption*, pp. 206, 210; cf. Hooker, *The Soules Implantation* (1637) pp. 215–16.

[23] William Greenhill, *An Exposition Continued upon the Fourteenth [to] ... Nineteenth Chapters of Ezekiel* (1651) p. 42; compare John Cotton's advice to his protégé, Ralph Levett, *MHSC* 2nd ser., 10 (1823) pp. 183–4.

[24] J. Bossy, 'Blood and Baptism: Kinship, Community and Christianity from the Fourteenth to the Seventeenth Centuries', in *SCH* 10 (1973) pp. 129–43, esp. 139, 143.

Doe not blanch, doe not dawbe with bad morter, sow no pillowes: but rather pluck off mens mufflers and vizors, and cry as Boanerges did, Awake O dead, slothfull, subtill heart! Be not beaten off from this, by the peoples unthankfulnesse, and repining.[25]

For John Rogers, one of the principal reasons for having a close working knowledge of one's flock was to gain an insight into the sins which were to be so denounced.

Thus Ministers shall know the better how to preach aptly, according to their peoples necessities, who else shall but preach generally and uncertainly: his Ministery is also the more like to prevail, when he comes home close to the peoples hearts, and toucheth their very faults; thus also shall he know the better whom to admit to the Sacrament.[26]

In Thomas Hooker's work, the necessity of such preaching, regardless of expectations of peaceableness, is made most explicit. Preaching is necessarily disruptive: his images, like those of Daniel Rogers, cast the Word as a plough, 'to plow up the fallow ground', an axe wielded by the 'skilful and strong arm of a cunning Minister', to 'take off the knotty untowardness in the Soul' or, perhaps most strikingly, as a purgative:

Strong Physick either Cures or Kills, either takes away the disease, or life of the Patient; so it is with a spiritual and powerful Ministery, it will work one way or other, either it humbles or hardens, converts or condemns those that live under the stroke thereof.[27]

Preaching to particular sins in particular sermons was a subject that Arthur Hildersham treated at length. The best preachers were 'wont to reprove the sinne boldly, and without partiality, and plainely, and particularly, so as the party they desired to reforme, might knowe himselfe to be meant', a standard he applied even to those who preached before kings. At the same time, the preacher was to take care to 'have due respect to the persons whom he doth reprove. The sinnes of superiors and magistrates, though they may be reproved, yet not with that bitternesse as other mens'.[28] Greenhill was less reserved: 'The Embassadors of God and Christ must neither flatter the persons, nor feare the faces of the greatest among the sons of men.'[29]

This rather bleak view of the pastoral vocation must be qualified in two

---

[25] Daniel Rogers, *A Practicall Catechisme*, pp. 69–70.

[26] John Rogers, *Exposition*, p. 625, cf. 62, 624, 630. This last remark is intriguing, especially as Rogers was parish lecturer and never held a cure of souls; cf. Arthur Hildersham, *CLII Lectures*, p. 48.

[27] Hooker, *Application of Redemption*, pp. 205, 215; cf. Daniel Rogers, *Practicall Catechisme*, p. 93.

[28] Hildersham, *CLII Lectures*, pp. 48–9.

[29] William Greenhill, *An Exposition Continued*, p. 42.

ways. Firstly, while it may be true to suggest that this was predominantly an expression of Puritan priorities, it was not theirs alone. Robert Sanderson, the Calvinist conformist bishop, would have recognised some of these emphases. In 1627, he told a Paul's Cross audience that 'In our preaching we should rather seek to profit our hearers, though perhaps with sharp and unwelcome reproofs, than to please them by flattering them in evil.'[30] Secondly, it is not the case that godly ministers were wholly neglectful of the ministry of reconciliation, or that a parish blessed with a minister of this stamp was necessarily riven by disputes caused by such pulpit denunciations. The impression received is that such 'particularising', as contemporaries called it, was not especially common. The Lincolnshire parishioners of John Vicars took their minister to the Court of High Commission after a specific accusation delivered during a sermon, but John Rogers felt that a spirit of reconciliation overwhelmed feuds of all kinds in Dedham. Of his congregation, he wrote: 'I found you, by the care and diligence of my worthy predecessor, in a peaceable state. Thus through Gods mercy, have you continued without rents or divisions, sidings or part taking, in peace and unitie these three and twenty years of my abode with you ... As few or no suits of Law have been found amongst you, but difference eithere betweene yourselves agreed or by indifferent neighbours compounded; so do still in the name of God.'[31] The same ideal of reconciliation was attributed to Rogers by his successor, Matthew Newcomen:

> His humble heart did soon make peace
> by arbitration wise,
> All jars and strifes he made to cease,
> twixt neighbours that did arise.[32]

This impression of harmony is bolstered by a survey of the ecclesiastical court evidence and also by Dr Pennie's intensive study of the parish.[33] Similarly, Stephen Marshall can be found trying to reconcile a husband and wife whose marriage was crumbling. Only after a year of such attempts did he present Peter Lynwood, the lover of Robert Clewes' wife, who had

---

[30] P. Lake, 'Serving God and the Times: the Calvinist Conformity of Robert Sanderson', *JBS* 27 (1988) pp. 81–116, quoted at p. 88.

[31] S. R. Gardiner (ed.), *Reports of Cases in the Courts of Star Chamber and High Commission, Camden Soc.* n.s., 39 (1886) p. 199; John Rogers, *Treatise of Love* (1632) ep. to the congregation of Dedham.

[32] Anon., *A Mournefull Epitaph upon the Death of Mr John Rogers* (1642) BL Luttrell I, 125 (C. 20 ff. 3–5) stanza 17. For the attribution to Newcomen, John Collinges, 'To the Reader' J. F. [John Fuller?], in *The Dead Yet Speaking* (Norwich, 1679).

[33] Pennie, 'Evolution of Puritan Mentality'. One exception to this pattern was a violent dispute over seating in church which was dragged through the Archdeacon's court in 1633: ERO D/ACA 49 ff. 25r, 27r, 41v, 48r, 55v, 83r.

finally left the marital home. In Finchingfield, the pattern was generally an attempt to deal with discord internally, and efforts at discipline were matched by the provision of social amenities.[34]

That there was a concern for peace and harmony in the parish seems undeniable; that biographers such as Samuel Clarke placed it higher among godly priorities than many divines of the previous generation seems plausible. While Clarke often employs the common opposition of Boanerges and Barnabus, sons of thunder and reconciliation respectively, and applies both titles to the same minister, no contemporary referred to John Rogers other than as Boanerges, the son of thunder; the same applies to Samuel Fairclough and would be appropriate for many of their godly colleagues.[35]

However, we will understand the identity and experience of the early modern clergyman only if we remember that he was exactly that: a clergy*man*. The identity of the cleric has to be understood as drawing upon and relating to conceptions of masculinity and femininity.[36] Even a superficial discussion reveals ambivalences in clerical discourse that have profound consequences for identity, piety and experience. The Reformation, of course, had a considerable effect on the question of the gender implications of the priesthood. No longer were priests members of a separate and celibate estate. While the priest no longer stood in for, and represented, the God made male flesh, the marriage of the clergy drew attention to their masculinity, reduced the sexual ambivalence of the pre-Reformation priesthood and perhaps made more likely the addition of masculinist authority to the clerical estate. In addition, this question cannot be completely separated from the changing social position of the clergy. This issue is still much debated, but it seems not unreasonable to suggest that for the university-educated elite, into which the vast majority of the clerics discussed here fell, the godly ministry was enjoying a period of rising social status, moving towards the position described by Brian Heeney as 'a different kind of gentleman'.[37]

In this situation, it is possible to see the minister as a type of masculinity writ large, a kind of superman. He draws fully upon the authority and

---

[34] GLRO DL/C 322 f. 139; Webster, *Stephen Marshall and Finchingfield*, pp. 5–9.

[35] See, for instance, Clarke (1662) p. 263; Clarke (1683) pp. 20, 287–88; Clarke (1677) p. 131. Samuel Stone called Thomas Hooker a 'son of thunder' in his 'In Obitum Viri Doctissimae Thomas Hookeri . . . ' in Hooker, *A Survey of the Summe of Church Discipline* (1648) sig. C3; cf. Daniel Rogers, *Practicall Catechisme*, pp. 69–70.

[36] It must be made clear at this point that I am considering the relationship of a series of ideal types, a series of gender ideologies. The reality, while not completely separable from the image, is rather more complex.

[37] B. Heeney, *A Different Kind of Gentleman: Parish Clergy as Professional Men in Early and Mid-Victorian England* (Hamden, Conn., 1975).

power of patriarchy supported, to a large degree, by biblical sources. The cleric, as we have seen, draws identity above all from speaking, predominantly in the sermon, speech invested with the authority implied in 'the Word of God'. The contrast to the Pauline injunction on women's silence in church is starker than for any other men. In contrast to the ideal type of their female charges, the godly clergy were active, in the world, with a public duty. They earned the honorific title 'Master', and were accorded, by virtue of their office, a degree of the honour so central to early modern masculinity. In addition, many of the epithets applied to the godly clergy have clear masculine connotations: charioteers, prophets, apostles and even gods. One demand for reform pleaded for ministers as 'Gods Messengers and Embassadors'.[38] Another saw ministers as ambassadors, fathers, guides, builders, warriors, prophets and shepherds in one paragraph.[39] Richard Baxter compared his role to that of physicians and lawyers but most often to that of military men.[40] Thomas Hooker was comparatively modest in his version: 'I am a poor ambassador sent from God to do his message unto you; and although I am low, yet my message is from above.' Smectymnuus used the same image with less modesty: 'all Ministers are Gods Messengers and Embassadours, sent for the good of the Elect'. When Hooker returned to the subject on another occasion, the task required masculine physique: 'the minister must hew your hearts, and hack them, he must frame and fashion your souls before they can be prepared'.[41] For Robert Pricke, ministers 'are called Spirituall Fathers, because they begette and change men anew'.[42] John Collinges referred to ministers as spiritual fathers, prophets and ambassadors. He went on to describe John Carter as 'the Lords Vinedresser, the Shepherd of the flock', and turned to a slightly less flattering image of leadership with the minister as 'a Belweather which leads the Flock of Sheep'.[43]

On the other hand, there is a strong element in clerical discourses that works against the clergy's place in contemporary masculinities. The idea of 'ministry' placed clergymen in a number of roles that were antithetical to

[38] Green, 'Reformed Pastors and *Bon Curés*', p. 240; Smectymnuus, *An Answer to a Booke Entitled, An Humble Remonstrance* (1641) p. 53.

[39] *A Parte of a Register* (1593) p. 203.

[40] Richard Baxter, *Gildas Silvianus: the Reformed Pastor* in *The Practical Works of Richard Baxter* (London, 1830) p. 98 and ch. 2 sect. I *passim*.

[41] Thomas Hooker, *The Danger of Desertion* (1631) in Williams *et al.* (eds.), *Writings*, p. 244; Smectymnuus, *An Answer*, p. 53; Thomas Hooker, *The Preparing of the Heart for to Receive Christ* (1640) reprinted in L. Ziff (ed.), *The Literature of America: Colonial Period* (New York, 1970) p. 158.

[42] Robert Pricke, *The Doctrine of Superiority, and of Subjection, Contained in the Fifth Commandment* (1609) sect F2.

[43] John Collinges, *Elisha's Lamentation for Elijah* (1657) pp. 6, 8, quotes from pp. 18, 7. A belweather [bellwether] is a large castrated sheep.

early modern masculinity. Both social and gender positions were undercut by the traditional ban, usually observed by parochial ministers, on clerical hunting and the usual exclusion of the godly clergy from office holding, a source of male honour in this society.[44] The familiar coupling of 'magistracy and ministry' can be read as a gendered binary opposition, the former to the latter as male to female. 'Ministry' has connotations of service and placed the clergy in roles of nurturing and caring; the sacraments, despite Reformation changes, still placed the clergy as providers of food and sustenance; spiritual comfort, a central role of the pastoral clergy and the whole rhetoric of service modified clerical masculinities. The image of Christ as the husband of the Church, for instance, gave clergymen a range of positions. On the one hand, it provided ministers with the image of a role as a proxy husband.[45] Christ's proposal could also be discussed with the ministry as the best man.

The Church as it is the house of God; so it is also the spouse of Christ: Ministers are the friends of the Bridegroom, and of the Bride. The ministers have done their work in preparing the Bride for the Bridegroom; as also in ministering to her when she is married. But in Betrothing her to Christ, the Bride in that work, must herself profess her own acceptance of the Lord Jesus, and subjection to him.[46]

Less moderate preachers could take the gender reversal possibilities a little further. Some could go so far as to present the ministers as breast-feeding mothers. For one, the minister is 'a Father to beget us with the immortal seed of the word, a Mother to nourish us up in the same'.[47] George Gifford, the preacher at Maldon, used this analogy: 'Wee doe all know this, that when a childe is borne, if it be alive and in health, howe much it doth covet the mothers breast, and howe sweete the milke is unto it; in the like manner, when a man is borne of God in the new and heavenly birth, he hath a vehement desire and longing after Gods word, it is marvellous sweete and delectable unto him . . . We must labour therefore by reading and hearing the word preached, by meditation and earnest prayer to come to the true understanding and right use of the sacred word of God.'[48] According to Thomas Shepard, 'Dish milk and slit milk may convey some nourishment, but breast milk hath spirit going with it; good books may be blessed, but there is not that spirit in them as in lively dispensations of

---

[44] R. B. Manning, *Hunters and Poachers: a Cultural and Social History of Unlawful Hunting in England 1485–1640* (Oxford, 1993) pp. 177–8; A. J. Fletcher, 'Honour, reputation and Local Office-holding in Elizabethan and Stuart England', in A. J. Fletcher and J. Stevenson (eds.), *Order and Disorder in Early Modern England* (Cambridge, 1987) pp. 92–115; M. James, *Society, Politics and Culture: Studies in Early Modern England* (Cambridge, 1986) pp. 308–415.
[45] Collinges, *Elisha's Lamentation*, p. 9.
[46] John Cotton, *The Way of Congregational Churches Cleared* (1648) pt. II p. 27.
[47] *A Part of a Register*, p. 203.   [48] George Gifford, *Foure Sermons* (1598) sig. f2.

the gospel by ministers themselves.'[49] For John Collinges, ministers 'are Fathers and Mothers too, Gal.4.19. *My little Children* (saith Paul) *with whom I travel in birth, till Christ be formed in you.* [Gal.4.29.] They are nursing Fathers, and nursing Mothers. The word is the Saints milk. As new born Babes desire the sincere milk of the word, that you may grow thereby. [1 Pet.2.2.] If the word be milk, the Ministers mouth is the breast, through which this milk runs into the bowels of the people.'[50] John Cotton agreed when he wrote: 'In the hearing of the Word, we are come like New born babes, desiring the sincere milk of the word.'[51] This image, an adaptation of I Corinthians 3.1–2, was so common that it provided the title for a series of catechisms by godly ministers. William Crashaw, Henry Jessey, Hugh Peter and John Syme are among the clerics who issued a pamphlet called *Milk for Babes* or something similar.[52] Samuel Crook was said to have 'adminstred . . . rationall unadulterated milk for Babes in Christ, . . . and strong meat for grown men'.[53] In a passage disparaging silent ministers, Arthur Hildersham complained that 'it were as intollerable bondage and tyranny to binde Gods people to rest upon the ministry of such as can not instruct them, as it were to compell infants to abide with such nurses as have neither sucke nor foode to give them'.[54] Less frequently, ministers working for the reformation of the church might be mid-wives: 'This is the day of the Churches travel, and she hath a hard labour to bring forth a settlement of truth, and reformation: the Ministers of the Gospel are as Midwives, to facilitate the birth.'[55] These various roles, each with gendered inflections, were listed in a parenthetical address *ad clerum* by Joseph Bentham:

You fathers begetting, 1 Cor 4.14. Mothers travailing in birth, Gal. 4.19. And nurses, 2. Thess. 2. Feeding soules to eternal life: You Shepheards to draw waters out of the wels of salvation, not for beasts, but men: . . . You Ambassadors of the Lord of Glory, co-workers with, and labourers for God: Angels of the Churches; salt of the earth; lights of the world; and men of God.[56]

---

49 Thomas Shepard, *Parable of the Ten Virgins*, in *Works* (Boston, Mass., 1853) vol. II p. 497.

50 Collinges, *Elisha's Lamentation*, p. 8. Travel, of course, means travail.

51 John Cotton, *A Practical Commentary, or an Exposition . . . [on] John* (1656) p. 338.

52 William Dickinson, *Milk for Babes. The English Catechisme, Set Downe in the Common-prayer Booke, Breifly Explaned* (1628); William Crashaw, *Milke for Babes. Or, a North-countrie Catechisme. Made Plaine to the Capacitie of the Countrie People* (1618); Hugh Peter, *Milk for Babes, and Meat for Men* (1630); John Syme, *The Sweet Milke of Christian Doctrine: in Question and Answer* (1617); Robert Abbot, *Milk for Babes* (1646); Henry Jessey, *A Catechisme for Babes* (1652); John Cotton, *Milk for babes* (1646); John Cotton, *Spirituall Milk for Babes* (1668). John Carter published a work called *Milk for Children*, which has not survived: Clarke (1662) p. 7.

53 Ibid., p. 36.　　　54 Hildersham, *CVIII Lectures upon the Fourth of John*, p. 253.

55 Collinges, *Elisha's Lamentation*, p. 33.

56 Joseph Bentham, *The Christian Conflict* (1635) p. 85.

In short, clerical masculinity was ambivalent. A space was opened up where ministers could see themselves in female roles and accordingly, in certain circumstances, appropriate 'women's symbols'. Indeed, as will emerge, it may not be excessive to argue that clerical piety drew upon, was perhaps even structured through, a series of male/female oppositions which the clergy were able to negotiate through the ambivalence of their gender identity.

II

If, in image at least, the emphasis on spirited preaching with a qualified neglect of the demands of social harmony is characteristic of the godly view of the ministry, albeit without being unique to that view, is this a sufficient account of the godly ministry? Clearly, it is not. We have to go further in a number of directions. Can we uncover common ground in the matter that preoccupied the ministers in their preaching? We have to remember that the role of the minister involved much more than preaching. We have touched upon some of the private duties of the godly cleric in considering patterns of sociability, but public duties were not exhausted with the sermon. We have to turn to the role of the sacraments in the godly ministry. Did the eucharist have a place in the religiosity of the godly? How far can we excavate the devotional life of the godly cleric?

The first question seems, on the surface, the easiest. Surely, given the vast tomes of sermons published by ministers in this period, we have better access to the early modern pulpit than any other, perhaps including the pulpit in the recent past? Approached a little more critically, the task appears less simple. In the first place, how far is a sermon preached the same thing as a sermon published? The audience is substantially different: it takes a great deal more commitment to buy a substantial volume than to attend a parish church. Printed collections of sermons are for the committed, if not necessarily the converted. This must make the assumption (of which I have been guilty) that we have direct access to early modern sermons problematic. We are slowly learning more on these issues: others are far more qualified than I to do more than raise the question.[57]

In any case, it must be acknowledged that the surviving material is a negligible fragment: Stephen Marshall preached on average three times a week from the early 1620s to his death in 1655; John Rogers delivered sermons at a similar rate from the 1590s to 1636, so each minister must

---

[57] Arnold Hunt is completing a Cambridge PhD that will illuminate this point. For now, see G. Selement, 'Publication and the Puritan Minister', *WMQ* 3rd ser. 37 (1980) pp. 219–31.

have stood in the pulpit over three thousand times. Those sermons that were published or that have left some record in manuscript notes clearly represent a meaningless proportion in statistical terms, and those ministers who left less record than men such as Marshall and Rogers are the vast majority. Moreover, most divines regarded the press as a pale shadow of the pulpit, deserving of little active cultivation. John Rogers, for instance, responding to criticisms of the first edition of his *Doctrine of Faith*, that the uses 'are very short and weak in comparison of that they were in preaching', agreed and claimed not to know 'how to mend it, unless I had preached them over again, or had more leisure to enlarge them than I can attain to'.[58] For these reasons, I am pessimistic about the value of studies which make large claims for the precise rendering of the thought of these ministers. This is to take issue with two strands of the current historiography, principally as produced by two groups of scholars: firstly, those identified by David Hall as 'seminary historians,' whose studies tend to assume that the published works of seventeenth-century divines lend themselves to systematic analyses as rounded systems of theology, occasionally neglecting the social and polemic contexts that bring such writings to print; secondly, to question some literary scholars whose analyses tend to rely upon techniques developed for more carefully authorised texts. Similarly, content analysis may be misapplied if it is used to tell us much about what happened in pulpits.[59]

However, this is not to suggest that nothing can be done or that the preoccupations of ministers are necessarily beyond the grasp of the historian. There is enough evidence to encourage us to reconstruct the intent of some godly ministers with some confidence, without forgetting the limits of the possible or doing violence to the provisory nature of our conclusions. Moreover, precisely because our main resource is the printed sermon, we know most about those ministers held in highest esteem by their colleagues and about the subjects they were most prepared to release into the uncontrollable public sphere of print.

In their stated priorities and in the estimation of contemporaries, there is a remarkable unanimity in the assessment of the subject of the godly ministry. Stephen Marshall stated plainly that 'the excellencie of a Ministry is in the light that it carries', and again, 'the clearer any Ministry is in the

---

[58] John Rogers, preface to *Doctrine of Faith* (1632) n.p. Thomas Goodwin told Samuel Hartlib that there were 'Few good English bookes, the best th[ing]s are kept in Mens studies in MS so that hee counted those which Cotton only had done were worth all that ever was printed.' SU Hartlib MS 29/2/53b–54a; cf. G. Selement, 'Publication . . . '.

[59] This is not, of course, to suggest that these scholars produce nothing of value, and I rely heavily on the work of seminary historians below. For the historiography, D. D. Hall, 'On Common Ground: the Coherence of American Puritan Studies', *WMQ* 3rd ser. 44 (1987) pp. 193–229, although he is less pessimistic regarding the possibilities of these works.

discoverie of Christ the more excellent it is'.[60] For Daniel Rogers, the preaching of the Word was first and foremost 'the seed of immortalitie' and the minister was 'the true arbiter or middleman to convey from God to [his congregation] the Lord Jesus in all his good things'.[61] Quite simply, the minister's duty was conversion: 'What a minister should chiefly desire for his people, even that they may be brought in God's favour by Christ, have their sins forgiven, Christ made theirs and they assured thereof.'[62] Although the minister could help the process along by example and pastoral advice, preaching was 'the meanes which the Lord hath sanctified, and by which he hath beene wont to worke repentence, and grace in his people': 'the Preaching of the Word is the Instrument of Regeneration to beget men again to God . . . To this end we must preach those points most diligently and carefully, that be most essentially necessary to work conversion, we must beat upon mens misery, labour to bring them to Faith and Sanctification, &c. without these all other points will be unprofitable: Unpreaching Ministers have no possibility of winning souls.'[63]

In broad terms, preaching was divided into two forms: preaching of the Law and preaching of the Gospel. Both were necessary; the Law to inspire 'Legal terrors,' 'to separate . . . sinne and the soule', 'though it be a handwriting against us', and the Gospel to apply the promises of Scripture to redeem the contrite sinner.[64] John Rogers was equally explicit in his understanding of the ministerial role that John Preston called 'fullones animarum' – fullers of souls. Ministers must be persuaded

that we preach the law to the people, open the Ten Commandments, show people their many sinnes, and breaches thereof, then Gods judgements against sinne and sinners, to humble them and prepare them for God . . . Wee must not affect the title to be Ministers of the Gospell onely . . . For the law though it work no grace, yet it makes way for it, as the needle sows not the cloth, but makes way for the thread.[65]

The dichotomy between Law and Gospel was not the ultimate expression of their understanding of conversion. The ministry focused on a much more intricate examination of the experience of this process. For the godly ministers, the *ordo salutis*, or way of salvation, was a delicately structured pattern, Scripturally determined and susceptible to scientific description and application to the experience of those moved by their preaching. It is not necessary to detail the complete process as described in the literature of

---

[60] Stephen Marshall, *A Sermon Preached . . . Januar. 26, 1647* (1648) pp. 3–4.
[61] Daniel Rogers, *Catechisme*, p. 109; *A Treatise of Two Sacraments*, p. 128.
[62] John Rogers, *Exposition*, p. 13; cf. pp. 572, 613.
[63] Hildersham, *CLII Lectures*, p. 18; John Rogers, *Exposition*, p. 694; cf. Rogers, *Doctrine of Faith*, p. 53.
[64] Daniel Rogers, *Catechisme*, p. 93; Thomas Shepard, *Parable*, pt. II p. 91.
[65] John Preston, *The Golden Scepter* (1638) p. 40; John Rogers, *Doctrine of Faith*, pp. 97–8. The same image is used by William Perkins, *Commentarie upon Galatians* (1617) p. 246.

practical divinity and in sermons; the seminary historians have anatomised the prescriptive literature, particularly in the context of colonial New England.[66] In its fullest account, the process began with the decree of election, but the efforts of the preachers tended to focus on the workings of the decree on the scale of the individual life. The degree of preparation required before faith could take hold was a matter of some disagreement, although all ministers seem to have agreed that the heart must be prepared. Rather than the sudden Damascene conversion, experimental Calvinism favoured models that regarded conversion as a process, a movement of several stages: Election, Vocation, Humiliation, Contrition, Justification, Adoption, Sanctification and Glorification. Saints could discover the various movements of the *ordo salutis* within these.[67] There was always a strain within godly divinity that allowed for variety in the form of the narrative but, on the whole, Thomas Shepard's voice is representative. He insisted that the form of the *ordo salutis* was Scriptural and therefore unchangeable: we must 'crook not God's rules to the experience of men, . . . but bring men unto rules, and try mens estates herein by that . . . We are not in this or any other point to be guided by the experience of men only.' We must 'attend the rule' and allow people to 'stand or fall according to the rule'.[68] Richard Baxter was exercised for many years by doubts concerning his own salvation, chiefly because 'I could not distinctly trace the workings of the Spirit upon my heart in that method which Mr Bolton,

---

[66] Modern treatments of the *ordo salutis* in an historical context begin with Perry Miller, *The New England Mind: the Seventeenth Century* (Cambridge, Mass., 1939) and Miller, 'The Marrow of Puritan Divinity,' in his *Errand into the Wilderness* (Cambridge, Mass., 1956). The best treatment of the theology of grace is D. D. Wallace, *Puritans and Predestination: Grace in English Protestant Theology, 1524–1695* (Chapel Hill, N. C., 1982). R. T. Kendall's *Calvin and English Calvinism to 1649* (Oxford, 1979) has been influential in recent years, despite a number of flaws. N. Pettit, *The Heart Prepared: Grace and Conversion in Puritan Spiritual Life* (Yale, Conn., 1966) and J. von Rohr, *Covenant and Grace in Puritan Thought* (Atlanta, Ga., 1987) are useful (but note important criticisms of Pettit in Kendall, pp. 4–5), despite a tendency, common in a good deal of this literature, to make too little of the distinction between prescriptive and descriptive works. This is not a criticism that can be applied to C. L. Cohen, *God's Caress: the Psychology of Puritan Religious Experience* (Oxford, 1986); ch. 3 of this work, pp. 75–110, is the best discussion of the *ordo salutis*. Among English studies that have engaged with this material: P. Lake, *Moderate Puritans and the Elizabethan Church* (Cambridge, 1982); Lake, 'Calvinism and the English Church, 1570–1635', *PP* 114 (1987) pp. 32–76; Lake, 'Calvinist Conformity of Robert Sanderson', *PP* 114 (1987). For a fuller account of the literature and some discussion, Webster, 'Godly of Goshen', pp. 107–12.

[67] See, for instance, S. Bush, *The Writings of Thomas Hooker: Spiritual Adventures in Two Worlds* (London, 1980) pp. 146–230; Cohen, *God's Caress*, pp. 75–110; Webster, 'Godly of Goshen', pp. 103–21.

[68] Thomas Shepard, *The Sound Beleever* in *Works* vol. 1 p. 140; cf. Arthur Dent, *The Plain Mans Pathway to Heaven* (1601) p. 32; Richard Sibbes, *The Bruised Reed and the Smoaking Flax* (1630); Thomas Goodwin, *A Childe of Light Walking in Darkness* (1636) p. 74 for a more moderate line.

Mr Hooker, Mr Rogers and other divines describe', and it was not until the third quarter of the seventeenth century that he 'understood that God breaketh not all mens hearts alike'.[69]

Setting out the path of the *ordo salutis*, defining the proper shape of the conversion process, and policing the boundaries of godly experience were the major themes of godly preaching as evinced by both surviving traces and contemporary estimates. Thomas Hooker's *corpus*, in particular, with the exception of his late work on ecclesiology, a few occasional sermons and his exposition of the Lord's Prayer, is an extensive treatment of exactly this theme, covering some four thousand pages.[70] He first preached through the *ordo salutis* as a fellow at Cambridge, for which 'he entertained a special Inclination . . . and the Notes of what he then delivered were so esteemed, that many copies therof were transcribed and preserved'. While at Chelmsford, he delivered his doctrine again, 'in a more popular way', from which most of the published versions were taken, and after his emigration he was prevailed upon to 'go over the Points of Gods Regenerating Works upon the soul of his Elect' once again. Manuscript notes of these sermons were similarly prized and circulated.[71]

John Rogers was remembered by one of his pupils, over forty years after his death, as a 'grave, severe, solid Divine', whom few heard 'without trembling at the Word of God'. The verses Matthew Newcomen composed upon his death claimed,

> His life Gods glory did advance,
> his doctrine good and plaine:
> And by Gods holy ordinance
> he many a soule did gain.[72]

Rogers' reputation has been made clear in the testimony of Thomas Goodwin, and in the attempts of Thomas Hooker to gain a preaching post close to Rogers. Hooker contributed a preface to the second edition of *The Doctrine of Faith* in which, according to convention, he refused to praise Rogers:

And in my silence the souls in heaven now blessed, and many hundreds of the saints brought to God by his ministry, are as large Letters, and the best of his commendation, as Paul speakes [2 Cor.3.1], read of all and known of all.[73]

[69] Matthew Sylvester (ed.), *Reliquiae Baxterianae* (1696) p. 69.
[70] S. Bush, Jr., 'Establishing the Hooker Canon,' in Williams *et al.* (eds.), *Thomas Hooker: Writings*, pp. 378–89, with a complete bibliography.
[71] Mather, III pp. 65–6; Philip Nye and Thomas Goodwin, 'To the Reader', in Hooker, *Application*, n.p.
[72] J. C. [probably John Collinges], 'To the Reader', in J. F. [John Fuller?], *The Dead Yet Speaking* (Norwich, 1679) n.p.; *A Mournefull Epitaph*, stanza 8.
[73] Hooker, preface to Rogers, *Doctrine of Faith*, n.p.

Both the works published in Rogers' lifetime, of course, were taken up with issues of the life of faith and its manifestations: in this case, the published work and the preoccupations of the preaching career seem coterminous. Newcomen recalled that:

> Most faithfully he preach't Gods will,
> with wisdome from above,
> And left for to direct us still
> his booke of faith and love.[74]

Similar claims can be made for the published works of Thomas Shepard, despite occasional pieces publicising the evangelical work among native Americans and contributions to the ecclesiological debates of the 1640s.[75] However, ministers whose published *œuvre* is devoted to other issues routinely served up a diet of regenerative exhortation from the pulpit. Thomas Weld left a body of work devoted to polemical and propagandist themes, but his regular preaching in old and New England was focused on the pursuit of conversions.[76] Stephen Marshall, who has been characterised as an archetypal 'political Puritan', owed his reputation among contemporaries to what Giles Firmin called 'catecheticall divinity'. In the mid-1630s, his work on free grace and the Sabbath was warmly anticipated and he was famous throughout his life as a painful preacher capable of moving the most stubborn hearts. As with Hooker, notes of his sermons were shared among voluntary groups of Christians. Where such notes have survived, the subjects are almost exclusively devotional, developing Christological themes, calling for conversion and repentance, a major (and neglected) aspect of his more famous fast sermons.[77]

[74] *Mournefull Epitaph*, stanza 23.
[75] See the three-volume edition of his works (Boston, Mass., 1853). The dangers of equating published works with pulpit preaching appear in David Leverenz's account in *The Language of Puritan Feeling: an Exploration in Literature, Psychology and Social History* (New Brunswick, N. J., 1980) p. 194, where there is a discussion of 'the greater part of his sermons' without making it clear how narrow the evidential basis is.
[76] See, for instance, the sermons reported in G. Selement and B. Woolley (eds.), *Thomas Shepard's Confessions, PCSM 58: Collections* (1981) pp. 76–80, and John Shaw's account in 'The Life of Master John Shaw', in *Yorkshire Diaries and Autobiographies of the Seventeenth and Eighteenth Centuries, Surtees Soc.* 65 (1875) p. 124. Samuel Rogers credited Weld with the first stirring of his conversion: it 'being holydaye; Mary Adams, our maide asked mee if I would go to heare Mr Wells at Terling, to which I answered yea; and so went skipping but why? the main cause that drew me (as I remember) was that I might see a new towne, and heare a new Man; Athenian as I was I desired noveltyies, though with an unknown god; but god had another end, though I knew nothing well, mr wells his mourneful prayer melted me into teares (as I thinke) but his sermon especiallye . . . and made mee come sobbing home'. QUB Percy MS 7 ff. 3–4. Rogers was fourteen years old at the time.
[77] H. Trevor-Roper, 'The Fast Sermons of the Long Parliament', in *Religion, Reformation and Social Change* (London, 1967) pp. 297–8; Giles Firmin, *A Briefe Vindication of Mr Stephen Marshall* appended to his *The Questions between the Conformist and the*

As I have shown elsewhere, it is possible to take an element of the *ordo salutis* and show that many ministers, preaching in a number of different pulpits, handled the same issue, accorded it the same place in the *ordo salutis*, and even explicated the theme with the same metaphors, hammering a common message home time and time again. Having performed such an exercise for the treatment of the theme of Adoption, a stage in the life of a fairly advanced saint, we can see that regular intercourse, in conferences and in fasts, fostered an extremely tight consensus on the minutiae of soteriological theology.[78]

This is not to say that there were no variations and no disagreements among the godly ministers. Kendall's account of the differences between John Cotton's attitude to, for instance, preparation for faith and that of Hooker and Shepard was anticipated by Perry Miller and Alfred Habegger,[79] and, more importantly, it was a matter of contemporary note, too. In their introduction to Hooker's *Application of Redemption*, Thomas Goodwin and Philip Nye were concerned that Hooker demanded too much of his auditors, 'perhaps by urging too far, and insisting too much upon that as Preparatory, which includes indeed the beginnings of true faith (and a man may be held too long under John Baptists water)'.[80] In private, Goodwin had previously been prepared to go much further, telling Samuel Hartlib that

Hooker is a severe and Crule man like John Baptist, urges too much and too farre the Worke of Humiliation. [Goodwin] Would not have it [viz. Hooker's *Unbelievers Preparing for Christ*] come abroad bec[ause] he was Erroneous in it, making a difference of one that shal be saved and Not too wide making it not true grace which indeed it is.[81]

Nonconformist (1681) pp. 4, 24, where Marshall seems to have been preaching through the *ordo salutis*; SU Hartlib MS 29/2/48a; Henry Walker, *Spirituall Experiences of Sundry Beleevers* (1651) pp. 16, 59, 79, 377–81, where notes of his sermons contributed to the conversion of a member of Henry Walker's congregation. See also the sermons edited by Firmin: Stephen Marshall, *Works* (1661), a number of sermons preached in London between 1649 and 1655. MS notes can be sampled in CUL Add MS 3320 f. 217; BL Add MS 39940–2 *passim*; Webster, *Stephen Marshall and Finchingfield*, pp. 3–5; see also B. Spinks, 'Brief and Perspicuous Text; Plain and Persistent Doctrine: Behind "Of the Preaching of the Word" in the Westminster Assembly', in M. R. Dudley (ed.), *Like a Two-Edged Sword: the Word of God in Liturgy and History* (Norwich, 1995) pp. 91–111.

[78] Webster, 'Godly of Goshen', pp. 113–19.

[79] Kendall, *Calvin*, pp. 110–17, 125–38; P. Miller, ' "Preparation for Salvation" in Seventeenth Century New England', in *Nature's Nation* (Cambridge, Mass., 1967); A. Habegger, 'Preparing the Soul for Christ: the Contrasting Sermon Forms of John Cotton and Thomas Hooker', *AL* 41 (1969) p. 346. Cohen, *God's Caress*, p. 84n takes issue with their account of Cotton's belief, but without denying that they differed.

[80] Philip Nye and Thomas Goodwin, 'To the Reader', in Hooker, *Application of Redemption*, n.p.

[81] SU Hartlib MS 29/2/56a.

Even within Hooker's circle, there was some dissent. Nathaniel Ward, for instance, shared some of Goodwin's misgivings. According to Giles Firmin, Ward, his father-in-law, 'use[d] to tell Mr Hooker that he made as good Christians before they come to Christ as ever they were after by his preaching'.[82] Of these disagreements, we should note two points. For our present purposes, such questions are differences of emphasis within an agreed framework. All godly ministers accepted that redemption was a process rather than an event. The exact duration and order of each phase and the signs of its presence in the saint were legitimate grounds for debate, but the basic structure was common ground, and the possibility of the saint's discerning of the movement of the spirit within him or herself was commonly accepted. Equally, it was generally felt that it was exceedingly difficult to make more than a judgement of charity regarding the presence of saving grace in others. It is worth concluding this account with a reservation: it has proved impossible to trace a direct link between piety and ecclesiology. All those who were to emerge as Congregationalists were devoted to some sort of experimental Calvinism, but this does not mean that all experimental Calvinists were closet Congregationalists. The same can be said of Presbyterians, primitive episcopalians, and those who were untroubled by the place taken by bishops in the early Stuart Church of England.

III

Preaching, of course, was not the only part of divine service. Arthur Hildersham divided the ordinary means for seeking assurance into two fields. We will come to the second category, the 'inward and spirituall' means below; but he also addressed the 'outward and bodily' means. Here he placed reading and hearing the Word in first place: 'this is said to be the maine end, for which God ordained the preaching and ministery of his Word'. He went on, however, to devote equal parts of his lecture to the benefits of the Lord's Supper and prayer.[83] The 'conscionable use of the Lords Supper' was the 'second ordinance of God that hath great force to work and preserve in us assurance of Gods favour in Christ, and to recover it when it is lost'.[84] Before we move on to the 'inward and spirituall'

---

[82] The earliest version of this anecdote is in a letter to Richard Baxter from Firmin dated July 1654, DWL Baxter MS 59.4.284, in which Firmin canvasses Baxter's opinion of Shepard's *Sound Beleever*, and especially for 'yor judgement of his Preparations: & of his Humiliation that wee might be quick though wee thinke God will nevere give us his love p. 154 so 147. 148 a hard chapter.' Firmin, of course, went on to question the soteriology of Hooker and his circle, taking issue especially with Shepard, Hooker, John and Daniel Rogers, in *The Real Christian* (1670). He repeats the anecdote above at p. 19 of this work.

[83] Hildersham, *CLII Lectures*, pp. 632–8, quoted p. 632.   [84] Ibid., p. 635.

means, we must turn our attention to the Eucharist. It may seem a little surprising to move from the sermon, generally accepted as the *sine qua non* of godly ministry, to the Lord's Supper, a rather neglected topic in studies of godly piety and one seen as peripheral.[85] To some extent, this assessment goes against clerical appraisal. According to John Brinsley, the sacraments 'in their right use are amongst the principall of those meanes ordained by the Lord, to keepe us from backsliding: and so for the preservation & increase of grace' and 'a gracious and a speciall meanes for the increase of our assurance'.[86] William Perkins was prepared to make it clear that 'a Sacrament is not absolutely necessary [to salvation], but only as it is a proppe and stay for faith to leane upon', but on the other hand he concluded that 'the preaching of the word, and administration of the Sacrament, are all one in substance, For in the one the will of God is seene, in the other heard'.[87] The assessment of John Rogers was subject to fewer qualifications. For him, 'The Word and Sacraments be the two breasts of the Church'. To move from a weak to a strong faith, he exhorted his congregation 'with all diligence and care to attend upon the means, publike and private, as hearing the Word, prayer, receiving the Sacrament, reading, meditation, and holy conferences'. Hildersham saw the sacrament as 'a Feast wherein every Christian soule may receive more sound joy, and comfort then by any meanes that God hath given us under heaven besides'. With 'conscionable use', the Eucharist was a rival to preaching: 'there is not more virtue in any ordinance of God to confirm us in the comfortable assurance of God than this, if it be worthily received'.[88] John Preston regarded the sacrament as 'among the maine helpes' of grace.[89]

Accepting that the godly ministers held the Lord's Supper in high esteem, what were the benefits available, and how were they to be gained? The

---

[85] A spendid trans-Atlantic account is provided by E. Brooks Holifield, *The Covenant Sealed: The Development of Puritan Sacramental Theology in Old and New England, 1570–1720* (London, 1974) esp. pp. 33–41, 51–61, 109–38; K. Stevenson, *Covenant of Grace Renewed: A Vision of the Eucharist in the Seventeenth Century* (Norwich, 1994) provides a useful survey, but the only godly minister to receive detailed attention is Richard Baxter. For an illuminating comparison see B. D. Spinks, 'Two Seventeenth-Century Examples of *Lex Credendi, Lex Orandi*: the baptismal and eucharistic theologies of Jeremy Taylor and Richard Baxter', *SL* 21 (1991) pp. 165–89. A helpful overview is provided by S. Mayor, *The Lord's Supper in Early English Dissent* (London, 1972). I have also benefited from the stimulating assessment in J. Houston, 'Transubstantiation and the Sign: Cranmer's Drama of the Lord's Supper', *JMRS* 24 (1994) pp. 113–30.

[86] John Brinsley, *The True Watch and Rule of Life* (1637) p. 185.

[87] William Perkins, *Workes* vol. I (1626 edn) p. 72; vol. II (1617 edn) p. 73; cf. John Preston, *Breast-Plate of Faith and Love* (1634) p. 73.

[88] John Rogers, *Doctrine of Faith*, pp. 215, 238; Hildersham, *CLII Lectures*, pp. 265, 407.

[89] Preston, *Breast-Plate*, p. 58; cf. Thomas Brooks, *Heaven on Earth: a Treatise on Christian Assurance* (Edinburgh, 1982, first pub. 1654) p. 306; John Dod and Robert Cleaver, *Ten Sermons Tending Chiefely to the Fitting of Men for the Worthy Receiving of the Lords Supper* (1632) p. 95.

Eucharist was a presentation of Christ's sacrifice on the cross, a confirmation of the covenant of grace, the consequence of that sacrifice, a vehicle of grace and an aid to memory. As John Beadle put it, 'not only a representing, a sealing, and a conveying signe, but a commemorative signe'.[90] Godly ministers, of course, subscribed to the Protestant rejection of transubstantiation, but this did not deny the presence of Christ. Perkins made this clear:

We hold and beleeve a presence of Christs body & blood in the Sacrament of the Lords Supper: and that no fained, but a true and reall presence which must be considered two waies, first, in respect of the signes, secondly in respect of the communicants.[91]

One of the advantages of the form of the supper was the familiarity of the materials. The bread and wine were 'but ordinary and base creatures', which made them 'excellent meanes, to seal up remission of sins, and confirm the whole Covenant of life everlasting'.[92] Communion 'afresh exhibits and gives him to us . . . yea and not darkely, but in a very familiar manner, under ordinary signes subject to all our senses'.[93] The human experience of bread- and wine-making provided a metaphor for Christ's suffering:

Seeing there is such a nature in the creature that the outward things have suffered many injuries before they became good food, as the corne being cutte down in its perfite age, pressed out of his husks with the flaile, losing all his intralles with the violence of the Mill, and after passing through the parching hands of the Oven is made good bread; so the flesh of Jesus Christ went under many paines, and the blood of Christ as the grape in its most flourishing estate was pressed out of the veines, and sustained hard passions, and shall nothing of us suffer with him?[94]

If recipients followed the advice of Robert Bolton, they would gain great spiritual benefit by meditating on the metaphors available in each of the minister's actions, all of which represent 'the spirituall, eternall, and invisible actions of God the Father, for the God of our Soule'. In taking hold of the bread and wine, the minister 'doth signifie and represent Gods sealing and setting apart of Christ for the great work of Mediation between God and Man'.[95] John Brinsley similarly set out appropriate matters of meditation for his readers from the preparation of the elements, through

---

[90] John Beadle, *Diary or Journal of a Thankful Christian*, p. 6; cf. Perkins, vol. I pp. 71–2.

[91] Ibid., vol. I pp. 589–90.

[92] Thomas Taylor, *A Precedent for Preachers* in *Works*, p. 454.

[93] Rogers, *Doctrine of Faith*, p. 214.

[94] Richard Greenham, *Works* (1601) p. 430; cf. Richard Sibbes, *The Complete Works* (ed. A. B. Grosart) (London, 1862–3) vol. IV p. 66.

[95] Robert Bolton, *Three Treatises* (1634) pp. 40–2, quoted p. 40; cf. Lewis Bayly, *The Practice of Piety* (1610) pp. 349–51; Thomas Hooker, *The Paterne of Perfection* (1640) pp. 375–6.

the breaking of the bread and pouring of the wine to the reception and the aftermath, laying out a spiritual journey that would maximise the benefits.[96]

The primary benefit for a communicating member of the godly was assurance, a renewed conviction that one was among the elect.[97] 'The nature of a seal is to make things sure and firm among men; so the supper of the Lord is Christ's broad seal, it is Christ's privy-seal, whereby he seals and assures his people that they are happy here, that they shall be more happy hereafter, that they are everlastingly beloved of God, that his heart is set upon them, that their names are written in the book of life.'[98] To get the full benefits it was necessary to undertake some preparation for the sacrament.[99] Richard Vines repeated Perkins' assurance that fasting was not necessary before the supper, but otherwise the preparation process was rigorous.[100] The properly prepared recipient was to bring knowledge, faith, repentance for sins and 'Charitie towards men'. Later writers made greater demands for self-examination: 'As a souldier is accoutred and furnisht with such weapons, as in fight are to be exercised and used, and therefore a Christian that would try or know his own fitnesse or worthinesse, considers first what graces are to be set on work in the act of receiving, and then examines whether he have them before-hand, or no.'[101] A period of self-examination was to be undertaken to discover whether 'wee have attained unto a compettent measure of Repentance, Knowledge, Faith and Love: which if we can finde in our selves, we may resolve our hearts in that Point of generall Examination, and conclude, that wee are within the Covenant of Grace, and have Communion with Christ Jesus, and therefore are in state to be Communicants at his Table'.[102] If communicants found this difficult, they could first turn to God, and then 'use the aid of the faithfull, which may by their faith carrie thee, as men did the sicke of the palsie upon their shoulders, and laide him before Christ'.[103] Daniel Rogers made the link between humility and the support of the godly explicit: 'Gods people

[96] Brinsley, *True Watch*, pp. 194–201.
[97] Richard Rogers, *Seven Treatises*, pp. 233–7; Arthur Hildersham, *The Doctrine of Communicating Worthily in the Lords Supper* (1619) p. 23; John Preston, *A Preparation to the Lords Supper* (1638) p. 121.
[98] Thomas Brooks, *Heaven upon Earth*, p. 27.
[99] See J. E. Booty, 'Preparation for the Lord's Supper in Elizabethan England', *ATR* 49 (1962) pp. 131–48. Booty provides some interesting material to compare and contrast with godly prescriptions, but does not address the similarities or differences between the godly and the mainstream.
[100] Richard Vines, *A Treatise of the Institution, Right Administration, and Receiving of the Sacrament of the Lords Supper* (1657) p. 28; Perkins, vol. I p. 596; vol. II p. 82.
[101] Ibid., vol. II pp. 81–2; Vines, pp. 278–9; cf. Jeremiah Dyke, *A Worthy Communicant: or, a Treatise Shewing the Due Order of receiving the Sacrament of the Lords Supper* (1642) esp. pp. 33–8; Brinsley, *The True Watch*, pp. 183–5, 188–94; Holifield, pp. 56–7.
[102] Dod and Cleaver, *Ten Sermons*, p. 2.   [103] Perkins, *Works*, vol. I p. 76.

so oft as they draw neere to him in duties, dare not rush upon him, but first humble themselves in dust and ashes, as most base wormes and corruption. Then they pray for assistance in the ordinance, meditate and conferre about the right doing, and the fruit of it.'[104] As Richard Sibbes put it: 'It is one branch of the Communion of Saints, to regard the judgement of others.'[105] The product of preparation should be humility. 'If thou thought thyselfe fit [for communion], thou shouldest not have it; even therefore because thou feelest thyselfe unfit, the rather thou shalt be received to mercy'; 'The sense of unworthinesse is our worthinesse; A little vessel that is empty, will receive more than a great one that is full; A broken Christ requires a broken heart'.[106] It may have been a result of the rising demands for preparation that some came to be convinced that communion could be a source of conversion. In his attempt to persuade the troubled Joan Drake to communicate, John Dod was reported to have said that 'the Sacrament was not a comforting, strengthening, building up Ordinance onely, but also a converting and healing power being therein for help of the sick and diseased, a reviving quickning Ordinance also; so as all ought to participate in the same'.[107] In the 1630s, the godly who shared in 'the holy duty of religious conference' convinced their minister, Robert Bolton, that the sacrament was a converting ordinance and in the 1640s this became a bone of contention, especially between William Prynne and the Scottish Commissioners.[108] John Beadle and Richard Vines complained that the subject had changed from a unifying to a divisive issue, 'an apple of strife'; 'when any listen to seducing spirits, and separate from this ordinance, they grow sowre and sullen to their dearest friends'.[109]

It was vital to become a worthy receiver: God could punish unworthy receipt by letting the plague run through a society. He had 'shewed himselfe so severe to his owne people, for their unreverent comming to this Sacrament'.[110] 'For certainly the blessed Sacrament will be your bane, if you come to it in malice. Nay, I dare confidently affirme, it were a matter of lesse danger to you, to eat a morsell of Rats-bane, then to eat the holy Bread; to drinke a cup of poyson, then to drinke of that Blessed Cuppe, if you come to it in malice.' Communicants must be thorough in their preparation, for 'if you be unworthy receivers, you cannot doe your selves

[104] Daniel Rogers, *A Treatise of the Two Sacraments of the Gospell* (1635) p. 267.
[105] Richard Sibbes, *The Art of Selfe-Judging* in *The Saints Cordiall* (1658) p. 92.
[106] John Preston, *The Cuppe of Blessing* (1633) p. 22; Vines, pp. 280–1; cf. Sibbes, *The Art of Selfe-Judging*, p. 79.
[107] Jasper Heartwell, *Trodden Down Strength* (1647) p. 87.
[108] John Humfrey, *A Second Vindication of a Disciplinary, Anti-Erastian, Orthodox Free-Admission to the Lords Supper* (1656) Epistle to the Reader; Holifield, pp. 109–38.
[109] Beadle, *Diary or Journal*, p. 31 (quoted); Vines, pp. 102, 247.
[110] Brinsley, *The True Watch*, p. 190.

a worse turne, than to offer to come to the Sacrament without faith, to provoke *God* more, *to eate and drinke your own damnation*'.[111]

If the process of preparation and receiving the benefits of the Lord's Supper seems a solitary activity, we are neglecting some aspects made central in the godly vision. We have already noted the help offered to struggling communicants by godly society, but further identification with the godly was a possible result of the sacrament. After Perkins noted that the ends of the sacrament were to renew assurance, to mark the true church and to preserve the doctrine of the gospel, he went on to claim that the Lord's Supper could 'binde the faithfull' in their loyalty and gratitude to God, and that it 'is the bond of mutuall amity betwixt the faithfull'. The Communion of Saints, joining the earthly godly with their fellows in heaven, appeared in the accounts of sacramental rewards printed by Robert Bolton, William Gouge and on to Richard Baxter.[112] A principal gain of the godly perspective on communion was exactly that, the *koinōnia*, the spread of unity and the bond of love among the communicants, the universal communion of Christians with Christ, and with one another in Christ. If the recipients were to follow John Brinsley's pattern, they would be 'Beholding them who communicate with us, to stir up our hearts to beare a loving affection, as to them, so to all Gods people, being partakers with us of Jesus Christ, and admitted with us into the same high dignity.'[113] In his preparation for the sacrament, Charles Chauncy followed the note of his desire for union with Christ by a rigorous test of the adequacy of his 'Brotherly Love'.[114] For Thomas Goodwin, the first purpose of the sacrament was a greater union with God, the second was to be 'a communion, the highest outward pledge, ratification and testimony of love and amity among his members themselves, . . . a love-feast, in that they eat and drink together at one and the same table'.[115] Edward Reynolds said that the Lord's Supper was 'the sinew of the Church, whereby the faithfull, being all animated by the same Spirit that makes them one with Christ, are knit together in a bond of Peace, conspiring all in a unity of thoughts and desires . . . so that the most immediate effect of this Sacrament is to confirme the Union of all the members of the Church each to other in a Communion of Saints, whereby their prayers are the more strengthened, and their adversaries the more resisted'.[116] In short, as Dod and Cleaver put it:

---

[111] Hildersham, *CLII Lectures*, p. 112; cf. p. 266; John Preston, *Breast-Plate*, 2nd numb. p. 90; 1st numb. 207; cf. ibid., 73–4; Perkins, *Works*, vol. I p. 76.

[112] Perkins, *Works*, vol. I p. 72; Robert Bolton, *Directions for a Comfortable Walking with God* (1630) p. 36; William Gouge, *Works* (1627) vol. I p. 242; Richard Baxter, *Works* (London, 1830) vol. XXIII p. 302.

[113] Brinsley, *The True Watch*, p. 197.   [114] Mather, III p. 138.

[115] Thomas Goodwin, *Works* (Edinburgh, 1861–5) vol. II p. 292.

[116] Edward Reynolds, *Meditations on the Holy Sacrament of the Lords Supper Written many yeares since* (1638) pp. 102–3.

'The Lord's Supper is ordained as a Seale of the mutuall fellowship and communion of Gods people, as with their Head Christ, so with one another.'[117]

It is, of course, insufficient to end this assessment with the prescriptive material; therefore, it is necessary to turn to the place of the sacrament in the piety of individual ministers. At one extreme, communion appears rarely in Samuel Ward's diary: it is mentioned twice, on the first occasion to note his negligence in preparation, both regarding his own worthiness and his failure to encourage the preparation of a fellow student; on the second simply to note his 'lasines in not rising early inough to prepare my self to the worthy receit of the communion'.[118] This stands in stark contrast to the records of Samuel Rogers and Thomas Shepard. Both prepared at some length, making great efforts to embrace the helpful humiliation. Rogers began two days before the delivery of the Lord's Supper.

This is the preparat: oh my sin; this body of death lyes heavye, ease me (deare god) in the sacrament; I am tyed by sin, unloose me, I am pressed downe by it, lift thou up mine head, then shall I praise thee with cheere;

Having worked so hard, the day after he received the sacrament, 'a feast of fat things', Rogers could feel the benefits:

I find some fruite by the sacrament this day; the lord hath banished evell in some measure; melted my hearte, made it stoope to him, fetched down deadness over which he hath given me a victory; He hath calmed my impetuous sp[irit]: these are fruites of a sacrament, and no wonder that it is better with me than befoore.[119]

On one occasion he ignored the warning of Perkins concerning fasting in preparation and conducted a private fast as part of his preparation, finding the Lord 'very gracious; he makes my heart bleed for the times and inlarges mee yet to mourne and wrestle'. The result was a very successful communion. He marked his journal with an asterisk, his usual practice to make his best days stand out for re-reading, concluding that: 'This is a day of gladnes and ioy.'[120] He received comparatively little when he had prepared too little, falling back on God's promises, which, as John Preston had explained, almost restricted his ability to withdraw mercy.[121] On a more successful day, he found an enhanced union with God, one of the available

---

[117] Dod and Cleaver, *Ten Sermons*, p. 13.

[118] M. M. Knappen (ed.), *Two Elizabethan Puritan Diaries*, pp. 106–7, 116.

[119] QUB Percy MS 7 f. 24.

[120] Ibid., ff. 341–2. Fasting was recommended for preparation by Joseph Bentham, and practised by the godly woman Mary Gunter; Jonathan Burr, preacher at Rickinghall in Suffolk, and his wife held a day of private fasting before each Communion day: Clarke (1683) p. 138; Mather III, p. 79. See Booty, 'Preparation for the Lord's Supper', p. 143.

[121] QUB Percy MS 7 ff. 29–30; John Preston, *The Cuppe of Blessing* in *The Saints Qualification* (1634) pp. 548, 551.

gains listed by Perkins, and regarded himself 'Refreshed by the publique means'.[122]

Thomas Shepard recorded his preparation at rather greater length, noting his sins of neglect and the elements he lacked. He found that he neglected his private duties 'toward myself, to my wife, child, family, church, companions abroad, not instructing, exhorting, quickening, being an example to them'. The causes were ignorance, 'unsavoriness', pride, lukewarmness, 'idleness and sluggishness' and 'apprehension of unfruitfulness', a set close to those outlined by Perkins.[123] In each period of preparation he found humiliation, in wants of wisdom, in the sense that his sins were 'depriving me of mutual communion with God'. 'On the sacrament morning I felt my nakedness and felt in some measure the evil of my sin which made me resolve against all sin.'[124] Shepard's experience of the sacrament was much more Christological than that of Rogers; he sought to gain comfort from Christ's presence. In one communion he was appalled at his inability to 'see Christ in these plain, familiar things, wherein he humbles himself to be seen of us'.[125] He gained spiritual comfort from the sacrament as a seal of the covenant of grace, as Rogers did, but took this further: 'I saw also that the elements were not only seals to assure me that Christ's word should be made good to me believing, but also that Christ by sacramental union was given to me.'[126] On one sacrament day, 'I saw I did come to Christ, thirst after Christ, and take Christ and prefer him above all things . . . This did much affect my heart for a while, and it was sweet to think that the Lord should die for me and pardon me.'[127] Rogers never matched Shepard in the union with Christ, but he found his greatest help in a renewed sense of godly society:

Saboth; and sacrament at Coleman: broken to pieces with ioy; drunk with comfort; this is a day of reioicing, and strength; for the ioy of the l[or]d, hath bin my strength; A sweet communion of Saints, at mr Rouls his house at dinner; one of a sweet, godly spirit; and now I lye downe with praises.[128]

As the administrator of the Lord's Supper, there were additional responsibilities for the godly minister. Given that one of the benefits of the Eucharist was a renewed sense of the Communion of the Saints, and given the consequences of admitting unworthy communicants, it was necessary

---

[122] QUB Percy MS 7 f. 325; Perkins, *Works*, vol. I p. 72.
[123] McGiffert (ed.), *God's Plot*, p. 123.
[124] McGiffert (ed.), *God's Plot*, pp. 180–2, 186–7 (quote from p. 186).
[125] Ibid., pp. 151–2. He was following the emphasis of Samuel's father, Daniel Rogers in this: Daniel Rogers, *A Treatise of the Two Sacraments*, 'To the Reader'.
[126] McGiffert (ed.), *God's Plot*, p. 112; QUB Percy MS 7 ff. 175, 347; cf. McGiffert (ed.), *God's Plot*, pp. 180, 195–6, 216–17 and esp. 224.
[127] Ibid., pp. 195–6.   [128] QUB Percy MS 7 f. 335.

to eliminate such members of one's congregation from the communion. John Rogers, as we have seen, mentioned this as part of the pastoral responsibility: the minister should be well acquainted with his parishioners in order the better to judge their admissibility to the supper.[129] This could lead, of course, to social eructations within the community and an appearance by the minister before the ecclesiastical court. In Essex this does not seem to have been the case, perhaps because of the dominant position held by the godly in the higher reaches of the parishes, but some instances do appear in Northamptonshire. In the mid-1620s, Robert Bincks, the minister of Braunston was cited for having examined a couple of his parishioners prior to Easter communion as they were suspected of criminal practices.[130] John Barry and Anthony Stackhouse became involved in similar disputes, the former on the grounds of a parishioner's inadequate understanding of the ritual, the latter for a reported appetite for incontinence. Barry's views were so strongly held that he was forced to cancel one Eucharist altogether.[131] The vicar of Stamford, in Lincolnshire, John Vicars, was brought before the High Commission, among other things, for administering a monthly communion, 'and before it to exercise on Friday and Satturday, which he call preparacions', excluding those who failed to attend from the Lord's Supper.[132] As the Lord's Supper was part of the institutional ritual of the Church of England, we may have been encouraged to regard the calls for godly social unity as a foolish ideal. However, the commitment of godly ministers to this ideal seems to have created a potentially divisive exercise within the parochial duties of the godly ministry.

Given the time spent on preparation, the possibilities of greater union with Father, Son and Holy Spirit, renewed assurance and an enhanced sense of the Communion of Saints, it comes as no surprise to find that practice of the Lord's Supper was important to godly ministers. With hindsight, it makes more comprehensible the attention they paid to the place of the communion table. The table placed centrally, physically making clear the communion in the social sense, was much more a re-enactment of godly society than the eastern site of an altar, isolating the individual communicant and 'limiting' the communion to one with Christ. While the dangers of similarity to Roman Catholic forms in the eyes of the godly should not be understated, the changes of the 1630s inhibited the benefits the godly sought in the Lord's Supper. The availability of the benefits of communion was fragile and could be lost through the inadequacy of the individual

129 Rogers, *Exposition*, p. 625.   130 NRO CB 56a f. 340.
131 NRO CB A43 ff. 30–31; A30 f. 8; 52 f. 36.
132 S. R. Gardiner (ed.), *Reports of Cases in the Courts of Star Chamber and High Commission*, Camden Soc. n.s., 39 (1886) p. 204.

saint. In Laudian reforms, they came under additional threats, external ones which should be resisted in the interests of godly piety.

The subject of the godly ministry seems clear. In stated priorities, in the bulk of surviving material and in the contemporary view, the sermon was the means God had chosen to perform his regenerative work. The godly ministers were to propound the nature of this work in sermons and to provide examples of godly practice in their own lives. In both these roles, the requisite self-examination and education, in theory and practice, placed a considerable stress upon the spirituality of the godly minister, in itself helping to explain the enhanced appetite for godly clerical sociability, an appetite that could only be expanded by the need to acquire the substantial pastoral skills required to offer comfort and guidance to their congregations.

6

Religiosity and sociability

I

At this point we can turn away from some of the more public aspects of godly spirituality and examine some of the 'inward and spirituall' pieties that interested Arthur Hildersham.[1] From this, as will become clear, it is useful to return to questions of godly sociability. The conviction that saints could find evidence of their election in this life is a critical point in any attempt to explain the individual spiritual practices of the godly. Devotional exercises have to be understood in the context of experimental Calvinism. Experimental Calvinists gave more than a theoretical assent to the dogmas of the *ordo salutis*, they made the search for the marks of election central to a practical divinity.[2] Stephen Marshall identified two forms of the knowledge of spiritual life: the first was theoretical, the second, 'experimental, and practical, and real and convincing. Now the notional knowledge . . . by the Common light that accompanies the Ministry of the Word, may break in upon some men: but for the experimental, real inward knowledg of it, they will be strangers to it.'[3]

From the 1580s, a steady stream of devotional manuals was produced as a consequence of this outlook, with a great deal of advice contained tending to encourage self-examination. Perhaps the most famous of these works was the *Seven Treatises* of Richard Rogers. The fourth treatise, of 150 pages, is the 'treatise of the daily direction', setting down in great detail the most spiritually effective way for the aspiring saint to lead his or her life.[4] Richard's nephew, John Rogers, adopted his uncle's term when he described his own version of the daily direction, which he held to be a vital part of the godly person's life:

1 Arthur Hildersham, *CLII Lectures on Psalm LI* (1635) p. 638; see above, p. 112.
2 R. T. Kendall, *Calvin and English Calvinism to 1649* (Oxford, 1979) esp. pp. 1–13.
3 Stephen Marshall, *Works* (1661) 2nd pag. p. 8.
4 Richard Rogers, *Seaven Treatises* (1603). I have used the expanded edition of 1627.

He that makes Conscience of his Ways, and to please God his only Way, is to take him to a Daily Direction, and some set rules, thereby looking constantly to his heart all the Day . . . if a man tie not himself thus to Rules, his heart will break from him, and be disguised one way or another . . . and so he shall never live anytime together in peace.[5]

The discipline began with rising, 'To begin the Day with Meditation, Thanksgiving, Confession and Prayer: to put on my Armour', and continued with constant introspection and examination of one's conduct in all relationships, with family, parishioners and fellow-ministers: 'To Watch and Pray oft and earnestly in the day, for holding fast this Course: to hearten on my self hereto by my own experience'.[6] The meditations and dealings of the day were to be drawn together in the evening, 'shutting up the Day in Examination, and viewing it over', 'to peruse and examine the several parts of my Life every evening, how this Course hath been kept of me, where it hath to keep it still, where it hath not, to seek pardon and recovery'.[7] Similarly, Thomas Shepard exhorted his readers to 'renew morning and evening by sad and solemn meditation, the sense of Gods love to you in Christ, and in every duty he sets you about, and love will love and like the yoke, and make the commandments that they shall not be grievous to you'.[8] Arthur Hildersham saw this practice as an important means of fostering repentance:

He that would be able to confesse his sins unto God aright, must use to take a dayly account of himselfe, and of his wayes. This examination of our selves, wee find oft prescribed in the word, as a speciall meanes, and help to bring us unto true repentance, *Lamentio.* 3.40. *Let us search, and try our wayes, and turn againe unto the Lord Psal* 4.4. *Tremble, and sinne not, examine your owne heart upon your bed.* And on the other side, the neglect of it, is mentioned as a chiefe cause, and signe of impenitency. *Ieremy* 8.6. *No man repented him of his wickednesse, saying, what have I done?*

A further fruit of such self-examination, he made clear in a later lecture, was 'profitable and necessary for a man that would get or preserve or recover the assurance of Gods favour, to observe diligently his owne wayes'.[9] Thomas Brooks argued that by 'a serious examination of a man's own estate, he may know whether he hath faith or not, whether he be Christ's spouse or the devil's strumpet, whether there be a work of grace

[5] The fragment, entitled 'Sixty Memorials for a Godly Life', is appended to Cotton Mather's brief biography of Nathaniel Rogers, John's son: Mather, III pp. 109–13. Numbers refer to Rogers' own ordering. This section is no. 48.
[6] Ibid., nos. 2, 3, cf. 7, 10.   [7] Ibid., nos. 47, 2.
[8] Thomas Shepard, *Certain Select Cases Resolved* in *Works* (Boston, Mass., 1853) vol. I p. 325.
[9] Arthur Hildersham, *CLII Lectures*, pp. 197, 641.

upon his heart or not'.[10] Self-examination, combined with a 'care to keepe a good conscience'. 'a consideration of the experiments wee have had of Gods favour', and a 'renouncing of our selves' were the four principal means to gain assurance.[11]

We should not take this interest in the 'self' and the renunciation of the self solely as a metaphor. What we are dealing with here is the maintenance, indeed the construction of a self. It is too easily assumed that ideas of the self are given, almost ahistorical. Here it is only necessary to direct attention to the work of anthropologists, who have shown that self is a cultural construct, capable of change and in need of maintenance.[12] In addition, the question is still more clear cut in this context as it becomes clear that the godly demanded a thoroughgoing destruction of conventional selfhood in the cause of creating the 'new man' of Colossians 3.10.

Herein lies the key to understanding the daily discipline described above. In the course of the conversion experience, widely regarded as a vital part of the life of a member of the elect, the saint was systematically to remove all vestiges of carnal identity, seen as stumbling blocks on the path to sanctification. The tensions and ambiguities, as well as the necessity of this project, are apparent in a sermon by Stephen Marshall, delivered in 1649.[13] His text was Matthew 16.24, focusing on the passage 'let him deny himself, take up his cross and follow me'. Marshall identified two selves, one to be denied, one to be taken to Christ. Moreover, he distinguished four branches of this divided self. Firstly, there is the sinful self: although all selves are corrupt, this self is materially corrupt, it is 'the body of lusts and corruption which every man in the world have in him from his Mother's Wombe'. Secondly, there is the natural self, the wisdom, understanding, and will, with 'all natural endowments and accomplishments'. Thirdly, there is the worldly self, that constructed through social and economic relationships; and, lastly, there is the religious self, that which performs holy duties and has virtues.[14] It is not that this last must be made predominant within the divided self: all are equally wicked and self-denial must be total – 'all the

---

[10] Thomas Brooks, *Heaven on Earth: a Treatise on Christian Assurance* (Edinburgh, 1982, first published 1654) p. 26.

[11] Hildersham, *CLII Lectures*, p. 638.

[12] See, for instance, C. Geertz, '"From the Native's Point of View": On the Nature of Anthropological Understanding', in *Local Knowledge* (London, 1993) pp. 55–70; M. Rosaldo, 'Towards an Anthropology of Self and Feeling', in R. Shweder and R. Levine (eds.), *Culture Theory: Essays on Mind, Self and Emotion* (Cambridge, 1984) pp. 137–57. A thoughtful account of issues of self and identity can be found in M. Freeman, *Rewriting the Self: History, Memory, Narrative* (London, 1993).

[13] Stephen Marshall, *Works*, Sermon 4. Compare Jeremiah Burroughes, *The Rare Jewel of Christian Contentment* (1648) esp. ch. 5, sect. I and Isaac Ambrose, *Prima, Media and Ultima* (1674 edn.) pp. 119–54.

[14] Marshall, *Works*, pp. 92–5.

comprehension of this must be abominated and renounced'. The aim is a life wholly centred on Christ, bereft of self-interest. 'There is an absolute impossibility . . . that ever the soul should cordially close with Christ until it do totally renounce itself.'[15] As Sarah Wright summarised the task, the Christian's true happiness 'lies in being emptied of all self, self refined as well as gross self; and being filled with a full God'.[16] For Hildersham, the renunciation of the self would lead to the self of the saint 'resting onely upon the free grace of God in Christ'.[17] In a sermon on the same text as Marshall's, Thomas Taylor demanded that 'all selfe-respects, selfe-seeking, selfe-aymes must be renounced and the Christian wholly vanish into nothing'.[18] Self-denial, or, as Marshall put it, 'continual self-abhorrency',[19] was intended to create a vacuum that might be inhabited by divine plenitude. However, Marshall recognized that the state of selflessness, even with the aid of the Holy Spirit, is an unattainable goal: even a preoccupation with righteousness is a way of life with Self as the end, 'whosoever [*sic*] I make use of, it is my self that I set in the throne'. The solution is a degree of denying self-reflexivity: 'study to know what thy sins are, and who thou art, that art a sinner'.[20] The disciplines of self-denial and self-examination are designed to turn the necessary condition of selfishness to the creation of a self-abnegating selfhood.[21]

The diary was a prime instrument in this self-examination, providing an external, material site for a sufficiently distanced perspective to aid self-assessment. This is related to the value placed by the godly in memory: given the doctrine of perseverance, that once one knows oneself to be a member of the elect, even in the darkest times, one remains so. 'Every experiment of Gods former goodnesse is a strong prop for our faith for the future.'[22] As I have argued elsewhere, one of the consequences of the part played by the diary in clerical spirituality was a repetitive, cyclical form of piety, constantly rehearsing the *ordo salutis* and attempting to take a middle path between despair and 'security', too great a sense that one is saved.[23] One of the principal ways to maintain this critical position was the exercise of humiliation. According to John Preston, 'the more empty the soule is, the more a man is humbled, the more he sees into himselfe (as faith

---

[15] Ibid., pp. 97, 116; cf. Richard Sibbes, *Christs Exhaltation Purchast by Humiliation* (1639) p. 94.

[16] Sarah Wright, *A Wonderful and Profitable Letter Written by Mrs Sarah Wright* (1656) p. 5.

[17] Hildersham, *CLII Lectures*, p. 638.

[18] Thomas Taylor, *The Principles of Christian Practice* in *Works* (1653) p. 5.

[19] Marshall, *Works*, p. 30.   [20] Ibid., pp. 96, 122–3.

[21] For further examples and a good account of the tensions involved, see S. Bercovitch, *The Puritan Origins of the American Self* (London, 1975) ch. 1, esp. pp. 15–24.

[22] John Beadle, *The Journal or Diary of a Thankful Christian* (1656) p. 181.

[23] T. Webster, 'Writing to Redundancy: Approaches to Spiritual Journals and Early Modern Spirituality', *HJ* 39 (1996) pp. 33–56.

comes with an empty hand) the faster hold is laid on CHRIST'. 'And take this withall, Humiliation doth not weaken assurance, but workes the contrary: Indeed the less sincerity, and the lesse mourning for sin, and the less Humiliation, the less assurance . . . Therefore a man should make a daily practise of Humiliation, for it is to a mans great advantage, it is a thing too much omitted, we should take time for it.'[24]

In this context, it is worthwhile returning to the ambivalent gender positions in godly clerical images touched upon earlier.[25] This comes through most clearly when we are reminded that ministers themselves can be the bride of Christ. Peter Bulkeley explained that it 'is a marriage-covenant that we make up with God, therefore we must doe as the Spouse doth, resigne up our selves to be ruled and governed according to his will'. The relationship between a Christian and God could be summed up 'as it is betweene man and wife, though shee be foolish, passionate, and wilfull; yet these doe not breake the Covenant of marriage, so long as she remained faithfull'. For Thomas Shepard, the role of a subordinate wife was a source of comfort. 'Weaknesses do not debar us from mercy, nay, they incline God the more. The husband is bound to bear with the wife, as being the weaker vessel; and shall we think God will exempt himself from his own rule, and not bear with his weak spouse?'[26] What emerge here are the advantages possessed by women in the eyes of godly clergymen. Humility and subordination were spiritually valuable and, if a woman was trained correctly, these were things that came naturally. As Daniel Rogers put it:

Nature hath put a fircenesse into the female . . . therefore the she-Beare and the Lyonesse are the most raging and cruell. But grace make that naturall impotency of the woman, turne impotency for God . . . their nature (being fearfull) hath ever been prone to superstition . . . Men's spirits are hardier, doe not so easily feare Majesty, tremble at judgements, beleeve promises, shun sinne, love God, as women: so that when they are in the way, none are better.[27]

Thus, according to the godly clergy, the weaknesses and dangers of femininity could be turned into sources of valuable obedience and a useful sense of inadequacy. At its worst, this led to gender reversal in times of a

[24] John Preston, *The Saints Qualification* (1637) pp. 28–9.
[25] See above, pp. 101–5.
[26] Peter Bulkeley, *The Gospel-Covenant: Or the Covenant of Grace Opened* (1651) p. 103; Shepard, *The Sincere Convert* in *Works*, vol. I p. 50; cf. William Bridge, *The Sermons* (1656) p. 93. At a late stage in this section, I benefited from reading a draft of S. Hardman Moore, 'Sexing the Soul: Gender and the Rhetoric of Puritan Piety', forthcoming in *SCH*. I am grateful to Susan for providing the draft and for discussions of the bride of Christ metaphor.
[27] Daniel Rogers, *Matrimoniall Honour* (1640) p. 309. More generally, see the examples in A. Porterfield, *Female Piety in Puritan New England: the Emergence of Religious Humanism* (Oxford, 1992) pp. 40–79.

sense of distance between God and the minister. At a bad time, Thomas Shepard expressed his low state in these terms:

> I was not sensible of his glory, love, beauty, majesty. And hence I had no sense of God. And hence I saw with sadness my widow-like separation and disunion from my Husband and my God, and that we two were now parted that had been nearer once.[28]

However, the gender reversal appears more often in positive moments. After Samuel Rogers had suffered a long period of spiritual insecurity, he found solace in illness, a comfort that was usually associated with women.[29] At one point, he noted in his diary: 'The lords hand is upon me in a 5. fit; but gentler still; I find my heart ready to be weary, and cast downe, but I gather up my selfe in the Lord, and have new comfort, and strength in him'.[30] Far more frequently, he recorded his comfort in forms drawn directly from the Song of Songs: 'I lye downe in thyne armes'; 'I find abundance of gods presence for my heart lyes in his armes'.[31] Through illness, he found the prescribed female passivity that made him appreciate the mercy of God.

This was the only occasion covered in his diary that Rogers benefited from illness, but throughout his records he pleaded for humiliation through Canticles. 'Oh that my husband would kisse mee, with the kisses of his mouth and refresh my pore decayed soule and raise it up somewhat'; 'when shall I lye in the embraces of Jesus Xt; when will he kisse mee with the kisses of his mouth, amongst those that excell in vertue'.[32] After one good sermon, he made the connection explicit:

> Something refreshed by mr Fullers sermon marriage of Xt, and ye soule; and by the communion of saints; oh more brokeness, tenderness, sweetness in thy love, some of the marriage love of my husband.[33]

---

[28] M. McGiffert (ed.), *God's Plot: the Paradoxes of Puritan Piety Being the Autobiography and Journal of Thomas Shepard* (Amherst, Mass., 1972) p. 98.

[29] C. W. Bynum, 'Women's Stories, Women's Symbols: a Critique of Victor Turner's Theory of Liminality', in C. W. Bynam, *Fragmentation and Redemption: Essays on Gender and the Human Body in Medieval Religion* (New York, 1991) p. 48; Porterfield, *Female Piety*, p. 15; M. G. Mason, 'The Other Voice: Autobiographies of Women Writers', in J. Olney (ed.), *Autobiography: Essays Theoretical and Critical* (Princeton, N.J., 1980) p. 213; M. B. Rose, 'Gender, Genre, and History: Seventeenth Century English Women and the Art of Autobiography', in M. B. Rose (ed.), *Women in the Middle Ages and the Renaissance: Literary and Historical Perspectives* (Syracuse, N.Y., 1986) pp. 261–2; W. Martin, 'Anne Bradstreet's Poetry: a Study of Subversive Poetry', in S. M. Gilbert and S. Gubar (eds.), *Shakespeare's Sister: Feminist Essays of Women Poets* (Bloomington, Ind., 1979) pp. 21–2.

[30] QUB Percy MS 7 f. 310.

[31] QUB Percy MS 7 ff. 319, 313. For the centrality of the Song of Songs, see R. Tudur Jones, 'Union with Christ: the Existential Nerve of Puritan Piety', *TB* 41 (1990) pp. 200–2; G. Nuttall, 'Puritan and Quaker Mysticism', *Theology* 78 (1975) pp. 518–31; J. C. Brauer, 'Types of Puritan Piety', *CH* 56 (1987) pp. 48–9.

[32] QUB Percy MS 7 ff. 62, 218.   [33] QUB Percy MS 7 f. 174.

More often, the power of gender reversal and the Song of Songs was so deeply inscribed that it came automatically when Rogers came to spiritual comfort. 'I will lye downe in the armes of g.[od] who hath spoken peace to me, and hath supported me.'[34] In a moment of supreme humility, in dealing with the inevitability of death in the introduction to his will, Robert Bolton turned naturally to the parable of the ten virgins. His conclusion was that 'I have thought it my dutie (that I may the more readily accompany the bridegrome with my lampe light at whatsoever houre of the night he shall come) to dispose of those things wherew[i]th God hath blessed me by this my last will and testament'.[35] It seems that the ambiguities of the clerical image opened a space for the expression of comfort through gender reversals. It seems to have been a preponderantly clerical emphasis, although Jerald Brauer noted that it was a favoured approach of the layman, Francis Rous.[36] Another lay person who took the image to her heart was Joan Drake, who received guidance from John Dod, Thomas Hooker, John Preston and James Ussher. When her mother visited, she found her daughter all dressed in white; she asked why this was so, and Joan replied: 'So I am Mother (said she) a Bride now trimmed for Christ the Bridegroome', requesting that she should be buried in these clothes.[37] Although the image was generally absent from the diary of Robert Woodford, at the end of the volume he recorded a prayer from 1640, describing himself as 'thy poore creature. to whom thee hast given not sense & reason but hast caused also thy spirit to breake upon me & hast embraced me in the everlasting armes of thy love, & kissed me with the kisses of thy mouth'.[38] At this point, the main lesson we may take from this form of spirituality is the strenuous, painstaking, almost punishing examination of godly piety, deliberately fostering a sense of humility and inadequacy in the individual saint. The demands of humiliation and penitence at the heart of Puritan religiosity help to make the forms of voluntary sociability rather more comprehensible.

II

It is, I think, possible to find a literature of exhortation and recommendation that is the ideological concomitant of the patterns of clerical sociability discussed in previous chapters. Moreover, it is linked to the style of divinity

---

[34] QUB Percy MS 7 f. 334.   [35] NRO Northampton Wills 1631–6 S.2.90.

[36] Brauer, 'Types of Puritan Piety', pp. 53–6; cf. Francis Rous, *The Mysticall Marriage, or Experimentall Discoveries of the Heavenly Marriage betweene a Soul and her Saviour* (1635) pp. 318–47.

[37] Jasper Heartwell, *Trodden Down Strength* (1647) pp. 151–3, quoted at p. 152.

[38] NCO MS 9502 25 January 1640 (p. 555).

fruitfully labelled 'experimental predestinarianism' and may be a way to explain the apparent prevalence of clerical collegiality among those divines within this tradition. Among the ways of increasing faith, John Rogers stressed

societie and conference with our fellow-brethren; especially some experienced Christian or faithfull Minister, and revealing unto them our doubts, is a noteable meanes. For they may much confirme us, by their counsells and consolations fetched out of the Word, and by theire owne experience laid before us; for it availes much our comfort to heare that others have been in our case, and yet now strong in Faith.[39]

Similarly, Richard Sibbes, the greatest of spiritual physicians, recommended 'Christian society with the Saints of God, to whom you might make known your griefs, and by whom you might receive comfort from the Lord and encouragement in your Christian course'. He held that it was dangerous to neglect 'the benefit of their holy conference, their godly instructions, their divine consolations, brotherly admonitions and charitable reprehensions'.[40] This was a resource that the insecure divine might use, but also a duty to offer similar help to others when his spiritual life was more settled. The saints had an obligation to have a care for each other's spiritual health and also 'to the soule in admonition, exhortation, consolation and prayer, which are the principall and profitable fruits of our love one to another'.[41] The benefits of such conference went beyond the occasion of meeting: the communion of the saints

be the most usefully and can doe us good, by their counsell, example, prayers, when we be present, yea absent from them: He that walkes with the wise, shall be the wiser (Prov.13.10); much good may we learne, and comfort may wee get, by conversing with them that be truely godly.[42]

Sibbes preached that the 'communion of saints is chiefly ordained to comfort the feeble-minded and strengthen the weak'.[43] However, no saints were so strong in their faith that they could afford to neglect these means: Thomas Taylor stressed that 'Godly society, and listening to private admonition . . . is made a means to keep us from departing from the living God'.[44] According to Thomas Hooker, 'even the best of Gods servants need seasonable Counsell and Advise',

. . . the strongest bones need sinewes, an Armie cannot lack the least bone; the greatest Pillars have need of these things: So in the Church, the strongest members

---

[39] John Rogers, *Doctrine of Faith* (1636) p. 216; cf. Thomas Shepard, *Subjection to Christ in all his Ordinances* (1657) pp. 48–52.
[40] Richard Sibbes, *A Consolatory Letter of an Afflicted Conscience* (1641) pp. 1, 4.
[41] John Rogers, *Treatise of Love* (1632) p. 173.   [42] Ibid., p. 149.
[43] Richard Sibbes, *The Complete Works* (ed. A. B. Grosart) (London, 1862–3) vol. I p. 122.
[44] Thomas Taylor, *Works*, p. 488.

in the same need advice, and support; the richest man must use the Market; so none can live without the Market of the Society of the Saints.[45]

However, the support mechanism had a theological dimension that went beyond counsel. In itself it played a part in the search for assurance. 'We shall show that wee have a lively faith, by loving the Saints in whom Gods Image shines most, and from whom wee may get most good.'[46] Sibbes went so far as to call conference 'a sanctified means', and recommended, 'Use we the company of those that are good for by conference God works strangely many times'.[47] Daniel Rogers included 'Conference' among the helps that God had given the Church, and gave the practice a broad definition:

Q. What is Conference? A. A wise and loving laying together (by two or more) of such things as concerne the glory of God and our spirituall edifying for mutual information and quickening.[48]

This sociability came to be a way of measuring godliness in biographies. Thomas Cawton was commended because the 'society he conversed with was of those that were painful and pious, he kept no company with bad company, such as loved God were his friends, such as would come together to pray, and confer about religion, and strengthen one anothers hands against profaneness and ungodliness, such were his delight, and with such he would be very familiar and open hearted'.[49] This was a major lesson taken from the deathbed of Thomas Peacock. 'One asked him, Do you love such an one? his most dear, and worthily dear friend. Yes. Why? For his goodnes. Why then you are Gods childe, for by this we know we are translated from death to life, because we own the brethren'.[50] The same position was taken by Thomas Taylor, concluding that 'True love of brethren is the first fruit of faith'.[51] Such society among the saints was to be contrasted to the common sociability of the unregenerate and became part of the practice that marked the godly as a separate caste, a process that was sharper among the godly within the church than for those who took the practice to what may seem its logical conclusion, as Patrick Collinson has persuasively argued.[52] The godly were obliged to join with the profane in

45 Thomas Hooker, *The Christians Two Chief Lessons* (1640) p. 3.
46 John Rogers, *Doctrine of Faith*, p. 377; cf. p. 238.
47 Richard Sibbes, *Works*, vol. VII p. 170.
48 Daniel Rogers, *A Practicall Catechisme, 3rd Edition much Enlarged and Corrected* (1640) pt 3 p. 108 (following p. 108 and preceding p. 109, but also numbered p. 108).
49 Anon., *Life and Death of Thomas Cawton* (1662) p. 9.
50 Robert Bolton, *The Last Visitation, Conflicts and Death of Mr Thomas Peacock B. D. Published by E[dward] B[agshaw] from the Copie of that Famous Divine Mr R. Bolton* (1660) p. 20.
51 Thomas Taylor, *Christs Victorie over the Dragon* (1633) p. 557 (misnumbered 337); cf. John Rogers, *Treatise of Love*, p. 137.
52 P. Collinson, 'The Cohabitation of the Faithful with the Unfaithful', in O. P. Grell, J. I.

public worship, 'the congregation is like to common pastures that are common for every man's cattle', but 'it is the duty of all saints of God not to close in communion and unnecessary company and inward familiarity with those that are the deniers of the power of godliness'.[53] The consequence was to be a firm division between the saints and the world. William Gouge urged the godly to be 'wise in making choice of your company. You that have escaped sundry dangers on sea and land . . . that have had any other evidence of Gods speciall providence and favour, let not play-houses, let not tavernes, let not assemblies of profane persons, of swearers, of drunkards, of riotous and licentious persons, be the places whither you resort to recount the deliverances which God hath given you. This rather beseemeth such as have vowed vowes . . . to Devils, then to the great Lord of heaven and earth. Associate your selves with the Saints, with such as feare God, with such as may incourage you in that which you do well, and instruct and direct you in that whereof you are ignorant, and wherein you do amisse'.[54] Robert Bolton made it clear that the scorning of the saint 'is a certain mark thou are a limb of Satan'.[55] As John Yates claimed:

A Saint is the World's spectacle and a very gazing stocke, as if he were as much runne out of himselfe and madde, as he is runne from the world and his merry company.[56]

Daniel Cawdrey argued that the godly should have 'no fellowship with the unfruitfulle works of darknesse' as the 'Saints shall be their judges'. The godly shall reprove the profane, 'by abstaining from their company'.[57] As Jeremiah Burroughes saw it, 'To complaine of Gods servants, that they are singular from others, is all one, as if you should complaine of Pearles, that they are more glistering than dirt and gravell'.[58] Even according to the peaceable John Rogers, the consequences of this social separation were not to be regretted:

There's a near conjunction between believers: They are fellow brethren, of the best brotherhood . . . This rebukes them that scoff, like Ismael, at the term of Brethren

Israel and N. Tyacke (eds.), *From Persecution to Toleration: the Glorious Revolution and Religion* (Oxford, 1991) pp. 51–76; cf. P. Lake, 'William Bradshaw, Antichrist and the Community of the Godly', *JEH* 36 (1985) pp. 570–89.
53 Thomas Hooker, *The Carnal Hypocrite* (1638) (delivered c.1626) in G. H. Williams, N. Pettit, W. Herget and S. Bush, Jr (eds.), *Thomas Hooker: Writings in England and Holland, 1625–1633, Harvard Theological Studies* 28 (1975) pp. 110, 113.
54 William Gouge, *The Saints Sacrifice: or, a Commentarie on the CXVI Psalme* (1632) pp. 199–200.
55 Robert Bolton, *A Cordiall for a Fainting Christian* (1644) pp. 10–11.
56 John Yates, *The Saints Suffering and the Saints Sorrows* (1631) pp. 217–18.
57 Daniel Cawdrey, *Three Sermons* (1641) p. 23.
58 Jeremiah Burroughes, *A Gracious Spirit a Choyse and Pretious Spirit* (1638) p. 152.

or Brotherhood, who yet can be content to have a Brotherhood between themselves, in swaggering, lewd companionship, &c.[59]

The 'brotherhood of the saints' was seen as a source of individual spiritual improvement. 'By being much in the company of the godly, you will come to see some beames of the excellency of the their spirits shine out to you, whereby you will see that your spirits are not like theirs, that they are in a happier condition than you; you will soone discerne, that they are men in a nearer reference to God than you.'[60] Jeremiah Burroughes laid stress upon the good examples available in spiritual sociability: 'If the godly be of such excellent spirits, then converse and communion with them is a most blessed thing; no greater heaven up on earth than this; for here you may see the beauty and lustre of Gods graces shining, the brightnesse of which darkens all the beauty and glory of the world to a spirituall eye.'[61]

The fruits of this sociability could be considerable. John Cotton claimed that

if you take but two or three of things that are well kindled, and they will set all a fire that comes nigh them . . . the breath of such Christians, is like bellows, to blow up sparkes one in another, and so in the end, they breathe forth many savoury and sweet expressions of the hearts, and edifie themselves by that mutuall fellowship one with another.[62]

The potential benefits were so great that 'our joy cannot be full, except we inioy union with him, and communion with his Children'.[63] Love of the godly was a sign of love to God. John Preston made this clear when he claimed that 'a man could not love the Lord unless he first learn to love the Brethren'; elsewhere, he went further, stating that 'to love all grace, to love all holinesse in all the Saints, wheresoever it is found, it is an infallible signe that thou lovest the Lord *Jesus*'.[64] Brotherly love was more than a sign of the saint's love for God; it was a helpful route to such love:

Dost thou love the Saints, those that are like him, those that are of such a disposition as God is of? Shall a man say hee loves the purity and holines of God; which he hath not seen, which is hidden from his eyes, when he doth not love the holines and the purity that he sees in his Saints? For there it is taught in a visible manner in the creature, where you may see it more proportionable to you. It is a

---

[59] John Rogers, *A Godly and Fruitfull Exposition of the First Epistle of Peter* (1650) p. 667; cf. John Rogers, *Treatise of Love*, p. 168, where he rebukes Ishmael again and asserts 'yet wee are not to bee ashamed of this name, see God so speakes'. See also Hooker, *Carnal Hypocrite*, p. 112; Rogers, *Exposition*, p. 337; and Thomas Taylor, *Peter his Repentance*, Sermon III in *Works* (1653).

[60] Jeremiah Burroughes, *A Gracious Spirit*, pp. 238–89.   [61] Ibid., pp. 173–4.

[62] John Cotton, *Christ the Fountaine of Life* (1651) p. 148.

[63] John Cotton, *A Practicall Commentary upon the First Epistle Generall of John* (1656) p. 1.

[64] John Preston, *The Saints Qualification* (1637) pp. 29–30; John Preston, *The Breast-Plate of Faith and Love* (1630) 2nd pag. p. 100.

hundred times more easie to love godlinesse in the Saints, then in God himselfe, because he is remote farre from us, and they are amongst us, and are visibly seene. Therefore except thou love the Saints, which thou seest holinesse in; except thou seest thy heart inwardly, to love them with a naturall affection, as it were, that thou lovest them whether thou will or no, thou dost pretend.[65]

These means could provide a helpful boost to assurance. One of the advantages of keeping a diary, claimed John Beadle, was that it 'will much enlarge our hearts in kindnesse and compassion to our brethren; for because (as the psalmist saith [16.2–3]) our goodnesse cannot extend to God, it shall to the Saints that are in the earth [1 John 3.14]. And surely he that loveth God, loveth him also that is begotten of God. And such love to the Saints is very profitable. 1. For the present; so it is a good evidence that we are past from death to life, because we love the brethren. He that loveth not his brother abideth in death.'[66] As Thomas Brooks put it, 'Love to the Saints, for the image of God stamped upon them, is a flower that grows not in nature's garden. No man can love grace in another man's heart but he that hath grace in his own.'[67]

This pattern of sociability, it must be noted, appeared across the spectrum of godly ministers: a few examples from many might be cited to make this clear. For the resolution of 'weighty matters', William Gouge recommended meditation and conference, stressing that conference 'may be more useful . . . because thereby we have not only our help, but also the help of others'.[68] Robert Bolton, an Oxford man, commended 'an humble mutual intercourse and communication of holy conference, heavenly counsel, spiritual encouragements, consideration one of another, [and] confirmation in grace'.[69] Thomas Taylor agreed: 'Godly society, and listening to private admonition and exhortation . . . is made a means to keep us from departing from the living God'.[70] John Preston drew these themes together:

Keep in the fellowship of the Saints, for they receive from Christ onely, as they are knit and compacted together: if the branch be divided from the tree and the roote, there is no growth. Let them look to it that take no heed of their company. There are many mutuall desires to be performed together, by which the Saints grow: be one of their fellowship in conference, praying, &c. if thou wouldest grow.[71]

In the dramatic, scripted conversation at the execution of John Barker, the

---

[65] Ibid., 1st pag. pp. 228–9; cf. Thomas Brooks, *Heaven on Earth*, p. 248.
[66] John Beadle, *Journal or Diary of a Thankful Christian*, p. 178.
[67] Brooks, *Heaven on Earth*, pp. 248–9.
[68] William Gouge, *A Commentary on the Whole Epistle to the Hebrews* in his *Works* (Edinburgh, 1856–62) vol. I p. 206.
[69] Robert Bolton, *Works* (4 vols., 1641) vol. III p. 344.
[70] Thomas Taylor, *Works*, p. 488.
[71] John Preston, 'The Churches Carriage', in *The Golden Scepter* (1638) p. 97.

vicar of Pytchley, the love of the godly as a source for assurance was one of the last lessons to be taught. Barker constantly regretted the ways in which his immorality might affect the image of Puritans in the eyes of the ungodly. The three ministers who attended to him before his execution, John Ball, Daniel Rogers and Daniel Cawdrey, offered him comfort from this: 'then sayd they this is a good argument that yor are translated from death to life, because you love the bretheren & wish their salvation: the Church triumphant and the Church millitant are such as doe belong each one to other'.[72] The last word may be given to Paul Baynes, a native of Wethersfield, who exercised his ministry elsewhere. In a letter copied by Nehemiah Wallington into his own letterbook, Baynes wrote, 'the communion of the saints must be a point of practice, as well as an article of belief'.[73]

These injunctions, for conference and separation, applied to godly laity as well as ministers. However, we may profitably apply them to ministers to a greater degree, for three reasons. Firstly, and most contentiously, it might be argued that the intensity of the application of experimental Calvinism that characterised Shepard's experience was more prevalent among ministers than all but the most godly laity,[74] less for reasons of zeal than as a result of educational experience, which may make ministerial spirituality more completely theologised, although no more deeply felt. An Elizabethan call for greater sociability among godly ministers was based on their rarity and, we may note, the godly ministers saw this as a form of defence against the ungodly.

Are good Ministers too thinne sowne? are there so fewe of them? then let all good and godly ministers *give the right hand of fellowship* [Gal.2.9] one to another, and ioine together in love; and by that meanes arme themselves against the scorne and contempt of the world: we see they that are of a kindred, or a brotherhood, or any kind of society, the fewer they are, the more closely doe they combine, the more firmely do they hold together against forraine force: so ought Gods Ministers to doe, because their number is so small: if they were many, lesse danger in their disunion. But seeing they are so fewe, the more it concerneth them to cut off contentions, and all occasions of debate, and to ioyne hand in hand against these common adversaries.[75]

---

[72] NRO Isham (Lamport) 2570 MSS f. 5r. For the context and a full account, see P. Lake, '"A Charitable Christian Hatred": the Godly and their Enemies in the 1630s', in C. Durston and J. Eales (eds.), *The Culture of English Puritanism, 1560–1700* (London, 1996) pp. 145–50.

[73] Quoted in P. Seaver, *Wallington's World: a Puritan Artisan in Seventeenth-Century London* (London, 1985) p. 131.

[74] On this issue see, for instance, ibid.; G. Aylmer, 'Collective Mentalities in Mid-Seventeenth Century England: I The Puritan Outlook', *TRHS* 5th ser., 36 (1986) pp. 1–25; C. L. Cohen, *God's Caress: the Psychology of Puritan Religious Experience* (Oxford, 1986) chs. 5–8; P. Caldwell, *The Puritan Conversion Narrative: the Beginnings of American Expression* (Cambridge, 1985).

[75] William Perkins, *Works* (1618) vol. III pp. 433–4.

Secondly, for the necessary rigours of preparation for the delivery of sermons. It will be clear by now that the exhortations for 'spirit preaching' involved deeply experimental study and meditation: as Daniel Rogers suggested: 'Studie we our selves first, then the Scriptures, and the Spirit of Convincement shall follow us, which the world shall not resist'.[76] Thirdly, and less contentiously, it was less possible, for professional reasons, for a minister to look to a lay person, however godly, for counsel and advice, than to another minister. John Rogers advised, 'get under the droppings of a profitable and settled ministry',[77] and Sibbes suggested that peace could best be found 'if they would advise with their godly and learned pastors and friends'.[78] William Ames saw preachers as a major source of godly zeal: 'we ought to associat with them, that have the zeale of God, *Pro* 22. 24 25. & 27.17. Among such we must especially desire those Ministers whose tongues have been touched with a coale from the Altar, *Esay* 6'.[79] In another context, John Rogers made a related point very forcefully:

Ministers are fittest to teach Ministers, and to judge of their actions. True people may and ought try our Doctrine, modestly and humbly, they may also mislike and speak against foul things in our life and conversation, but of things not so apparent, people must not be ready to censure, much less think to teach their ministers: For the spirits of the Prophets are subject to the prophets. (1 Cor.14.32)[80]

Clearly, if clerical insecurities were to be paraded before the laity, no matter how godly, a serious undermining of clerical status would result. The prophetic status of the godly preaching minister could not hold with such frailties and so, in addition to their role to refer their own ills, first and foremost, to those 'of their tribe'.

We might suggest that the construction of a godly self described above retained some of the characteristics described by Natalie Zemon Davis for a different context. For her, the early modern self was defined by relationships and connections as much as by boundaries, was 'prepositional'.[81] It seems that the construction of the godly self meant emphasising a particular set of prepositions, integrating that self into the godly community. If we imagine the godly minister wrestling with God on his own, we have only part of the picture: the construction of the godly self was necessarily a communal activity.

---

[76] Daniel Rogers, *Practicall Catechisme*, pt. I p. 69.
[77] John Rogers, *Doctrine of Faith*, p. 253.   [78] Sibbes, *Works*, I p. 210.
[79] William Ames, *Conscience and the Power and Cases Thereof* (1639) Book 3 p. 59.
[80] Rogers, *Exposition*, p. 617.
[81] N. Z. Davis, 'Boundaries and the Sense of Self in Sixteenth Century France', in T. C. Heller, M. Sosna and D. E. Wellbery (eds.), *Reconstructing Individualism: Autonomy, Individuality and the Self in Western Thought* (Stanford, Calif., 1986) pp. 53–63, esp. 55–6; cf. V. Turner, 'Images of Anti-Temporality: an Essay in the Anthropology of Experience', *HTR* 75 (1982) p. 245.

We cannot use the example of Thomas Shepard to measure the proposition that the insecurity engendered by this style of divinity led to a greater sociability among clergy of this stamp: as we have seen, his career took him from the exercises of Emmanuel to Thomas Weld's Terling and thus into the supportive networks of Essex. Connections made here helped him through his unsettled period, and by the beginning of his surviving journal he was within the close-knit ministerial society of Massachusetts. For almost all of his life, he was firmly within the communion of saints and never far from the comforts of the godly ministry.

To assess the effects of the removal of such society, it is more fruitful to return to the experience of Samuel Rogers. Samuel had left home at the age of fifteen and a half to live at Felsted, 'where indeed I thinke, I got more good in 2 yeares with the blessing of god, upon the diligent labours of my godly master Mr Holbeach than I got in many twoos before'.[82] From Felsted he went to Emmanuel College, where he benefited from the pastoral care of his tutor, Mr Frost, and by December 1634, 'a companye of us have ioined together to meet often to pray together, and discourse'.[83] In August 1635, he left Cambridge for Bishops Stortford, where he was to be chaplain to Lady Mary Denny. Here the vicar was Richard Butler, a conformist whose preaching Samuel found formal and dull. He regretted Butler's 'heartless aching, litle life in it: oh a convincing ministry is worth a world'. He was offended by Butler's regular denunciations of Puritans: '29. [March, 1636] Saboath; Butler plays his parts, shews hims[elf]: in his colors ag[ainst]: zelotes; brings his 25 obii [objections] ag: common prayer, answers them, and railes'.[84] At Stortford Rogers found little comfort in public worship and less success in the Denny household. In October, he wrote,

> Saboath, sadded, because of Stevens the caviler: such an one in a company is like a dead fly in a box of ointment, makes the company unsavory; oh lord, that I might live among thy servants though with bread, and water: oh some way, some way make that I may serve thee sweetly, and not alwayes among bryars, and thornes and to wash Ætheopians.[85]

He attributed his own spiritual troubles to the lack of like-minded company, concluding that 'I want a good companion, unto whom I may unloade my selfe[.] I will, and doe looke to heaven but am troubled; I wil waite for the L[ord] will speake peace.'[86] He continually regretted this lack:

[82] QUB Percy MS 7 f. 3.   [83] QUB Percy MS 7 ff. 15, 16.
[84] QUB Percy MS 7 ff. 71, 103.   [85] QUB Percy MS 7 f. 171.
[86] QUB Percy MS 7 f. 85.

. . . but oh the want of a close lively preaching; good lord so provide for thy pore servant, that I may walke with life, savour and cheerfulnesse; the way to attain which is to lie under a convincing ministry.[87]

As he received comfort from people on their way to New England, Rogers came to see the colonies as a possible source of the spiritual stability which he lacked at Stortford. This perception of New England as a society of the godly was among the principal attractions for Samuel when, over a period of about two years, he considered emigration.

This day I part with G. Howe to New England. Oh how precious is the company of the saints, and the Lord rends them from us and gleans away the cheife and choise, and full eares.[88]

Such society was so important for his spiritual well-being, that his vision of Heaven became strikingly moulded by the patterns of religious sociability that he found so helpful on earth:

I have bin a litle in heaven now toward my lying downe; oh I can ioy in meditation that onlie a slight, giddy, proud, iolly wretch as I am. shall be rid of all my sloth; and sit downe in companye, with Abraham, Paul, my grandfather [Richard Rogers], and all other blessed saints, and angels, and be filled unto eternity, in the presence and full sight of God, whose countenances to see afarre of[f], while I live heere is worth a world.[89]

Richard Baxter used the same image at rather greater length. He relished the idea of 'sitting down with Abraham, Isaac, Jacob and all the prophets', imagining the activity of a number of Old Testament figures in heaven. He culminated with a collection of saints through history.

Will it be nothing conducible to the completing of our comforts to live eternally with Peter, Paul, Austin, Chrysostom, Jerome, Wickliffe, Luther, Zuinglius, Calvin, Beza, Bullinger, Zanchius, Paræus, Piscator, Camero; with Hooper, Bradford, Latimer, Glover, Saunders, Philpot, with Reighnolds, Whitaker, Cartwright, Brightman, Bayne, Bradshaw, Bolton, Ball, Hildersham, Pemble, Twisse, Ames, Preston, Sibbs? O 'foelicem diem' (said holy Grynæus) 'quam ad illud animarum concilium proficisar, et ex hac turba colluvione discedam!' O happy day, when I shall depart out of this crowd and sink, and go to that same council of souls![90]

---

[87] QUB Percy MS 7 f. 136.
[88] QUB Percy MS 7 f. 98. This understanding receives support from the perceptive discussion in A. Zakai, 'The Gospel of Reformation: Origins of the Great Puritan Migration', *JEH* 37 (1986) pp. 584–602 and contradicts the assessment of Kenneth Shipps in his 'The Puritan Emigration to New England: a New Source on Motivation', *NEHGR* 135 (1981) pp. 83–97. See below, ch. 14.
[89] QUB Percy MS 7 f. 92.
[90] Richard Baxter, *The Saints' Everlasting Rest* in *The Practical Works of Richard Baxter* (London, 1830) vol. XXII p. 122. John Wilson had a similar vision of heaven on his death bed, looking forward to his reunion with his friends, John Preston, Richard Sibbes, Thomas Taylor, William Gouge, William Ames, John Cotton and John Norton: Mather, III p. 47; Charles Chauncy required himself to feel the 'Love of the Godly Dead' as part of his

Towards the end of his time at Stortford, Samuel Rogers made frequent visits into Essex, to hear sermons and enjoy the company of godly society. Among the ministers and noble professors in and around Hatfield Broad Oak he began to find the support and society that he thought existed only in heaven:

I have bine at Hatfield, heard good old Mr Harrison; my heart inlarged in discourse, at Mr Barringtons; how sweet is it to be one heere in the companye of such as [are] from God.[91]

These contacts proved invaluable when the Denny household was at its most intractable. In the midst of the heavy plague of 1636, when he had quarrelled with his employer over his attempts to discipline drunken servants and over his treks into Essex, his only respite was in these meetings:

Now wee fast and pray at Hatfield wee give the whole day to god sweetly; in publique, and private together; the Lord goes out with mee, Lord heare, Lord heare, downe with plauge [*sic*.] sins, take away the stubble, that the fire of thy indignation may goe out; and lord the destroying angel stop him.[92]

Shortly afterwards, Samuel became involved with a fasting company in Farnham, led by William Sedgewick, the rector, and his former tutor, the deprived minister George Hughes.[93] Frequent trips to the neighbouring parish brought support and stability into his spiritual life, and the remainder of his time at Stortford, while less than serene, was characterised by what was to be a more manageable cycle of humiliation and assurance. It seems reasonable to apply Samuel's own diagnosis more widely to that religiosity that we have seen above in its public and private faces. Within months of beginning his journal, he was 'sweetly touched by Mr Marshalls sermon, but ready to drop againe; I have need of continuall underproppings to hold up my tottering soule'.[94]

---

preparation for communion: ibid., p. 138. The same vision was offered to John Barker before his execution. Barker hoped 'oh that I might see your faces in heaven: they told him, they hoped hee should though he went before them, oh what a merry ioyfull meetting shall wee have in heaven': NRO Isham (Lamport) MSS 2570 f. 5r; cf. John Bunyan, *The Pilgrim's Progress* (ed. R. Sharrock) (Harmondsworth, 1987) pp. 326–7, where Gaius traces Christian's relations through a genealogy of martyrs including Stephen, James, Peter and Paul and on through Ignatius, Romanus, Polycarp and Marcus of Arethusa.

[91] QUB Percy MS 7 f. 124.

[92] QUB Percy MS 7 ff. 176–7. For disagreements with Lady Denny, f. 157: 'I have had some bickering with her Ld: for backing her tipling servants; I told her highnes that it was fit they should rather be reproved, than backed; she a litle quailed; all the house ag[ainst]: mee as too strict; but I have comfort in it, at my lying downe'; for similar incidents with Lady Denny, and with his next employer, Lady de Vere, cf. ff. 161–2, 246, 248, 349, 356.

[93] QUB Percy MS 7 ff. 166, 181, 195, 204, 212, 239, 245. For Hughes and Sedgewick, see *DNB* and T. W. Davids, *Annals of Evangelical Nonconformity in the County of Essex* (London, 1863) pp. 566–7.

[94] QUB Percy MS 7 f. 30.

This cluster of traits, emerging from the relationship between discursive and experiential spheres, encourages a further perspective on these rituals of sociability. The exhortations in the literature of practical divinity in favour of godly conference clearly go beyond the demands of clerical collegiality and possibly exceed the needs of insecure faith. The vocabulary of these calls circulates around the notion of a brotherhood run out of the world, the fellowship of the saints and the communion of the saints. This rhetoric reflects Peter Lake's observation that the godly tended to elide the distinction between the visible and invisible church.[95] Daniel Cawdrey claimed that 'when Gods people meet together in any place, He is spiritually present with them not in regard to the place, but to the persons'.[96] John Rogers went further, suggesting that despite, or in fact in consequence of, the impossibility of certainty regarding the election of other people, the invisible church was present because there the elect were sufficiently predominant: he located the communion of saints, in a strict sense, not in the agglomeration of individuals, but in collective godliness.[97] It was perhaps William Gouge that took this furthest.

Places set apart for Gods worship are Gods houses. More than five hundred times is this title *house of God*, or *house of the Lord*, in holy Scripture attributed to places deputed unto divine service. And because worship is done to God, not onely in materiall Temples, but also in the communion of Saints, yea and in the bodies and soules of particular Christians, they are also called *Gods houses.*[98]

The maintenance of this vital communion demanded the recurring, constantly renewing cycle of sociability described above, not simply in response to theology. The majority in the Scots church shared the Predestinarian theology of the English godly, while firmly rejecting voluntary associations outside public worship.[99] The elect had no institutional basis in the Church of England, a body of undifferentiated sheep and goats. This placed the godly in a position fraught with tension: as Victor Turner observed, 'our sociability is mutable though we yearn for permanence'.[100] The society of the saints, therefore, was one which had to be constantly maintained, made and remade, defined and redefined. Godly society can be

---

[95] P. Lake, *Anglicans and Puritans? Presbyterians and Conformist Thought from Whitgift to Hooker* (London, 1988) pp. 28–9, 241–2; P. Lake, 'Presbyterianism, the National Church and the Argument from Divine Right', in P. Lake and M. Dowling (eds.), *Protestantism and the National Church* (London, 1987) pp. 193–224; Lake, 'William Bradshaw and the Community of the Godly', pp. 570–89.

[96] Daniel Cawdrey, *Superstitio Superstes* (1641) p. 14.

[97] John Rogers, *Godly and Fruitful Exposition*, p. 693.

[98] William Gouge, *The Saints Sacrifice*, p. 259.

[99] D. Stevenson, 'The Radical Party in the Kirk', *JEH* 25 (1974) pp. 135–65, esp. 142; D. Stevenson, 'Conventicles in the Kirk, 1619–37: the Emergence of a Radical Party', *RSCHS* 18 (1972–4) pp. 99–114.

[100] V. Turner, 'Images of Anti-Temporality . . .', p. 245.

seen as the result of the potentialities of a sect under the regime of a universal church. These potentialities were matched by equally strong universalist tendencies and commitments, but without suggesting that sectarian tendencies were inevitably fulfilled – they were, of course, heavily policed by godly writers – this perception makes more comprehensible Scottish unease at imported English practices of voluntary religion. In the eyes of the Scots, in their adequately reformed church, the structures of the divine order were expressed, as far as was humanly possible, within the institution of the Kirk. Closer to our own object of study, this incomprehension is paralleled in the exchange between Thomas Hooker and John Paget: Paget asked if fasting and prayer were allowed outside public worship and concluded that they were not; Hooker concluded that far from being allowed, they were, in some circumstances, necessary.[101] To Paget and the Scots, there was no need for the active remaking of godly society; such activity was, implicitly, a suggestion that the institutions of the church were an insufficient reflection of God's plan. In England, even when godly writers rejected the necessity of disciplinary reform, the reproduction of the communion of the saints reveals a sectarian ethos.

Leaving aside, for now, the ecclesiological consequences of this view, we may suggest some tentative conclusions from our study of religion and society. It is, perhaps, helpful to imagine this relationship as a system of cultural reproduction,[102] with all the efforts of preaching, conference, intra- and extra-mural education, fasting and prayer added to the prescribed disciplines of personal, private devotion, working together in an internally coherent and, evidently, very successful strategy for the replication of more godly ministers, for the reproduction of godly society. This was a system where precept and practice reinforce and reproduce each other but where practice could also turn back upon, and alter, precept. We can consider the results of this system as what sociologists call 'habitus', a set of deeply internalised dispositions that limit without determining the actions of individual agents.[103] In fact, the godly habitus sets boundaries, not only to action, but to subjective experience itself.

The habitus is cultural, that is, it is learned. However, it is most successfully inculcated once it is naturalised: when the precepts are so deeply internalised that they become barely conscious, when individual and social practice come to mesh effectively with experience. It is a system

---

101 Williams *et al.*, Document 8, Question 18.
102 P. Bourdieu, *Outline of a Theory of Practice* (Cambridge, 1977) pp. 30–58; P. Bourdieu, 'Cultural Reproduction and Social Reproduction', in R. Brown (ed.), *Knowledge, Education and Social Change* (London, 1973) pp. 71–112; cf. the essays in C. Jenks (ed.), *Cultural Reproduction* (London, 1993).
103 Bourdieu, *Outline of a Theory of Practice*, pp. 72–95.

which practical divinity describes but also inculcates in conjunction with practice: godliness is learned through individual and social practice. We should be careful not to make too rigid a distinction between precept and practice – reading and hearing are means,[104] are forms of practice – or ignore the fact that habitus is inculcated through both explicit and implicit forms, in the discursive and non-discursive spheres.[105]

However, this model should not be taken as wholly deterministic. The habitus is not homogeneous and this, added to the reciprocal relationship between precept and practice opens a considerable space of individual agency. The habitus is a social phenomenon, but it is embodied in individual agents,[106] who experience social circumstances and in turn act upon them.[107] These factors, as we have seen, allow for internal change. Practices are produced in and by the encounter between the habitus and its dispositions on the one hand; on the other, they operate and are modified by the demands, constraints and opportunities of the social field to which the habitus is appropriate or within which the actor is moving.[108] A social field may be (and in complex societies usually is) inhabited by other habituses placed in differential power relations. The habitus operates in relation to this contested social field – the same habitus can produce very different practices, depending on what is going on in the field and can be transformed by changed circumstances there.[109] Without ignoring internal dynamics of change, these shifts in the social field prove to be extremely important in our case, relating directly to the question of the changing expressions of godly society under Jacobean and Caroline conditions.

It should be stressed that much of the habitus we have been describing, especially in Jacobean conditions, was not in conflict with, indeed was considerably reinforced by, the dominant forces in the social field. Godliness was never a counter-culture and, as Professor Collinson observes,[110] constituted something like a moral majority in the earlier period. The Caroline changes and their consequences will be discussed in greater detail later. Here we may pause to note an added consequence of the forms of religiosity we have described. Although the changing relationship between

---

[104] Richard Rogers, *Seven Treatises*, pp. 371–81.
[105] Here I give rather more emphasis to explicit forms than Bourdieu tends to: see the account in R. Jenkins, *Pierre Bourdieu* (London, 1992) pp. 74–84, but cf. P. Bourdieu and J.-C. Passeron, *Reproduction in Education, Society and Culture* (London, 1977) p. 31 and *passim*, where he gives more emphasis to explicit 'pedagogic work'.
[106] Bourdieu and Passeron, *Reproduction in Education*, p. 205.
[107] E. P. Thompson, *The Poverty of Theory and other Essays* (London, 1978) p. 199.
[108] P. Bourdieu, *The Logic of Practice* (Cambridge, 1990) pp. 52–65; P. Bourdieu, *Language and Symbolic Power* (Cambridge, 1991) pp. 37–42.
[109] P. Bourdieu, *In Other Words* (Cambridge, 1990) p. 116.
[110] See, for instance, P. Collinson, *The Puritan Character: Polemics and Polarities in early Seventeenth-Century English Culture* (Los Angeles, Calif., 1989) p. 13.

habitus and social field is most likely to be experienced at the level of the individual, in godly experiences of struggle, opprobrium and persecution, or power, approval and preferment, because the godly minister is so thoroughly integrated in networks of consultation, spiritual sociability and communal ways of thinking, changes in the position of the habitus were internalised as a collective experience. As we will see, individual experiences, especially of the negative kind, were collectivised and magnified in the process. This made the perceived persecution of the individual the persecution of the group and, by the logic of godly rhetoric, opened the possibility of a perception of persecution of the visible church.[111]

IV

The preceding account may seem more than a little static: the Church of England was anything but unchanging in the period under review. It is particularly necessary to consider change in the fifteen years before the calling of the Long Parliament. Change among the godly will be considered in detail in the next section; here I will limit myself to considering how the religious practices that came to dominate the church from the late 1620s affected the vision of the ministry and devotional life outlined above.

Firstly, I will give a brief account of the alternative view of the ministry that informed Laudian policy, and then go on to examine the changes in policy that depended upon this view and touched directly on the ministry of the godly clergy.[112] Lastly, I will suggest some ways in which the new conditions interacted with the piety discussed above to produce a potentially explosive mixture.

For the alternative view of the ministry that became orthodoxy in the 1630s, as for much of what became Laudian policy, we have to go no further back than the writings of Richard Hooker.[113] In his attempts to produce a positive ideal to set against late Elizabethan Presbyterian propagandists, Hooker created a system of ecclesiology, a doctrine and vision of the church that undermined Calvinist assumptions of the purpose of the church militant. With specific regard to the ministry, he produced a view focused on the intercession of public prayer rather than on instruction and exhortation from the pulpit. He reinstated the sacraments as the central drama of Christian life, suggesting that they were 'the

---

111 Aspects of this argument receive support from P. Lake, '"A Charitable Christian Hatred": the Godly and their Enemies in the 1630s', pp. 145–83, and D. Willen, '"Communion of the Saints": Spiritual Reciprocity and the Godly Community in Early Modern England', *Albion* 27 (1995) pp. 19–41.

112 I will discuss trajectories of resistance and compliance in chapters 8–12.

113 For what follows I rely principally on P. Lake, *Anglicans and Puritans?* ch. 4, and esp. pp. 169–71, 176–7, 213–17.

ordinary means to eternal life'. This sacramental emphasis allowed him to raise the status of a reading ministry which could serve a broadly defined community of Christians. While he did not deny the importance of preaching *per se*, the natural consequence of his view was to diminish the role of the preacher. Puritans, of course, made large claims for the ministry, but in Richard Hooker's vision, the parochial minister was to take his authority from a priestly role, not from his resemblance to an Old Testament prophet. As Lake concludes, 'For the first time since the beginning of the reign English protestants possessed a rhetoric of self importance which could be applied to the general run of ministers without embarrassment'.[114]

Hooker's heirs in the first decades of the seventeenth century, men such as Lancelot Andrewes, John Howson and John Overall, added anti-Calvinism to this equation and helped to pave the way for the rise of the Durham House group under the patronage of Richard Neile. During the 1620s, the Durham House clergy captured crucial centres of influence, and in 1625 the accession of Charles brought to the throne a monarch upon whom they could rely to support their innovative programme.[115] Among their first successes was the proclamation of June 1626, 'for the establishing of the Peace and Quiet of the Church of England', which attempted to suppress debate over the works of Richard Montague. With the declaration along similar lines prefaced to the November 1628 reissue of the 39 Articles,[116] it seemed to the godly that they were no longer to uphold the doctrine of predestination, the grounding of the whole scheme of experimental Calvinism. It is not of the essence here whether Bishop Laud and the King were genuinely motivated by a desire for peace, as Peter White

[114] Ibid., quotes from pp. 176, 217.
[115] For this account, and much of what follows, I have relied upon N. Tyacke, *Anti-Calvinists: the Rise of English Arminianism c.1590–1640* (Oxford, 1987) esp. chs. 5 and 8, and *passim*; A. Foster, 'Church Policies of the 1630s', in R. Cust and A. Hughes (eds.), *Conflict in Early Stuart England* (London, 1989) pp. 193–223; P. Lake, 'Lancelot Andrewes, John Buckeridge, and Avant-Garde Conformity at the Court of James I', in L. L. Peck (ed.), *The Mental World of the Jacobean Court* (Cambridge, 1991) pp. 113–33, and the debate brought together in K. Fincham (ed.), *The Early Stuart Church, 1603–1642* (London, 1993). This view is not uncontested: see esp. P. White, 'The Rise of Arminianism Reconsidered', *PP* 101 (1983) pp. 34–54; K. Sharpe, 'Archbishop Laud', *HT* 33 (1983) pp. 26–30; K. Sharpe, 'The Personal Rule of Charles I', in H. Tomlinson (ed.), *Before the English Civil War* (London, 1983) pp. 53–78, and N. Tyacke and P. White, 'Debate: the Rise of Arminianism Reconsidered', *PP* 115 (1987) pp. 201–29.
[116] For the proclamation, J. F. Larkin (ed.), *Stuart Royal Proclamations* (Oxford, 1983) vol. II pp. 90–3; for the preface to the 39 Articles, S. R. Gardiner (ed.), *Constitutional Documents of the Puritan Revolution 1625–1660* (Oxford, 1979) pp. 75–6. It is worth stressing that neither specifically mentioned predestination, although James I's earlier directions for preachers of 1622 did, for which see E. Cardwell, *Documentary Annals of the Reformed Church of England* (Oxford, 1844) vol. II, p. 202.

suggests;[117] rather, what is crucial is how the moves were perceived. We can turn to a petition circulating among 'faithfull, obedyant, peaceable, and conformable' ministers of the diocese of London, during 1629. It was felt that the King's

> sayed edicts are soe interpreted, and pressed upon us, as we are not a little discouraged and deterred from preaching those saving Doctrines of Gods Free Grace in Election & Predestination which greatly confirme our fayth of eternal salvation, and fervently kindle our love to God . . . Soe as wee are brought into a greate Stayte eyther of incuring Gods heavy displeasure if wee doe not faithfully discharge our Embassage, in declaring the whole Counsell of God, or the danger of being censured for violators of your Majesties sayed Actes.[118]

It became a commonplace perception among the godly that the declaration was only enforced on the Calvinist side: these 'Declarations and Inhibitions, being observed by many Ministers, but not so, by the Arminian-faction, was a mighty means to increase them, and to suppresse Orthodox-Doctrines'.[119] Even if the strictures on debate had been evenly enforced, the strain would have been greater on the godly: John Rogers quoted William Perkins with satisfaction on the absolute necessity of handling the doctrine of God's eternal decree.[120] To see the ecclesiastical authorities as hostile to the preaching of the basis of practical divinity was a considerable stress upon the godly ministry. For these same authorities to pursue what was seen as a policy hostile to preaching generally was still more stressful. In December 1629, Royal Instructions were issued from the King to the bishops which required afternoon sermons to be converted to catechising sessions; lecturers were to read divine service, wear the surplice and, more importantly, single lecturers (as opposed to members of a combination) 'be not suffered to preach, till he professes his willingness to take upon him a living with a cure'.[121] These directions were sufficient in themselves to cause offence among the godly ministers, but tensions were exacerbated by suspicions that worse intentions lay behind the instructions. Within weeks William Greenhill was writing to his patron, Lady Jane Bacon:

> Since I wrote to your Ladyshipp the Byshops have received instructions from the king, for they make him the author of all. And they are touching Byshops retiring to their owne seas, Catechizing in the afternoons Gentlemens restraint from keeping of chaplaines or scholars in their houses. Lecturers reading of prayers in their habits & surpluces Constantly on weekedayes and others. They had thought to have chopt

---

[117] White, 'Rise of Arminianism', p. 50; White, *Predestination, Policy and Polemic: Conflict and Consensus in the English Church from the Reformation to the Civil War* (Cambridge, 1992) pp. 282–4, 286, 293–9.

[118] SP 16/408/325.

[119] John Vicars, *The Schismatick Sifted* (1646) p. 16; cf. Thomas Edwards, *Antapologia: Or, a Full Answer to the Apologeticall Narration* (1644) pp. 241–2.

[120] John Rogers, *Exposition*, p. 254.   [121] Cardwell, *Annals*, pp. 229–33.

them all downe at a blow but that was too violent, they will take a milder course weary all men out with imposition of heavy burdens that they will hardly touch with one of their fingers. it makes my heart bleede to thinke of the miseries that by such men and their projects are coming uppon the Xurch wch I beseech the Lord of his infinite mercy to uphold and preserve in dispight of all the oppressors thereof.[122]

As in the writings of Richard Hooker, the correlative of a diminished respect for preaching was a heightened emphasis on the liturgy. The strain here was less the raised status of prayer *per se*, as the new standing of *set* forms of prayer. As so often, John Rogers was the voice of authentic old English Protestantism:

Some will pray, and they think that as good as preaching. A. Its monsterous wickedness for any to put down any Ordinance that God hath set up, under color of setting up any other: These two Preaching and Prayer, be inseperable companions, and must go together, & none pray more, than they that make most conscience, and have profited most by Preaching . . . and what Prayer is it that they talk so much of, but Book prayer to serve a turn? which though it be not amiss, as a staff till a man can go of himself, yet its not as conceived prayer, much less to be set up with the casting down of Preaching . . . to thrust out preaching, that were abominable; Pray as much as you will, but neglect not preaching.[123]

The very real changes of emphasis, and the hostile perceptions that made them still more damaging, must have seemed wholly designed to undermine the exercise of a godly preaching ministry: not only was the sacramental priesthood raised at the expense of the ministry of the Word, and set forms preferred to spirited exposition in prayer and pulpit, but the voluntary religious exercises that form the natural means of spiritual support came under increasing official disapproval. Stephen Marshall summarised godly perceptions of the changes at his first opportunity to preach to the House of Commons. He bemoaned the profanation of the Sabbath, the suppression of preaching, and the corruption of divine worship.[124] Godly ministers were forced to ask themselves whether their vision of the ministry was so far compromised by the objectives of what they saw as recidivist authorities that the continuation of their ministry was impossible. Set against the pastoral imperatives of conversion and witness that made the liberty of preaching so precious to the godly ministers, this amounted to an almost intolerable strain: the preacher was faced with a choice between a silence that offended against a deeply ingrained preaching vocation or an unconscionable compromise with an alien conception of their given task.

Marshall's first indictment of the Laudian programme concerned the 'miserable defection' in doctrinal matters: a reference to the Arminianism

---

[122] ERO D/DBy C24 f. 19.   [123] John Rogers, *Exposition*, p. 234.
[124] Stephen Marshall, *A Sermon Preached before the Honorable House of Commons. November, 17, 1640* (1641) pp. 32–5.

perceived to motivate the policy. The reality of William Laud's own doctrinal position and the theological roots of the ecclesiastical policies of the 1630s have been debated, with less than conclusive results,[125] but it seems less contestable that the changes were attached to Arminian doctrine, at least within godly perspectives. The godly response to that perception has been dealt with elsewhere[126] and will be touched upon in the next section, but I will close this chapter by suggesting a reaction that struck deeper into godly consciousness.

Here, we may turn again to Thomas Shepard's experience. Jeremiah Burroughes could have been thinking of his friend when he warned that 'nothing is so delicate and tender as the life of grace'.[127] For the experimental Predestinarian the way of faith was strenuous and demanding, and the temptations of alternative creeds were considerable. Shepard had flirted with Antinomianism when he heard of the 'Grindletonians' while he was at Cambridge, and the 'deep temptation' to 'forsake the scriptures and wait for a spirit to suggest immediately Gods inmost thoughts towards me' recurs throughout his journal.[128] McGiffert suggests that 'it seems plausible to suggest that in putting down the Antinomian apostate [Anne Hutchinson], Shepard was suppressing the Antinomian propensities of his own passionate spirit'.[129] At other times, Shepard wrote, 'I saw my heart popishly inclined' and of 'many horrid temptations of atheism, Judaism, Familism, Popery, despair as having sinned the unpardonable sin'.[130] For a piety as frail as this we may suggest two possible responses to the advance of Arminianism. Firstly, the undermining of the doctrine of perseverance was to remove the hope that lay in the accumulation of delicate assurances: the natural response was horror and anger. Secondly, the heightened evaluation of human abilities and of the role of the will in conversion offered what seemed a seductive proposition to the embattled saint. Shepard certainly saw Arminianism in this light: 'it is a good speech of Doctor Ames; Arminian universall grace (as they describe it) may be the effect of a good dinner sometimes'.[131] Could it be more than speculative psychobabble to suggest that the violence of some godly reactions to Arminianism was linked to this insecurity? Might it be possible that Shepard's loathing of Laud, 'a fierce enemy to all righteousness and a man

---

[125] See esp. the works by White and Sharpe cited above, n. 115; cf. White, *Predestination, Policy and Polemic*, pp. 276–86, and N. Tyacke, 'Archbishop Laud', in Fincham (ed.), *The Early Stuart Church*, pp. 51–70.

[126] E.g. Tyacke, *Anti-Calvinists*, ch. 8; W. Hunt, *The Puritan Moment: the Coming of Revolution in an English County* (London, 1983) chs. 10, 11.

[127] Jeremiah Burroughes, *Foure Bookes* (1659) p. 103.

[128] McGiffert (ed.), *God's Plot*, pp. 42, 164.   [129] Ibid., p. 28.

[130] Ibid., pp. 114, 73.   [131] Shepard, *Certain Select Cases*, p. 30.

fitted of God to be a scourge to his people', was a reflection of his self-loathing in regard of his weak grasp on Assurance?

Broader thoughts may be stimulated by Dr Kendall's suggestion that the rejections of Antinomianism in the Westminster Assembly, the apotheosis of the experimental Predestinarian tradition, produced statements of the doctrine of faith and assurance that were all but identical with those of Arminius. Moreover, the heightened voluntarism of the Westminster documents was achieved despite the rejection of the dangerously voluntaristic doctrines of preparation promoted by Essex divines such as Hooker, Shepard and John and Daniel Rogers.[132] In the polemical conditions that obtained between 1618 and the mid-1640s, it was scarcely possible to make the short step from experimental Predestinarianism to Arminianism: what for Kendall is merely a theological boundary was a social and existential Rubicon for the godly. Even so, some divines within this tradition dipped their toes in these decades, and in the new environment after the Westminster Assembly figures like John Goodwin and, most notably, Richard Baxter could take the crucial step which recast Arminianism as a tenable position for divines who rejected the sacerdotal accoutrements of Laudianism.[133] Goodwin was at the heart of the experimental predestinarian position in the 1630s, and Baxter's search for a new grounding of security led him back to the writers he called 'affectionate practical English divines', and these writers, whom he continued to revere to the end of his life, helped him to a new, Arminian, synthesis.[134] Perhaps Thomas Shepard would have found a more settled devotional life had this option been available to him.

To return, for the present, to the godly view and experience of the ministry, we may sketch elements of a view that can, not unprofitably, be labelled 'Puritan'. Much of this view overlapped with a view which formed the common ground of English Protestantism: the stress on preaching, sometimes, it seemed, to the derogation of all else, the necessity of spirited denunciation of sin and sinners; a plain style and an intention to move

---

[132] R. T. Kendall, *Calvin and English Calvinism to 1649* (Oxford, 1979) pp. 210–12, 198–200.

[133] One such divine was Anthony Wooton, accused of Arminianism by George Walker. It may be significant that Wooton was influenced by Alexander Richardson, and also that he was an early opponent of Richard Montague. Thomas Gataker accused Richardson of a dangerously raised view of human abilities that resembles John Goodwin's early work. George Walker, *A True Relation* (1642); Thomas Gataker, *An Answere* (1642); Anthony Wooton, *A Dangerous Plot Discoverd* (1626).

[134] For Goodwin's work in the 1630s, SU Hartlib MS 29/2/53a; E. More, 'John Goodwin and the New Arminianism', *JBS* 22 (1982) pp. 50–70. For Baxter, see W. Lamont, 'The Rise of Arminianism: a Comment', *PP* 106 (1985) pp. 227–31; Richard Baxter, *A Christian Directory* (1673) pp. 922–8 where he praises the work of Hooker, Rogers, Shepard, Burroughes and Marshall.

congregations to reformation of life. Some elements received a heavier emphasis among those who were judged to be 'the hotter sort of Protestants': a particular relish for the nuanced exposition of the processes of conversion; an experimental style of divinity rooted in private devotional exercises and a consequent vision of a community of saints, supporting, exhorting and defining themselves against their less zealous neighbours. John Rogers made it clear that these spiritual nourishments were best available in combination. The means 'whereby we may increase from a weake to a strong faith', he concluded, were 'with all diligence and care to attend on the means, publike and private, as hearing the Word, prayer, receiving the Sacrament, reading, meditation, and holy conferences'.[135] Given the fragility and importance of the godly self, the perception that any or all of these means came under threat was unlikely to produce a gentle acquiescence.

[135] John Rogers, *Doctrine of Faith*, p. 238; cf. Daniel Rogers, *Practicall Catechism* (1640) p. 108; Thomas Brooks, *Heaven on Earth*, p. 306.

Part III

'THESE UNCOMFORTABLE TIMES': CONFORMITY AND THE GODLY MINISTERS 1628–38

Delivering his last provincial account in 1632, Archbishop Abbot informed the King that 'there is not in the Church of England left any inconformable minister which appeareth', although the bishops of London and Lincoln had been forced to deprive two or three divines, 'whom no time can tame, nor instruction conquer'. Six years later, William Juxon, the Bishop of London, made his annual report to Abbot's successor, William Laud, and, after taking note of a brief squabble in the city occasioned by 'some overnice curiousities' expressed in the pulpit, claimed 'there is but one noted refractory person that stands out in that diocese, and he is now under suspension'.[1] These accounts present, from either end of the decade, a diocese essentially at peace, with the occasional disciplinary duty and an infrequent need for peacemaking falling under the pastoral eye of the bishop. The task of this section is to scratch beneath the surface of this picture to test its validity, to see if this was a decade of tranquillity and to measure the perception of the ecclesiastical establishment against that of the godly ministers. In the course of the discussion a number of themes emerge: firstly, I will examine in a little detail the experience of Thomas Hooker between 1628 and 1633 to see how debates among the godly, particularly regarding the Prayer Book ceremonies, underwent a crucial transition during these years. The issues which animate these ministers lead us to variations in response to changing perceptions: it becomes possible to discuss different trajectories of experience and gain an insight into their doubts and resolutions. These phenomena can then be placed into the context of the experience of Essex in these years through an examination of the structure and operation of the ecclesiastical courts and the conduct of visitations. Through a consideration of the ecclesiastical government of Essex and the dioceses of Norwich and Peterborough we can begin to build an understanding of the perceptions of the godly ministers of the county to place against those of the establishment quoted above.

[1] William Laud, *The Works of William Laud, Anglo-Catholic Library* (ed. W. Scott and J. Bliss) (Oxford, 1847–60) vol. V pp. 310, 356.

7

Thomas Hooker and the conformity debate

I

For two of the leading lights of the godly ministry, the years between 1628 and 1633 had been extremely unsettled. The conference which Thomas Hooker had organised had operated with relative impunity during the episcopate of George Montaigne. Late in his reign Montaigne had brought Hooker before his court at Little Baddow and required him to obtain a licence as a schoolmaster. Hooker was questioned for absenting himself from communion in his home parish, Little Baddow, but he claimed to take the sacrament in the neighbouring parish of Chelmsford. Although this was strictly illegal, he doesn't seem to have been troubled any further. Montaigne came to hear him preach at Chelmsford, commended him, 'and desired him, for his sake not to meddle with the discipline of the Church – the field was large enough besides. And he did promise him to do so.'[1]

The peaceable days under Montaigne were coming to a close, however. According to Peter Heylin, the King regarded Montaigne as 'a man inactive . . . one that loved his ease too well to disturb himself in the concernments of the church'. Charles resolved to reform the clergy of the diocese 'by placing over them a Bishop of such Parts and Power as they should be unable either to withstand or afraid to offend'.[2] Montaigne was appointed to the see of Durham, in effect a demotion, and he was replaced by William Laud.

By May of 1629, Laud had turned his attention to Hooker, whose suspension was mooted. Hooker must have realised that the new regime was not going to continue the qualified tolerance of Montaigne and although Samuel Collins had attempted to win him for conformity, all Hooker asked was that he should not be brought into the Court of High

---

[1] GLRO DL/C 624 f. 209; GL 9537/13 f. 10; A. Clark, 'Dr Plume's Pocket Book', *ER* 14 (1905) p. 67.
[2] Peter Heylin, *Cyprianus Anglicus* (1671) pp. 165, 169.

Commission and be allowed to leave the diocese untroubled.[3] The response of Arthur Duck, Laud's chancellor, to the compromise proposed by Collins does not survive, although Hooker was called into the High Commission. However, Collins was still sufficiently optimistic about the possibilities of a compromise that he rode to Chelmsford on Monday, 29 May 1629, to sound Hooker out. However, he found that Hooker had left for a visit to his native county of Leicestershire, and that he didn't intend to return to Essex before his court appearance on the first day of the following term.[4] Hooker still had family in the area, although his friend Francis Higginson had set sail for New England in April. He may well have visited another friend, Arthur Hildersham, the veteran radical of Ashby-de-la-Zouch.[5] From Leicestershire, he travelled to London and made his first and, it seems, inconclusive appearance before the court. By July he had returned to Chelmsford, still, it seems, free from suspension. Towards the end of that month he was met at Chelmsford by Roger Williams, at the time chaplain to Sir William Masham. Together they rode to Boston and with John Cotton travelled on to Sempringham, where, with John Winthrop, Emmanuel Downing and others, they conferred at the home of Theophilus Clinton, the Earl of Lincoln, on 25 July 1629, discussing the settlement, finance and the government of the proposed Massachusetts Bay colony, and the task of converting the native Americans. As they rode north, Cotton, Hooker and Williams, to be associated with the genesis of three colonies, Massachusetts, Connecticut and Rhode Island respectively, discussed on horseback the problem of separation and the Book of Common Prayer. Hooker and Cotton were united in opposing the younger radical's complete rejection of the liturgy, holding that it was lawful to use selected passages in divine service.[6] The return journey from Sempringham was the last Hooker and Cotton were to see of each other for nearly four years.

Upon his return to Chelmsford, Hooker took up his tasks of preaching, instruction and conference once more, to the extreme annoyance of John Browning, rector of Rawreth, a parish some nine miles south of Chelmsford.

---

[3] SP 16/152/113.
[4] SP 16/154/567. This was probably 6 July: R. G. Usher, *The Rise and Fall of the High Commission* (Oxford, 1913) p. 259.
[5] The possibility of a meeting between Hooker and Hildersham is given additional force by an aside in his preface to Ames' *Fresh Suit* regarding recent controversies in Leicester, and his possession of notes written by Hildersham, condemning the work of John Burgess, the author confuted by Ames. See Hooker's preface in G. H. Williams, N. Pettit, W. Herget and S. Bush, Jr (eds.), *Thomas Hooker: Writings in England and Holland, 1625–1633, Harvard Theological Studies* 28 (1975) pp. 334, 357–9.
[6] S. L. Caldwell (ed.), *Complete Writings of Roger Williams* (New York, 1963) vol. IV p. 65; G. H. Williams, 'Life of Thomas Hooker', in G. H. Williams *et al.*, *Writings*, pp. 17–18.

Browning, a former chaplain of Lancelot Andrewes and a man wholly in accord with Laudian principles, wrote to Laud on 3 November to offer his help in bringing Hooker to book. Browning alerted Laud to Hooker's troubles when he had been in the diocese of Winchester, and wondered if Hooker might prove to be exercising his ministry unlawfully, as he would have done if Andrewes had excommunicated him.

It may be thought (I confess) strange [he wrote], that now & not before, I have addressed my selfe in this kind to your Lordshipp. The reason may be this, amongst others; because I expected that the party being called in Question (as I have heard) before the High Commission, might without our subsidiary helpe & aide, be otherwise reduced to order, or punished for disorder: but hearing at last no farther of any such preceedings; I have adventured as you see.

He offered the assistance of his friends, and his own service, in the matter,[7] and Laud seems to have accepted his offer, for Browning set about organising a petition to the bishop from 'the conformable part' of the clergy of Essex, calling for a more rigorous enforcement of ceremonial conformity. The petition must have come to the attention of the godly ministers, as a rival petition was quickly circulated among them and presented in advance of that in favour of conformity. Although Browning's petition did not mention Hooker by name, the intention was plain and the response made the issue still more clear:

Whereas we have heard that your honour hath been informed against Mr Thomas Hooker, preacher at Chelmsford, that the conformable ministers of these parts desire his removal from the place, we whose names are hereunder written, being ministers in the partes adjoining all beneficed men, and obedient to His Majesties ecclesiastical laws, doe humbly give your Lordship to understand that we all esteeme and knowe the said Mr Thomas Hooker to be for doctryne, orthodox, and life and conversation honest, and for his disposition peaceable, no wayes turbulent or factious, and so not doubting but he will contynue that good course, commending him and his lawfull suite to your Lordships honourable favor, and entreating the continuance of his libertye and paines there, we humbly take our leave.[8]

The signatories do not represent, as Nicholas Tyacke suggests, a geographical division of religious loyalties in the county: the Warwick powerbase of Rochford hundred is almost entirely unrepresented in the godly petition, despite the presence of many ministers who we can confidently suggest

[7] SP 16/151/12. For Hooker's earlier troubles, see above, pp. 10–11.
[8] SP 16/152/4; 151/45. Both petitions and the signatories are printed in T. W. Davids, *Annals of Evangelical Nonconformity in the County of Essex* (London, 1863) pp. 153–61, with some corrections noted in H. Smith, *The Ecclesiastical History of Essex under the Long Parliament and Commonwealth* (Colchester, 1933) pp. 36–7.

would be sympathetic,[9] and the fact that only beneficed ministers were asked to sign, and the consequent omission of stipendiary lecturers, clearly a tactical decision, devalues the petition in this respect. Rather, the petition reflects the location of Hooker's closest friends: the signatories appear in significant clusters, one in the south-west of the county, close to Nathaniel Ward at Stondon Massey and Jeremiah Dyke at Epping, another around Chelmsford and Little Baddow, a third in north-central Essex, around Felsted, Finchingfield and Wethersfield, and a couple of signatories at the east end of the Stour valley, around Dedham. It may be indicative of the sociability of these clerics that a petition of forty-nine beneficed ministers could be raised at such short notice. The document was in Laud's hands by 10 November 1629, a full week before Browning's petition. However, it comes as no surprise to discover that Laud responded more positively to the second petition: whatever other virtues Hooker's supporters ascribed to him, he could not be described as 'conformable'. This was the crucial word, and the deliberate moderation of his petitioners seems to have been insufficient even to win Hooker a little more time. On 10 December 1629, upon his refusal to subscribe at Chelmsford, Hooker was suspended from the ministry. No specific charges were brought, but he was required to place a bond of fifty pounds to guarantee his later appearance at the Court of High Commission.[10] His activities after the appearance at Chelmsford are unclear: it seems likely that Samuel Collins' fears were realised, that 'if he be suspended . . . its the resolution of his friends and himself to settle his abode in Essex, and maintenance is promised him in plentifull manner for the fruition of his private conference.'[11] His bond was placed by a tenant of the Earl of Warwick, and the protection the Earl afforded Hooker was remembered with gratitude by Hooker's friends. Thomas Hill promised that

God who is faithful, will not forget your labour and cost of love to the truly reverend man of God Mr Thomas Hooker . . . when he was persecuted by the Archi-flamen of Cant.[12]

Hooker returned to Leicestershire, pausing to preach at Great Bowden in the south-east of the county, a prospect sufficiently attractive to encourage

---

[9] N. Tyacke, *Anti-Calvinists: the Rise of English Arminianism, c. 1590–1640* (Oxford, 1987) pp. 188–92; for Rochford, W. Hunt, *The Puritan Moment: the Coming of Revolution in an English County* (London, 1983) pp. 202, 203, 269, 274; R. Cust, *The Forced Loan and English Politics, 1626–28* (Oxford, 1987) pp. 277, 288; *VCH Essex* iv, pp. 47, 181, 287; P. Morant, *History and Antiquities of Essex* (1768) vol. II pp. 75–102.
[10] GL 9531/15 f. 22v; Mather, III p. 61.   [11] SP 16/162/113.
[12] Thomas Hill, ed. dep. to William Fenner, *Wilful Impenitency* in Fenner's *Works* (1651) n.p.

people to take the trip across Northamptonshire from Wilby to hear him.[13] He took further advice among his clerical friends and came to the conclusion that there was no profit to be had in attending the court, and the forfeited bond was paid by friends around Chelmsford. In all likelihood, these friends were members of the voluntary community to which Hooker ministered in Little Baddow and the surrounding parishes. As John Eliot recalled:

I have known before I came to N. E. in the B[ishop]s times, a company of Christians who held frequent communion together, used the censure of admonition, yea and of excommunication, with much presence of Christ, only they had not officers, nor the sacraments; and, notwithstanding their liberty together, they held publicke parochial communion so far as avoided offence, and interested themselves in all good meanes for the publicke good of the parish where they lived.[14]

Hooker seems to have been unsettled, but as yet unresolved as to where his future lay. On 2 October 1630, he was deprived, but he responded unfavourably when John Humfrey, Emmanuel Downing and others gave him a call to New England in early December.[15] Isaac Johnson and his associates in London were unsure how to proceed, whether to visit him or to write again, and it was, as yet, unclear whether Hooker would stay in England and devote himself to writing, or leave the country in order to exercise his ministry.[16] However, he responded more enthusiastically when Stephen Offwood wrote on behalf of members of the English Reformed Church at Amsterdam to invite him to become co-pastor with the senior minister, John Paget. It is not possible to show why the Netherlands seemed a more attractive proposition, but we may suggest that the presence of William Ames and Hugh Peter in the Low Countries encouraged him, and that a place across the North Sea seemed to allow continued contact with friends in East Anglia in a way that a trans-Atlantic post seemed to preclude. In 1630 New England had yet to attract the leading lights of the ministry: perhaps it seemed a poor career move at this stage, although that was to change in later years. Hooker was by no means the only divine to choose the Netherlands over New England, at least initially. In any case, it

[13] NRO PDR CB61 unfol. The curate at Great Bowden was William Lenerish who was called before the ecclesiastical court with a long list of nonconformist charges, including an allegation that he had spoken against bowing or bending the knee at the name of Jesus 'saying that it was an unlawfull & superstitious thinge & not warranted by god or gods word': LRO 1D 41/4/vi/109. His successor, in 1632, was John Palmer, who had been at Emmanuel College in the early 1620s. The rector was Christ's College, Oxford: John Nichols, *The History and Antiquities of the County of Leicestershire* (1798) vol. II pt. ii p. 475. Sir John Lambe's notes made in preparation for the metropolitical visitation of 1634 noted that Great Bowden was renowned for 'many Puritans and conventicles': SP 16/535/26.

[14] Mather, III p. 61; DWL Baxter MS 59.2.274.

[15] GL 9531/15 f. 22v; *MHSC* 4th ser. 6 (1863) pp. 11–12.   [16] Ibid., p. 31.

was apparent that England in 1631 was not a place that would allow him to exercise his ministry. In April he delivered his farewell sermon, a powerful jeremiad in which he warned that God was near to departing England because worship had become so sullied: 'it is God's ordinances purely administered that brings God's presence to a people'. He sustained an audacious metaphor of God as a peddler who finds his goods out of favour:

God is packing up of his gospel, because none will buy his wares nor come to his price . . . Oh therefore my brethren, lay hold on God, and let him not go out of your coasts . . . [S]top him at the town's end, and let not thy God depart. Oh England, lay siege about him by humble and hearty closing with him . . . Suffer him not go far, suffer him not to say: 'Farewell' or rather 'Fare ill, England.'

In the tradition of the jeremiad, Hooker allows that God is not yet gone, and may yet be persuaded to stay:

If he may have his own worship, you please him wondrous well. You must dress his dishes according to his tooth; but if you put poison into his meat, if you mingle the traditions of men with God's worship, then you discontent him . . . Lay aside, therefore, all your superstitions and erroneous opinions of God and do it according to his will in his word revealed. And then you please him, indeed.[17]

Perhaps, like his divine peddler, Hooker still hoped for England's reformation, and so was not prepared to go as far as New England. If this was so, his qualified optimism cannot have been encouraged, for the pursuivants of the High Commission were dispatched to apprehend him, presumably for preaching despite his deprivation, and he took ship for the Netherlands while they were hot on his tail.[18]

Hooker arrived in the Netherlands in June 1631. He spent around twenty months there, a period if anything less settled than the previous two years in England. He had walked into a power struggle within the Amsterdam church, and although he managed to keep out of the bitterest exchanges between John Paget and the elements of his congregation who had called Hooker, he experienced, alternately, humiliation and frustration in Amsterdam. Ultimately, Paget made it impossible for him to stay, and he withdrew to act as John Forbes' assistant in his Prinsenhof church. He was still unsettled, writing to John Cotton that the 'state of these provinces, to my weake eye, seems wonderfully ticklish and miserable. For the better part, heart religion, they content themselves with very forms, tho' much

---

[17] This sermon was published as *The Danger of Desertion* (1641) and other versions. Quotes from the edition in Williams *et al.*, *Writings*, pp. 236, 246, 249. On the jeremiad form, see S. Bercovitch, *The Puritan Jeremiad* (London, 1978).

[18] Mather, III p. 61.

blemished.'[19] Between January and March 1633, he had returned to England in order to settle his family affairs and determine anew whether his future lay in New England or the Netherlands. He seems to have visited Essex briefly to discuss his plans with some of those resolved to emigrate in order to enjoy his ministry, then to have travelled to Towcester, where Samuel Stone kept him one step ahead of the pursuivants, and then down to Ockley in Surrey, to the home of Henry Whitfield. Here he met John Cotton for the first time since the ride back from Sempringham.[20]

The intervening years had been equally unsettled for John Cotton. He had been protected in his nonconformity at Boston for many years, but in the early 1630s one parishioner, alienated when the town's regulation of morals turned upon him, resolved to inform against the nonconformist practices of the corporation and was persuaded to give evidence against Cotton. In early 1632 Cotton was called before the High Commission and went into hiding while he took advice on the best course of action. Having been assured by John Dod and others that flight was permissible, he resolved to follow Hooker to the Netherlands. Travelling in disguise and under an assumed name, he made his way to the coast, but there he was met by a kinsman who persuaded him to stop in London before his departure. From there he was to go on to Henry Whitfield's house.[21]

II

At Ockley, Hooker, Stone, Whitfield and Cotton were joined by a number of other important divines from London and Cambridge. A conference had been called to persuade Hooker and Cotton of the necessity of compromise, that such prominent preachers should not be lost to the English church. The struggles of Hooker and Cotton had been far from private affairs: when Hooker's case was heard Samuel Collins reported that 'all men's heads, tongues, eyes are in London, and all the counties about London taken up with plotting, talking and expecting what will be the conclusion of Mr Hooker's business', and that the discussion 'drownes out the great question of tonnage and poundage';[22] the informant against Cotton was denounced in John Rogers' Dedham pulpit where the judgement of God

---

[19] The best account of this period is K. L. Sprunger, 'The Dutch Career of Thomas Hooker', *NEQ* 46 (1973) pp. 17–4. The letter to Cotton is preserved by Mather, III p. 62.

[20] Sprunger, pp. 19, 43–44; Mather, III pp. 62, 218.

[21] Mather, III pp. 17–20; John Norton, *Abel Being Dead yet Speaketh* (1658) pp. 20–1; L. Ziff, *The Career of John Cotton: Puritanism and the American Experience* (Princeton, N.J., 1962) pp. 65, 69–70; D. D. Hall, *The Faithful Shepherd: a History of the New England Ministry in the Seventeenth Century* (New York, 1972) pp. 75–6.

[22] SP 16/144/567.

was called down upon him;[23] William Speed reported from Chichester that Hooker was attacked;[24] Richard Everard wrote to his mother-in-law, Joan Barrington, that 'we heare that Mr Hooker's case will goe very hard against him, the byshoppe is so sett against him':[25] and in Herefordshire, prayers were offered up for both Hooker and Cotton from February 1633.[26] Across the country preachers, aware of the painful ministry of the two men by acquaintance or reputation, contemplated their cases, and the result was the clandestine conference at Henry Whitfield's house. Here issues which were becoming unavoidable were weighed and discussed among the most prominent godly clergymen: Whitfield was a conformist and he was joined by Thomas Goodwin, Philip Nye, John Davenport, William Twisse and others to press the case for conformity.[27] There were few occasions as dramatic as the Ockley conference, but the issues debated there were to be forced into the attention of many more ministers in the years that followed. Indeed, Philip Nye kept a manuscript account of the conference, which he circulated, very cautiously, among sympathetic clergy. William Speed had access to it, but Nye would not even discuss it with Samuel Hartlib. Robert Dawlman, a London printer who had published works by Hooker, Thomas Shepard, Thomas Goodwin, Jeremiah Burroughes and Richard Sibbes, felt that the manuscript should be published, but Nye refused. The London minister, Thomas Edwards, had seen the manuscript, claiming to know 'something of the story of Master Goodwins first comming to fall of[f]

---

[23] Mather, III p. 19. The informant, naturally, died of the plague shortly afterward, Norton, *Abel Being Dead*, p. 20. Such denunciations seem to have been a habit of Rogers': he was reported to have expressed his amazement that the godly minister Thomas Wilson had been able to continue preaching in Canterbury, '*so neere the Throne of the Beast*': Richard Culmer, *Cathedrall Newes from Canterbury* (1644) p. 12.

[24] SU Hartlib MS 46/6/28b.   [25] BL Egerton MS 2645 f. 75.

[26] BL Add MS 70062 unfoliated, heads of prayer for fasts dated 22 February and 12 April 1633. Prayers were also offered for the 'suppression of popery & Arminianism', 'for a happy meeting in Parliament', for the 'Children of Affliction' and 'the Case of the Feffeese'.

[27] The main sources for the conference are Norton, *Abel Being Dead*, pp. 20–1, 32–3; John Cotton, *The Way of the Congregational Churches Cleared* (1648) pt. I p. 24; Mather, III pp. 20, 218; SU Hartlib MS 29/2/45b–46a. These sources establish the presence of Cotton, Davenport, Nye, Goodwin, Whitfield and Twisse. Hooker is not mentioned by Mather, which may in part be due to his familial pride in his maternal grandfather, who certainly gets star billing in Mather's account, but also because Mather's chief sources for Hooker's life, his widow and John Eliot, were not with him at this stage. His presence can be suggested by more than the chronological possibility: he was with Cotton and Stone immediately after, when they sailed for New England; Mather mentions that Whitfield housed Hooker during this time and left a glowing tribute to his learning and skill in debate, and John Davenport was shown the answers Hooker composed in reply to John Paget's twenty propositions, before he (Davenport) resigned his living at St Stephen's, Coleman Street, in December 1633. This was, I suggest, at the Ockley conference or around this time: Mather, III pp. 64, 218; I. M. Calder (ed.), *Letters of John Davenport* (New Haven, Conn., 1937) p. 54; John Davenport, *An Apologeticall Reply to a Booke Called an Answer to the Unjust Complaint of W. B.* (Rotterdam, 1636) p. 112.

from the ceremonies, having seen and perused the Arguments that past between him and Master Cotton, and some others'.[28]

Nye's manuscript does not seem to have survived, but it is possible to reconstruct some of the debate. The conformists urged 'all their Arguments for Conformity together with Mr Byfield's, Mr Whately's and Mr Sprints'.[29] We may not be able to reproduce the whole debate, but we have access to the published arguments of the three ministers named by Mather. The argument forwarded by Whately, the 'roaring boy of Banbury', seems to have been along the lines that questions of ceremonial conformity were strictly subordinate to the imperatives of spirited preaching, and that preoccupation with such issues was evidence of a proud spirit in need of greater mortification:

There be some, that if they can outstrip the common sort a little, and keepe a course of religious exercises in their families, and flocke to good Sermons, and then be hot and sharpe against Bishops and Ceremonies, and crie out against the faults of the times, and blame Magistrates and Ministers, and every mans faults, with a great storm of words, that in the Campe of Christians, whereas they are not able to show any sinfull lust and affection mortified in them.[30]

Whately attributed such 'vaine disputations of men of corrupt minds' above all to pride:

Such be called mad, doating, or busie questionists, or disputors, as give themselves to contend about every matter, (even of small moment, as of the Moone shining in the water, or wearing of a comely Surples) and through Pride so to trouble themselves. As many doo about the orders of our Church, established neither for superstition nor Idolatry . . . but to keepe comlinesse, uniformitie, and order in the Church: this satisfieth my conscience, and what should I seeke to alter the decree of a whole Parliament.

In summary, 'A foule puddle the more it is stirred, the more it stinketh.'[31] For Whately, too much time was spent on 'indifferent things, by troubling a mans minde with unnecessarie scruples, making him to shunne them as

---

[28] SU Hartlib MS 29/2/46a; 46/6/15b; 29/2/23a; H. R. Plomer, *A Dictionary of Booksellers and Printers who Were at Work in England, Scotland and Ireland from 1641 to 1667* (London, 1907) s.v. 'Dawlman'; he also published works of Robert Sanderson, Henry Burton, Peter Sterry and Jeremiah Dyke, and was the printer chosen for the *Apologeticall Narration*. For Edwards, Thomas Edwards, *Antapologia: or, a Full Answer to the Apologeticall Narration of Mr Goodwin, etc.* (1644) p. 17.

[29] Mather, III p. 20.

[30] William Whately, *Mortification, A Sermon* (1623) pp. 169–70; on Whately, see W. Haller, *The Rise of Puritanism* (Columbia, S.C., 1938) pp. 92, 103; P. Collinson, *The Birthpangs of Protestant England* (London, 1988) pp. 68–9, 71–3; *DNB* and J. B. Blackenfield, 'Puritans in the Provinces: Banbury, Oxfordshire, 1554–1660', PhD Yale University (1985) *passim*, and esp. pp. 260–86, 453–83.

[31] Whately, *A Sermon on Pride* (1602) pp. 17–18, 20. Elsewhere in this sermon he berates 'these schismatickes of Martins crew', p. 47, referring to Martin Marprelate.

sinnes. This is the fault of many a sanctified but over tender conscience.'[32] In the end, there was simply no point to such arguments. He advised godly people to avoid 'al iangling and frivolous disputes about unnecessary quirkes and quiddities, and matters of ceremony, and disputable points in things externall (wherewith some doe onely take up the time and trouble themselves, and the Church, without edification)'.[33] We will see something of this position in the experience of John Rogers.

It is clear how it must have been answered by Hooker and Cotton. Hooker's most recent work had been to write a preface for William Ames' *A Fresh Suit against Human Ceremonies in Gods Worship*; while Ames rebutted the arguments of his father-in-law, John Burgess, Hooker surveyed the arguments that the godly raised for conformity. To those who argue, with Whately, that energy is wasted on ceremonial controversies, Hooker asked:

But alas, these men, have they taken the arguments into serious consideration? Have they labored to search and examine the strength of them? Have they propounded them to such who are held most able and judicious of the other opinion, who do not find themselves yet persuaded? Alas, here is deep silence! Where is that ancient rule: 'Audi alteran partem' [Listen to the other side]? Where is that charge of the Apostle, 1 Th[ess] 5:21: 'Try all things.'[34]

Refutation of Whately's position did not necessarily make for principled nonconformity, but merely re-opened the debate. The conformists were not yet convinced, and would propound the arguments of Nicholas Byfield, formerly the preacher at nearby Isleworth. He may well have been a friend of Henry Whitfield; he was certainly a figure, like Whately, whose arguments would carry some force among the godly. He was no fawner upon bishops: he wrote, with an outrageous comparison, that 'we may see . . . that Christ and true Christians may be persecuted and monstrously abused in Spirituall Courts as well as Temporall. Christ never had worser enemies, nor more corrupt or malicious than Churchmen. In his owne person none hated him more deadly than the Priests and great Spirituall

---

[32] Whately, *A Pithie, Short and Methodicall Opening of the Ten Commandments* (1622) p. 32. In the light of these positions it is perhaps surprising to find Whately presented in the court of the Bishop's Peculiar of Banbury in 1607 for omitting prayers for the bishops, for not reading the Book of Common Prayer and neglecting baptism, and also for administering the sacrament to parishioners who refused to kneel and for preaching against the ceremonies. In March 1613, four parishioners were presented for refusing to kneel, and Whately and his sidesmen (though not his churchwardens) refused to set their names to the presentment, S. A. Peyton (ed.), *Churchwardens' Presentments in the Oxfordshire Peculiars of Dorchester, Thame and Banbury*, Oxfordshire Record Society Publications 10 (1928) pp. 202, 209.

[33] Whately, *The New Birth, or, a Treatise of Regeneration* (1618) p. 172.

[34] Williams *et al.*, *Writings*, pp. 333–4.

Counsellors of the State Ecclesiasticke.'[35] Neither was he unduly attached to the ceremonies. In his discussion of Colossians 2. 16–17, he argued:

These words may be referred either to Gods children, or to false teachers. In the first sense, it is thus: 'Let none condemne you,' that is, doe not show such love to these ceremonies hereafter, that thereby you incurre iustly the blame and censure of Gods children. And if they bee referred to false teachers, then it is thus: let no man whatsoever persuade you that are condemned, or iudged of God for omitting the observation of the Ceremonies; care not for their censures, never trouble your conscience above it.[36]

Despite this low opinion of the machinery and ceremonies of the church as established, Byfield took his stand for conformity. Part of his argument overlaps with Whately's. In company, the godly are to 'avoide vain ianglings and contradictions of words, such as are, 1. Doubtful disputations about Ceremonies, and things indifferent, which may entangle the weak, and keep them from more necessary cases and knowledge.'[37] His priorities mirrored those of Whately:

some there be that preach of Christ, but it is chiefly of his Crown and Scepter: they are never so kindled, till they get into questions of Church-Government: they teach their hearers the doctrine of reforming of churches, when they had more need to teach them how to reforme themselves, and their households.

He disapproved of 'a contentious zeale such as theirs that make needlesse rents in the church'.[38] The ceremonies 'are but shadowes of that substance which now we have, and therefore it is a foolish thing to strive about the shadow when we have the substance'.[39] These resemble the positions advanced by John Davenport in the mid-1620s, when he wrote to Alexander Leighton in a similar attempt to win a troubled nonconformist around: 'For is it not worke enough to preach unles we dispute also? or, if we must dispute, were it not better to unite our forces against those who oppose us in Fundem[en]talls than to be divided amongst ourselves about Ceremonialls? Who can, without sorrowe, and feare observe how Atheisme, Libertinisme, papisme and Arminianisme, both at home, and abroad have stolen in, and taken possession of the house, whilest we are at strife about the hangings and paintings of it?'[40] Similarly, Byfield offers advice for men in the position of Hooker and Cotton, which may have been pressed at the conference. Follow Christ's example, he suggests: when

[35] Nicholas Byfield, *The Rule of Faith* (1626) p. 358.
[36] Nicholas Byfield, *An Exposition upon the Epistle to the Colossians* (1627) p. 75.
[37] Nicholas Byfield, *The Marrow of the Oracles of God* (7th edn, 1630) p. 56.
[38] Nicholas Byfield, *Exposition*, pp. 174, 194.   [39] Ibid., p. 75.
[40] Calder (ed.), *Letters of Davenport*, pp. 23–4; cf. BodL Tanner 75 f. 132 where William Bedell takes the same position in a discussion with Samuel Ward in the demands for subscription after the Hampton Court Conference.

called before the court, the officers are convinced that his doctrine is subversive, but when 'he answers about his doctrine, it is in generall and sparingly, to teach us wisdom in evill times, and to learn how to bridle our tongues, when we speake before men in authority, especially if they are enimies to religion'.[41]

However, he offers a more pressing argument for conformity. As the ceremonies were 'things indifferent', *adiaphora*, they can justly be ordered by the state, and the godly are bound to observe them.

Lastly, in that is said, Christ was buried after the manner of the Jewes burying, it shews plainly, that respect is to be had to the customes of any country or place where we live, and that Gods servants have beene careful to observe them, and not willing to give offence by crossing such customes. This is true of all customes that are not sinfull, and against the word of God; though they be such usages as are not commanded in Scripture: for this manner of buriall was no where commanded in Gods word, and yet the custome prevailes, and good men observe it.[42]

Hooker considered this position, which he calls the 'statist', to be among the most despicable: 'your statist is most gross to whom his religion is as his coin. All that goes for current gospel with him that is stamped with the authority and allowance of the state. He is hovering betwixt several religions that he may take any for his turn, waits and eyes to see which side is like to prosper, that so he may be of the safest side.'[43] Beyond this, Hooker emphasised the limitations upon the church's authority, which, it may be noted, appear in a crucial qualification of Byfield's argument:

Not that I detract any due respect and esteem which each man should have both in opinion and affection of the true Church of Christ. I know she is the spouse of Christ; yet but the spouse. It is enough that she is next to her head, the Lord Jesus. She must not usurp to be head; her power is subordinate, not supreme. Mt.28:20; *ministerium*, not *imperium*.[44]

The issue had turned on to the authority of the church: as Cotton might testify, this was one of the factors that persuaded him to neglect the ceremonies many years earlier. His first reason was a response to the preface of the Book of Common Prayer, which enjoined the ceremonies as 'neither dumb nor dark, but apt to stir up the dull minde of man to the remembrance of his duty to God, by some notable and speciall signification, whereby he may be edified'. In this, Cotton was reproducing an argument that had been voiced by fellow ministers of the diocese of Lincoln at the beginning of the century. In the new context, however, Cotton had more to add:

---

[41] Byfield, *Rule of Faith*, pp. 360–1.

[42] Ibid., p. 441. The same argument appears as a lesser refrain in Whately, *Ten Commandments*, pp. 55–6, but it is a major theme in Byfield's defence.

[43] Williams *et al.*, *Writings*, p. 325.   [44] Ibid., p. 327.

The second was the limitation of Church-power (even of the highest Apostolicall Commission) to the observation of the Commandements of Christ, *Matth. 28. 20.* which made it appear to me utterly unlawfull, for any Church-power to enjoyn the observation of indifferent Ceremonies which Christ had not commanded. And all the Ceremonies were alike destitute of the commandement of Christ, though they had been indifferent otherwise, which indeed others have pleaded they were not.[45]

According to Mather, Cotton pressed the case of the second commandment, and, it seems, persuaded the conformist divines that the ceremonies were not matters indifferent, but were idolatrous. As Hooker had pressed in his farewell sermon: 'To bow at the name of Jesus [Phil.2.10] is not meant at the word *Jesus*; for to give him the bow is to commit syllabical idolatry.'[46]

If Hooker and Cotton were successful in convincing the company of the idolatrous nature of the ceremonies, they still had a further case to answer. John Sprint, a former nonconformist, presented the case for conformity with the assumption that he was to persuade divines 'to practice inconvenient, scandalous and hurtful ceremonies'. His position was not that the ceremonies were matters of no importance, or that they were lawfully imposed by the church, but to press 'the imputation of a sinne upon the sufferers of silencing for not conforming'. His case thus related precisely to the situation of Hooker and Cotton. He argued that the practice of suffering deprivation for not conforming to the ceremonies was against the word of God:

One ground is this: where two duties doe meet, a greater and a lesse, whereof both cannot be done at the same time, the lesser dutie must yield unto the greater. . . The practice thereof (of suffering deprivation for nonconformity) causeth to neglect a greater duty for the performing of a lesse.[47]

He was suggesting that however obnoxious the ceremonies might be, it was a sin to lose the liberty of preaching in order to avoid using them. Hooker was familiar with this argument and would not allow it:

Others of this rank [clerics] plead the love of their people, the necessity of preaching, and hope of doing good, how precious mens pains are, and what need of labourers in the vineyard. And therefore conclude: if all men should sit downe in silence, as some do, the ruine of the church must needs follow. They confess, its true indeed, these popish relics, which are the bane of the churches peace, being unprofitable and needless, nay scandalous and offensive, should be removed. But

---

[45] John Cotton, *The Way of the Congregational Churches*, pt. I pp. 18–19; *An Abridgment of that Booke which the Ministers of Lincoln Diocese Delivered to his Maiestie upon the First of December Last* (1605) pp. 35–6. I am grateful to Peter Lake for drawing this earlier work to my attention.

[46] Mather, III p. 20; Williams *et al.*, p. 249; cf. SP 16/280/33: where William Dobson is accused of preaching that such action was 'to bowe to 5 l[ett]res or to a worde'.

[47] John Sprint, *Cassander Anglicanus: Shewing the Necessitie of Conformitie to the Prescribed Ceremonies of our Church, in Case of Deprivation* (1618) 'To the Reader', pp. 2, 15; cf. Joseph Bentham, *The Societie of the Saints* (1630) p. 36.

when they weigh that heavy charge: 'Woe if I preach not the gospel [I Cor.9.16],' they are then willing to bear all than to deprive the Church of the benefit, and the souls of Gods people of the profit and comfort, of their ministry!

Hooker sees this as a cover for naked self-interest, and ridicules the notion that God would need such tainted service, that He 'could not bring his servants to his own haven without the devils boat', and observes that the gospel profited more from the martyrdoms of Queen Mary's reign than from all the preaching of the reign of King Edward.[48]

Sprint's argument depended upon a particular view of the ceremonies which was impressed upon him by his Archdeacon, Samuel Burton. He had been asked, 'whether I would rather suffer death, than use them [the ceremonies] in a church professing the foundation, and urging them as things indifferent, not pressing them, as binding conscience in themselves, or as needful for salvation?' He had come to the conclusion that as the ceremonies were not to be held as the *sine qua non* of the ministry, as they might be altered in the future, and as they were not pressed upon those with scruples, they might be used with a clear conscience.[49] This was the view of a man living under the moderate regime of Archbishop Abbot; clearly, in Hooker's view, this was no longer the case:

Consider beside[s] how many poor ministers are under pressure, some fled, some imprisoned, many suspended, themselves and their families undone. Why, will you not suffer them to lie in the dust, but will you trample upon them even unto death? . . . Is not the fury of the bishops yet fierce enough, their rage not sharp enough, but you must set them on and strengthen their hands to strike harder? Lastly, is not cringing at altars, bowing at the name of Jesus, like to be brought in and practiced with great forwardness . . . ? Thus is the foundation of superstition laid, the gospel stopped, and an open way made for Popery; and you are the persuader, the encourager, yea, defender of all these. How will you answer this at the Great Day?[50]

For Hooker and Cotton and now, as they were persuaded of the justice of the nonconformist case, for Goodwin, Davenport, Nye and Whitfield, the tenor of the times had invalidated Sprint's argument: they believed the ceremonies to be pressed unduly upon those with scruples regarding their lawfulness, and could no longer be used with a clear conscience.

III

After the conference, Hooker and Cotton resumed their disguise, rode to the Downs with Samuel Stone and, in July 1633, they boarded the *Griffen*. As the ship was to take on provisions from Yarmouth in the Isle of Wight

---

[48] Williams *et al.*, *Writings*, pp. 329–30.
[49] Sprint, *Cassander Anglicanus*, 'To the Reader', p. 18 and *passim*.
[50] Williams *et al.*, pp. 372–3.

where pursuivants were in waiting, the two older ministers remained incognito until they were well out at sea. Once they were safe all three ministers took on a daily round of worship, with Cotton preaching in the morning, Hooker in the afternoon and Stone in the evening. This was the first opportunity Hooker had enjoyed to exercise his ministry on a regular basis since late 1629.[51]

For those who remained, the conference changed their lives. Stephen Goffe reported that the conference 'hath convinced Mr Damport & Mr Nye two of the great preachers of the city that kneeling at the sacrament etc is plaine idolatry, & yt for that reason Mr Damport hath absented himself every sacramental day wch is once a month since Christmas'.[52] Philip Nye abandoned his lectureship at St Michael's Cornhill in London and eventually took ship for Arnhem; Thomas Goodwin resigned his living at Trinity College in Cambridge to his friend Richard Sibbes (Hartlib noted that he 'seemes to stagger bec[ause] of the ceremonies') and 'desires alwaies to live in the Colledge where he meanes now et then to preach et to perfect a book in Pr[actical] Divin[ity]'. This he did until he joined Nye late in the decade.[53] Henry Whitfield abandoned his conformist practices. He kept his living for some time, enlisting the help of John Stoughton to hire a curate to read prayers and assist in the administration of the Lord's Supper, and thus hoping to elude the censures of the ecclesiastical courts. In 1639 he too left England and founded Guildford, Massachusetts.[54] For John Davenport the changed circumstances are a little better documented. We have seen how he remonstrated with Alexander Leighton for raising the disputed ceremonies. He had, he claimed, won his father and uncle for the cause of conformity, and convinced George Montaigne that he was conformable when he was elected vicar of St Stephen's Coleman Street in London.[55] In 1631 he had endured a much sterner test when his discontented curate, Timothy Hood, passed information to Bishop Laud. Davenport defended himself and announced his conscience settled on the surplice, the liturgy and on receiving the sacrament kneeling. Laud was satisfied that he had 'settled his judgement' and was accordingly surprised, upon returning from Scotland in July 1633, to discover that Davenport had been convinced of the contrary view, and was reported to have fled to Amsterdam. As Davenport told Lady de Vere: 'The trueth is, I have not forsaken my ministry, nor resigned up my place, much less separated from the church, but am onely

---

[51] Mather, III pp. 20, 62.   [52] BL Add MS 6394 f. 144.

[53] R. Zaller and R. L. Greaves (eds.), *Biographical Dictionary of British Radicals in the Seventeenth Century* (Brighton, 1982–4) s.v. 'Nye, Philip'; SU Hartlib MS 29/2/2b, 6a, 55b; 'The Life of Dr Thomas Goodwin', in Goodwin's *Works* (1704) vol. V, xvii–xviii.

[54] SP 16/284/6; Mather, III p. 218.

[55] Calder (ed.), *Davenport Letters*, pp. 14–23; SP 14/173/43; 14/173/58.

absent a while to wayte upon God, upon the settling and quieting of things, for light to discerne my way, being willing to lye and dye in prison, if the course may be advantaged by it, but choosing the rather to preserve the liberty of my person and ministry for the service of the church elsewhere if all dores are shutt against mee here.' He went on to explain:

> The onely cause of my present sufferings is the alteration of my judgem[en]t in matters of conformity to the ceremonies established whereby I cannot practice them as formerly I have done. Wherein I doe not censure those that doe conform (nay I account many of them faithfull, and worthy instrum[en]ts of Gods glory, and, I know that I did conforme with as much inward peace, as now I doe forbeare, in both my uprightnes was the same, but my light different.)[56]

His fresh light took him to Amsterdam in November 1633, for a space of three or four months, or so he intended. While he was absent, Laud, now Archbishop, called him into the High Commission, effectively blocking his retreat. Davenport's time in Holland was no more rewarding than Hooker's. He returned to England in April 1636, gathered a company from his former parish, and, after delays, sailed for New England.[57] His long career as patriarch of New Haven has been described elsewhere:[58] here we may perhaps note that the end result of his new light took him to a stricter practice in political and religious rights than Hooker's neighbour colony, forcing Davenport to oppose union with Connecticut in the early 1660s. It might be suggested that men like Davenport had further to fall than Hooker, and they landed harder, and, perhaps, meaner.

---

[56] Calder (ed.), *Davenport Letters*, pp. 33–8; H. Trevor-Roper, *Archbishop Laud* (London, 1965) p. 142; Laud, *Works*, vol. V pp. 318–19.
[57] Calder (ed.), *Davenport Letters*, pp. 38–40; John Davenport, *An Apologeticall Reply*, esp. pp. 107–11.
[58] I. M. Calder, *The New Haven Colony* (Hamden, Conn., 1970).

⫷ 8 ⫸

Trajectories of response to Laudianism

I

From the experience of the Ockley conference we can learn, in particular, four important lessons. The first is the existence of a constituency among those recognising themselves, and recognised, as ministers of the godly sort, which might perceive the controverted ceremonies as unprofitable and not tending to edification, and even as an evil to be suffered rather than merely *adiaphorous*. These ministers might administer the sacrament to those who knelt, might use the sign of the cross in baptism and wear the surplice, holding them to be enjoined by lawful authority, holding controversy to be unprofitable or seeing them as a necessary price to be paid for the liberty to preach, which, as we saw in earlier chapters, was at the centre of their vocation. It would be an error to call such ministers 'conformist', although they might write to, or confer with, their brethren to persuade them to use the ceremonies or to leave the controversies over them. It is perhaps more accurate to call such ministers 'conformable', that is, capable of conforming, without being committed to a defence of the ceremonies in any positive sense.[1]

Secondly, we can see that members of this constituency were coming under pressure. Goodwin, Nye, Davenport and Whitfield changed their practice after the Ockley conference, a decision directly contrary to the best hopes of a settled life and the peaceful exercise of their vocation. It is possible to suggest that they changed their practice without changing their judgement: the arguments of those I would like to call 'conformable', of Whately, Byfield and especially Sprint, were conditional. Whately believed that for men to introduce new ceremonies, not for the enhancement of worship, 'but alone for solemnitie and orders sake' was to abuse

---

[1] Bishop Harsnett, admittedly not the most objective analyst, coined the phrase 'conformable Puritans' for those who subscribed without considering the controverted ceremonies to be lawful: K. Fincham, 'Episcopal Government, 1603–1640,' in K. Fincham (ed.), *The Early Stuart Church, 1603–1642* (London, 1993) p. 77.

167

worship.[2] Byfield warned his readers not to 'shew such love to these Ceremonies hereafter, that thereby you incurre iustly the blame and censure of Gods children' and advised adherence to the custom established, provided that the customs were not sinful or against the word of God.[3] Sprint allowed that to suffer deprivation was a sin only as long as the ceremonies were not pressed too hard on those with scruples.[4] If these conditions were seen to be breached, the adherence of the conformable ministers was no longer to be expected. It will be a major task of what follows to see how and why and where this perception developed and what the consequences were.

Thirdly, we should avoid the academic temptation of seeing these debates out of context. Context is, in fact, crucial to the persuasive powers of godly ministers. The deprivation of ministers like Hooker, Cotton and others critically changed the context. Arguments in favour of conformity were, while they were in office, practical concerns for the godly minister. In this situation, casuistical positions encouraging compromise must have seemed fairly persuasive. Once one had suffered the attentions of the ecclesiastical courts and the High Commission and lost one's living, the debate became, to a degree, academic. The principled, aggressive position of a resolution of no compromise regarding ungodly ceremonies became, in a sense, of less cost. In addition, the deprivation created a number of authoritative martyrs with voices, considerably more persuasive than they had been before their struggles with the persecutory hierarchy. This was a fear raised among Sprint's arguments for conformity.[5] Perhaps this helps to explain why Hooker and Cotton managed to persuade their brethren that times had changed.[6]

Fourthly, we have encountered two trajectories of response to these dangerous times, one of which has loomed large in recent discussions, one of which has been a little neglected. The first is the godly minister driven into nonconformity, or even hostility to the ecclesiastical authorities by the Laudian reaction. Such men were, we have been told, among the settled ministry, anti-formalist but firmly within the establishment. It may be that

---

[2] William Whately, *A Pithie, Short and Methodicall Opening of the Ten Commandments* (1622) p. 61.

[3] Nicholas Byfield, *An Exposition upon the Epistle to the Colossians* (1627) p. 75; Byfield, *The Rule of Faith* (1626) p. 441.

[4] John Sprint, *Cassander Anglicanus: Shewing the Necessitie of Conformitie to the Prescribed Ceremonies of our Church, in Case of Deprivation* (1618) 'To the Reader'. In 1634 an unnamed minister told Samuel Hartlib, 'Of Cerem[onies] they are not so profitable. 2. They are not to be opposed by privat men. Nor ought any to separate for them. if they be urged they loose their Nature et wee can not yeeld. Bowing etc at the name etc if it be done with kn[owledge] etc. Not unlawful as a memorial.' SU Hartlib MS 29/2/3b.

[5] Sprint, *Cassander*, p. 65.

[6] My thoughts were encouraged in this direction by Frank Bremer.

it is not accurate to try to label such men 'Puritan' at all: their Puritanism was created by the changed polemical conditions of the 1630s.[7] The second trajectory is that followed by men like Hooker and Cotton, staunch and convinced nonconformists of the old school, who had come to their practice under the influence of men of the generation of Arthur Hildersham and John Dod. When the ceremonies were pressed the decision to accept deprivation or, if possible, to leave their lectures or benefices without being deprived, was no less painful, but was the necessary extension of their established practice. We can see other examples of both trajectories among the godly ministers of the East Anglian network, and learn that there were other responses.

We find something of the first pattern in the experience of Thomas Shepard. Having begun to preach at Earls Colne around June 1627, he quickly aroused the hostility of the neighbouring ministers and came under the watchful eye of the ecclesiastical authorities.

> . . . Satan began to rage, and the commissaries, registers, and others began to pursue me and to threaten me, as thinking I was a Nonconformable man (when for the most of that time I was not resolved either way, but was dark in those things.)[8]

No offence could be proved against him and no charges were brought, but he was marked out for Laud's attention when he succeeded Montaigne in July 1628. On his first visitation he required Shepard to give a certificate of his conformity. Shepard hesitated, but complied on 12 December 1628.[9] However, he was not clear of suspicion: he was further pressed to give evidence of his conformity in June of the following year; in August, his licence was inspected in the Archdeacon's court; in May 1630, he was asked 'to shew by what authoritie he exerciseth a lecture', and when Laud prepared to conduct his second visitation in person Shepard was among the ministers noted as 'not conformable in opinion or practice'.[10] The chron-

---

[7] See, for instance, P. Collinson, *The Puritan Character: Polemics and Polarities in Early Seventeenth Century Culture* (Los Angeles, Calif., 1989) pp. 14–15 and *passim*; R. Ashton, *The English Civil War* (London, 1978) ch. 5; W. M. Lamont, *Marginal Prynne 1600–1669* (London, 1963) esp. chs. 1 and 2, pp. 13, 19–21; 'Puritanism as History and Historiography', *PP* 44 (1969) pp. 133–46; F. Condick, 'The Life and Works of Dr John Bastwick 1595–1654', University of London PhD (1983) esp. chs. 1 and 2; P. Collinson, *English Puritanism* (London, 1983) pp. 32–9. To some extent, this is to conflate two models: those credal Calvinists labelled 'Puritan' in Laudian polemic and those conforming godly ministers driven from their conformity by Laudian policy.

[8] M. McGiffert (ed.), *God's Plot: the Paradoxes of Puritan Piety Being the Autobiography and Journal of Thomas Shepard* (Amherst, Mass., 1972) p. 48.

[9] GL 9537/13 f. 28r; GLRO DL/C 624 f. 384.

[10] GLRO DL/C 322 f. 45; ERO D/ACA 47 ff. 11v, 19r, 92v; SP 16/175/104, dated 25 November 1630. In July 1629, Shepard was presented (erroneously) for preaching without a licence and at the court hearing, a parishioner, William Adams, was presented 'for using certaine speeches tending to the contempt of ecclesiastical jurisdiction', apparently in

ology in his autobiography is somewhat muddled,[11] and he fails to mention that he delivered certificates of conformity, which may not be surprising, as the account was written in New England for his son's benefit, but his behaviour is consistent with his statement that he was not yet settled on the ceremonies. This was still the case when Laud followed up his information on 16 December, 1630. Shepard brought certain expectations to his interview: he was surprised when Laud did not ask whether he would subscribe or whether he was in any way conformable. The bishop seemed to be more interested in the source of Shepard's income, taking his refusal to conform for granted:

He asked me who maintained me all this while, charging me to deal plainly with him, adding that he had been more cheated and equivocated with by some of my malignant faction than ever man was by Jesuit, at the speaking of which words he looked as though blood would have gushed out of his face and did shake as if he had been haunted with an ague fit, to my apprehension by reason of his extreme malice and secret venom.

He went on to suspend Shepard from all ministerial functions. Shepard thought he might be allowed to convert his lecture into Sunday afternoon catechising sessions, in line with the Royal Instructions of December 1629, but Laud replied: 'Spare your breath: I will have no such fellows prate in my diocese. Get you gone, and now make your complaints to whom you will!'[12]

Having been silenced, Shepard lodged with the Harlackdens in Earls Colne and applied himself to patristic studies. Over the following six to eight months, 'the Lord let me see into the evil of the English ceremonies, cross, surplice and kneeling'. At the beginning of September 1631, Laud returned and summoned him to Peldon, where he was again ordered to leave the diocese; two days later, Shepard was barracking Laud at the Dunmow demonstration and began the troubled peregrinations which brought him fresh light concerning the ceremonies and, eventually, the hierarchy of the church, and took him to New England where he landed in early October 1635.[13]

Parallels can be drawn with the experience of Nathaniel Rogers,

---

response to the court's interest in Shepard. Perhaps it was this outburst that generated the greater interest: ERO D/ACA 47 f. 11v.

[11] He mentions his first encounter with Laud as occurring shortly after the bishop's arrival, which would place it in late 1628. However, he explains that this was six months after the initial three years of the endowment of his lecture, which suggests a date around December 1630, which receives corroboration from other sources.

[12] GL 9531/15 f. 25r–v; McGiffert (ed.), *God's Plot*, pp. 48–9; Thomas Prince, *A Chronological History of New England* (Boston, Mass., 1826 edn) pp. 338–9. Prince writes, 'I have by me a manuscript of Mr Shepard's, written in his own hand, in which are these words.'

[13] McGiffert (ed.), *God's Plot*, pp. 50–64.

although the disenchantment of the melancholy and sickly son of John Rogers lacks the drama of Shepard's radicalisation. After his education at Dedham and Emmanuel College and a spell as a chaplain, possibly in the household of the Cranes in Coggeshall, where he married the wealthy clothier's daughter, he became curate to Dr John Barkham, the dean of Bocking. The appointment raised a few eyebrows, as Barkham was a great friend of William Laud, but at this time, very much his father's son, he 'applied his Thoughts only to the main Points of Repentance from dead works, and faith towards God', in which he excelled.[14] In fact, Giles Firmin recalled that Nathaniel refuted his father in his own pulpit, moderating his doctrine of faith to general applause while his father stood by.[15] After his conversion to Congregationalism, Nathaniel Rogers wrote, in 1643:

Its no small joy to think how many now look upon that truth [of church government] with patience and inquisition, that thought it a note of pride or hypocrisie to be meddling withall.[16]

In the early phase of his career, he would have been among them. He worked in peace under Dr Barkham, until mid-1631, when Thomas Hooker related his own reasons for nonconformity to the young divine. Shortly afterwards, Rogers officiated at an important funeral without the surplice. Dismayed, Dr Barkham made it plain that he could not tolerate such a stance from his curate. Rather than bring ecclesiastical discipline to bear upon Rogers, Barkham encouraged him to leave of his own volition. As Mather observes, the circumstances fell out well for Rogers: he was unlikely to have survived the 1631 visitation, but stepping into the vacant rectory at Assington, some ten miles from Dedham, he was over the diocesan border and enjoyed the liberty of his ministry for another four years.[17] Rogers arrived before the middle of September 1631, and quickly established himself among the Suffolk godly. His patron was Brampton Gurdon, an old friend of his father's, and through him moved into the circles of the Barnardiston and Winthrop families. At Assington, he shared his pastoral burden with Henry Jessey, Gurdon's chaplain and another radical influence.[18]

In this environment, watching the rule of Bishop Laud south of the Stour and the gathering storm in the diocese of Norwich, in the company of such

[14] Mather, III p. 105.

[15] Giles Firmin, *The Real Christian* (1670) 'To the Reader'.

[16] Nathaniel Rogers, *A Letter Discovering the Cause of Gods Continuing Wrath against the Nation, notwithstanding the Present Endeavours of Reformation* (1644) p. 6.

[17] Mather, III p. 106.

[18] N. Evans (ed.), *The Wills of the Archdeaconry of Sudbury 1630–1635, Suffolk Record Society* 29 (1987) p. 142 no. 335: the will of Thomas Downham, dated 13 September 1631, leaves money to Rogers to pay for renovations to his house, and to Jessey 'for his pains'. MHSC 4th ser. 6 (1863) pp. 457, 546; ibid., 5th ser. 1 (1871) pp. 84, 197.

as Jessey, Rogers came to see the church as more and more corrupt. In his report to Laud after the provincial visitation of Norwich diocese in April 1635, Nathaniel Brent wrote that 'one Mr Nathaniel Rogers, minister of Assington, is an absolute nonconformitan. I am told he hath resigned his benefice, purposing to go into New England. However, I have suspended him de facto, though if he have resigned, the suspension will be but brutum fulmen.' As Mather wrote, 'perceiving the Approaches of the Storm towards himself, did out of a particular Circumspection in his own Temper, choose rather to prevent than to receive the Censures of the Ecclesiastical Courts'. Rogers sailed for New England in June 1636.[19] As with Shepard and Davenport, once the times brought new light concerning the ceremonies, much more was opened up to question. Of the English church in the 1630s and before, from the perspective of the 1640s, he wrote,

the Lord Jesus [had] not been set up in his throne, but iniquity established therein by a Law: . . . contrary to the testimony of many able, worthy Confessors, Cartwrights, Brightmans, etc. by their pens and sufferings; prevailing against that precious blood of holy Bates and others in prisons, the impoverishing [of] families and obscuring of men of choice abilities . . . cast aside for rotten trash, the starving of many Congregations, robbed of their profitable and painefull pastors . . . the best Congregations forced to prostrate themselves to the tyranny of men over their consciences, and the most sacred parts of his worship corrupted with superstitious mixtures.

In the same work, he asked whether Parliament had done penance for allowing the former corruption of the church, and admitted,

yea so I write as one that acknowledge my selfe to have had a share in those provocations and pollutions, and want yet an heart to be meetly sensible of the wrong done to the Lord Jesus therein.[20]

Unlike Davenport, Rogers' conversion led him to despise his former conformity and, by inference, those who continued to adhere to the corruptions of human worship.

In this conclusion, he was joined by his uncle, Daniel Rogers. The lecturer of Wethersfield, however, did not reach this position through the ceremonial equivalent of a conversion experience; in his response we can find something more akin to the second trajectory outlined above, that of the old nonconformist. In one of what he seems to have been aware would be his last sermons at Wethersfield for the foreseeable future, Daniel Rogers warned the ministers who attended his weekday lecture to avoid the tacit approval of unlawful forms:

---

[19] Mather, III p. 106; SP 16/293/218; *MHSC* 4th ser. 6 p. 560.
[20] Nathaniel Rogers, *A Letter*, pp. 4–5.

Let him beware lest he lend that authority and strength which God hath put upon his person, to countenance, backe and support any base dishonour of God, any the least affront given to the Commands of God . . . be thou closely subiect to God.

He preached against those godly ministers who fell off from obeying a divine command 'and consult with flesh and blood, the consequences of such an obedience to God: and if they finde, that it is like to become any prejudice to their state and liberty, they thinke it a very rationall thing to obey man before God'. In particular, he pressed the example of the godly man of Judah (1 Kings 13) who was slain by a lion after allowing an old prophet to deflect him from his mission to denounce Jeroboam's 'altar policy'.[21]

Rogers made it clear that his own course of action was decided: under the head 'Godly Ministers must not onely use, but also lay downe their parts and services if God so require', he explained that a preacher should not be so in love with his ministry that he becomes unwilling to embrace silence if God requires it:

The onely triall of the denying of your owne parts for God is, if when God calls for them in sacrifice, you be as willing to make shipwracke of them, as to improve them. Be not more anxious for God than he is for himselfe: for he can make the stones cry, although you should hold your peace.[22]

This is not to say that Rogers was prepared meekly to yield his place. In July 1631, ahead of the visitation, he canvassed support among his neighbouring ministers, asking them to certify his conversation and good life to Bishop Laud, in similar terms to those employed to defend Hooker two years earlier. Among those moderates prepared to offer such support were Samuel Collins and the aforementioned Dr Barkham. It is not clear whether a petition was raised,[23] but any such persuasions carried little weight with Laud. When the visitation arrived at Braintree on 4 September 1631, Daniel Rogers was asked to subscribe. He flatly refused, and his licence to preach was suspended. As he was a lecturer only, no further action was needed to deprive him of his income and place. He was to remain under this suspension for the rest of the decade, devoting himself to writing on family duties and the sins of the times.[24]

[21] Daniel Rogers, *Naaman the Syrian, his Disease and Cure* (1642) pp. 524–5. In the dedicatory epistle he refers to 'these my last Lectures which I preached at my last farewell to publicke'.

[22] Ibid., p. 78.

[23] SP 16/196/61. This letter from Collins to Arthur Duck, dated 13 July 1631, is badly torn. He asks that his certificate be delivered with that of Dr Barkham 'if it may doe him [Rogers] good and us noe hurte'.

[24] GL 9531/15 f. 25r–v; SU Hartlib MS 29/2/7a–b; 29/2/51a.

II

The issues and the proper responses were not so clear to all godly ministers. I have mentioned that William Twisse attended the Ockley conference without discussing his reaction to the arguments that proved so persuasive to the other ministers present. In order to correct the impression given so far, that ministers among the spiritual brotherhood fell into one of two categories, the old nonconformist and the new, equally heroic in the sacrifices made in the rejection of Laudianism, it is worth considering Twisse in a little more detail.

Twisse spent his mature years exercising a pastoral cure at Newbury in Berkshire after a glittering academic career. He refused prestigious offers of preferment, including a prebendary stall at Winchester cathedral, although he was tempted by the offer of the Earl of Warwick of a Northamptonshire benefice. His contributions to soteriological debates won him the offer of a professorial chair at the University of Franeker, formerly occupied by William Ames. His learning was held in high esteem by James I, who accepted his scruples regarding the first issue of the Book of Sports, and Robert Baillie, who claimed, 'he is doubtless the most able disputter in England'.[25] Twisse came to the Ockley conference as a divine whose opinion Cotton valued: he brought with him notes he had made on Cotton's manuscript answers to a neighbouring divine who had consulted him on the decree of reprobation, written about 1618. He asked Cotton to make a copy and return the original, although in the event, Twisse procured another copy and Cotton, grateful for the brotherly admonitions of Twisse, took them to New England and cited them in his own defence in his reply to Robert Baillie in 1648.[26]

However, Baillie's approval of Twisse was qualified: when Twisse was unanimously elected Prolocutor to the Westminster Assembly, Baillie described him as 'very learned in the questions he has studied, and very good, beloved of all and highlie esteemed; but merely bookish . . . among

---

[25] There are lives of Twisse in Clarke (1683) pp. 13–18; *DNB* and J. Reid, *Memoirs of the Westminster Divines* (Paisley, 1811) pp. 37–67, whence the biographical details are taken. For his contributions to the contemporary polemics, S. Hutton, 'Thomas Jackson, Oxford Platonist and William Twisse, Aristotelian', *JHI* 39 (1978) pp. 635–52; P. White, *Predestination, Policy and Polemic: Conflict and Consensus in the English Church from the Reformation to the Civil War* (Cambridge, 1992) pp. 257, 263–4. For Baillie, D. Laing (ed.), *Letters and Journals of Robert Baillie* (Edinburgh, 1841–2) vol. I p. 303.

[26] Twisse's comments were published in 1646 as *A Treatise of Mr Cottons Clearing Certaine Doubts Concerning Predestination, Together with an Examination Thereof.* Cotton cites the work and gives some of the background in *The Way of Congregational Churches Cleared* (1648) pt. I pp. 29, 32–4. Cotton was replying to Robert Baillie's *A Dissuasive from the Errours of our Time* (1645).

the unfittest of all the company for any action'.[27] It seems to have been this side of him that was to the fore at the Ockley conference: Goodwin dismissively told Hartlib, 'Twist was none in these controversies.' He had announced himself unversed in these issues and hoped for further conference to settle himself.[28] We are fortunate that he chose Joseph Mead as a counsellor, for their correspondence is preserved and allows us to reconstruct Twisse's concerns, a third trajectory of response. His correspondent, Mead, had become a fellow of Christ's College, Cambridge, in 1613, and remained so for the rest of his life. He was an Essex man, educated at Wethersfield under Richard Rogers and tutored at Christ's by Daniel Rogers.[29] He enjoyed enormous prestige as an academic, particularly for his work on the Apocalypse and Biblical chronology. Stephen Marshall held his work *de Daemons* to be 'the learnedest peece that ever hee had seene'.[30] He was, however, very much an academic: in April 1634, after hearing two sermons at Great St Mary's in Cambridge, Samuel Rogers announced himself: 'As you may suppose after 2 Mary sermons, Mr Meads, and Mr Howletts; Dry like the sermons in matter of any spiritual life; and so unfitted for tomorrow saboath.'[31] This perspective, as we will see, shapes the correspondence between the two divines.

Although Twisse does not seem to have been as dramatically convinced as some of his fellows at the conference, his mind was troubled by some of the issues raised there. In addition to his usual queries regarding the conversion of the Jews and on millennial issues, he began to solicit Mead's opinion on ceremonial subjects:

> . . . it makes me willing to know what you think of Genuflexio versus Altare, which now grows rife, and begins to challenge subscription as licita; like as genuflexio at the name of Jesus as pia ceremonia; and where we shall end I know not.[32]

Mead was pleased to settle his friend's concerns: many years earlier he had treated this question in his *concio ad clerum* for his divinity degree, although he felt that the present atmosphere made open discussion of such subjects more difficult.

> . . . the Times, when my thoughts were exercised in those Speculations I spoke of, were times of better awe than now they are; which preserved me from that immoderation which I see divers now run into, whether out of ignorance or some other distemper I cannot tell.

---

[27] Laing (ed.), *Letters and Journals*, vol. II p. 108.
[28] SU Hartlib MS 29/2/45b. On another occasion, Goodwin denounced Twisse even more intensely, telling Hartlib that 'Dr Twist speakes like a Miles Gloriosus as if hee had done so much in Learning as the King of Sweden in Warre': 29/2/56a.
[29] W. Haller, *Liberty and Reformation in the Puritan Revolution* (New York, 1958) p. 49.
[30] SU Hartlib MS 29/2/32b.
[31] QUB Percy MS 7 f. 36.   [32] Joseph Mead, *Works* (1672 edn) p. 817.

His defence rested upon a distinction between *imago* and *locus*. While it was flat idolatry to worship an image, places could be invested with sacred properties and it was not spiritually unlawful to genuflect towards such places. Indeed, Mead suggested that the Reformed churches, 'out of extream abomination of Idolatry', had been too severe in their removal of distinctions between sacred and profane. He admitted, 'you see hereby what a mungrel I am. I know not how you will like it, I know how full of prejudice in these Things most of our Divines are.'[33]

Twisse responded favourably to Mead's ideas. Mead had thought that Twisse would know his distinction, but, Twisse wrote, 'truly I never did, but somewhat have I heard another way'. He willingly subscribed to the distinction, clarifying Mead's notion of locus by offering the alternative *Signum praesentiae*. He wondered whether the Lord's Table was the only site of sacred authority; it is indicative of the ingrained primacy of preaching that he argued for equal reverence to be placed in the font, where baptism is administered, as in the pulpit, 'where God speaks to us', although preaching, of course, had never been a sacrament. In his speculations around this question we find a rare indication that *avant garde* ceremonialist arguments had made some headway among the godly ministry. Twisse mentioned,

yet I have heard that one who much furthereth these course should give us a reason thereof, that Hoc est Corpus meum is more with him than Hoc est Verbum meum.[34]

The discussion proceeded along fairly academic lines: Mead admitted that this was the limit of his interest as he was no practitioner. Twisse was more concerned with how the ceremonies operated in the parishes. He wondered 'Whether Bodily Gesture alone be fit to be urged or practiced in entring into Gods House; the outward adoration without the inward, the one without the other, being no better than Hypocrisy.' Such ceremonies might be inoffensive in themselves, yet 'these days are full of Formality'. In these circumstances, he feared that:

Things lawful in themselves become unlawful by accident; as when they are superstitiously practiced, though not by ourselves, yet by concurring in the same act, we may scandalize by countenancing the Superstition of others.

At this stage, in mid-1635, Twisse was still unconvinced either way. He resolved to take the new arguments and confer with other divines, hoping to find a way to tread lawfully and safely in 'these uncomfortable days'.[35]

The tone of the correspondence changed dramatically at the beginning of the following year, when it came to Twisse's attention that Mead had preached a sermon favouring the ceremonies. He sternly rebuked Mead

---

[33] Ibid., pp. 818, 829, 819.   [34] Ibid., pp. 821, 822.   [35] Ibid., p. 822.

and reminded him that he had suggested 'that the times wherein we live are the times for the slaughtering of the Witnesses', which were to precede the battle of Armageddon:

And if it be so, how sorry should I be to observe that you should have a hand in the slaughtering of them? as namely by promoting of such courses and countenancing them, for not conforming whereunto many are like to be slaughtered, that is, according to your interpretation, turned out of their places.

The middle ground was becoming increasingly difficult to defend without offending even the mildest of the godly. From Mead's point of view, the question was one open to objective academic examination; from Twisse's perspective, the conditions in the parishes were such that public airing of opinions which might be licit in discussions among divines was to endanger the godly ministry. His intensified sensitivity may be traced to his ongoing struggle over the failure to rail in the communion table at Newbury following the metropolitan visitation of 1634.[36] Twisse recalled that Mead expressed approval of Lancelot Andrewes' ceremonial in the chapel of Pembroke College; he could fully concur that devotion was a worthy aim, but also recognised that eminent divines of that time, the opening years of the century, had been concerned, and that such issues were still more controverted in the present time:

Indeed the Matter of Bowing at hearing the name of Jesus is nothing pleasing to some in these times . . . And I remember how faintly Mr H. carries himself in this; and others, in pleading for it, most of all urge this, that no body is troubled about it but now more than enough must yield or suffer – I never had experience of the practice till now, and that makes me the bolder to write as I do.[37]

Mead's wounded reply points up the differences among the godly: he denied promoting the ceremonies, either standing at the *Gloria Patri* or bowing to the altar or at the name of Jesus. He admitted that he had touched upon the issue of bowing, we may presume in terms similar to his *concio ad clerum*, which, in the changed polemical conditions of the 1630s, must have seemed little short of a betrayal of the persecuted godly. In practical terms, he pointed out that he had not bowed to the altar upon leaving the pulpit at Great St Mary's, as others had done. Moreover,

I have urged no man at any time to use any of these Ceremonies, nor conformed myself to any of them, till I saw them prevail so generally as I should have been accounted singular.[38]

This account of a newly conformist Cambridge accords with Samuel

---

[36] Ibid., p. 845; BRO D/A2/c.77, *Acta* (Berkshire Archdeaconry) 1635–6 ff. 81–2; D/A2/c.78 *Acta* (Berkshire Archdeaconry) 1636–7 f. 255. I am grateful to Mike Norris for drawing this conflict to my attention and for providing me with the references.
[37] Mead, *Works*, p. 845.   [38] Ibid., pp. 848–9.

Rogers' perception upon his return to his old college, Emmanuel, at the end of March 1636. In his diary he wrote:

Lord stay my heart, and cause mee to walke closely with thee, though I see [the] Universitye; even my own colledge much declined and vanishing into shadowes and formalitye; many of the fellows bowing at Jesus; Lord be merciful to the place.

He was shocked to find the 'cursed formalists' even in his own college chapel and feared that his scruples would prevent him from taking his degree. On the day of the Commencement he prayed, 'oh the poore university, Lord pitty it in the general consent to superstition, and will worship; it is a sinful decaying universitye, oh the strange change in 7 years'.[39]

Mead saw himself as prudently conforming with the majority to avoid being 'accounted singular'. He was incredulous at Twisse's accusation that such an action put him among the slaughterers of the saints of Revelation 16.6:

But you would not have me have any hand in killing the Witnesses. God forbid I should; I rather endeavour they might not be guilty of their own deaths. And I verily believe the way that many of them go is much more unlikely to save their lives, than mine. I could tell you a great deal here, if I had you privately in my chamber, which I mean not for any mans sake to commit to paper.[40]

This was an atmosphere in which the words and deeds of godly ministers were to be closely watched and mutual incomprehension and recrimination followed easily. The middle ground occupied by those enjoining silence and compromise was increasingly unstable, despite the best efforts of moderate ministers. Even as Twisse found himself moving from the difficult terrain of the middle ground towards those divines who accepted that the times had invalidated Sprint's argument, he was looking for a way back. He still hoped that Mead could offer some assurance.

I doubt not but whensoever I am put unto it, I shall find you the readier to afford me your best satisfaction; for certainly I will neglect no means to keep me out of the paw of the Lion as well as I can.[41]

Seeking such help had been condemned by Thomas Hooker, from the perspective of those for whom the arguments against the ceremonies were uncontestable:

If some searching truth delivered in publicke, presse him, or some syncere hearted friend perswade him to a further inquiry, he seeks after the truth, as a coward doth for his enemy, being afrayd to find it. Loath he is, to be in the society of such, whom he conceaves, to be either ludicious in their dispute, or Zealous in their course, against this trash . . . When he goes for counsel, and direction, it is to some such

[39] QUB Percy MS 7 ff. 106, 107, 133.   [40] Mead, *Works*, p. 849.   [41] Ibid., p. 847.

Authors, who write for the things he would practise, or consult onely with those men, that professe to mayntayne them, & so they make up the match at midnight.[42]

Hooker's invective, even allowing for hyperbole, completes a triangle of incomprehension. The suffering nonconformist sees cowardice and hypocrisy in the conscience-stricken conformable minister, who sees a dangerous consequence in the naivety of the godly conformist, who sees two over-tender consciences. Mead ended his reply by regretting the new atmosphere:

Sir, I can remember when you understood me more rightly, and interpreted my freedom with much more candour. To tell you true therefore, I am somewhat suspicious lest the air of Cambridge did you some hurt. But let that pass.[43]

The notorious fenland miasma is not admissible as an agent of religious conflict, but when such tensions and fractures occur within godly society to a greater degree than had been the case, and godly ministers respond to a perception that the times have changed and become more dangerous, we have to look for an explanation. As part of the danger was seen to be in the way that the ceremonies were newly pressed, perhaps we can build some understanding of this situation through an examination of the machinery and operation of the ecclesiastical authorities.

[42] G. H. Williams, N. Pettit, W. Herget and S. Bush, Jr (eds.), *Thomas Hooker: Writings in England and Holland, 1625–1633, Harvard Theological Studies* 28 (1975) p. 332.
[43] Mead, *Works*, p. 850.

9

The ecclesiastical courts and the Essex visitation of 1631

I

The lowest level of ministerial discipline in Essex was the archidiaconal court. Three archdeacons had jurisdiction in the county: the largest archdeaconry, which took its name from the county, included the deaneries of Barking, Barnstaple, Chafford, Chelmsford, Dengie and Ongar, taking in the southern and central parts of the county; the north-east fell under the Archdeacon of Colchester, covering the deaneries of Tendring, Colchester, Lexden and Witham, and also the north-westerly deaneries of Newport and Sampford; between these areas, part of the archdeaconry of Middlesex took in Harlow, Dunmow and Hedingham deaneries. Small areas fell under other authorities as the fossilised remnants of pre-Reformation jurisdictions: the tiny deanery of Bocking was directly answerable to Canterbury; part of the civil hundred of Tendring was a Peculiar of the Earl Rivers, and the lands formerly governed by Waltham Abbey retained the right to hold their own court under the jurisdiction of the bishop of London's Commissary in London, Barking and Middlesex. The Liberty of Havering, Writtle and Roxwell constituted a Peculiar of New College, Oxford. For visitation purposes the archdeaconry of Colchester split into three circuits: one for the separate area in the north-west, with the court held at Walden or Henham; a second for the Colchester and Tendring deaneries, with the court at Colchester; and the court for Lexden and Witham at Kelvedon. The archdeaconry of Essex, despite its size, was covered by only two circuits: Barking, Ongar and Chafford were governed by a court sitting at Romford; Chelmsford, Rochford, Barnstaple and Dengie deaneries reported to a court which usually sat at Great Baddow or occasionally Chelmsford. The Essex part of the archdeaconry of Middlesex does not seem to have been visited by the archdeacon before the Restoration; his place was supplied by the commissary of the Bishop of London in Essex and Hertfordshire, who held, and exercised, the right of visitation over a number of parishes scattered through the county. His court dealt with cases in Finchingfield and Castle Hedingham, for instance, within the archdeaconry of Middlesex, which were technically beyond his jurisdiction. The commissary normally held his court at Braintree, Dunmow and Bishops Stortford. The archidiaconal courts visited every spring, with the exception of those years in which there was an episcopal visitation, when archidiaconal business was suspended.[1]

The archdeacon's courts were principally concerned with the regulation of the behaviour of the laity. They were entrusted, along with other courts, with the presentment of adulterers, drunkards and the like, alongside non-communicants, recusants and schismatics. With regard to ministerial discipline, their power was considerable but limited. The archdeacons had access to the three lowest forms of punishment available to ecclesiastical courts. The lowest was a canonical admonition, which amounted to a warning, and was usually applied when an obligation had been neglected, but it was felt that the defendant was reformable. Although an admonition carried no real penalty, the court would generally require certification of the action in question, and admonitions were frequently acted upon. The second censure available to the archdeacons' courts was suspension, which was of two kinds. Suspension *ab officio et beneficio* applied only to the clergy: it meant the removal of the right to preach, to administer the sacraments within the province and from the profits of any ecclesiastical office.[2] Suspension *ab ingressu ecclesiae* could apply equally to both clergy and laity, and took away the right to attend church, to receive the sacraments and other ministrations. For a lecturer or a stipendiary curate, suspension could amount to the end of one's ministry, at least in the place involved. Beneficed ministers, however, retained the fruits of their freehold, and both types of suspension were normally regarded as of a temporary nature; suspension was a penalty for failing to appear in court when cited to do so, or for simply absenting oneself from visitation. Rights were

---

[1] F. G. Emmison, *Elizabethan Life: Morals and the Church Courts* (Chelmsford, 1973) introduction and *passim*; J. Anglin, 'The Court of the Archdeacon of Essex, 1571–1609', University of California PhD (1965); the jurisdictions and sources, though not the practices are sketched in F. G. Emmison, *Guide to the Essex Record Office* (Chelmsford, 1969) pp. 70–8. On the church courts more generally, see M. Ingram, *Church Courts, Sex and Marriage in England, 1570–1640* (Cambridge, 1987). The best-documented archdeaconry in the London diocese is outside Essex, in the archdeaconry of St Alban's. Despite the inhibition, the archdeacon of St Alban's visited even in years of an episcopal visitation; the inhibition was generally observed in Essex: R. Peters, *Oculus Episcopi: Administration in the Archdeaconry of St Alban's 1580–1625* (Manchester, 1963) p. 39 and *passim*; cf. R. Burns, *Ecclesiastical Law* (1767) vol. IV pp. 14–15. However, the suspension of archidiaconal business was relatively short lived, usually of a duration of around six to ten weeks, with business overlapping.

[2] Suspension *ab officio et beneficio* came to be limited to a maximum of three years, but this does not seem to have applied in this period: H. C. Coote, *The Practice of the Ecclesiastical Courts* (London, 1847) pp. 248–55.

restored when the duty had been performed and certified back to the court. On 10 December 1630, for instance, John Archer, one of the St Antholin's lecturers, was suspended as a suspected nonconformist. Within the week he had submitted, apologised and promised conformity and was thus restored to his post.[3] If a minister remained contumacious, the archdeacon could excommunicate him. Canon Law enjoined excommunication after one month of unrepentant suspension in the case of ceremonial nonconformity, and this pattern was extended to most disciplinary actions. Excommunication was of two forms: the lesser form deprived the offender of the sacraments and any share in public worship. This form thus resembled suspicion *ab ingressu ecclesiae*, but opened the offender to a greater penalty: after forty days the court was to proceed to a writ of *excommunicato capiendo*. In addition to the social and legal consequences of the greater excommunication, an excommunicate clergyman could not be presented to a benefice, and if he continued to officiate he was liable to deprivation.[4]

However, the greater excommunication was rarely applied in the archidiaconal courts. In Canon Law the archdeacon had the right to the full sentence of excommunication, but it was at the very limit of their authority. Canon 122 allowed the first three censures, but if a minister appeared in an archidiaconal court and was found guilty of an offence which merited either deprivation from his living or deposition from the ministry, sentence was to be withheld until the case could be dealt with by the bishop himself.[5]

In reality, the archdeacon's jurisdiction took its lead from episcopal practice. Throughout the period, the extant archdeaconry visitation articles are normally identical to those produced by the episcopal visitation. In terms of ministerial discipline the significance of the archdeacons was more as a vital link between a distant diocesan and the clergy under his care, affecting the efficiency of the episcopal visitation with its greater censorial powers. In addition to the three minor censures, the bishop could deprive a minister of his living, despite some fears that it was inappropriate for a freehold right to be removed by canon law and, less controversially, to depose an offender from the ministry.[6]

[3] GL 9531/15 ff. 23v–24v.
[4] Burns, *Ecclesiastical Law*, vol. II pp. 201–5. See also C. Hill, *Society and Puritanism in Pre-Revolutionary England* (London, 1964) pp. 343–69.
[5] Canons 109–12 and 122 deal with the archdeacons' courts. The 1604 canons (more properly the 1603 canons) are printed in E. Cardwell, *Synodalia: a Collection of Articles, Canons and Proceedings of Convocation . . . from 1547 to 1717* (Oxford, 1847) vol. II pp. 245–329.
[6] Burns, vol. II pp. 123–4; C. Hill, *Economic Problems of the Church from Archbishop Whitgift to the Long Parliament* (London, 1971) pp. 51–3, 58.

I will return to the conduct of episcopal visitations in the diocese of London later, but it is necessary to complete the account of the jurisdictions to which ministers were answerable. Beyond the diocesan level, of course, Essex was part of the province of Canterbury and thus subject to irregular metropolitical visitations, either by the archbishop himself or by his vicar-general, using the same machinery and most of the same procedures as the episcopal visitation.

All these jurisdictions were inherited from the pre-Reformation church with some modifications in procedure from subsequent canon law. The court which became most odious in the eyes of the godly ministry was a post-Reformation innovation, established by statute: the Court of High Commission in Ecclesiastical Causes. The Elizabethan Act of Supremacy empowered the High Commissioners to undertake the enforcement of such ecclesiastical discipline as might be required. As a statutory body the court was not strictly ecclesiastical, but a secular court dealing with religious affairs. Objections to the *ex officio* oath, whereby defendants undertook to answer truthful charges regarding which they had no previous knowledge and thus risked incriminating themselves, are well known, but the Court of High Commission also had secular punishments at its disposal which were not available to the regular ecclesiastical courts. The High Commissioners, under the Archbishop of Canterbury, could arrest, fine and imprison suspects, thus threatening liberty and wealth to a greater degree than the worst censures of the other jurisdictions. Moreover, the High Commission could pursue delinquents from one ecclesiastical jurisdiction to another. If suspects fled from one archdeaconry, or more frequently from one diocese to another, they could only be cited through the slow and complex procedure of request from one court to another. The High Commission employed pursuivants with freedom of arrest throughout the province, and it is these men who appear so often in accounts of the peregrinations of nonconformist ministers.[7]

The regular scenes of the episcopal visitation were less spectacular than the dogged pursuit of the High Commission pursuivants, but more the coinage of the ordinary experience of every minister. In all dioceses a newly inducted bishop was expected to conduct his primary visitation within a year of his arrival. In London, visitations continued on a triennial basis. The first action was the publication of visitation articles sent to the churchwardens of every parish detailing the expectations of the visitor and notifying the officers of the time and place of first appearance. For ministers the first contact with a new bishop would follow as the visitor traced the

---

[7] R. C. Marchant, *The Church under the Law: Justice, Administration and Discipline in the Diocese of York, 1560–1640* (Cambridge, 1969) pp. 4, 33–4; R. G. Usher, *The Rise and Fall of the High Commission* (Oxford, 1913); Hill, *Society and Puritanism*, pp. 333–42.

regular route through the diocese. With a show of welcoming pageantry, an hortatory sermon and a speech from the bishop, the visitation arrived. After his speech, the bishop would normally retire to an inn while his commissioners took a roll-call of the ministers summoned to each place, inspected licences to preach and teach, collected fees, swore in new parish officers and began summary interrogation of offenders. In Essex the company moved from London along the Colchester road, spending a day at Brentwood and another at Chelmsford in the archdeaconry of Essex, moving on to Colchester and then retracing their steps to Kelvedon, also in the archdeaconry of Colchester, before travelling west to Braintree and then Great Dunmow in the commissary of Essex and Hertfordshire, and then on to Bishops Stortford, just over the county border. At each stage, absentee ministers might be suspended and a date set for the return of bills of presentment or answers to the visitation articles. The correction courts normally followed seventeen days later to receive presentments and sit in judgement. The commissioners could refer intractable cases to the Bishop's Court of Audience, and the bishop might cite some cases into the High Commission. A fortnight after this stage, the circuit was revisited to complete cases, to certify penances and occasionally to try cases that had been missed in the previous sessions. The final stages sometimes visited smaller centres, concluding cases at inns in, for instance, Peldon or Lexden.

II

Such were the settled practices of the administration of the church. In answering the questions posed above, regarding the perceived change in ecclesiastical climate, we must first ask if these practices changed in ways that encouraged the godly to believe that the *modus vivendi* of the Jacobean church no longer applied. In some respects, the short answer is that the machinery of visitation was surprisingly constant. In the diocese of London, in contrast to that of Norwich, as we shall see, the structures of visitation were not notably transformed. The circuits remained constant: there is no sense in which pressure on the godly was increased by raising the visibility of the hierarchy. Large areas of the diocese remained free from the sight of the mobile court: the Dengie peninsular, the deanery of Rochford, the far reaches of the Stour valley, and the Rodings and Lavers in the west were scarcely troubled. Episcopal visitations remained an experience that ministers travelled to, rather than an all-seeing, intrusive presence prying into parochial practice. It is perhaps more fruitful to trace the progress of the machinery of the episcopal visitation.

Bishop Laud's primary visitation began two months after his elevation. In the articles he issued ahead of this event there were few indications of change: they were closely modelled on the 1605 articles used by Richard Vaughan in his primary visitation as the articles of all the intervening bishops had been. In the section regarding the clergy, there are occasional modifications which reveal subtle adjustments. Article 2 requires the use of the Book of Common Prayer in divine service. Laud reproduced Montaigne's article to the letter, adding only the clause 'without omission or addition'. With regard to the administration of communion he inserted an article which might seem to undermine the exercise of parochial discipline, asking

Whether hath your minister rejected any from communion, who were not by public presentment, or other open scandal, infamous and detected of some notorious crime by common fame, or vehement suspicion known in the parish?

Laud also revealed his concerns about unbeneficed lectures to a degree slightly greater than that of his predecessor, enquiring whether any lecturer was beneficed out of the diocese, or kept from his cure in the diocese by lecturing elsewhere, or whether he lacked a benefice at all. Finally, he tried to crack down on ministerial conferences by introducing an article asking

Whether at any meeting do they [the clergy], or any of them, preach, confer, or agree upon any private orders for divine service, prayers, preaching or form of divine service, than such as in the Book of Common Prayer, and by the laws established, appointed; or be drawers of others to such schismatical conventicles?

There was, however, no broadcasted change in altar policy, beyond the reproduction of an established article requiring the sacrament to be administered only to those that kneel, for the minister to take communion kneeling every time he performed the rite and to follow the service in the Book of Common Prayer, adding a final clause, 'And doth he deliver the bread to every communicant severally?' This last change may be seen to stress the priestly role of the minister against a vision of a minister officiating over a shared memorial, but it cannot be denied that these are minimal changes.[8]

Neither can the 1628 visitation be said to have struck hard against the godly ministers of Essex. Laud's first concern seems to have been with lecturers within the city of London, whose licences were thoroughly inspected through December and January 1628/9.[9] With his attention focused on the capital, Essex escaped relatively unscathed: Thomas

---

[8] William Laud, *The Works of William Laud, Anglo-Catholic Library* (ed. W. Scott and J. Bliss) (Oxford, 1847–60) vol. V ii pp. 397–404; STC 10262; K. Fincham, *Prelate as Pastor: the Episcopate of James I* (Oxford, 1990) p. 130. It might also be noted that Laud extended Montaigne's article on the Communion table, asking: 'And is the same Table so used out of divine service or in it, as it is not agreeable to the holy use of it, by sitting, throwing hats on it, writing on it, or is it abused to other prophane purposes?'

[9] GLRO DL/C 317 ff. 13r–14v, 20, 26, 35r, 49v, 63v.

Hooker was the only minister in the county to be deprived in this visitation.[10] This compares favourably with the record of George Montaigne in his last visit to the county. In 1627, he prosecuted two ministers for nonconformity, one of whom was deprived, the other submitted. However, there was a substantial qualitative difference: under Montaigne, the first minister troubled was Samuel Otway, rector of St Peter's, Colchester, who had preached a sermon against the order 'lately disperst throughout the whole diocese by his lordships command for observation of due reverence in time of divine worship'. This was the order Montaigne had issued in August 1627 requiring disciplinary action against those who refused to remove their hats during divine service, and also enjoined beneficed ministers and curates (though not lecturers) to use the liturgy before their sermons. The case against Otway was principally concerned with his impugning of the bishop's authority, with his neglect of the surplice a decidedly minor issue. In the event, Otway continued in his cure after subscribing to the Articles of Religion and preaching a recantation sermon.[11] The second minister to receive Montaigne's censure was John Newton of Stock, a notable example of the potential for conflict inherent in Puritan preaching priorities. He had preached on John 1.15 and moved on to condemn all festive survivals as 'a monstrous idolatry'. Generally, he announced: 'Whatsoever was done in the church [which] was not expressly commanded by the Word of God was wicked and sinful.' He denounced holy days and the general principle that places special significance on particular times or places irrespective of actions taken therein. At this point, a local gentleman, Richard Ball, stood up, took off his hat and ordered the minister: 'I pray you keep your text.' Newton did little to reduce the tension between them when he denounced Ball from the pulpit as a man who cheated the poor. From this incident, in 1622, Montaigne had tried to reconcile the factions that grew up around Newton and Ball without success. Evidence of Newton's nonconformity (and his unlicensed medical practice) only came up when Ball came to give evidence in court, and it was Newton's refusal to pacify his parish rather than his ceremonial nonconformity that led to his final deprivation in 1627.[12] In numerical terms, Montaigne may be said to have been more successful in his last visitation than Laud in his first, but the deprivation of a contumacious curate was nothing compared with the determined pursuit of a widely revered lecturer of Hooker's stature.

---

[10] The sources for the 1628 visitation are GL 9537/13; 9531/15; 9539A/1; GLRO DL/C 317; DL/C 624; DL/C 322; DL/C 343.

[11] GLRO DL/C 343 f. 32v; SP 16/43/20; 16/75/87.

[12] GLRO DL/C 314 ff. 130, 150v.

III

It was not until his second triennial visitation that Laud's arrival made its impact upon the Essex Puritan ministry. Two factors explain this delay. Firstly, Laud armed himself with additional means to combat what he saw as the disruptive elements in the church. Shortly after the dissolution of the 1629 Parliament, Laud consulted with Bishop Harsnett and submitted a series of 'Considerations for the Better Settling of the Church-Government' to the King.[13] Within weeks, the Considerations were issued, almost unrevised, as Royal Instructions to both archbishops. The bishops and archdeacons were to enforce the proclamations limiting debate and to turn their particular attention to stipendiary lectures. Afternoon sermons were to be converted into catechising by question and answer; every lecturer was to read divine service in his hood and surplice before his lecture; market-town lectures were 'to be read by a Company of grave and Orthodox Divines' from the same diocese; corporation lecturers were not to preach until they professed a willingness to take on a benefice (the 'Considerations' had suggested such a lecturer should not teach until he held a cure). The law restricting the keeping of chaplains to those socially qualified was to be more fully enforced, and the bishops were to 'take special care the Divine Service be diligently frequented, as well for Prayers and Catechisms, as Sermons'.

All these measures are fairly familiar. Less attention has been paid to article five of the Royal Instructions, which directed,

That the Bishops do countenance and encourage the Grave and Orthodox Divines of their Clergy; and that they use means, by some of their Clergy, or others, that they may have knowledge how both lecturers and Preachers within their Dioceses behave themselves in their Sermons, that they may take order for any Abuse accordingly.[14]

This was the second strand of Laud's strategy, to improve intelligence gathering within the diocese. Shortly after the Instructions were issued he wrote to his archdeacons, enclosing a copy of them. The archdeacons were to abstract the articles relating to lecturers, chaplains and divine worship, and deliver a copy to the parson and churchwarden in each parish. More-over, Laud required each archdeacon to return a list of all the lecturers within his archdeaconry, including those in the various peculiars. By Wednesday 3 February 1630, Laud expected to have details of the names, of every household keeping a chaplain without the sanction of the law. The

[13] Peter Heylin, *Cyprianus Anglicus* (1671) p. 188; William Prynne, *Canterburies Doome* (1648) pp. 368–9.
[14] John Rushworth, *Historical Collections* (1721) vol. II pp. 30–1.

archdeacons were to ensure that Laud was kept informed of the performance of the Instructions and, more importantly, of the names of those ministers who disobeyed.[15]

Laud slowly established a network of informants who could keep him abreast of parochial practice. They went beyond the archdeacons: he benefited from details provided by Thomas Wilborow, a minister of Pebmarsh in the extreme north of the county who held high sacramental views and lost his living in the 1640s; John Etheridge of Halstead, a pluralist; and Richard Hooke, rector of Little Baddow, another minister whose living was to be sequestrated. He followed up information given by men and women: Sir Thomas Wiseman, a member of a prominent recusant family of Rivenhall, Henry Neville of Cressing Temple, William Lynne of Little Horsley, near Colchester, one Mr Durden, schoolmaster of Coggeshall, a Goodman Chote and a Mrs Alleston in the north. In the main, the network was coordinated by Dr Robert Aylett, the Commissary of Essex and Hertfordshire, from his home, Feeringbury, a house belonging to the bishop between Feering and Coggeshall and very convenient for Kelvedon. Aylett was a well-connected ecclesiastical lawyer, a first cousin of Sir John Lambe, with whom he was sworn as a member of the High Commission in January 1629. During Laud's episcopacy he informed Laud directly of conditions in the county and thereafter sent his information to Lambe, who was dean of the Arches, and therefore technically had jurisdiction over the bishop's peculiars but who remained close to Laud as Archbishop.[16]

Both strands of this strategy were in place by the time Laud came to make his second triennial visitation. Thus the Instructions were incorporated into the visitation articles, which were otherwise more or less unchanged, and information was held by the end of November 1630 regarding eleven Essex ministers 'who are not conformable in preaching nor practice'. Two were reported for scandalous life, both in the Dengie peninsular. Seven of the remaining nine can be associated with Hooker's conference: Thomas Shepard, Thomas Weld, Daniel Rogers, Mr Seton, an assistant to Martin Holbeach in his Felsted school, Nathaniel Ward, John Beadle and John Rogers.[17]

---

[15] Ibid., pp. 31–2.

[16] SP 16/339/53; H. Smith, *Ecclesiastical History of Essex*, pp. 144–5, 112, 50, 118, 125, 49, 56; A. G. Matthews, *Walker Revised* (Oxford, 1988) pp. 169, 155; Venn; B. P. Levack, *The Civil Lawyers in England, 1603–42* (Oxford, 1973) p. 207; J. H. Round, 'Dr Robert Aylett', *TEAS* 10 (1909) pp. 26–34; J. H. Round, 'Robert Aylett and Richard Argall', *EHR* 38 (1923) pp. 423–4; SP 16/161/54; 163/45; 218/43; 223/4; 276/42; 351/100. Aylett later conducted Laud's provincial visitation in the Archdeaconry of Leicester: SP 16/263/67; 277/79.

[17] Laud, *Works*, vol. V ii pp. 401–2, 404; SP 16/175/104. Weld had been noted for further investigation during the 1628 visitation: GL 9537/13 f. 19.

At the first stage of the visitation it became clear that Laud's officials were targeting such ministers. On 16 December 1630, Laud followed up the information he had been given regarding the patron of Shepard's lecture and required Thomas Weld to subscribe. Weld first came to Laud's attention through the court of the Archdeacon of Colchester: in June 1629 the churchwardens were presented 'for suffering one Mr Peters [*sic*] a suspended minister to preach in their church'. They admitted that Hugh Peter had preached at Terling shortly before Whitsun, but added 'that they did not knowe either that he was a suspended [minister] or should preach there untill he was in the pulpett or who procured him to preach there, or gave him leave to do so'. The lecture was suspended while enquiries were made, but the godly of Terling presented an impenetrable front, and by the end of the month they had successfully petitioned the court for the relaxation of the suspension. Their petition was granted, with an order that the churchwardens should be more vigilant, keep the ordinary informed of visiting preachers, and deliver a copy of the order to their minister, clearly suspected by the court to be behind Peter's presence in Terling. The incident was not forgotten and, as Laud gathered information regarding the lecturers in his diocese, in May 1630, Weld was called before the Archdeacon's Court 'to shew by what authoritie he reads a lecture in his parish church upon the weeke daye'. Although Weld satisfied the court,[18] such dealings were enough to elicit Laud's investigations and bring Weld to the court at the end of 1630. The bishop did not bring any charges but required Weld to subscribe to the three articles. Weld tried to evade the demand, claiming that three men, two of them his neighbours, had bound land over to him on condition that he should not subscribe, referring Laud to Nehemiah Rogers of Messing for confirmation. Laud was unconvinced but allowed Weld three months to deliberate and seek counsel.[19] In the past, the inefficiency of the ecclesiastical courts was such that, having won time, a godly minister could be hopeful that no charges would be brought and he would be left unmolested for a further three years. This was no longer the case: at the end of Hilary term, Laud interviewed him again and sent Thomas Goad, former chaplain to Archbishop Abbot, who was to become Dean of Bocking shortly after, to try to win Weld around. After two months of this attention Weld realised that he was not going to be let off the hook and told the Consistory Court 'That his Lo[rdshi]pp had dealt most favourablie with him, & had granted him a long time to informe his judgement, But he was not yet persuaded in his conscience to subscribe nor desired anie longer time of Consultation.' Accordingly, on 1 July, he was

[18] ERO D/ACA 47 ff. 5r, 19r, 94v, unbound paper no. 1.
[19] GL 9531/15 f. 23; GLRO DL/C 319 f. 39.

suspended. This result came as no surprise to the godly: as John Humfrey wrote to John Winthrop in December 1630, 'Mr Weld of Essex is now upon the stage and expects his doome. I think hee will bee easilie for us.'[20]

He was still under suspension when Laud returned to the north of the county two months later. The court session for Colchester was transferred to Kelvedon to avoid the plague and there were thus two court days held there, 2 and 3 September. On the first day Laud spoke 'with much gravity and severity' against pride in the ministry, 'that they must have their plush and satin and their silken cassocks, and their bandstrings with knots', and promised that if any would inform him of scandalous ministers he would do his best to bring reform. Then the bishop retired to his chamber and Weld was called again. Once again Weld was asked to subscribe and replied simply: 'The Lord knows I cannot.' As Canon Law required, Weld was now excommunicated.[21]

IV

On the second court day at Kelvedon, Laud summoned John Rogers, the elderly lecturer of Dedham. He had been given information against Rogers but he was less certain of his nonconformity: he was told that Rogers 'hath beene much suspected, but hath protested his opinion to be for conformity in a Visitation sermon at Colchester'.[22] To understand his stance, and his experience at Kelvedon, we need a rather longer perspective. John Rogers was one of the few godly ministers with direct experience of the last full-blooded drive against nonconformity. At the 1605 visitation, he was a fairly youthful replacement for the recently deceased Edmund Chapman of the Dedham *classis*. A week before the visitation he crossed the border to stay in Suffolk, possibly with friends in Assington. Absence from the first stage of a visitation made any minister vulnerable to suspension, but by 3 October, when the churchwardens, George Lowe and Samuel Sherman, made their presentment and were interrogated about their lecturer, Dr Corbett, one of the commissioners, still had the order for Rogers' suspension in his hands and had not yet acted upon it. The churchwardens attempted to stall, trying, in particular, to conceal the fact that they knew Rogers to be unlicensed. Once Corbett had left, they raised about forty pounds, which was offered to Meredith Powell, the incumbent, for his resignation, presumably so as to nominate Rogers to the benefice. Bishop

[20] GL 9531/15 f. 24v; *MHSC* 4th ser. 6 (1863) p. 11. For Thomas Goad, who had attended the Synod of Dort: *DNB*; Venn; E. G. Beeton, 'Seventeenth Century Church Discipline', *HTM* 4 (1926) p. 27.

[21] *Winthrop Papers* (Boston, Mass., 1929–43) III p. 58; GL 9531/15 f. 24r.

[22] SP 16/175/104.

Ravis heard of these attempts and quickly put a stop to them. At this stage, evidence of Rogers' nonconformity came to the bishop's attention: he was told (by someone other than the churchwardens) that Rogers had impugned the recent canons on the liturgy and on the ceremonies; the Tuesday lecture began with a psalm and went straight on to the sermon. He occasionally took the Sunday morning service, using selected passages from the Book of Common Prayer. Sir Edward Stanhope, the bishop's vicar-general, who had helped to draft the 1604 canons, left instructions that Rogers was to attend upon the bishop for a licence to preach, and the churchwardens were to certify when this was done. They were also to warn Rogers that he should receive communion kneeling, attend morning and evening service and that 'he do turn his preaching into a sort of catechizing and . . . examine the younger sort in the principles thereof. And for his Tuesday sermon it is ordered that there be no sermon unless there be first public prayer read either by him or by Mr Sage the vicar before the sermon doth begin according to the Book of Common Prayer.' He was given until 14 November to carry this out, with the vicar-general holding the letter of suspension as a threat. Three weeks after this deadline had passed the churchwardens left a letter with William Brigg, a servant of the vicar-general's, certifying that Rogers was now licensed. No further action was taken. Nine days after the passage of the visitation, Rogers returned to the Dedham pulpit.[23]

In the following twenty-six years, as his reputation as a powerful preacher grew, Rogers established himself as one of the natural leaders of the Essex godly. Throughout his career he refused the surplice and used the ceremonies minimally, perhaps meeting the canonical requirement of reading the divine service and administering the sacraments twice a year using the Prayer Book ceremonies. Giles Firmin, who was close to Rogers during the 1620s, recalled that 'tho' he did conform, I never saw him wear a surplice, nor heard him use but a few Prayers; and those, I think, he said *memoriter*, he did not read them: but this he would do in his Preaching, draw his finger around his throat, and say, Let them take me and hang me up, so they will but remove these stumbling Blocks out of the Church'.[24] In the light of this evidence, it seems a little incongruous to discover that Rogers had declared himself for conformity. In reality, he had declared

[23] GLRO DL/C 305 f. 317; DL/C 338 pt. v f. 105. For the successive vicars of Dedham: C. A. Jones, *History of Dedham* (Colchester, 1907) p. 39. It is not clear whether the Dr Corbett mentioned here is the same man who later became such a powerful opponent of Puritanism in the diocese of Norwich: cf. Levack, *Civil Lawyers*, pp. 220–1; Emmison, *Elizabethan Life: Morals and the Church Courts*, p. 300, and below pp. 204–14.

[24] Cardwell, *Synodalia*, p. 278; Giles Firmin, *The Questions between the Conformist and the Non-Conformist* (1681) p. 12.

himself less a conformist than a conformable minister of the stamp of William Whately. He had declared to Dedham congregation that

> some spend all their zeale in crying out against Ceremonies, and neglect matters more belonging to edifying themselves and others. Some forsake their own Ministers when they preach, very uncharitably and indiscreetly . . . Now if a Minister, or any Christian shall shew his dislike of such courses in generall or rebuke any particular person for any of them, he is not to be ill thought of for doing so, while he loves them for those graces that he seeth to be in them, nor to be reputed a hater of Gods servants.[25]

He went beyond Whately's strictures on the conservation of energy for spiritual matters, to incorporate something approximate to Sprint's position on conformity. He was full of reverence for genuine martyrs – 'Happy are those that suffer for a good cause, for righteousness, for Religion, for conscience sake' – but cautioned, 'let us be careful that we suffer for righteousness and a good cause . . . Beware we suffer not as Separatist, that flie out against and from the Church . . . or for meddling with things or persons wherewith we have nothing to do; or for passing our bounds in things beyond our reach.' Among the things judged 'beyond our reach' were the issues of church government and the ceremonies. He stressed that there were no contentions about points essential to salvation, only about the government of the Church and the ceremonies, and that it was 'more seemly for Christians to mind the Doctrine of Faith, Sanctification, Love, etc., than to busy themselves about the Government of the Church'.[26]

If this seems a schizoid existence, practising nonconformity and professing a neglect of the issues that informed his practice, it was not unique among the godly divines of his generation. We have seen a similar pattern in the experience of William Whately and can perhaps understand it more fully through a third minister, Thomas Pierson of Brampton Bryan. Throughout his career Pierson neglected the cross in baptism and the surplice, yet when his curate stopped wearing the surplice, Pierson presented him in the ecclesiastical courts, as the unfortunate youth could give no adequate reason for his action, other than his master's example. Pierson told him 'that he must weare it, Unlesse he had cogent argument, wherein he could not satisfy his own conscience'.[27] The rationale for what seems slightly eccentric behaviour was that attitudes to the ceremonies were a personal matter: as they were not strictly unlawful, a minister should not be admired or reviled for his adherence to or rejection of them, but for his

[25] John Rogers, *A Treatise of Love* (1633) pp. 161–2.
[26] John Rogers, *A Godly and Fruitfull Exposition of the First Epistle of Peter* (1650) pp. 461–2, 240.
[27] BL Harl MS 7517 ff. 14–18, quoted at 17v–18r.

own godliness, and actively promoting nonconformity was to diminish that godliness.

By 1627, this settled position was coming to seem less than completely satisfactory. In that year John Rogers made a private resolution in his journal:

> If ever I come into trouble for want of Conformity I resolve with myself, by Gods assistance, to come away with a clear conscience, and yield to nothing in present, until I have prayed and fasted, and conferred: And though the liberty of my ministry be precious, yet buy it not with a guilty conscience. I am somewhat troubled sometimes with my Subscription, but I saw sundry men of good gifts, and good hearts, as I thought, that did so. And I could not prove that there was anything contrary to the word of God, tho I misliked them much, and I knew them unprofitable burdens to the Church of God. But if I be urged unto the Use of them, I am rather resolved never to yield thereunto. They are to me very irksome things, yet seeing as I was not able to prove them flatly unlawful, or contrary to Gods Word, I thought better to save my liberty with Subscribing . . . than to lose it, for not yielding so far . . . But it may be, I might not have been urged of a long time, or not at all, but might have escaped by Friends and Money, as before, which yet I feared. But it was my weakness as I now conceive it, which I beseech God to pardon unto me.[28]

This new resolution was still in Rogers' mind when Laud became Bishop of London. The 1628 visitation passed without incident,[29] but the new vigilance of the archdeacon brought censures 'for that being lecturer he dooth not reade divine service in the surplice according to his Maiesties Instructions'.[30] This brought him to Laud's attention and the bishop followed up his information on the second court day at Kelvedon, on 3 September 1631. Once again, Laud pressed subscription as a first test of orthodoxy. Rogers steeled himself, and refused. Laud 'told him how he had borne with him, and shewd how he must needs suspend him and so proceed if he reformd not to do all accor[ding] to Canon after a month to excom[municate] him, and then after a month to deprive him of the ministry, (so lying open also to a writ of excom[municato] cap[iendo]) as was read in the Canon'. Faced with the prospect of long court proceedings and the repeated demands that would be laid upon his resolution, Rogers balked and told the bishop that he would rather be deprived at once. Laud refused, and said that he would proceed according to law. Rogers was suspended.[31]

Attention passed quickly from Rogers as Laud turned his energies to his

---

[28] Mather, III pp. 105–6. Mather transcribes this from a manuscript of John Rogers which may have come into Mather's possession through Nathaniel Rogers, John's son. At the end, Mather observes, 'Reader, In this one Passage thou hast a large History, of the Thoughts and Fears, and Cares, with which the Puritans of those Times were exercised.' Ibid., p. 106.
[29] GL 9537/13 f. 28v.   [30] ERO D/ACA 47 f. 97v.
[31] *Winthrop Papers*, III pp. 58–9; GL 9531/15 f. 25r.

brief dismissal of Shepard 'as one that kept conventicles', and then became involved in a bitter argument with representatives from Colchester who hoped to install William Bridge as their new lecturer. Rogers may have stayed to watch all this, although it is perhaps more likely that he began the fifteen-mile horse ride home, for he had travelled very little since his lameness.[32] The first enforced break in a thirty-year preaching career must have given him a great deal to think about as he rode home.

V

The results of Rogers' agonisings will become clear, but if we follow the court to its next destination, we find the 4 September session seven miles down the road to Bishops Stortford, at Braintree. After the sermon, Laud called the godly ministers of the area and kept them before him while he checked his notes in a book that he carried. Among those present were Samuel Wharton of Felsted, Stephen Marshall of Finchingfield, Edmund Brewer of Castle Hedingham and Daniel Rogers of Wethersfield. The atmosphere must have been tense: Rogers, as we have seen, expected trouble, and Wharton and Brewer had been troubled for nonconformity in the past.[33] After closing his book, Laud commended each man 'for parts and paines and their lives' and then, as they relaxed, charged them all with nonconformity. Rogers made his position plain, but the others present all denied the accusations; they knew they were in a position of weakness, aware of the fact that Laud held information about them but unsure exactly what he knew. Marshall spoke for all of them:

Mr Mar[shall] said he was misinformed. Ay but said he [Laud] do you conforme always? He ans[wered] he did somet[imes] but not alwa[ys.] he was much employed in preaching and in catec[hising] the youth. The B[ishop] ans[wered,] your prea[ching] I like wel and your Catec wondrous well but I mislike your answers, (which he spoke angerly) you wear the Surplesse sometimes, and then you lay it aside from you for a long time, and what say your people then?[34]

This is a revealing scene in a number of ways: Laud interviewed the ministers in groups, making it difficult for any minister to seek compromise without losing face; he made it clear that he was informed regarding practice in the parishes; he commended them for their lives, as throughout the visitation he maintained a public concern to root out scandalous ministers, although the surviving records do not show any minister troubled for issues of this kind. Moreover, we find a preoccupation with catechising over preaching and, perhaps more importantly, a differential of expectation

---

32 *Winthrop Papers*, III p. 59; *MHSC* 5th ser. 1 (1871) p. 197; see above pp. 40–2.
33 GL 9537/11 f. 139v; ERO D/ABA 1 f. 126.   34 *Winthrop Papers*, III p. 59.

between the minister striving to be seen as conformable and the new stance of the bishop. We can compare this with the case of Thomas Juby, a vicar of Theydon Mount: when, in 1610, he was presented for neglecting the surplice, he testified that he had worn it sometimes, though not always. The case was dismissed.[35] In Marshall's case the end result was the same, but the impression given is very different. Even when no action is taken, the ceremonies seem to be pressed upon ministers regardless of any scruples they may have. In itself, this is an important truth – the quantitative assessment of the court record is insufficient to understand the impact of an episcopal visitation: interviews like this were remembered, related and spread among the godly. In addition, the court record fails to record those ministers driven to flight by the fears aroused by such relations: from 1631 alone, John Norton of Bishops Stortford, John Wilson of Sudbury and Hooker's former assistant, John Eliot, all left the diocese. It is important to note Laud's manner as well as the proceedings of his court, and even Clarendon, no friend to Puritans, attributed to Laud 'a hasty, sharp way of expressing himself'.[36] The result of his manner and the perception that the ceremonies were unduly pressed was the angry delegation that met the following day at Dunmow.

Two days before the court was held at Dunmow, a group of godly clerics met at Braintree. Thomas Weld, Samuel Wharton, Stephen Marshall, Nathaniel Ward, Thomas Shepard and Daniel Rogers 'consulted together whether it was best to let such a swine to root up God's plants in Essex and not to give him some check'. On 3 September, Weld and Shepard travelled together, discussing the options of emigration open to them, resolving to try Ireland and then Scotland rather than cross the Atlantic. When they arrived, Shepard entered the church, with Weld staying outside as his excommunication prevented him from setting foot inside. Shepard listened to the sermon, preached by Nehemiah Rogers, the vicar of Messing, justifying human inventions in divine worship, and after the sermon Weld entered and approached Laud. Laud pre-empted any remonstrance Weld intended to make: as he was to depose during Laud's trial, the bishop 'reviled me for impudency, as dareing to appear in his presence' and went on to threaten him with a summons from the High Commission Court for treading upon holy ground, this action intended to make Weld an example to all ministers. Weld claimed innocence from ignorance and William, Lord Maynard, a layman with Laudian sympathies, and Arthur Duck spoke up on Weld's behalf, claiming that they 'had allwaies found me a sober man', but Laud was resolved, 'protesting in general fury yt all ye friends I could

---

[35] O. U. Kalu, 'The Jacobean Church and Essex Puritans', University of Toronto PhD (1972) p. 165.

[36] G. Huehns (ed.), *Selections from Clarendon* (Oxford, 1978) p. 103.

make in England should not move him one haires breadth from his purpose against me'. Laud began to declare him prisoner to the pursuivant until Weld paid one hundred marks, promising to appear at the High Commission. Laud asked if Weld was intending to go to New England and if Shepard would go with him. At this point, Shepard was making his own approach and attempted to intervene, despite the warnings of others in the throng, and had to be restrained by Martin Holbeach, the schoolmaster of Felsted, 'a godly man [who] pulled me away with violence out of the crowd. And soon as ever I was gone the apparitor calls for Mr Shepard, and the pursuivant was sent presently after to find me out. But he that pulled me away . . . hastened our horses and away we rid as fast as we could. And so the Lord delivered me out of the hand of that lion a third time.'[37]

Despite the demonstration, there was no further ministerial discipline administered at Dunmow. As Laud moved out of Essex into Hertfordshire there was a time of quiet and reflection in the county. This was the silence that descends over a battlefield during a lull in the proceedings rather than genuine peace. Those ministers whose affairs with the court were unfinished had little time to consider their positions; those who had survived could assess the damage and offer advice before the third wave came to complete the visitation.

Thomas Weld had the prospect of a citation to appear in the Consistory Court at St Paul's on the afternoon of 5 October. By 18 September he must have made his final decision to leave as he allowed his curate, Nathaniel Bosse, to denounce his excommunication from the pulpit. He was to absent himself from the deprivation hearing at St Paul's and take ship for Amsterdam, leaving his family to enjoy the 100 pounds a year in land that had been settled upon his children upon his refusal to subscribe. In his absence, Laud complained to the High Commission, which completed Weld's deprivation for contumacy in January 1632. Bosse's denunciation was noted, and when the court returned he was presented for neglecting to read prayers on Wednesdays and holy days in the afternoon and for failing to catechise since Weld's departure. Not intending to deprive Terling of all ministerial leadership, Bosse submitted.[38]

---

37 M. McGiffert (ed.), *God's Plot: the Paradoxes of Puritan Piety Being the Autobiography and Journal of Thomas Shepard* (Amherst, Mass., 1972) pp. 50–1; Nehemiah Rogers, *A Sermon Preached at the Visitation of William, Bishop of London, 3 ix 1631* (1632); SP 16/499/87; on Maynard, see N. Tyacke, *Anti-Calvinists: the Rise of English Arminianism, c.1590–1640* (Oxford, 1987) pp. 192–4.

38 GL 9531/15 ff. 24, 25r; S. R. Gardiner (ed.), *Reports of Cases in the Courts of Star Chamber and High Commission, Camden Soc.* 39 (1889) pp. 260, 264; GLRO D/LC 319 f. 39. Bosse had been called before the court of the Archdeacon of Colchester in May for not using the surplice, for omitting parts of the liturgy, for baptising without the sign of the

Before the court returned in full, John Rogers had come to an uncomfortable decision. On the same day that Weld's excommunication was denounced, having had six weeks to consider life without the liberty to preach, he met the Commissary of Essex and Hertfordshire, Robert Aylett, in rooms he had taken at 'Le Taverne' in Lexden. Although Aylett had no jurisdiction in the area, Rogers applied to him to have his suspension lifted. Aylett suggested that the revocation of the suspension would have to be confirmed by the bishop himself, but he accepted Rogers' submission. Clearly, the capture of such a notable citadel for conformity had been Laud's intention. He had made the consequences of Rogers' refusal to subscribe very clear and, satisfied that Rogers' credit among the godly would be compromised by his submission, confirmed the revocation in January.[39] In fact, such was the esteem in which Rogers was held that his reputation survived this humiliation: his case makes an anonymous appearance in Hooker's preface to the *Fresh Suit*. In the only sympathetic example he gives of a conforming minister, Hooker describes his friend's case:

... some have openly protested, that if it were but half an hours hanging, they would rather suffer it than subscribe. (I speak but what I know.) But for them and theirs, to lie in the ditch and to be cast into a blind corner like broken vessels, yea, they and their families to die many hundred deaths by extreme misery before they come unto their graves, this they were not able to undergo; a condition, I acknowledge, which needs and deserves a great deal of pity and commiseration, since it is true that some kinds of oppression make a man mad.[40]

The third stage of the visitation was no less thorough than the first two. As already noted, the task of this stage was to follow up outstanding business and to pick up cases that had evaded the bishop on his first circuits. Nathaniel Ward, rector of Stondon Massey, fell into this last category. He had been noted as 'unconformist' during the 1628 visitation and marked out for further attention.[41] He was prominent in the information gathered before the 1631 visitation,[42] but failed to appear for the first two rounds. Ward was not, however, forgotten, and when the court returned to Chelmsford on 13 December, he was presented 'for not wearing the surplice for theis two yeares last past, And for that there were noe prayers constantly read in his church on Wednesdayes, Frydiaes and

cross, and for administering communion to people who refused to kneel. On this occasion he had also appealed for clemency and submitted, delivering a certificate of penance on 7 December 1631: ERO D/ACA 48 ff. 13v, 26v, 40r, 50, 90r.

[39] GL 9531/15 ff. 25–6; at the end of the resolution quoted above, Rogers had noted, 'This I smarted for in 1631. If I had read this. it may be, I had not done what I did.' Mather, III p. 106.

[40] G. H. Williams, N. Pettit, W. Herget and S. Bush, Jr (eds.), *Thomas Hooker: Writings in England and Holland, 1625–1633, Harvard Theological Studies* 28 (1975) p. 330.

[41] GL 9537/13 f. 16.   [42] SP 16/175/104.

holydaies'. The churchwardens attempted to evade substantive issues by submitting a well-worn evasion, presenting that 'the surplice is old and not fit to be used'. When Laud interviewed Ward more fully he charged him with rejecting the ceremonies and the Book of Common Prayer. The godly expected Ward to be put by, but he hoped to talk his way out of trouble, perhaps feeling that business begun at such a late stage could be delayed beyond the patience of a court which had been constantly on the road since August. He told Laud, 'There is one thing I confess I stick at, how I may say for any that die *In sure and certain hope*, or *We, with this our brother*', and so on. Laud was not one to be worn out by being asked to defend the liturgy. He made 'a large explication' until Ward pronounced himself satisfied.[43]

For the time being, Ward was left with the task of repairing the surplice and providing a certificate of restitution. Laud moved on, tidying up loose ends and completing the routine business of lay discipline. He admonished Weld's curate and instigated a presentment against Thomas Witham of Mistley, a friend of John Rogers, for neglecting the holy days. At Wethersfield, where Daniel Rogers still lay under suspension, the churchwardens, Thomas Digby and George Strawland, were presented 'for maintaining a lecture without any authority since Mr Rogers suspension'. It was discovered that 'divers have preached that have not observed the Kings instructions nor read prayers before their sermon therefore [it was ordered that] they will certify the names of such have preached there since Mr Rogers suspension'. At Braintree Laud found that his thoroughness had generated a new radicalism: Samuel Collins had not worn the surplice or used the blessing since the visitation. The churchwardens, John Dedman and Samuel Smith, were cited for not presenting his new nonconformity and, under pressure, admitted that they had been godfathers to children baptised without the sign of the cross.[44]

Despite this new business, Laud had not forgotten Nathaniel Ward. In relating the first exchange, Henry Jessey believed that Ward's strategy had been successful. Like Weld, he underestimated Laud's determination. Ward had watched his progress carefully and knew better. The day after his first interview, he wrote to John Cotton:

I was yesterday convented before the bishop, I mean to his court, and am adjourned, to the next term. I see such giants turn their backs, that I dare not trust my own weak heart . . . I pray therefore, forget me not, and believe me also if there be such a piece of neighbourhood among Christians.[45]

43 GL 9531/15 f. 38r; GLRO DL/C 319 f. 32; *Winthrop Papers*, III p. 60.
44 GLRO DL/C 319 ff. 39, 63, 77, 157.
45 The letter is printed in Thomas Hutchinson, *The History of the Colony and Province of Massachusetts Bay* (ed. L. S. Mayo) (Cambridge, Mass., 1936) vol. I p. 104n.

As Ward expected, the bishop returned to Stondon to interview him from 8 to 10 February 1632. Although he seems to have been aware that he was unlikely to escape, and had long been involved with the New England project, Ward was still prepared to try and talk his way out of trouble. Part of this may have been a pleasure in debate born of his legal training, but he also felt every possibility must be explored before emigration. He wrote:

I dare averre, that it ill becomes Christians any thing well shod with the preparation of the Gospell, to meditate flight from their deare Countrey upon these disturbances. Stand your grounds ye Eleazars and Shammahs, stir not a foote of ground so long as you have halfe a foote of ground to stand upon.[46]

During his long interview, Laud became convinced that Ward had a case to answer, and pressed him to subscribe. Ward opened further doubts and was given until 18 April to satisfy his scruples.[47] He was interrogated again in April and August. At his last interview, in September 1632, he made his final plea for a measure of tolerance, citing Romans 14.21. He said he 'would not offend his weak brother', and asked, 'why then should the Bishop offend him by imposing the Surplice? To that speech of Paul, Bishop Laud answered, Yea, Paul said so when he was alone, but do you think Paul would have said so, if he had been in a Convocation?' – as Giles Firmin observed, 'A rare Answer, worthy of a Bishop'. With this final invocation of authority to end debate, Ward was suspended and, a month later, excommunicated. On 10 December 1632, he suffered a final sentence of deprivation.[48]

The final member of the conference drawn to Laud's attention before the 1631 visitation was John Beadle, at the time rector of Little Leighs and chaplain to the Earl of Warwick, resident in his parish. At Leighs he seems to have been relatively immune, even to Laud's thoroughness. Once again, Laud's memory proved equal to his task. In the first months of 1632, the bishop had offered Samuel Collins the rectory of Barnston. Despite his troubles, Collins declined and recommended instead his kinsman, Beadle. Collins suggested that Laud should call both men to attend upon him when Beadle was to be inducted, and charge Collins with the task of reducing conventicles, to keep conformity in his administration of the communion and, perhaps most importantly, to make it clear that few things were spoken or acted in Braintree that failed to come to the bishop's attention.

---

[46] GLRO DL/C 319 ff. 249, 162; Nathaniel Ward, *The Simple Cobler of Agawam* (1647) pp. 23–4. Here Ward is referring to the disturbances within the English church during the 1640s, with particular reference to toleration. For New England, M. J. Bohi, 'Nathaniel Ward, Pastor Ingeniosus (?1580–1652)', University of Illinois PhD (1959) pp. 76–81.

[47] GLRO DL/C 319 f. 162.

[48] GL 9531/15 ff. 39v–41r; Giles Firmin, *Presbyterial Ordination Vindicated* (1660) p. 38; Laud, *Works*, V ii p. 318.

Collins hoped that this fearsome example would settle Beadle into conformable habits and perhaps win a little peace for Collins if it became known that he was under such pressure. In the event, Laud seems to have gone further and formally to have presented Beadle. It was claimed that he seldom or never read prayers or wore the surplice on Sundays, and usually read a lesson, sang a psalm and then went straight into the pulpit, that he had baptised his own child without the surplice or the sign of the cross, and that on the previous anniversary of the Gunpowder Plot he 'tooke an occasion to speake ag[ains]t the ignorance of the people and told them positively that it were a thousand to one if one of a hundred of them that were not booke-learnt were saved', and that in the same sermon 'he wished that those ministers that did not that day preach their tounges might cleave to the roofs of their mouthes and they never preach more'. The combined pressures of Collins and Laud prevailed, at least for the present, with the young minister: he submitted, promised conformity and subscribed, and thus was dismissed with a canonical admonition, the lowest censure available.[49]

VI

While the loose ends of visitation business were being tied up, the achievements of the earlier stages were being consolidated. The information networks which set the agenda for the visitation were called into play again, and Aylett sent conformist ministers to assess the extent of reformation and visited many churches himself, within and beyond his own jurisdiction, to make it clear that the absence of the bishop from the county did not mean the end of his scrutiny. His investigations yielded a mixed harvest: at Dedham he found that prayers were now read before the lecture but that Thomas Cottesford, the vicar, often ministered without the surplice, and so admonished him and reminded John Rogers of his submission; he found that Stephen Marshall was 'in all very conformable', and preaching only on the holy days; Thomas Witham of Mistley was also now conforming in his principle cure, although he delivered a weekly lecture at Manningtree, a chapel of ease, without the surplice, claiming that the chapel was unconsecrated and that he held a special faculty from the bishop; Edmund Brewer of Castle Hedingham had also taken steps towards conformity and now 'seldom omitted to wear the surplice'. Aylett demanded that the surplice should never be neglected, and the minister and churchwardens promised to observe his admonition. However, he found

---

[49] SP 16/216/207; 16/175/104; *HMC Report on Manuscripts in Various Collections* (London, 1914) pp. 3–4; GL 9539A/2 f. 6; 9539A/1 f. 18v; Laud, *Works* V ii p. 318.

that there were common attempts to evade the full effects of the Royal Instructions, with lecturers allowing curates to read prayers in the surplice before the lecture, but refusing to attend until prayers were over, 'which gives occasion to the people lightly to esteem of public prayers'. This was Samuel Wharton's practice at Felsted, and he was followed by John Michaelson at Chelmsford. At Wethersfield, Daniel Rogers was still attempting to provide for his parishioners: Aylett was 'credibly informed that Mr Attwood, a great unconformist, is there indeed a lecturer, admitted under the colour of being curate'. The churchwardens informed the Commissary's Court, which investigated, that since the receipt of an order from the bishop's officers making it clear that visiting preachers would be closely watched, the only minister preaching there had been Stephen Marshall and that he wore the surplice.[50] In addition, preachers were being invited to substitute for troubled ministers: at Dedham, Rogers' protégé, John Angier, was invited back and preached four times, and also delivered sermons at Boxted, Little Leighs, Castle Hedingham, Coggeshall and Earls Colne;[51] in the weeks that Nathaniel Bosse was suspended it was found that four different ministers had preached at Terling, including John Newton of Little Baddow and Mr Hill, curate at Felsted, and that none had worn the surplice.[52] Strange ministers had also appeared in the pulpits at Springfield, Boreham, Great Waltham, Braintree and Hatfield Broad Oak, and Stephen Marshall had procured a preacher for St James, Colchester.[53] In each case, the churchwardens had forgotten to ask to see the minister's licence and neglected to ask him to enter his name in the parish book for visiting preachers, although at Dedham, Samuel Sherman, who had

---

[50] SP 16/218/43; ERO D/ABA 5 ff. 135–6. The Commissary's Court, which resumed its business on 22 September 1631, was used to collect much of this information. The churchwardens of each of the ministers Laud had paid special attention to were questioned about their practice, and interleaved in the Act Book of the court are notes regarding the practices of the lecturers of Felsted, Wethersfield, Finchingfield, Walden and Castle Hedingham, which are clearly the source for the notes in the State Papers, ERO D/ABA 5 f. 133v. In relation to the supply of sermons at Wethersfield it is noteworthy that Walter Wiltshire, a Wethersfield Yeoman who was remembered in Richard Rogers' will and housed Stephen Marshall when he was lecturer in the parish, provided in his own will that, if the lecture he erected or supplemented in Wethersfield were to lapse, Marshall should receive the income from 105 acres of land to pay for a weekly lecture in Finchingfield: ERO D/P 119/25/195; Giles Firmin, *A Briefe Vindication of Stephen Marshall* appended to Firmin, *Questions between the Conformist and the Non-Conformist* (1681) pp. 4, 24; H. F. Waters, *Genealogical Gleanings in England* (Boston, Mass., 1901) vol. I p. 211.

[51] ERO D/ACA 49 ff. 133r, 136r, 139v, 159r; D/ABA 6 ff. 117v, 120r.

[52] ERO D/ABA 5 ff. 119r, 123v, 125r. Newton claimed that he normally wore the surplice at Little Baddow but that Terling did not possess a decent surplice. Despite these expedients, the Terling churchwardens were presented twice in May 1632 for failing to provide a sermon or service on Easter day, upon various holy days, or on the anniversary of the King's coronation: ERO D/ACA 48 ff. 147v, 166v.

[53] ERO D/ABA 5 ff. 118v, 119v, D/ACA 48 f. 93r.

covered for John Rogers in the 1605 visitation, had told the churchwardens at Dedham and Boxted that Angier, a relative, was licensed.[54] This issue caused further trouble at Dedham when the vicar, Thomas Cottesford, refused to allow the churchwardens, Francis Bought and John Heywood, to perform public penance for their negligence.[55]

Laud was not Bishop of London for long enough to make a third visitation. The submission of John Beadle, which proved to be illusory, marks the end of the business set out before the 1631 visitation and allows us some space for assessment. We have noted that Laud made very few changes to the machinery of discipline, the visitation articles and the court circuits. He did, however, substantially improve the detective structures in the diocese, employing the archdeacons' courts as well as conformist ministers and laypeople to gather information. In addition, he followed up his information with a greater energy and diligence than his predecessors had displayed:[56] the devices to delay or evade discipline employed by, for instance, Ward and Weld, were utterly unsuccessful. Moreover, a pattern emerges in his pursuit of those ministers he suspected as inconformable. His first move was to require them to subscribe, usually in the company of a number of other ministers, making the act a very public submission. If the minister refused to subscribe, Laud would then bring up the information he had gathered regarding the minister's inconformity. Once he had begun the process against a nonconformist minister it soon became clear that he would follow that process to its conclusion, either in complete submission or in the removal of the contumacious preacher. This is not to say that his approach was inflexible; if he felt that pressure or argument would win a minister for conformity, he would make the choices very clear and allow him time, but if he felt that the preacher was beyond the pale he could make it equally clear that there was no place for such a man in his diocese. On occasion his judgement was exact and his aim achieved: this was the case, for instance, with Thomas Weld and John Rogers. On others, he was mistaken, and appears less adept: his handling of Thomas Shepard and Stephen Marshall seems to fall into this category, the one driven into nonconformity and eventual exile, the other keeping the liberty of his ministry with a fresh sense of grievance. Finally, we may note that the

---

[54] ERO D/ACA 49 ff. 136r, 139v, 184r. Stephen Marshall had performed the same service for the strange preacher at Colchester: ERO D/ACA 48 f. 93r. The churchwardens' lack of curiosity is, to say the least, striking.

[55] ERO D/ACA 49 f. 160r.

[56] On former practice, see O. U. Kalu, 'Bishops and Puritans in Early Jacobean England: a Perspective on Methodology', *CH* 45 (1977) pp. 469–89; O. U. Kalu, 'Continuity and Change: Bishops of London and Dissent in Early Stuart England', *JBS* 18 (1978) pp. 28–45; K. Fincham, *Prelate as Pastor*, pp. 112–46, 212–47; Emmison, *Elizabethan Life: Morals and the Church Courts*, p. xi and *passim*.

response of the godly ministers was not wholly passive, and a series of strategies was evolved to cope with the changed circumstances. Neither was the response uniform: we shall see more clearly that disagreements among the godly regarding the correct reaction to greater pressure became an extra strain upon the godly community, revealing fissures that divided ministers who had seemed completely in sympathy with one another, and contributing to the diaspora of the Essex godly.

Juxon, Wren and the implementation of Laudianism

I

Archbishop Abbot died on 4 August 1633. It came as no surprise that William Laud was to be translated to Canterbury, a nomination of which he was informed within two days. On 6 August 1633, Francis Kirby informed John Winthrop, 'For domesticke newes it is bad. The bishop of Canterbury died the last saboth day, & his place (as I hear) the kinge hath bestowed upon the bishop of London.' It was less clear who was to succeed him at Fulham Palace: court sources believed Matthew Wren and the Bishop of Oxford, John Bancroft, to be the front runners, with the Bishop of Bath and Wells, William Pierce, to be another candidate. In the event, on 23 September the nomination went to William Juxon, until January the president of St John's College, Oxford, Laud's college. Since July, Juxon had been clerk of the King's closet, the royal confessor, and when he received his nomination for London, he was bishop elect of Hereford. Bearing in mind that each Archbishop of Canterbury since Whitgift had been translated directly from London, this was a fairly meteoric rise. Juxon was clearly the new archbishop's nominee: he recorded in his diary that he had secured Juxon's appointment so that he 'might have one that I trust near his majesty, if I grow weak or infirm, as I must have a time'.[1]

Juxon's Arminianism is rather more assumed than evident,[2] but it is

---

[1] H. Trevor-Roper, *Archbishop Laud* (London, 1965) pp. 144–5; *MHSC* 4th ser. 7 (1865) p. 15; SP 16/24/53; William Laud, *The Works of William Laud, Anglo-Catholic Library* (ed. J. Bliss and W. Scott) (Oxford, 1847–60) III p. 216. On Juxon see T. A. Mason, *Serving God and Mammon: William Juxon, 1582–1663* (London, 1985) esp. ch. 3, although it will become clear below that I differ in my assessment of his time as Bishop of London; and for a more anecdotal approach, W. H. Marah, *Memoirs of Archbishop Juxon and his Times* (Oxford, 1869).

[2] Tyacke describes him as an Arminian on the grounds of the religious propositions he drew up to be assented to by the ministers of his diocese, which will be discussed below, pp. 235–6, although he recognises that his chaplains cannot be located theologically with any precision: N. Tyacke, *Anti-Calvinists: the Rise of English Arminianism, c.1590–1640* (Oxford, 1987) pp. 208, 217–18. The only explicit identification of Juxon as an Arminian is

certainly accurate to describe him as Laudian. He had been close to Laud for some years, at least since they were fellows together at St John's College, Oxford, and his policy reflects this allegiance, although his theological stance is poorly documented. It is better to regard him, a little like Laud himself, as an administrator with a strong practical programme rather than any sort of theologian. His programme became clear as he prepared to conduct his primary visitation: the articles he issued continue and amplify Laud's concern for constant ceremonial conformity. He added the canonical authorities for each of his requirements and demanded that every minister should read the 1604 Canons once a year before divine service. For the surplice and the cross in baptism he applied Laud's aim of complete conformity without exception, as opposed to the former policy of occasional use of the ceremonies. He asked,

Whether doth your Minister use to signe Children with the signe of the Crosse when they are baptised, according to the Booke of Common Prayer, and the 30. canon: and doth he never faile to use the said signe of the Crosse?

The same formula applied to the surplice, whereas Laud had used the formula only once, in his article relating to the Book of Common Prayer. In addition, Juxon showed a greater interest in the observance of prayers for 'the whole Catholic Church Militant' and of divine service on the holy days, namely 'the Birthday of the Lord God, the feast of the Purification, the Annunciation of Saint Mary the Virgin, the Feast of the Ascension of our Lord God, the Nativity of St John Baptist, and the Feast of All Saints: and whether doth your Minister reade Evening Prayer upon these dayes following, viz. upon the Eve of the Birth of our Lord God, Easter Eve, and Whitsun Eve?' Finally, he reproduced in full the Royal Instructions regarding lecturers at the end of the articles, and enjoined churchwardens to certify whether their minister had read the Book of Sports, which had been reissued in October 1633, in the parish church.[3]

If this increased ceremonial pressure was to be the policy of the new bishop, the prospect of Juxon's visitation must have had the godly ministers of Essex fearing a repeat of the experiences of 1631. In the event the 1634 visitation proved to be a very different matter. From the first, Juxon found that his court duties interfered with the rigorous administration of his diocese and it was the outlying parts of his diocese that suffered (or benefited) from his neglect. He visited the City of London and Middlesex in

in the index. Mason admits that he left little evidence of his theological views, but claims that he 'demonstrated liturgical Arminianism' and refers to him unequivocally as an 'Arminian reformer': Mason, *Juxon*, pp. 15, 45–67, esp. 61–2. He is not one of the individuals discussed by Peter White in his *Predestination, Policy and Polemic: Conflict and Consensus in the English Church from the Reformation to the Civil War* (Cambridge, 1992).
[3] STC 10265.

person, but by the time the court moved into Essex, towards the end of 1634, he had passed the business entirely into the hands of Dr Arthur Duck, his chancellor. Duck was an able and prominent civil lawyer, whose incomplete commitment to Laudianism was firmly demonstrated in 1641 when he turned petitioner against the archbishop.[4] The preoccupations of the visitation reverted to pre-Laudian patterns in the main, focusing on traditional moral regulation. There seems to have been little attempt to use the intelligence structures so carefully constructed by Laud to set objectives for the court and still less attention to consolidation in the later sessions and in the archidiaconal courts as the visitation came to an end.[5]

The only issues which seem to have been pressed in ministerial discipline were the publication of the Book of Sports and the observation of the holy days. Edward Collins of Boxted, a friend of John Rogers pressed in the previous visitation, admitted he had not read the declaration at all and had held no service on St Jude's day.[6] In other parishes the churchwardens were required to certify that the declaration was published: this was the case in Dedham, Messing, St Leonard's, Colchester, Wethersfield, Little Dunmow and Barnston, but in no instance was the requirement followed up. It is hard to believe that certificates were meekly delivered up without making any impression on the surviving record. It seems more likely that no further action was taken.[7] The same appears to be true among those parishes where questions were asked with respect to the observation of the holy days.[8] For what might be called routine nonconformity, despite 'divers complaints about inconformity to the Church Discipline', in the whole diocese 'the proofs came home' against only four, three curates and a vicar. The vicar was Thomas Peck of Prittlewell, who survived to suffer deprivation after the Restoration. He was presented for administering the sacrament to parishioners who refused to kneel, for omitting the cross in baptism, and for neglecting the surplice. Upon his submission, no further action was taken. Two of the curates left no trace in the surviving court records, although Juxon claimed that they had submitted and promised conformity. The third, Philip Sanders, curate of Hutton, was suspended and left the diocese, although he had returned by 1637 and survived to

[4] *DNB* s.v. 'Duck'; B. Levack, *Civil Lawyers in England, 1603–42* (Oxford, 1973) pp. 225–6; Trevor-Roper, *Archbishop Laud*, p. 414. Juxon's relative laxity in visitation cannot, of course, be attributed entirely to his other duties: Laud managed to maintain his increased surveillance despite his own extensive secular role.

[5] The sources for the 1634 visitation are GL 9531/15; GLRO DL/C 320, 322, 326, 343; ERO D/AEA 40, D/ACA 50, D/ABA 7, D/ALV 2.

[6] ERO D/ALV 2 f. 24r. On Collins see A. G. Matthews, *Calamy Revised* (Oxford, 1934) s.v. 'John Collinges'.

[7] ERO D/ALV 2 ff. 36v, 37r, 40v, 45r, 63r, 65r, 66r, 157v–8r.

[8] E.g. ERO D/ALV 2 ff. 24r, 31r, 45r, 46v.

hold a sequestrated cure of Magdalen Laver, which he held till his death in 1652.[9]

Over the following two years the distractions that limited the effectiveness of Juxon's primary visitation multiplied. By April 1636, he was a member of the Privy Council, a commissioner of depopulations, first commissioner for licensing the retail of tobacco, new buildings in London, saltpetre and gunpowder, first commissioner of the Admiralty, and on 6 March 1636 he crowned his achievements when he became the first clerical Lord Treasurer since the reign of Edward VI. In addition, his chief officials, Arthur Duck and Robert Aylett, were increasingly occupied with High Commission business and other extra-diocesan concerns.[10] Placed against the activity Laud was able to maintain, Juxon's duties might not have led to a neglect of his diocese. In fact, his limited control of his territory had become apparent by the end of 1635, for Juxon's account to Laud for that year could only provide details for the City of London, three of his archdeacons failing to return any report at all to their bishop.[11]

II

All this is in stark contrast to the experience of ministers north of the River Stour. It is worth considering developments in the diocese of Norwich to make the contrast clear, to follow the fortunes of some of the ministers encountered in the discussions of godly society and conceptions of the ministry above, and also to illuminate further some of the themes of this chapter. In particular, I think it is profitable to focus on the primary visitation of Matthew Wren, who had been a candidate for the vacant see of London in 1633.

Wren succeeded to the large diocese upon the death of the indolent poet, Richard Corbett, in July 1635. He prepared his new see for his primary visitation with the publication of his articles. He issued two documents: firstly, 'orders, directions and remembrances', comprising twenty-eight articles, pressing the full observances of the rites of Common Prayer, requiring communion tables to be placed altar-wise against the east wall of the chancel and railed in, and demanded that pews should be orderly and uniform; secondly, a series of articles addressed 'to the Churchwardens, and any other of every parish, that shall be sworn to make presentments', a

---

[9] Laud, *Works*, V pp. 327, 28; ERO D/ALV 2 f. 109; H. Smith, *The Ecclesiastical History of Essex under the Long Parliament and Commonwealth* (Colchester, 1933) pp. 47, 50, 57, 108, 158, 270; T. W. Davids, *Annals of Evangelical Nonconformity in the County of Essex* (London, 1863) pp. 415–16; GL 9531/15.

[10] Mason, *Juxon*, ch. 5 and *passim*; J. H. Round, 'Dr Robert Aylett', *TEAS* 10 (1909) pp. 26–34; SP 16/263/67; 16/277/60; 16/277/79; *DNB* s.v. 'Duck'.

[11] Laud, *Works*, V pp. 322–33.

pamphlet of nine chapters and 142 sections, each with six or more questions. These related in particular to the conduct of the services, the character and activities of the minister, and the condition of the church, as well as traditional moral concerns.[12]

Among the godly, the articles were a subject of shocked correspondence and a cause of trepidation. Lucy Downing informed Margaret Winthrop in May 1636 that, 'The Bishop of Norwich, whose name is Wren, doth impose a hundred and 32 articles to the clergy in his diocese, some wherof they fear will be put by both Msr Lea and divers others wich thought themselves very conformable men.'[13] Robert Ryece, patron of Preston in Suffolk, some twelve miles from Dedham, made large extracts from the articles, which he sent to John Winthrop.[14] The fears of the godly proved to be entirely justified, for in Norwich the administration matched the intention: Wren sought, and gained, royal permission to spend several months in Suffolk, away from his episcopal houses, in order to oversee the visitation more closely, and in his chancellor, Clement Corbett, he had an able administrator whose fierce antipathy towards Puritans exceeded even his own.[15] The rigorous enforcement of his articles produced, in intensified form, the same disagreements among the godly as to the proper response to such pressure, as had been seen during the 1631 London visitation. For instance, as Lucy Downing had predicted, William Leigh, the parson of Groton who had been a candidate for Finchingfield along with Stephen Marshall and Daniel Rogers in 1625, was one of the ministers attracting Wren's opprobrium. Wren had noted, among the copious memoranda made during and ahead of the visitation, 'Groton, Mr Lee, every Holy day preaching, drawes all ye people of neighbouring parishes from prayers'. In March, Leigh was admonished for failing to read the Book of Sports and suspended until he certified his compliance. Robert Stansby, minister at neighbouring Little Waldingfield passed on the news to Leigh's former patron, John Winthrop, adding, 'but I lately hard ther was some hope of his

---

[12] *STC* 10298; the orders are bound up in manuscript with the British Library copy of the articles; Robert Ryece (see below) quoted from both; on the prevailing situation in the diocese, and on Wren, see R. W. Ketton-Cremer, *Norwich in the Civil War* (Norwich, 1985) chs. 3 and 4; on the pre-Laudian arrangement of church interiors see G. W. O. Addleshaw and F. Etchells, *The Architectural Setting of Anglican Worship* (London, 1948) pp. 30–63, 108–16; N. Yates, *Buildings, Faith and Worship: the Liturgical Arrangements of Anglican Churches 1600–1900* (Oxford, 1991) pp. 30–43; M. Chatfield, *Churches the Victorians Forgot* (Ashbourne, 1979) *passim*. It should be stressed that there were pre-Laudian communion rails in parish churches with altar-wise communion tables and in churches with the altar placed in the centre of the chancel: Addleshaw and Etchells, p. 118; J. C. Cox and A. Harvey, *English Church Furniture* (London, 1907) pp. 17–20 gives examples of both, but overstates their prevalence before the 1630s.
[13] *MHSC* 5th ser. 1 (1871) p. 11.
[14] Ibid., 4th ser. 6 (1863) pp. 407–8, 411–12.
[15] Laud, *Works*, V p. 339. On Corbett, see Ketton-Cremer, pp. 70–3.

liberty.' On the 5 April, Leigh failed to appear as required at Ipswich and was excommunicated. As for John Rogers, the penalty proved too great and within the fortnight he had submitted, and Stansby informed Winthrop 'that your old minister, Mr Lea, hath his libertye to preache, but on what conditions I know not'. Winthrop evidently received more details of Leigh's submission, for he wrote to Lucy Downing, his sister, in a sharply critical manner, appalled by what he saw as his friend's apostasy. Downing sent the letter on to a relation in Suffolk and, as it happened, Leigh was present when she received it. She, 'beinge a very poor clarke, desierd him to read it to her' with highly embarrassing consequences. Leigh wrote a long, wounded reply to Winthrop's aspersions, asking, 'Worthie friend, be iealous (yet with a godly iealousie) not with a carnall. Accept my defens, wch is in truth & playnnes of heart, as before God.' He expressed his astonishment at Winthrop's censures, disappointed at his lack of charity, an absence he was surprised to find 'in you a godly man yt knows what uproars are in our church, & that Gods ministers (especially such poore ones as my self) are in daynger of taking hurt, by reason of oppression & trouble'. He denied preaching in favour of the ceremonies, although he admitted that his practice had changed:

Know I am not more zealous of ceremonies this day, than when you first called me to Groton. I then wore the surpliss, lesse frequentlie for your sake; now more frequentlie for my ministries sake. Consider of it well; he yt judges he may wear the surpliss, & yet will not often, because he will not offend one, may he not weare it often, for the good of manie?[16]

Throughout the diocese, godly ministers were bewildered by the changed environment and many were similarly unsure of the proper response. It is clear that the experience tested the resolution of many godly ministers. For some, the confusion of these times would return to haunt them in the 1640s: attempts at compromise, grounded on a preaching vocation, could resurface in accusations of time-serving pragmatism. One such minister was Jeremiah Burroughes, Thomas Hooker's pupil, who provided a haven for Thomas Shepard and his pregnant wife while they waited for a ship to New England.[17] As one of the Dissenting Brethren, he found the vitriolic pen of Thomas Edwards turned upon him in his *Antapologia*. One accusation was that he had conformed in the 1630s, an imputation he responded to in his *Vindication*. His explanation gives an impression of the pressure under which the godly ministers found themselves, and also how that experience could change moderate men:

---

[16] BodL Tanner MS 68 ff. 212, 225, 30; *MHSC* 4th ser. 7 (1864) pp. 8, 12; ibid., 5th ser. vol. I pp. 13–14, 226–9.
[17] M. McGiffert (ed.), *God's Plot: the Paradoxes of Puritan Piety Being the Autobiography and Journal of Thomas Shepard* (Amherst, Mass., 1972) pp. 34, 62–3.

This conformity he [Edwards] speaks of was some ten years since, and though I did conforme to some of the old Ceremonies, in which I acknowledge my sinne; I doe not cast those things off as inconvenient or discountenanced by the state onely, but as sinful against Christ; yet I think there can hardly be found any Man in that Diocesse where I was, who was so eyed as I was, that did conforme less than I did, if he conformed at all. As for the new conformity, God kept me from it; . . . I see now what I did not; and I blesse God I saw it before the times changed.[18]

Burroughes made a crucial distinction between the 'old conformity' and the new, a distinction which seems to have become a commonplace. Thomas Edwards wanted to know whether the corruptions that the authors of the *Apologeticall Narration* considered intolerable were established by law, that is, the liturgy and government, or those 'innovations in the government and worship, as bowing to Altars, &c. which came of later days'. The question was important, as it had been claimed that all recognised the corruptions as sinfully evil. Edwards claimed: 'Now if you meane the first, that which usually was called, Old conformity, in opposition to the New: So I deny that all doe now generally acknowledge and decrie that as sinfully evill.'[19] Robert Stansby related the godly casualties after Wren's visitation in the same terms, noting: 'Mr Mott of Stoke & Nayland standeth suspended ab officio et beneficio for refusing the new Conformitie, as they call yt. My selfe was deprived of my parsonage July 18, 1636, by our B. , for refusing the old Conformity.'[20]

From Stansby's experience, we can reconstruct what he meant by 'the old conformity'. He was faced at Stowmarket, in October 1635, with a long and damning presentment from his churchwardens, who alleged that he never wore the surplice, never used the cross in baptism, only ever read selected portions of the liturgy 'but never all in one day', and chose his own texts, ignoring the lectionary. Stansby admitted the veracity of all these charges but hoped that his partial use of the liturgy might prove him 'conformable'. He regretted any offence his omissions might have caused and promised 'hereafter to carry & demeane him selfe more conformable'. His attempts to make himself appear moderate were to no avail, and similar charges were brought when he appeared before Wren at Ipswich on 18 July 1636. Again he promised to use more of the Book of Common Prayer, but told the court that he was not satisfied with the lawfulness of either the surplice or the cross in baptism. He had conferred on the issues with previous bishops, notably John Jegon and Samuel Harsnett, without success, although he had kept his liberty. Wren was not going to indulge his

---

[18] Jeremiah Burroughes, *A Vindication of Mr Burroughes against Mr Edwards his Foule Aspersions, in his Spreading Gangraena, and his Angry Antiapologia* (1646) p. 17.

[19] Thomas Edwards, *Antapologia: or, a full answer to the Apologeticall Narration* (1644) p. 15; cf. Robert Baillie, *A Dissuasive from the Errours of our Time* (1645) p. 55.

[20] *MHSC* 4th ser. vol. VII p. 9.

scruples and ordered him publicly to confess his fault in neglecting parts of the liturgy and to confer with learned men regarding the surplice and cross. Like Thomas Weld, Stansby realised that there was to be no escape and refused to make his confession, and was therefore suspended, and eventually deprived.[21]

The experience of Jeremiah Burroughes was similar, although he seems to have started from a lower plane of nonconformity. After his vocational training in Essex he had preached for some time at Bury St Edmunds and then become rector of Tivetshall in north Norfolk, travelling into Suffolk to join a combination lecture at Mendlesham, where Stansby, William Greenhill and Thomas Young, the Scottish Smectymnuan, also preached.[22] He was regarded with particular venom by Clement Corbett, who claimed he was, 'though but young, yet ancient in his inconformity, & universally followed as a popular Patriarck'. He was initially questioned for refusing to read the Book of Sports, but Corbett felt that there was more to his nonconformity than had yet appeared. He wrote to Wren: 'if your Lord[-ship] shall enjoin him to read Praiers when he commeth, he will be found stiff at [bowing at] ye Blessed name of o[u]r saviour. Your Lo. will find some other imperfections upon search.' Burroughes was suspended for these two offences and, despite the best endeavours of his patron, Lady Jane Bacon, Henry Rich, the Earl of Holland and others to secure his departure without censure, he was deprived and moved back into Essex, where he became a regular visitor at Little Leighs.[23]

John Carter, preacher at St Peter Mancroft in Norwich marketplace, was another who made the distinction between old and new conformity in his attempts to keep his place. He was the son of the eminent Suffolk divine of the same name, and father and son were acclaimed preachers up and down the Stour valley. Clement Corbett offered a different assessment of the younger man: 'For a Traducer he was very schismatically brede, his Father died in that shifted vaine.'[24] As with Burroughes, the bishop and his

---

[21] BodL Tanner MS 68 ff. 129–35, 334.

[22] For Burroughes' former practice, I see no reason to doubt his own testimony in the *Vindication*, despite Corbett's assertions (see pp. 209–10, below). In the context of the 1640s, there was little polemical leverage to be gained by confessing to former ceremonial conformity. There is a good deal of biographical information regarding Burroughes in K. Shipps, 'Lay Patronage of East Anglian Puritan Clerics in Pre-Revolutionary England,' Yale University PhD (1971) pp. 175–83. The Mendlesham lecturers are named in N. Evans (ed.), *The Wills of the Archdeaconry of Sudbury 1630–1635*, Suffolk Record Society 29 (1987) p. 263, no. 627.

[23] BodL Tanner MS 68 ff. 121, 180, 204, 248, 96, 7–9. Burroughes was not, as is often asserted, chaplain to the family of the Earl of Warwick.

[24] Clarke (1662) pp. 2–24; *Winthrop Papers* (Boston, Mass., 1929–43) I p. 43; for the younger Carter preaching at Wethersfield in late 1634, QUB Percy MS 7 f. 23; BodL Tanner MS 68 ff. 189–90.

chancellor required Carter to perform divine service, as public a test of conformity as can be imagined. Initially, he refused the ceremonies, for which he was suspended. In order to show his willingness to compromise, he tried again, and read the whole morning service in his surplice. However, he performed everything from the reading desk, and as Robert Ryece noted, 'Our Littargie [is] now devyded into 2 partes, the one to be readde in the reading desk, in the other, called the second service, to be read in the chancell, at the communion table'. Most godly ministers drew the same conclusion as Ryece: 'And to what ende is all this service & addoration of that invisible power unto which it is referred?' Similarly, Carter admitted that his conscience reached its sticking point with this ceremony, the heart of the new conformity. Initially, Carter tried to evade the rite: he knew that Canon 14 ordered ministers to read prayers 'in such place of every church as the bishop of the diocese . . . shall thinke meet for the largeness or straitness of the same so as the people may be most edifyed', and appealed to this provision, claiming that his congregation could not hear if he officiated at the east end of the chancel, a claim with some validity, for St Peter Mancroft, as its name suggests ('Mancroft' being a contraction of 'Magna Croft'), is a very large building. However, Carter's argument was rejected as equivocation, so he made one more attempt. He read the first part of the service from the reading desk, and then announced:

There is another part of divine service to be read: but I am commanded by authority to read it in another place, viz. at the communion table: & so commanded, as I must do it, or leave my ministry. I hope no judicious Christian will be offended at it: Seeing
1. It cannot possibly be unlawful to read the same service in any part of the church, being the whole temple is the house of prayer.
2. Being lawfull: the magistrate hath power to command it: so we are to preach, & practice obedience to governors:
3. Therefore this cannot be accounted a sufficient cause for any man to leave the ministry: God make us carefull in the maine things that concern our salvatio. [sic]

Having explained himself in his reading desk, he continued the service from the chancel. However much the equivocations infuriated Corbett, who felt that he 'hath playd fast & loose & Peeboe' with Wren, Carter eventually regained his place and became a thorn in the side of Wren's successor, Richard Montague. He was noted as 'not suspended; but will needs suspend himself; although he hath taken ye Oath of Canonical Obedience and promised, from time to time; all comaunded Conformity; as much, as a man, possibly can doe'.[25]

III

We may take notice of one final event in Wren's visitation. While he was in Ipswich, Wren asked his servants to hire horses, as he had business elsewhere. It appeared that all the horses were taken by townsfolk travelling to Dedham to hear John Rogers preach. 'Is the wynde at that doore?', asked Wren, 'I will soon ease that.' Accordingly, as Robert Aylett was reported to have confessed, Wren complained to Archbishop Laud, who ordered Aylett to silence Rogers. Aylett wrote to Dedham around June 1636, claiming that his order was to suspend the lecture as a risk to public health while the plague was at its height. Rogers complied, and after the harvest, when the sickness had abated, applied to renew the lecture. Aylett stalled, and Rogers eventually realised that 'there was a secrett determination wholly to supresse that lecture'. According to Robert Ryece, 'this strooke him to the harte, hastened all his natural maladies to his uttermost period'. Rogers died on 18 October 1636. Recording the same account of 'that cursed wren', Samuel Rogers noted that 'the L[or]d thus pluckes out our stakes that are sound out of the hedge, and rotten ones are full in; how soone is such an hedge pushed downe to let wrathe come in'.[26] William Prynne drew attention to the episode as a recent proof that bishops were 'Antichristian and Diabolicall', that they were 'altogether carelesse' of the souls of Dedham.[27]

All these events, which led to some forty godly ministers receiving some form of ecclesiastical censure, were watched with distress, anger and fear by the godly elsewhere.[28] It is easy to imagine the feelings of the many

[26] This anecdote only appears in godly sources, and is uncorroborated in the official record, and so may not be the whole truth, but here it is more important that it was a version believed by the godly. Informed of Rogers' death, Corbett was reported to have said, 'let him goe in reste, for he hath troobled all the country these 30 yeares, & dyd poyson all those partes for x myle round aboute that place'. *MHSC* 4th ser. 6 (1863) pp. 412–13; QUB Percy MS 7 f. 172.

[27] William Prynne, *The Unbishoping of Timothy and Titus* (1636) pp. 152–61, quoted pp. 152, 155.

[28] The figures for Wren's administration are taken from Tanner MS 68 ff. 122–3; cf. P. King, 'Bishop Wren and the Suppression of the Norwich Lecturers', *HJ* 11 (1968) pp. 237–54 (noting the important criticisms made in P. Collinson, *Godly People: Essays on English Protestantism and Puritanism* (London, 1983) p. 469). Wren's primary visitation passed into Puritan mythology: enumerating the dire consequences of rigorously pressed ceremonial uniformity, John Collinges, a former pupil of John Rogers and the son of Edward Collins of Boxted, listed the changes of Laud's 'new Edition of Impositions' and recalled: 'What havock these things made, is yet within the memory of many; and what disturbance Bishop Wren made in Suffolk, and other places, as several other Bishops that were [Laud's] Creatures did in other Dioceses, many alive know; multitudes of Ministers were again deprived and suspended. many undone in the High Commission.' John Collinges, *The History of Nonconformity* (1681) p. 24. In 1640 a soldier reported to be pulling down altar rails in the Stour valley was said to have adopted 'Bishop Wren' as his pseudonym, SP 16/463/27.

godly people who packed Dedham church when John Knowles of Colchester preached Rogers' funeral sermon. Even after death, Rogers was capable of delivering a powerful moral message: as Emmanuel Downing reported, the throng was such that the western gallery began to give way, some of the congregation squeezing out of the doorway and into the stairwell, others leaping down into the nave, 'but yt pleased God to honour that good man departed with a miracle at his death, for the gallery stood and the people went on againe'. The parallels with the tragedy at Blackfriars, where a company of Roman Catholics was less fortunate, were clear for the godly.[29] The effect of such apparent providences and persecutions was to produce an atmosphere of righteous anger and uncertainty: at the end of Wren's visitation Samuel Rogers wrote:

A deep sadnes hath taken hold on mee [from] many motions; the church of god held under hatches, the walls taken downe; pore Suffolk and Northfolk lying desolate by that cursed wretch wren; the plague abroad; this woeful place; in whose company as I am afraid to be for feere of some evell speech.[30]

These accounts helped to feed a perception of the godly ministry as a persecuted minority, even among those ministers who, according to the official record, were untouched by the visitation. The results of this perception will be discussed in greater detail.

[29] *MHSC* 4th ser. 6 (1863) p. 47; on Blackfriars and the Protestant response, see A. Walsham, '"The Fatall Vesper": Providentialism and Anti-Popery in Late Jacobean London', *PP* 144 (1994) pp. 36–87.
[30] QUB Percy MS 7 f. 184.

11

The diocese of Peterborough: a see of conflict

If we turn to the other county favoured by Emmanuel College, Northamptonshire, we find interesting contrasts and similarities. In some respects the differences can be traced to the different pre-history of the diocese of Peterborough as well as the character of the members of the ecclesiastical hierarchy. Northampton developed a fervent radical Puritanism rather earlier than the eastern counties, especially to be found in the orders of 1571 adopted in Northampton, matching a considerable provision of godly sermons and exercises with a vigorous combination of civic and spiritual government, associated in particular with the evangelism of Percival Wiburn, a former Marian exile.[1] In the 1580s, Northamptonshire developed three well-organised *classes* with some notes of synodical authority, and Sir Richard Knightley provided a temporary home for the press that produced the virulent Marprelate tracts against episcopacy.[2] Godly ministers in the county and former Northamptonshire incumbents resident in London were crucial in the plans and organisations related to the Hampton Court Conference.[3] In broader terms, the creation of Peterborough as a new diocese at the Reformation, one partitioned off from the vast diocese of Lincoln, created administrative and disciplinary problems, with poverty, uncertainty over the roles of archidiaconal and consistory courts, and the difficulties following from the placing of the cathedral in Peterborough, at some distance from Northampton, the main town in the county.[4] Perhaps as a consequence of the Elizabethan experi-

---

[1] W. J. Sheils, 'Erecting the Discipline in Provincial England: the Order of Northampton, 1571', *SCH Subsidia* 8 (1991) pp. 331–45; Sheils, 'Religion in Provincial Towns: Innovation and Tradition', in F. Heal and R. O'Day (eds.), *Church and Society in England: Henry VIII to James I* (London, 1977) pp. 168–9.

[2] W. J. Sheils, *The Puritans in the Diocese of Peterborough 1558–1610, Publications of the Northamptonshire Record Society* 30 (Northampton, 1979) pp. 51–60.

[3] Ibid, pp. 73–9.

[4] W. J. Sheils, 'Some Problems of Government in a New Diocese: the Bishop and the Puritans in the Diocese of Peterborough 1560–1630', in R. O'Day and F. Heal (eds.), *Continuity and Change: Personnel and Administration of the Church in England, 1500–1642* (Leicester, 1976) pp. 167–87.

ence of Puritan radicalism, the diocese developed a hierarchy with an early devotion to comparatively 'high church' worship, nominally under the rule of Bishop Dove but, given his effective withdrawal into retirement after the 1605 disputes over subscription, under the activism of John Lambe, the chancellor from 1615 to 1629 and a prominent aid at the Court of Arches thereafter.[5]

I

In the diocese of Peterborough there was a considerable emphasis on the structures and furniture of the parish church. Some of this work may have been relatively uncontroversial. In 1634, Oundle acquired a new spire, the roof of Polebrook was repaired and Higham Ferrers replaced a damaged west end with a new tower and spire, Archbishop Laud subscribing towards the cost of the latter.[6] This work cannot all be described merely as maintenance of decayed buildings, however. Peterborough was one of, if not the, first dioceses to implement the Laudian altar policy.[7] At the end of 1634 the Consistory Court paid close attention to the position of the communion table, whether it was 'cancelled in' and whether silver plates were provided for the bread. At this stage, the responses were disappointing and the similarities in the explanations suggest that some discussion had produced suggestions for passive resistance, or at least this is evidence of a common mind-set on these issues. Cranford St Johns admitted that they lacked a silver plate for the bread 'unlesse ye Cover of the Challice is meant thereby', and went on to agree that the communion table was lacking rails, stressing that 'yet it is not prophaned'. The neighbour of Cranford St Johns, Cranford St Andrew, claimed credit for having the table at the east end of the chancel, and delivered the same request for leniency: 'it is not cancelled in, yet it is not prophaned'. It may be that this was judged as the best response to the practical reason for communion rails, that they would prevent the possibility of profanation by canine urination.[8] Similar defences of such inadequacy were common. At Cold Higham there was no railing

---

[5] J. Fielding, 'Arminianism in the Localities: Peterborough Diocese, 1603–1642', in K. Fincham (ed.), *The Early Stuart Church, 1603–1642* (London, 1993) pp. 93–113 provides an overview of the early Stuart context; for Lambe, see pp. 99–103. Fielding uses the term 'proto-Arminianism' but, as he points out, the issue of soteriological theology took a marginal place in these disputes, so I have not adopted his nomenclature.

[6] NRO PDR Misc. Doc. X650 no. 1. Polebrook may also have acquired a new pulpit and simple benches in the south transept at the same time: N. Pevsner, *Northamptonshire* (Harmondsworth, 1961) p. 378.

[7] N. Tyacke, *Anti-Calvinists: the rise of English Arminianism, c.1590–1640* (Oxford, 1987) pp. 204–5.

[8] NRO PDR CB64 ff. 42, 40.

and the paten was still used for the 'holie bread'; Pattishall also lacked railing and there was 'noe silver plate but pewter for the holy bread'.[9] Some parishes delivered practical excuses: Thomas Williams, the curate of Lilbourne, had baptised using a bowl in the font for the past year, claiming that the font would not hold water, although the visitors may not have been convinced, as Williams was also presented 'for reportinge yt the Bishop of this Diocesse is a superstitious Bishop for yt he bowes to ye Altar and at ye name of Jesus'. Barton Seagrave explained their lack of railing at greater length, blaming poverty, the size of the chancel and concerns about safety.[10] Perhaps the most common response was a plea for time. At Ringstead the position of the pulpit was said to cause 'Inconveniencyes', and the churchyard was insufficiently fenced to exclude swine and cattle. All such inconveniences would be eliminated 'if it please your Worships to commande us give way to the settling of it'. Higham Ferrers admitted that their church was not in 'sufficient repaire, but we are repairing it with all care & speed, and therefore desire favor from the Court to certify of our performance thereof the next visitation'.[11] Burton Latimer lacked rails, 'but wee have spoken for the same to be done and it is in hands a doing'. Flore had neither rails nor silver plate 'for the providing whereof wee crave tyme', a plea repeated by Whitfield for the provision of a surplice and at Stowe-Nine-Churches, where the church was 'nowe downe and uncovered'.[12] This seems to be the same expectation that was seen in Essex, that if one survived the present visitation the case would not be pursued.

On the other hand, All Saints and St Peters of Northampton offered no explanation for their failure to move the table, to rail it in or (in the case of St Peters) to provide a plate for the bread.[13] Godly rule was so well established in Northampton that nothing had been reformed by October 1637 when the metropolitical visitation arrived. The churchwardens had set the furniture table-wise. Robert Woodford, the godly steward of the town, anticipated the approaching court with concern, noting in his diary that there was to be 'a general visitation of Churches in this diocese, by some of the worser sorte of divines, & by paritors &c to observe the standinge of the tables whether altarwise or not, & to set them so. Oh Lord looke uppon us in mercy it is an evill time & the prudent hold their peace who so departeth from evill maketh himselfe a prey, Oh Lord some helpe

---

[9] NRO PDR CB64 ff. 102, 105.   [10] NRO PDR CB64 ff. 72, 160.
[11] NRO PDR CB64 ff. 11, 30.
[12] NRO PDR CB64 ff. 47, 67, 112, 106. The lack of railing at Burton Latimer was probably due to the reluctance of the parishioners, as Robert Sibthorpe, one of the leading Laudian clergymen in the diocese, had been rector of the parish since 1629.
[13] NRO PDR CB64 ff. 75, 80.

from heaven for the Lords sake.'[14] His fears were not ungrounded and accordingly, the visitors delivered a lengthy report on St Peters. The churchyard mounds were said to be too low and 'much rubbish lyeth ag[ains]t the church wales to ye ruining of ye same'. 'The churchyard is basely defiled w[i]th excrements and it appeares that there is usuall evacuating ag[ains]t the church walles at the doores and at the most eminent ends and frontispieces thereof.' (Daniel Cawdrey drew attention to the fact that under the government of the 1630s, the churchyards 'were grown so holy that if a beast did touch them' they were considered to be profaned.) The condition of the ceiling of the vestry was in poor repair, the walls needed plastering and whitewashing, and the floor needed re-paving; various parts of the floor throughout the church were 'uneven, rough and broken in divers places', requiring 'hewen squared stone beseeming soe beautifull a fabrick and the house of God'. There were many complaints about the seating: there was too much seating too far east in the chancel; some seats were 'too high by 3 inches'; some were in need of boarding or paving. Many were held together with inappropriate boarding 'fitt for nothing, but to hide sleepers' and likely to make it difficult to spot non-kneelants at communion. At the west end the seats were too close to the font and thus likely to prevent the minister from kneeling during the prayers at baptism. The cross at the east end of the chancel had been replaced by the town's arms 'as if it were the townes church and not Christs'. The seats in the chancel had prevented the movement of the table and so the visitors ordered them to be cleared for thirteen feet at the east end, the table moved and railed and a 'kneeling bench' supplied.[15] Thomas Ball was thus cited, admonished for his negligence, and ordered to supervise the required repairs. In November, Woodford noted that the table was 'removed to the very top', and he asked God to 'establish us in thy truth & for Xt his sake root out all superstition & idolatry'.[16] The table was, however, neither secured nor railed and this led to the churchwardens being cited in mid-December, Clarke and his colleagues enjoining them to do so 'but they both refused and answered them boldly', earning the applause of Woodford for 'their courage & confidence of fayth & wisdome

---

14 NCO MS 9502 3 September, 1637, 31 August 1637 (pp.19, 17). For Woodford, see J. Fielding, 'Opposition to the Personal Rule of Charles I: the Diary of Robert Woodford, 1637–1641,' *HJ* 31 (1988) pp. 769–88. The diary is unpaginated; Dr Fielding has given page numbers, a practice I have followed in parentheses but, to aid reference checking, my primary notation is through dates. With some exceptions in the later parts of the diary and a few prayers transcribed in the last few pages, the diary follows a strict chronological pattern.
15 SP 16/370/50; Daniel Cawdrey, *Superstitio Superstes* (1641) 'To the Reader'.
16 NCO MS 9502 12 November 1637 (p.57).

for the Lords sake'.[17] At the end of December, the wardens continued to bring down the table 'from the top & set it long wise in the body of the Chancell', earning excommunication in January 1638, a sentence that was overturned in March, an answer to Woodford's prayers.[18] Clarke met with some success, however: in the middle of March the seats at the east end were pulled down and the tables were receiving rails in the altarwise position.[19] The following day Woodford reported that the 'rayle in the Chancell is now so almost up and its confidently reported that the sickness is in the towne', implying that this was cause and effect, an argument that a Mr Bernard was to deliver in a sermon in August at Wilby.[20] In June Clarke accurately reported this perception to Sir John Lambe, and also that the rail had been cut in pieces and the table moved into the centre of the chancel. Ball's piety, his sympathetic biographer noted, gave him the resolution to stay in the town during the plague to offer comfort.[21] As late as March 1639 communicants were still receiving the sacrament either sitting or leaning at All Saints.[22] Slightly later, a Northampton resident, Humphrey Ramsdell, made a complaint. The table had been returned to the east end and railed in, but lay people joined the minister within the rails. James Cranford, the rector of Brockhall, had delivered a sermon condemning ceremonies, especially bowing to the altar, as that suggested that God could be confined in a narrow room, and also spoke against the burning of candles, as that implied that God needed light. When Daniel Rogers, the schoolmaster, administered the sacrament, he delivered it to communicants sitting, the same being true of Ball and the curate, Charles Newton. Rogers had told Ramsdell, evidently a man in favour of Laudianism, that he would have a quieter life if he left the town, apparently a common perception among the godly, for when Ramsdell, 'the superstitious fellow[,] was indicted for nightwalking & punished for an affray', Woodford prayed for God to 'convert him if it be thy will or remove him from this towne for the Lords sake'.[23] There was a final attempt to impose the ceremonies on Ball, forcing him to leave the table at the east end, to renew the railing, to stay within the rails at the time of communion and to distribute the elements only to those who came to the rails and knelt. This attempt, it seems, was

[17] NCO MS 9502 16 December 1637 (p.81).
[18] NCO MS 9502 31 December 1637, 12 January 1638, 9 March 1638, 13 January 1638 (pp.95, 107, 140, 108).
[19] NCO MS 9592 16 March 1638 (p.144).
[20] NCO MS 9592 17 March 1638, 19 August 1638 (pp.145, 224).
[21] SP 16/570/57; 16/393/15; John Howe, *Real Comforts. a Sermon Preached at the Funeral of Thomas Ball* (1660) pp. 49–50. It is perhaps unnecessary to make it clear that this Samuel Clarke was not the post-Restoration godly hagiographer.
[22] SP 16/414/63.
[23] SP 16/474/80; NCO MS 9502 6 September 1637 (p.22).

made too late in the decade to be enforced before the decline in the powers of the ecclesiastical authorities.[24]

If the intransigence of All Saints demonstrates long-term resistance, in the short term it barely compares with the behaviour of William Castell, the rector of Courteenhall during the 1637 visitation. Charged with making changes to the liturgy, with never wearing the surplice, with using an alternative to the catechism in the Book of Common Prayer, hindering the churchwardens in their attempt to rail in the communion table, and harassing his parishioners playing on the bowling leys, presumably on the Sabbath, Castell showed his short temper when the church was visited by Emanuel Arundel, the minister of Stoke Bruerne appointed as one of the commissioners for the deanery of Preston. Arundel complained that the rails were not correctly positioned and ordered Mr Pidgeon, the apparitor, to measure the table. Castell initially refused to allow any alterations, claiming that he could live as well in New England as in Courteenhall. When Pidgeon moved towards the table, Castell pushed him away and called him 'Rogue, Rascal & cur with other Disgraceful names'. He defiantly asserted that his parishioners did not approach the rails during communion, that they should not and that he would never encourage them to do so, adding, almost to complete his offences, that it was inappropriate to bow at the name of Jesus.[25]

Rather less sensationalist forms of resistance to the altar policy appeared elsewhere, albeit ones which also attracted disciplinary action. Daniel Cawdrey placed the table altar-wise but moved it table-wise at communion. Thomas Harris and Thomas Perkins both refused to deliver the bread and wine to communicants kneeling at the rails.[26] After receiving an admonition and fearing for his deprivation, Miles Burkitt, a vociferous opponent of Laudianism, made the railing of the altar meaningless by joining the lay communicants beyond the rails, taking the elements to those who would not come up to receive and then by assisting one of his churchwardens, Paul Garner, to move the table into a table-wise position in the middle of the chancel.[27] He made his awareness of the threat of discipline clear in his Christmas Day sermon on Coll.1.14 saying 'I doubt [not] I shalbe taken away from yo [sic] before I make an end of my text but Woe be to the heads that plotted it and woe be to the tongues that swear'd it and woe be to the hands that belied it'. This was not an empty threat. As he was aware

---

[24] SP 16/570/57.

[25] SP 16/366/17. Castell was an unusual godly minister, extremely litigious and, from 1629 to 1633, a pluralist, holding the rectory of Dennington in Suffolk while he was still rector of Courteenhall: P. Gordon, 'William Castell of Courteenhall: a Seventeenth Century Pioneer of Missionary Work', *NPP* 8 (1993–4) pp. 354–62.

[26] NRO PDR Church Survey 1637 ff. 93, 142; CB A63 f. 381.

[27] SP 16/393/92; cf. 16/406/88.

that one of his parishioners, Henry Sutton, was an informant for the authorities, Burkitt had a hand in having two horses driven into the church during the service and took the opportunity to deprive Sutton of his office as parish clerk.[28] He apparently took similar action against a local tanner, Henry Folwell, threatening him with legal action relating to unauthorised building on Burkitt's fee simple to intimidate Folwell and prevent him from giving evidence against his minister in the Court of High Commission. Another informant, Nicholas Gare, was brought before Sir Richard Samuel for unspecified misdemeanours during Burkitt's first clash with the authorities, a possibility which Gare feared would be repeated when Burkitt was summoned for a second time.[29]

In a more celebrated case, close attention was paid to the ministry of Charles Chauncy, an acolyte of Alexander Richardson. His troubles began when he was vicar of Ware in Hertfordshire. In April 1630 he was called upon to answer a series of largely liturgical charges: he was said to omit the Athanasian creed, the litany and the exhortation in the marriage ceremony 'with my body I thee worship' as well as failing to wear the surplice or use the cross in baptism. He had neglected worship on saints' days, and canonical services on Wednesdays and Fridays, or at least failed to exhort his parishioners to attend on those days. In addition, he had made various speeches in praise of the godly, claiming that those called 'Puritanes are the chariotts & horsemen of Israell and those that stand in the gappe', speeches said to disparage the authority of the church, and anticipated changes in church and state, denouncing the fact that 'Idolatry was admitted into the Church', leading some families to prepare for emigration to New England, in Chauncy's case a self-fulfilling prophecy. He had not followed the changes insisted upon by the Instructions, neither reading the service nor catechising before his lectures 'out of a meere fond affectation of singularity, because you would seeme to be more precise than other men, and in very truth you doe affect the name of a Puritane'.[30] His initial response was a mixture, defending or at least explaining his speeches while asserting his conformity in the particulars charged. The commissioners handed the case to Bishop Laud, who extracted a more complete submission.[31]

The parish seems to have been divided, for this submission brought peace only in the short term. In June 1634, after Chauncy had left his benefice at Ware and become vicar of Marston St Lawrence in south Northamptonshire, he was called into the High Commission Court with a former parishioner, Humphrey Packer. The case was brought by Sir Thomas Fanshawe and Isaac Craven, the new vicar of Ware, initially for a speech

[28] SP 16/395/79. [29] SP 16/387/70; 339/59.
[30] SP 16/164/40. [31] SP 16/165/10, 16; 167/33.

delivered in a private house against the communion rail. The offence was made more public at the consecration of Fanshawe's new chapel in the south transept, decorated with ornate panelling and rails for the table. Chauncy was commanded to be present at the consecration, at which Laud, Fanshawe and others bowed to the altar before communion.[32] Having placed Chauncy in this difficult position, his opponents called a general meeting of the parishioners and agreed that the table should be moved to the chancel and railed in, with a bench attached for kneeling, an alteration which received Laud's approval. Chauncy, of course, disapproved, stating that if it was done he would leave Ware, suggesting, perhaps not inaccurately, that this was an attempt to drive him out. He did indeed depart, moving to Marston, where he was visited by Packer, the latter having refused to leave his seat to receive the sacrament, and Chauncy returned to Ware to stay at his friend's house. During this visit, Chauncy denounced the altar rails, declaring 'that it was an Innovation, a snare to mens consciences, superstitious, a breach of the second commandment and An addition to Gods worship'. Not surprisingly, Packer agreed, saying that the altar rail would serve a better purpose in his garden.[33]

At his condemnation, Chauncy made a call for leniency, pointing out that, since his move to Marston, he had 'in testification of his conformity' had the table railed in the chancel, leading the commissioner to contact his new bishop to enquire about his new conformity. He pleaded that these objections had not been produced by a dislike of the rails themselves so much as a lack of 'sufficient authority', and pointed out that he had had a rail set up upon his arrival at Marston St Lawrence. His parishioners supported him in this, affirming that the table was railed in at the upper end of the chancel and that communion was administered to kneeling communicants. They admitted that the table was moved into the body of the church at the time of the Lord's Supper, reiterating Chauncy's plea to established practice, stressing that this was 'according to the direction given in the rubric'. A second certificate was delivered by nine neighbouring clergymen, attesting to Chauncy's piety, education and beneficent life. On the negative side, evidence was also provided that he didn't always wear the surplice, that he failed to bow at the name of Jesus, and that he did not stand at the reading of the Gospel. Any protection Chauncy may have gained from these certificates was, however, undercut by evidence submitted by two of the principal Laudian agents in the diocese, Samuel

---

[32] SP 16/261 ff. 60, 89; N. Pevsner, *Hertfordshire* (Harmondsworth, 1953) p. 259; Charles Chauncy, *The Retraction of Mr Charles Chauncy, formerly Minister of Ware in Hertfordshire Written with his own Hand before his Going to New England 1637* (1641) 'To the Reader', p. 17.

[33] SP 16/261 f. 298.

Clarke and Robert Sibthorpe, showing that, even though the table was at the east end of the chancel, it was set table-wise and enclosed with a rail 'little bigger in Compasse than the table is, like a sheeps pen or cage, and there is no bench around it'. In addition, they affirmed that the table was moved, that communion was given to lay people from other parishes, and that it was also given to non-kneelants. This last complaint is revealing. The first certificate, pleading credit for Chauncy's willingness to administer to those who knelt, operates within the Jacobean mentality of heterogeneity and partial conformity; the last within the Laudian demand for perpetual and complete uniformity.[34]

It will come as no surprise to discover that Chauncy was found guilty of his offences. He did, however, receive what might be seen as a degree of leniency in the sentencing. He was not deprived of his new benefice, receiving only an admonition, providing that he refrained from bringing any of the ceremonies into disrepute by word or deed. Chauncy was, however, required to make a lengthy submission in court, acknowledging his guilt and penitence, declaring that his conscience was now persuaded that kneeling at communion was a lawful and commendable gesture and that the approval of the rails and bench by the ordinary was sufficient authority.[35] If his conscience had been convinced, it did not remain so. In his will, written some forty years after his submission, he recorded his regret, holding himself to be 'a Child of Wrath, and sold under Sin, and one that hath been polluted with innumerable Transgressions and Mighty Sins . . . especially my so many sinful Compliances with and Conformity unto Vile Human Inventions, and Will-Worship and Hell-bred superstition, and Patcheries sticht into the Service of the Lord'.[36] His immediate response was to write a retraction of his submission which was, in fact, a mixture of retraction and self-defence. He explained his former statement that he did not object to the moving of the communion table *per se*: furniture placed table-wise could be seen as an idolatrous altar no less than one 'such as stand Dresserwise', the difference being in the spiritual condition of the observer. Like William Twisse, he expressed little concern about bowing to the table, asking only that if this was done, should not one also bow to the font and pulpit, and that if rails were built to protect the table from dogs, then why weren't the pulpit and font similarly protected?[37] Chauncy defended Humphrey Packer's remark regarding the rails, revealing the different perspectives of the disputants. For Chauncy, Packer's denunciation was merely an expression of disapproval of the policy; for Laud, it was a 'blasphemous speech' as this wood was 'destined for holy use'.[38] He went

---

[34] SP 16/261 f. 298, 302/16, I, II, III, 311/33.   [35] SP 16/324 f. 5.
[36] Mather, III p. 135.   [37] Chauncy, *Retraction*, pp. 8–9, 15, 29.
[38] Ibid., pp. 35–6.

on to ask himself that if the altar policy was one of the 'diabolical inventions in Gods worship' which were 'urged and imposed', then why did he make his submission? He admitted that 'Tis true, that by the perswasion of friends, thus far I yielded', an act of which he was very ashamed, and asked,

onely let this be added, which I must needs speake for caution to others, that I perceived evidently whilst I was conformable in my judgement, that I must needs give way to the Rail, or whatsoever innovations, upon the same grounds that I conformed upon. But the Lord be thanked, that though I was a servant of sin, yet he hath at the last subdued my soule to obey from the heart the forme of Doctrine to which I am delivered.[39]

II

As we have seen in chapters 7 and 8, the godly were divided over issues relating to ceremonial conformity. Two ministers of the Northamptonshire godly went so far as to preach and eventually print their arguments in favour of conformity. Joseph Bentham, whose moderation preserved his licence to preach at the Kettering combination lecture, in a series of sermons concerning godly society pleaded for conformity on the grounds of the preservation of peace. He asked that 'those who are strong would beare with the weake' and that the weak 'would not contemne the strong'. Such parties were encouraged to minimise the expression of their differences by Romans 14, a crucial text in this debate. The ceremonies were things indifferent in their being, 'neither good nor bad in their owne nature'. This meant that they could be seen in contrast to 'necessaries': for the latter one could sin in 'the doing, not doing, and in the manner of doing', whereas for the former, sin was only a possibility in terms of the manner of doing. If one had knowledge of the indifferency of a ceremony, had faith, and performed the ceremonies in love, one did not sin. Provided that one had the proper internal perceptions, one could perform outward gestures without the danger of hypocrisy. Thus, if the minister possessed this adequate spiritual outlook, he 'may yeeld to some things inconvenient for the peace of this society'.[40] This appetite for ceremonial 'unanimous uniformity' was strengthened by the authority of the church in setting warrantable public gestures to avoid the dangers of 'breaking the bounds of comelinesse and order': 'this being a principall preventing preposterous

---

[39] Ibid., pp. 38–9.
[40] Joseph Bentham, *The Societie of the Saints* (1630) pp. 35–6. On the side of the conformists, the crucial text is v.1. 'Him that is weak in the faith receive ye, but not to doubtful disputations'; for the nonconformists, perhaps v.15: 'But if thy brother be grieved with thy meat, now walkest thou not charitably. Destroy not him with thy meat, for whom Christ died.'

censuring and condemning of others'. Bentham was willing to stress that in themselves the ceremonies were neither sufficient nor primary in worship, and not necessary in private. Without suitable spiritual conditions, 'that is both preposterous, and hypocriticall'. The worship of the 'soule, heart, mind, and spirit' should go first. Kneeling was not necessary in all times of public worship or for all people, as it would be 'Hurtfull to the impotent, lame, sick, sore, *&c* and inconvenient if it should hinder the minister's capacity to be heard, but it was helpful in invocation or prayer, not least as an aid to proper humiliation. Given these reserved approvals of such ceremonies, it was suitable to kneel 'because [it is] commanded, *Ps*.75, 6, 7 *Isa*.45.23. and consonant to the practise of the most pious people, 2 *Chron*.6.13'.[41]

Edward Reynolds held forth at greater length in a sermon delivered on a rather more sensitive occasion, delivering a visitation sermon at Daventry in July 1637. He too focused on Romans 14, warning of the dangers of disagreements between weak and strong Christians, pointing out that Paul was 'premising a most wise and pious maxime, That weake Christians ought to bee plied and cherished in the maine matters of Religion, and not perplexed with impertinent disputations'.[42] Like Bentham, he stressed the values of peace, and restated John Sprint's argument that 'wee ought not by impudent and immoderate pertinacy in smaller things to disturbe or hazard the worke which God hath set us to doe'. Reynolds distinguished between 'the foundation and superstructure' of divine worship, calling upon ministers with scruples to reform their consciences:

Things standing, I say, *by themselves alone*, as meates and drinkes in the Church of that time did. Otherwise when any materiall Act doth intervene to alter the *indifferency* of the thing (though not in its *nature*, and as to *Liberty of Conscience*, yet in its use, and as to *Liberty of Practice*) as an act of Soveraigne *Authority*, in this case men should labour to rectifie their judgements, that they may not lie betweene the two difficulties of a doubtfull Conscience on the one hand, and an undutifull practice on the other.[43]

He reproduced the position that John Davenport had used in the 1620s to urge ceremonial passivity upon Alexander Leighton, calling for Protestant unity against their enemies: providing there is

---

[41] Joseph Bentham, *The Christian Conflict* (1635) pp. 264–5. Here Bentham was working through a major theme of less moderate proponents of ceremonial uniformity: see P. Lake, 'The Laudian Style: Order, Uniformity and the Pursuit of the Beauty of Holiness in the 1630s', in K. Fincham (ed.), *The Early Stuart Church, 1603–42* (London, 1993) pp. 161–86.

[42] Edward Reynolds, *A Sermon Touching the Peace & Edification of the Church* (1638) pp. 2–3.

[43] Ibid., pp. 3–4, 6–7, 4.

agreement in *Fundamentall Truths*, and in the *Simplicity of the Gospell*, wee ought rather to deny our wits, and to *Silence our disputes* in matters meerely *notionall* and *curious*, which have no necessary influence into faith and godly living, than by spending our pretious houres in such impertinent contentions, for gaine of a small Truth to shipwracke a great deale of Love, and while wee perplex the mindes of men with abstruse and thorny Questions, wee take off their thoughts from more necessary and spirituall employments.[44]

Such a discipline would be spiritually advantageous to the godly, producing charity and peace, while providing a useful source of humility. In these circumstances, the authority of the church became central. Concluding with a section on the calling of bishops, Reynolds identified four necessary attributes of a bishop. After piety and a good life, learning and a devotion to preaching, his model bishop was to exercise 'Discipline and fatherly Government, to keepe the stones of the Building in order, and to reduce all unto decency and beauty: for as God must be served with holinesse, so it must be in the *Beauty of Holinesse* too, and Unity is the beauty of the Church. *Behold how pleasant it is for Brethren to dwell together in Unity.* [Psalm 133.1]'[45]

Although Robert Woodford reported two sermons at Northampton, one by Richard Trueman, the vicar of Dallington which 'dealt faythfully and boldly (out of 16.Deut.4. heare or I shall go) against Idolatry & super-stition', another by Thomas Ball 'against idolatry & persecutors of Xtians', and a 'good discourse with Mr [Daniel] Rogers who seemes to loath vayne ceremonies',[46] I have come across no godly responses to these particular sermons, but it is a little difficult to imagine that many godly ministers would find these stances especially persuasive, particularly the pleas of Reynolds for peace, charity and love in the context of a visitation late in the 1630s, just as we saw the conformable positions inhabited by Davenport, Goodwin, Nye and others in the 1620s become less tenable in the 1630s. If we compare these calls with the perspectives enunciated by Daniel Cawdrey in a series of sermons that were not considered fit to print until the early 1640s, we can see the other side of the division and one which, in these circumstances, many godly ministers would have found more persua-sive. Considering the position of the communion table, Cawdrey drew attention to the spiritual gains to be had from paying close attention to the preparation of the bread and wine. To make the most of the possibilities of edification from these actions, all communicants should watch the minister at work. 'For which reason our Church hath ordered that the table should

---

44 Ibid., pp. 14–15, 24.   45 Ibid., pp. 19–20, 42–3.

46 Trueman was called into the court and, according to Woodford, 'they threaten him that he is like to loose his life for the sermon he preached here' and he was, indeed, suspended: NCO MS 9502 27 August 1637, 25 February 1638, 9 June 1638, 2 and 3 September 1637 (pp.11, 132, 104, 19–20).

at the administration of the Sacrament stand in the body, that is in the midst of the Church or Chancell, that people might come round about it to behold the particulars before mentioned.'[47] Bowing to the table would hinder the visual benefits of the ceremony and, as the elements had not changed their essence, such bowing was, in effect, to worship a piece of furniture. Such behaviour would offend even the Catholics: 'Why Sir, not onely many Protestants, but even Papists doe condemne you, if so you doe, for the greatest Idolaters in the world, and worse than Papists themselves, who have their God alwayes in a Box upon the Table, lest they should worship a peece of wood.'[48] The same spectacular insult applied to bowing to the elements of the communion, 'because all adoration of a creature, is Idolatry against the second Commandement; Thou shalt not bow down to it, nor worship it, *&c* and therefore Papists themselves, to justifie their Adoration of the Host, as they call it, are forced to flye to their Transubstantiation, and imagine the bread to be turned into their God; For they confesse, if it were not so, but remained still meere bread, they were most grosse Idolaters.'[49] Regarding the authority of the church, Cawdrey reproduced, albeit in a relatively moderate form, the argument that Hooker and Cotton had used at Ockley. The ceremonies might be indifferent and in these conditions, objections would be gently expressed. It was lawful to bow to any part of the church, east, west, north or south, 'and no way is limited by God'. Conformists would infer, then, that this was a legitimate arena for the authorities to determine 'which way men shall direct their posture of Adoration, and having determined, shee must be obeyed'.[50] However, while Cawdrey was willing to allow the church the power to govern matters of indifferent ceremony, there were further conditional questions to be considered:

And they are these, 1. Of Order and *decencie*. 2. All *appearance of evill* must be avoided, and things of *evill report*. 3. All *occasions of superstition* are to be prevented as much as may be. Now if the church should determine our posture to be this way onely directed, almost all these rules would thereby be infringed. For, not to speake of the violation of Christian libertie (if so it were determined) the three rules are all hereby violated.

Compulsory conformity in indifferent matters was beyond the authority of the church, 'the Church cannot command the use of everything indifferent in the service of God'.[51] He brought his argument to a climax by inverting the argument Bentham and Reynolds had delivered, returning to Romans 14:

We suppose they doe forget another rule of the Apostle, concerning the use of

---

[47] Daniel Cawdrey, *Superstitio Superstes*, p. 29.   [48] Ibid., p. 22.
[49] Ibid., p. 24.   [50] Ibid., p. 26.   [51] Ibid., p. 27.

indifferent things; They that are strong ought to beare with the infirmities of the weake, and not to please themselves with displeasing others . . . And therefore we thinke they ought to bee so farre from despising them that use it not, that they themselves ought not to use it, being confessed an indifferent thing, and yet of evill report, and carrying with it a face and appearance of superstition, and lastly, (which is not least considerable) not yet determined by the Church.[52]

If we lack the details of debates among the godly considering ceremonial conformity, this does not mean that the new policies were accepted or rejected passively by godly society. When the Book of Sports was reissued and all ministers required to read it to their parishioners, Nicholas Estwick of Warkton reported to his friend, Samuel Ward, the master of Sidney Sussex College, Cambridge, that there had been a great deal of discussion among godly ministers. He hoped that Ward would declare that he accepted the casuistry that would permit moderates to avoid discipline in the ecclesiastical courts on this matter.[53] He had found his own conscience very tested over the Book of Sports; it had 'caused much distraction & griefe in many honest mens hearts in our Diocesse', especially for those who had read the book. Despite those accepting compromise, albeit with troubled consciences, Estwick had heard that almost sixty ministers still refused 'to publish it'. The very prospect of the deprivation of such ministers distressed Estwick: 'what a losse yt would be amongst us & what a blowe it would give to the power of religion your Worship apprehendeth'. At this point, in early 1634, he remained unsettled. He was not sure that recreations on the Sabbath were unlawful. Estwick accepted the importance of the Sabbath, but 'whether yt day is so strictly to be kept yt all parts used for time according to ye booke & ye rules prescribed for things of such nature do violate ye law of ye Sabbath, I am not able to determine'; on the other hand, many of the games that were to be permitted were seldom 'without sin & many times with great disorder'. He expressed some feeling of resolution, claiming to inhabit a conformable position, being unwilling to suffer for disobedience 'to mans laws in point of Ceremonie', but prepared to suffer in defence of the Sabbath. However, having said this, he went on to consider the possibility of reading the book, 'not looking at ye contents but at his authority which commands the publication thereof', that is, extending legitimate authority on ceremonies to include the Book of Sports. He professed a wish that must have been shared by many of his colleagues, that the reading 'might have been done by Proclamations published by Cryers at the Market Crosses & not by Gods ministers in our holy churches', before going on to mention a second form of avoiding the unconscionable act of reading the book himself, that a minister with a troubled conscience might cope with baptism by allowing a 'conformable

---

[52] Ibid., p. 28.   [53] BodL Tanner MS 71 f. 187.

curate' to use the sign of the cross, so such a minister might do something similar with the Book of Sports.[54]

We do not know if Estwick overcame his conscience, although he does seem to have been free from censure in the courts. What is more important to note is that this is further evidence of the inadequacy of counting heads to understand the troubles of the 1630s. It is insufficient simply to provide lists of deprived preachers, for ministers may have overcome their consciences, but only after intense cogitation and such matters were, to say the least, hardly a way to win popularity with godly society. We do know that a number of other ministers were not able to make any compromise, even though they knew they were being closely watched. Jeremiah Whitaker refused to read the book despite, according to Simeon Ashe, suffering numerous 'commands and threatenings pressed upon him'. Such obdurate ministers reads almost like a roll call of the godly clergy: Andrew Perne, John Baynard, John Barker, Francis Turland, Phineas Cockraine and Charles Newton never overcame their scruples. Their geographical concentration between Northampton and the eastern border of the county may indicate an effective intelligence network in that area or perhaps a reciprocal encouraging of consciences among the clergy.[55] In the west of the county enquiries showed that all parishes at least possessed the book, with two exceptions, the parishes of Marston St Lawrence and All Saints, Northampton, the homes of Charles Chauncy and Thomas Ball respectively.[56] Some ministers went further than a simple refusal, three actually preaching against the book. These ministers, William Price, Henry Raymond and William Spencer, represented old and new nonconformity, Spencer having formerly made compromises to maintain his preaching vocation, but finding the book to be the final straw.[57] William Price allowed his parish clerk to read the book at the end of the service while he was present, but he stood to one side with his fingers in his ears while the reading went on. On another occasion, he preached against the book, arguing that it was closer to God's law to perform agricultural work on the Sabbath than to dance. In any case, he was reported to have made the newly permitted recreations an academic question by encouraging the clerk to lock the church door during the service in the winter so that no parishioner could leave until the end of the service, which he extended to

---

[54] Bodl Tanner MS 71 ff. 186–7. The first wish was for the book to be delivered in a way closer to the Jacobean precedent when ministers were not required to read the book to their congregations; a slight but significant difference.
[55] Simeon Ashe, *Living Loves betwixt Christ and Dying Christians* (1654) p. 57; SP 16/308/52; NRO PDR CB A63 ff. 177, 181, 202.
[56] NRO PDR X2159/5/11.
[57] NRO PDR A63 f. 175; SP 16/280/54; 308/52; 266/54; 531/135.

ensure that divine worship finished after dark, thereby rather limiting the recreational choices available to the ungodly.[58]

III

The few preachers who can be shown to have denounced the Book of Sports cannot be taken to represent the whole resistance to the changes in ecclesiastical policies. On an individual level, George Catesby held forth on his disapproval of the new policies as a whole. He expressed his dislike of the surplice, derided bowing to the altar and even threatened to stone a fellow clergyman, William Churchman, for having 'committed Idolatry' in adopting this ceremony, referring to him as a 'foole, asse and knave'. He also disparaged the High Commission Court (in which he was shortly to appear) and announced his approval of Henry Burton's *For God and the King*, dismissing Peter Heylin's reply, *A Briefe and Moderate Answer*, by throwing it to the ground.[59] Catesby was not the only clergyman to give voice to his objections. In 1635, Thomas Hill told his congregation that these 'were ye dayes of persecution long since profesied (of yt they must arise themselves ag[ains]t it)'; John Mayo was noted for his condemnation of idolatry, that 'he mayntayned that it is utterly unlawfull to have the picture of Christ[,] though we have known Christ after the flesh know we him so no more'.[60] In the course of passing on information to John Lambe, Bishop Lindsell denounced Andrew Perne as a 'hollow pillar of Puritanisme'. In addition to his edited highlights of the Book of Common Prayer, delivered without a surplice, Perne was said to have 'complained much of ye overfloweings of Popery every where in this land, & wished or hoped, yt god would raise up a standard to hinder it'. He had also managed to delay the turning of his afternoon sermons into catechising sessions by asking if the Directions were for lecturers only.[61] If the target of Perne's disapproval was not obvious, a heavily qualified compliment delivered by Samuel Craddock, the vicar of Thistleton, in the ecclesiastical court, was a little more specific: 'he dyd say that he did know two or three worthy B[isho]ps in England. And said also that he was very sorry that Dr Piers should be Bp for he was a very good man in his place . . . and when he did hear of the order of prayers w[hi]ch was used in the Cath[edr]all church of Peterb, and of the boweinge [to] the Altar there, he said it was wonderfull.'[62]

More communally, a public fast was called in Northampton on 21 June 1638, with Thomas Ball preaching in the morning, Charles Newton in the afternoon. The subject matter does not seem to have been offensive, but

---

[58] SP 16/280/54. [59] SP 16/375/82. [60] SP 16/308/52; 474/80.
[61] SP 16/251/25. [62] NRO PDR CB65 f. 79.

Robert Sibthorpe noted that neither minister prayed for archbishops or bishops, that neither ended his sermon with the Lord's Prayer, and that no one present used 'any of the Reverend gestures or rites or ceremonies enioyned'.[63] The discipline applied to Miles Burkitt seems to have had little effect. He attended one fast at Marston St Lawrence for the deliverance of William Prynne and Henry Burton and, 'about the tyme of Mr Burtons passing through his parrish and since his admonition', he called a public fast, and 'hee declared in the Pulpitt that though the faithfull were molested persecuted and Wept yet they would contynue faithfull'.[64] Charles Chauncy seems to have been similarly unreformed, despite his submission to the High Commission Court. In mid-1637, Samuel Clarke reported that Chauncy 'mends like sowre Ale in summer'. It had been Chauncy who had called the public fast in June. Two preachers occupied the pulpit for around seven hours, speaking to a full church, for 'the whole tribe of Gad flocked thither', around sixty from Northampton, accompanied by Lord Saye and Sele. The end of the fast was to join in prayer for the deliverance of Burton, Bastwick and Prynne from persecution.[65]

Perhaps the most substantial clerical conference came in late August 1640. Around thirty ministers came together at an inn, the Swan, in Kettering, twenty-one of whom dined there. Most of the major figures of the saints attended: Thomas Ball, Andrew Perne, Daniel Cawdrey, Thomas Harris, Thomas Clarke, William Spencer, Jeremiah Whitaker, John Gill and James Cranford of Peterborough diocese were joined by William Burroughs, George Goodman and another Leicestershire minister. They met to discuss the 'etcetera' oath, recently passed by the Convocation, which remained sitting after the dissolution of the Short Parliament. They had received six or seven arguments against the oath from London ministers, probably including John Goodwin, Edmund Calamy, Cornelius Burges, Charles Offspring, John Downham, Arthur Jackson and Joseph Brown, more from the 'western ministers', and Jeremiah Whitaker led the production and discussion of new reasons. The oath was seen as a dangerous precedent, opening the way for other such oaths; in any case, the oath was illegal (presumably because it was passed after the Convocation should have finished). It was also seen as clashing with the Royal Supremacy: taking the oath bound one to refuse consent to the altering of the church government, and thus if the Crown were ever to alter the discipline people would be bound to oppose the Crown. This last objection was the centre of a petition to the King on behalf of the 'Ministers, Schoolemasters and Practitioners of Physick' of Bristol and Dorset, presumably the western ministers mentioned above. The Kettering meeting concluded with a

---

[63] SP 16/393/75.   [64] SP 16/406/88.   [65] SP 16/361/67.

resolution never to take the oath, and that the ministers would rather lose their livings than do so. Having dealt with the oath, the meeting moved on to the Scottish occupation of the north of England. They had a book entitled *The Intentions of the Army of the Kingdom of Scotland* read to them. Lambe reported that the book 'swarmes about London, (and here too)'. The book stressed that the Scots had petitioned the King for the removal of grievances and that, having promised to satisfy their petition, he had forgotten this promise, blocking maritime trade and threatening them with his army. In these circumstances, the Scots had been forced to invade, 'knowing that neither the law of god nor the Lawes of Nations did alow of that they did, but necessitie had no law'. They pleaded for financial support, promising to hurt no man, woman or child, wanting only the two chief evil counsellors, Laud and Strafford, to be brought to justice. Cranford emphasised that 'their coming was only for peace'. The potential charge of treason was undermined by drawing attention to the fact that the Scots had not used up all their supplies, drawing upon voluntary relief from the English, and noting that the English army 'embraced them and offered to be on their side'. The Scots pointed out that they did not need the English army to fight for them as they had not come for military action, but to have some abuses reformed, that is, Laud and Strafford and 'some other'.[66]

IV

We may close by drawing attention to the ways in which the diocese of Peterborough resembled and differed from the other sees we have examined. At the level of the enforcement of Laudian policies, it seems clear that this fell more upon the shoulders of the lower levels of the hierarchy than in the dioceses of London and Norwich. Bishops Dove, Piers, Lindsell, Dee and Towers were sympathetic to the changes, making their implementation possible, but the imposition itself fell more to the surveillance and activism of Sibthorpe, Clarke and Sir John Lambe, although the latter was, in the 1630s, a relatively remote guiding influence. Although Bishop Dee was more energetic than his predecessors in imposing the ceremonies, the activism of his deputies ensured the success of Laudianism in Peterborough. Had it not been for the work of Sibthorpe and Clarke, Northamptonshire

---

[66] SP 16/465/8, 12, 44. The 'Mr Gill' may have been William Gill, a former student of Christ's College, Cambridge, who had been ordained in Peterborough in 1618; the 'Mr Clarke' may have been Burtin Clarke, a Leicestershire man who had studied at Emmanuel and Clare Colleges, Cambridge, graduating in 1632. The London ministers named here are among those reported to have met concerning a petition against the oath: SP 16/263/54. For the Dorset petition, which was reportedly circulated by Richard Bernard, John Talbott, vicar of Milton Abbot, and Robert Welstead, rector of Bloxworth: SP 16/467/63, 63II.

and Rutland would have more closely resembled the diocese of London in its time under Juxon.

In terms of the response of the godly ministers, there is a rather surprising difference. The demonstration at Dunmow is a clash showing resolution and courage, but is unique in the eastern counties. Peterborough, as we have seen, produced a number of instances when godly ministers, offended by the proposed changes, were willing to denounce them from the pulpit, to make their objections clear to visitors and even, on occasion, to express them in physical terms. It may be that this willingness to resist can be traced to the earlier polarisation of the diocese: Peterborough had a tradition of opposition between bishops and Puritans, while London, for instance, had enjoyed the rule of godly bishops like John King or peaceable diocesans like George Mountaigne. This resolution to stay and fight may help to explain the fact that few of the ministers willing to emigrate and begin anew in New England or Holland came from this diocese, in sharp contrast to the numbers who left East Anglia and Essex. This is not to say that Northampton ministers were wholly hostile to the colonies of New England. In 1641, William Castell published a petition promoting the missionary campaign to convert the native Americans. The seventy ministers whose signatures were attached to the petition reveal the geographical breadth of the clerical network. Six of the Scottish ministers in London added their names to the English supporters. The English ministers ranged from John White of Dorset, William Ford of Somerset in the west, Stephen Marshall and Samuel Joyner of Essex, John Ward of Suffolk, Jeremiah Burroughes of Norfolk in the east, and John Rawlinson of Derbyshire. The clergy from London included Edmund Calamy, George Walker, Joseph Caryl, Adoniram Byfield and William Price. At the heart of the petition were twenty-five ministers of Castell's own diocese, including Daniel Cawdrey, Jeremiah Whitaker, James Cranford, Daniel Rogers and William Spencer.[67]

The lack of emigrants draws to our attention two other absences, the first of which may help to explain the small contribution of Peterborough ministers to New England. While Northamptonshire ministers do not seem to have been tight-lipped in their expressions of disapproval, there are few signs of any demand for changes in church government and even fewer complaints about Arminianism. As we will see, the former is not proof that ministers of this diocese were unanimously content with episcopacy. There

---

[67] [William Castell], *A Petition of W. C. Exhibited to the High Court of Parliament* (1641) pp. 16–19. The other Northampton ministers were John Barry, Samuel Craddock, David Ensme, Edmund Castell, Samuel Moyle, Benjamin Tomkins, Richard Cooke, Richard Trueman, John Guderick, Edmund James, John Baynard, George Jay, Francis Atterbury, Jeremy Stephens, John Ward, Peter Fawtract and William Malkinson.

were several Puritans prepared to attack individual bishops in sermons and elsewhere, but this was to criticise the individual, not the office. Disgust with individual bishops opened the way to advocation of alternative ecclesiologies, but this was not the necessary outcome. There is a small hint of the practice of particular church discipline in the refusal of John Dod to read out in church the sentence of the ecclesiastical court on a fornicator of his flock because the young man had already taken penance before his fellow parishioners before he had been examined by the archdeacon in 1633.[68] Otherwise, there was silence. For the matter of Arminianism, Bishop Lindsell is the only bishop of Peterborough who received the accusation of such adherence, probably with some justice.[69] Although godly ministers were not reluctant to hold forth against changes in ceremony and furniture, they were more likely to link these changes directly with Popery than Arminianism, perhaps a further symptom of the earlier, and more irreducible, dichotomies of the diocese.

[68] NRO PDR CB A55 f. 298.
[69] Tyacke, *Anti-Calvinists*, pp. 36, 118–19.

12

The metropolitical visitation of Essex and the strategies of evasion

I

For the godly ministers of Essex, the examples related by correspondence and word of mouth made Archbishop Laud's metropolitical visitation, imminent in Essex, an object of intense concern. A week ahead of the disciplinary circuit's return to the county, William Munning, a friend of Robert Ryece and minister of Good Easter, near Felsted, wrote to New England:

> Wee have noe newes heere worth the relating, onely wee heare, that the Archbps Metropoliticall Visitation is (once againe) coming downe into this county. What effects it will produce I am not prophet sufficient infallibly to foretell: but (if wee may ghesse by the proceedings of Pope Regulus [Wren] in our next neighbour and native diocese) it is to be feared that wee shall have more loste groates swept out of the house, instead of the duste, to the little laude of our good huswifery.[1]

Perhaps some of this fear can be explained by the unfamiliarity of the metropolitical visitation: the provincial discipline was normally exercised as soon as practicable after the installation of a new archbishop, and there had not been such a visitation since 1613. However, Munning grounded his fears in what he knew of the proceedings in Norwich and, no doubt, in what was remembered of the diocese's last encounter with Laud.

The intervening period had been characterised by perhaps the worst possible combination of policy and practice. The public face of Juxon's episcopacy threatened the full vigour of Laudianism, while the application of his policy was sufficient to arouse hostility without being thorough enough to silence dissent. The published views expressed in diocesan and archidiaconal visitation articles pressed ceremonial conformity with greater urgency than previously had been the case, and in 1635 Juxon drew up a series of articles to be subscribed by ministers in the diocese. The subsequent history of the articles is not clear, but it seems very unlikely that they

---

[1] QUB Percy MS 7 ff. 172, 184; *MHSC* 5th ser. 1 (1871) pp. 235–6.

were pressed in the diocese without recorded protest. Even if, as I believe, the articles never passed beyond the inner circles of the Privy Council, they merit a little attention. There are two drafts extant, which vary a little; combined, they require ministers to assent to the following:

1. That a man once baptized is truly regenerate.
2. That a Minister is tied in conscience to deliver the Eucharist to none but those who kneel.
3. That a canonical minister may have more than one benefice.
4. That bowing at the name of Jesus is a pious ceremony.
5. That a minister's pronouncing absolution is more than merely declarative.
6. That Christ descended locally into hell.
7. That the office of Bishops is by law of God.
8. That it is lawful to bow to the altar.
9. That the Church of Rome is a true church & truly so called.
10. That clergymen have rights to temporal goods in God's church.
11. That the voice of the people is not required in the election of the minister.[2]

The articles could scarcely be better calculated to offend the godly ministers. While they cannot convincingly be used to prove that Juxon was an Arminian, they do reflect a vision of the church that contrasts sharply with a model that had formerly held sway. He echoes a forty-year-old attempt doctrinally to isolate Puritanism,[3] and generally reflects a priestly conception of the ministry and a Hookerian vision of the church. Here it is more important to suggest that the public policy rooted in such a vision, without effective disciplinary mechanisms, would produce a rising level of disenchantment which could be transmitted, if not freely, at least discreetly, by the many godly ministers still active in Essex. Samuel Wharton, for instance, could vent his spleen when he visited Chelmsford to preach in 1635, for which he received a canonical admonition and submitted, whereupon 'any further censure is forborne'. Essex became a refuge for ministers pressed elsewhere, as for Jeremiah Burroughes and similarly for Edward Sparrowhawke, who withdrew to Coggeshall when he was suspended from his curacy and lectureship at St Mary Woolchurch in London. More seriously, the county became, with the city of London, a centre for the dissemination of radical pamphlets criticising the Laudian regime, including, of course, those produced by the 'martyrs' Prynne, Burton and Bastwick. The achievement of Juxon's regime was to produce a reservoir of angry ministers without removing their means of expression.[4]

2 SP 16/534/145; 308/43. Articles 10 and 11 appear only in the second document; in other respects the two are similar, with insignificant variations in wording. Both are dated 1635, and the second is in the hand of Edward Nicholas.
3 Article 6; cf. D. D. Wallace, 'Puritan and Anglican: the Interpretation of Christ's Descent into Hell in Elizabethan Theology', *AFR* 69 (1978) pp. 248–86; P. Lake, *Anglicans and Puritans? Presbyterian and English Conformist Thought* (London, 1988) pp. 239–40.
4 William Laud, *The Works of William Laud, Anglo-Catholic Library* (ed. J. Bliss and

A case in point is Thomas Weld's replacement, John Stalham. He was attracted by the parish's reputation for traditional voluntary religious exercises, by 'that inviting report which was given of you that you were a fasting and praying people: which I found true, among the best of you, who gave me a call hither'. At his first settlement he observed the ceremonial of the Prayer Book, 'through inconsiderate timidity and temerity'. However, presented by his congregation with Weld's 'example of Non-Conformity to Prelaticall injunctions', Stalham was eventually 'convinc'd . . . of my folly' and became a practising nonconformist. He enjoyed 'Preaching liberties (with some success) all the Prelates times', although he admitted that these years were endured 'in weaknesse and in fear and in much trembling'. His survival was not without incident: in 1634, the churchwardens were required to report on 'whether the parishioners receive the communion kneeling', and two years later the Archdeacon of Colchester pressed them to ensure that the communion table was railed in. Stalham, however, escaped without censure. These twin themes of fear and unpunished nonconformity might be taken as the leitmotif of Juxon's episcopate.[5]

II

The court action requiring the construction of an altar rail at Terling brings us to an aspect of Laudian policy neglected so far. As we have seen, the church interior and the conduct of the 'second service' were major concerns in the dioceses of Norwich and Peterborough. By contrast, although the refurbishment of St Gregory's by St Paul's in the City of London provided the initial test case on Laud's policy in November 1633, in the outlying parts of the diocese enforcement was sporadic and ineffectual. There were no novel articles on the position of the communion table or the furniture of the chancel before 1637, although Robert Aylett made some personal attempts to force churchwardens to provide communion rails. The 1633 archidiaconal visitation at Colchester showed a detailed interest in the furniture of chancels, and the first order to provide rails round the communion table was given to the churchwardens of Kelvedon, a parish neighbour to Aylett, who was prominent in the visitation. This initial effort was not entirely successful, for Aylett had to clarify his order, instructing the churchwardens, in December 1635, 'to remove the rail about the Communion Table and to get it up close to the east end of the Chancel

---

W. Scott) (Oxford, 1847–60) V p. 338; P. Seaver, *The Puritan Lectureships: the Politics of Religious Dissent, 1560–1662* (Stanford, Calif., 1970) p. 258.

[5] John Stalham, *Vindiciae Redemptionis* (1647) 'To My Beloved Brethren and Neighbours in Terling'; ERO D/ALV 2 f. 24r; D/ACA 52 f. 157v. On Stalham, T. W. Davids, *Annals of Evangelical Nonconformity in the County of Essex* (London, 1863) pp. 486–9.

wall, and to enlarge the said rail so as the minister may go about the table within the rail as the judge ordered'. At the same time, he ordered the parishes in and around Colchester to provide rails. A number of parishes failed to provide certificates showing that the work had been done by January 1636, and at this point opposition escalated beyond dumb insolence. James Wheeler, the churchwarden of St Botolph's, was among the strongest opponents, and he suffered excommunication and defied the High Commission. He was forced to flee, to his financial ruin, although he extracted a degree of revenge when he gained a judgement against Aylett in 1642.

In June 1636, Aylett informed Sir John Lambe that

> I have caused many of ye communion tables in my officiality to be railed in and ye people to come up and kneel to receave at ye raile (though with much opposition especially in great clothing townes because they see no such thing, as they say, in ye churches in London).

The silence of the articles on this issue, and the failure to implement the policy in the city suggests that this was Aylett's own initiative, rather than a drive led by Juxon. This suggestion is given added force by the distribution of those parishes questioned on the issue before the metropolitical visitation: they are all either close to Aylett's home, under his jurisdiction as Commissary of Essex and Hertfordshire or parishes that often sent cases to the Commissary court. This view is confirmed by Peter Heylin's account, which credits Aylett, without mentioning Juxon. It is clear that Aylett regretted the lack of unified direction on this issue, for his letter to Lambe continued,

> . . . since our articles books for ye metropoliticall visitation were delivered they have found an article wch, as they conceave, gives them leave to remove their table at ye time of celebration and place it as it may be most convenient for ye parishioners to come about it and receave, wch in some places, where ye minister is willing to please his peoples undoes all wch I have done, and lays on mee an imputation, as yf it were mine own invention, crossing ye articles delivered by his Graces visitor.[6]

If the articles had been published by June 1636, the godly ministers of

---

[6] For Aylett's orders, ERO D/ACV 5 f. 37v; D/ACA 51 ff. 8v, 15v, 27v, 38r, 50r, 61r, 62v, 71, 72, 78v, 81r, 87; Peter Heylin, *Cyprianus Anglicus* (1671) pt. II p. 27, dating his initial drive to 1634. Orders were also given in Great Sampford, Henham and Walden, in the north west of the county by the archdeacon's surrogate, Nicholas Gray: ERO D/ACA 53 ff. 31, 42v, 66, 82v. On altar policy generally, see N. Tyacke, *Anti-Calvinists: the Rise of English Arminianism, c.1590–1640* (Oxford, 1987) pp. 197–216; on Colchester, *Lords' Journals* iv pp. 156–7; N. C. P. Tyack, 'The Humbler Puritans of East Anglia and the New England Movement: Evidence from the Court Records of the 1630s', *NEHGR* 138 (1984) pp. 91–4; SP 16/327/101. It must be noted that if Aylett produced his own visitation articles for the parishes under his jurisdiction, none has survived.

Essex had a long time to wait 'in fear and in much trembling' as the main business of the court was postponed while the plague was at its height. As their use in opposing Aylett shows, the articles were closely scrutinised. Those who hoped to gain some leverage from the articles on church furniture were encouraged by the question of 'whether is the same table placed in such convenient sort within the Chancell or Church, as that the Minister may bee best heard in his Prayer and Administration: and that the greatest number may communicate'.[7] This demand was no more than the canonical requirement; in fact, this sets the pattern for the visitation, for generally the articles were no more strict than Laud's diocesan articles and depended upon rigorous administration. The only new article was a consequence of the previous deprivations, asking

Whether your Minister or any other, having taken holy Orders, being now silenced or suspended, or any other person of your knowledge, or as you have heard, hold any conventicles, or doth preach in any place, or use any other forme of Divine Service than is appointed in the Book of Common Prayer: if yea, then you are to present their name, and with whom?

The question acknowledged that there was a pool of disenchanted ministers who had been neither reformed nor forced to leave by Laud's attempts and who, perhaps, had been inadequately supervised by Juxon. Archbishop Laud used the time between June 1636 and early 1637 to make good his friend's neglect. The visitation in the diocese was to be conducted by the archbishop's vicar-general, Sir Nathaniel Brent, and he received a long list of ministers suspected of various offences. His information on this occasion came less from the archidiaconal courts as from sympathetic ministers: only Thomas Wilborow, one of Laud's principal informants, acted as a surrogate in the Consistory court. Laud had gathered details of nine nonconformist ministers, and every one appears in Brent's report. In addition to rejuvenating the intelligence networks neglected by Juxon, Laud worked hard to consolidate his authority over the smaller jurisdictions, the peculiars and the foreign churches. The evidence of the call book and Brent's report indicates that in this he was wholly successful.

Brent met with less success in terms of ministerial discipline. The visitation moved into Essex at the end of February 1637. At Brentwood, John Morse was examined following information that he had neglected the surplice, administered communion to sitting parishioners, and 'delivers not the Cup severally to every communicant as the 21st Canon enjoins'. Brent found it difficult to press the charges successfully. He reported that

He confesseth himself to have bin faultie in former tymes, but protesteth that of late yeares he hath been very conformable, and vowed very seriously that he will

---

[7] STC 10265.5.

always soe conforme hereafter. I could not finde noe proofes of more than he confessed, & therefore I gave him a canonicall admonition, and so dismissed them.

On the same day Brent was informed that Philip Sanders, the curate troubled by Bishop Juxon in 1634, 'lurketh around Burntwood and as it is thought doth much hurt among people inclyned to faction'. He could not be apprehended, and all Brent could do was recommend that the High Commission look for him. Similarly, at High Laver he felt that Sir William Masham, 'a very factious Puritan', should be investigated, but Brent had moved on and could only ask Robert Aylett to follow up his suspicions.

The same impression is gained from the following day's business at Chelmsford. John Newton of Little Baddow, it was reported, 'omitteth the blessed Name of Jesus wheresoever he meeteth it in reading of the second lesson'. Like Morse, he 'confesseth he was inconformable before your Grace did visit as Bpp of London. But professeth that he was then convinced and hath continued conformable ever since.' At Chelmsford too, suspended ministers were causing trouble; in particular, two curates, suspended by Laud, were in the area. Brent felt that he could find out their names, 'but I feare it would be hard to find the parties'.

At Colchester on 3 March, Brent found that Earls Colne remained a town of religious troubles. The Harlackdens, great friends of Thomas Shepard and Samuel Rogers, had encouraged the aged minister, John Hawksby, to conduct nonconformist baptisms and communions. Hawksby was very distressed at the court's attentions. 'The man is very old and weake; he would have fallen downe upon his knees, but that I held him up; he wept very much, and asked pardon, and vowed a constant conformity hereafter. Upon the earnest entreaty of divers grave ministers, whoe undertook for him, I freed him from the suspension wch I had laid on him.'

The court moved on to Kelvedon, where Brent found little amiss, for which he gave full credit to Aylett. This was in contrast to Braintree, where the court arrived on 6 March. Brent had been told that Stephen Marshall 'omitteth the blessed Name of Jesus whensoever he speaketh or readeth the Blessing, saying thus "The grace of our Lord and Saviour, the love of God, and the fellowship of the Holy Ghost . . . "'. Once more, Brent found his investigations frustrated, reporting,

Mr Marshall Vicar of Finchingfield (mentioned in the paper) is held to be a dangerous person, but exceeding cunning. Noe man doubteth but that he hath an inconformable hart, but externally he observeth all. I could not prove upon him the omitting of the blessed name of Jhesus (as is expressed in the paper) nor anything els concerning the Ceremonies of the Church. It is fit in myne opinion that Mr Chancellor of London should have a watchfull eye over him, in regard he governeth the consciences of all the rich Puritans in those parts, and in many places farre remote: and is growen very rich.

Without proof, Brent dismissed him 'with as many admonitions as I thought fit, and he promised obedience in the highest degree. Yet I fear it will be but superficial.' He had less difficulty proving that Edmund Brewer was inconformable: he had been told that Brewer usually baptised without the sign of the cross, that he gave the communion to those who refused to kneel and tried to make his neighbour ministers do the same. Brewer confessed to all this and added that his use of the surplice was no more than occasional. He apologised and announced that in future he would be more conformable. Brent suspended him, but, at the request of John Barkham and other ministers present, this was changed into a canonical admonition. Once again, Braintree brought rumours of the activities of contumacious preachers; in particular, John Davenport was said to have been in the area, and also at Hackney, where he must have been visiting Lady de Vere. Brent reported: 'I am told that he goeth in gray like a country gentleman.'

At Dunmow, on 7 March, Brent ran into more frustrations. He was given a great deal of secret information, but found proof scarce. Samuel Wharton, whose preaching had been sufficiently offensive to penetrate the somnolence of Juxon's diocesan administration, was questioned in line with Laud's information, but he claimed to have been completely reformed by the 1631 visitation. Brent's information proved this a lie and Wharton, along with the curate of Wethersfield and others, was dismissed. As Brent moved out of the county, his hopes for further reformation were still quite high. He knew that there was a great deal of work to do, but in a number of cases noted, 'I am confident it will be done if the motion is seconded in the Visitation of the next summer', or that because 'the relaxation cometh so fast I had no time to examine the business. But Mr Chancellor of London may do it the next summer when he visiteth.'[8]

This confidence in Juxon's administration was, as we will see, misplaced, but the authorities did not have to wait until November, when the episcopal visitation was due, to find that the peace of the county was more apparent than genuine. Many ministers must have shared Samuel Rogers' feelings; when the first round of the visitation reached Bishops Stortford, he noted,

Ab: the cursed visit: D. Duck plays the base wretch; and Mr Crausn in his sermon;

[8] For Brent, *DNB*. He was first advanced by Abbot, the previous archbishop, and supported Parliament in the Civil War but this may have something to do with his falling out with Laud over the latter's strict and intrusive visitation of Merton College, Oxford, of which Brent was warden, in 1638. For the visitation, Laud's information and Brent's report: GL 9537/14; SP 16/339/53; 16/351/100. For Thomas Wilborow, e.g. ERO D/ALV 2 ff. 110, 118, 127, 160; for Harlackden, M. McGiffert (ed.), *God's Plot: the Paradoxes of Puritan Piety Being the Autobiography and Journal of Thomas Shepard* (Amherst, Mass., 1972); QUB Percy MS 7 ff. 70–6, 244–6 etc.

all formality and bitter speaking ag[ainst] sermons; L[or]d ease us, and unclothe these wolves or their sheepskins.[9]

Not all the godly ministers were so discreet. While the court was concluding its business in Essex, on 7 March, Edward Sparrowhawke, a minister among the spiritual brotherhood of the Stour valley in the 1620s who had recently sought refuge in the county,[10] preached against Laudian policies at Coggeshall. Brent had clarified altar policy by publishing orders for the setting up of altar rails at each point on the visitation circuit; Sparrowhawke rejected such policy in the strongest terms. His text was Jerem. 8.20, 'The Harvest is passed, the summer is ended, and we are not saved.' He enumerated the judgements upon the land: bad harvests, the plague, recession and the 'doubling of taxes'. These continued, he claimed, because 'we do not search out the true causes; our Altars and such superstitious adoration, bowing at names and such new idolatrous mixtures of religion, and the treading down of God's people; and until these causes cease, the Plague will not cease'. As Aylett observed, 'you shall see by these enclosed notes that Mr Vicar general was no sooner gone out of the country but one sets up to confute what he had delivered'. Aylett made it clear that it was necessary for the full machinery of surveillance, that he had helped Laud to construct, to be reactivated at the diocesan level. He suggested, 'the best way were a letter from the Secretary of State by a messenger to Sr Thomas Wiseman, Mr Henry Neville, and such others as they will assume into their company. If I be called, my service shall not be wanting.' It is noteworthy that Aylett did not look to the archdeacons, and also that he admitted: 'Mr Neville next week goes into Leicestershire and yf he be gone wee have not so forward and active a man, and therefore I could wish haste.' He advised that Sparrowhawke's study should be searched along with those of his brother, John, Edmund Brewer, the father and son John and Nathaniel Dodd, vicar and curate of Coggeshall respectively, and that of Robert Crane, Sparrowhawke's brother-in-law, whose daughter had married Nathaniel Rogers.[11]

It is especially significant that Aylett addressed his advice to his relation, Sir John Lambe, and not Juxon, for the consolidation of Brent's visitation depended upon the bishop's coming disciplinary circuit. It does not seem that his advice was acted upon, for if Edmund Brewer's study was searched,

[9] QUB Percy MS 7 f. 261. I have been unable to identify the preacher.
[10] On Sparrowhawke's connections see above, pp. 46–7. Sparrowhawke's sons were educated at Felsted under Martin Holbeach: F. S. Moller (ed.), *Alumni Felstedienses 1564–1691* (London, 1931).
[11] SP 16/350/54. Sparrowhawke compared Charles I to Manasseh, who had erected altars to strange gods and consorted with witches and wizards. The whole eighth chapter of Jeremiah reinforces the depth of Sparrowhawke's disenchantment.

his manuscript tract 'of the unlawfulnes of diocesan bishops' would surely have brought him into more trouble.[12] In the event, Juxon's administration remained ineffective. Laud reported to the King that 'My lord treasurer complains, that he hath little assistance of his archdeacons; and I believe it to be true, and shall therefore, if your majesty think fit, cause letters to be written to them, to awake them to their duties.' Juxon mentions that twenty-five ministers had appeared before Brent earlier in the year, but merely observes that 'there is as good order taken with them as could be', and the information he had received from Laud's vicar-general does not seem, as Brent had hoped, to have formed the agenda for the episcopal visitation. The only information available to Arthur Duck, who conducted the entire visitation, was a list of those ministers questioned in the diocesan court in 1634. The effects are clear: Stephen Marshall, for whom Brent recommended 'a watchful eye', was not troubled at all. Finchingfield presented a few recusants and cases of incontinency, but there was no report of ways of worship in the parish church.[13] In the whole county, only two ministers were troubled in the courts. The first was John Borodale, preacher of Steeple Bumpstead, who had been an associate of Marshall's in distributing William Prynne's tracts from Cambridge into Essex.[14] On Monday 17 December 1637, he was presented for not bowing at the name of Jesus. Required to give full canonical conformity, Borodale gave a reply that deserves quoting in full:

the said Mr Borrodell maide answer and alledged that he gave ye same reverence to the name of Jesus that he gave to the name of God or to the third person of the holy Trinitie wch he expressed sometimes by lifting up his eies or inclining his head and sometimes by bowing of ye bodie wch he saith he conceaveth satisfieth ye Canon.

His equivocation was unacceptable and he was suspended; but within a month his suspension was relaxed, although there was no certificate of his conformity.[15]

The second minister to receive the court's censures was Edmund Brewer of Castle Hedingham, already frequently encountered. He was cited on the same day, and seems to have been practising occasional conformity: he was accused of omitting sections of the liturgy, 'for not wearing the suplic [*sic*] and hood constantly in time of prayer, and for not baptising constantly with the signe of the crosse', for not conducting divine service on Wednes-

---

[12] SU Hartlib MS 29/2/25a.   [13] Laud, *Works* V p. 348; ERO D/ALV 2 f. 243.
[14] Above, p. 87; SP 16/144/10; 16/141/17; 16/142/22; 16/144/48. Borodale was Ralph Josselin's teacher and lived to lead the Hinkford *classis* in the 1640s. Marshall preached his funeral sermon: A. Macfarlane (ed.), *The Diary of Ralph Josselin 1616–1683, Records of Social and Economic History* n.s. III (London, 1976) pp. 3–4; Davids, *Evangelical Nonconformity*, p. 287; Anon., *The Godly Mans Legacy* (1681) p. 22.
[15] ERO D/ALV 2 ff. 247v, 298v.

days and Fridays, for not catechising, for not bowing at the name of Jesus, and for administering the sacrament outside the rails, perhaps the most complete collection of offences in any presentment. Brewer replied that 'he conceaved that he had given Mr Chancellor satisfaction for his said omissions and therefore desired to be dismissed or to be respited till he could come to London to answer the same before the said Mr Chancellor'. Although his attempts to play one court off against another were ingenious in the light of the poor communications between diocese and province, Brewer had won too high a profile for Duck to let this indictment pass. Brewer was suspended until June the following year. On the 19th of that month he appeared again; he was offered absolution and the end of his suspension upon certification of his bowing at the name of Jesus and correct administration of the sacrament. He refused, and on 27 June 1628 was pronounced contumacious.[16]

We may note an unintended consequence of the impact of Laudianism on the county, a changed leadership of Essex clerical Puritanism. It will have become clear that Stephen Marshall was on the rise from the late 1620s. In 1629, he was awarded his divinity degree, owing to the patronage of Sir Nathaniel Rich. Questions were raised regarding the validity of his master's degree, sufficient to prevent him taking the BD exercise. An intervention from the Earl of Holland, Rich's kinsman and the new Chancellor of the University, made it possible for Marshall to perform the requisite English and Latin sermons, in which he chose to preach against idolatry, to general applause.[17] After the 1631 visitation, with men such as Hooker, Ward and Weld set to emigrate, and Daniel and John Rogers silenced or broken, Marshall became the leading godly minister in the county, advising the noble professors and deeply involved in schemes such as John Dury's. By 1637, Nathaniel Brent believed that 'he governeth the consciences of all the rich Puritans in those partes, and in many places far removed'. His advice was sought by Sir Robert Harley regarding a potential preacher for one of his Herefordshire cures, and he played his part in the provision of Welsh-language preachers and possibly also in the Feoffees for Impropriations.[18] His new prominence was approached by that of Matthew Newcomen. Intriguingly, he had been curate to the conformist Nehemiah Rogers at Messing in 1632, but was trained in the household of John Rogers and succeeded him as lecturer at Dedham upon the death of the more famous

---

[16] ERO D/ALV 2 ff. 247v, 327v, 328r.

[17] SP 16/114/79; CUL Add MS 3320 f. 217; Thomas Fuller, *The History of the Worthies of England* (ed. J. Nichols) (London, 1811) pp. 52–3; Venn, s.v. 'Marshall'; Anon., *The Godly Mans Legacy*, pp. 26–7; cf. B. Donegan, 'A Courtier's Progress: Greed and Consistency in the Life of the Earl of Holland', *HJ* 19 (1976) pp. 317–53.

[18] SP 16/351/100; BL Add MS 70062 (unbound papers); I. M. Calder, 'A Seventeenth Century Attempt to Purify the Anglican Church', *AHR* 53 (1948) p. 764.

Rogers in October 1636. Perhaps drawing upon the reputation of his predecessor, he quickly established himself, preaching up and down the Stour valley and coming into contact with Thomas Young, the Scot who had been preaching at Stowmarket since 1628, after a period of training in Thomas Gataker's household seminary at Rotherhithe. By the calling of the Long Parliament, Newcomen, as Edmund Calamy's brother-in-law and a prominent preacher in the county of the Barringtons and the Earl of Warwick, was well set to take his place in the twice-weekly meetings at Calamy's house.[19]

III

Though the godly ministers could not know it, this was the last complete diocesan visitation Essex was to see before the civil war. The casualties over the previous six years had been heavy and conspicuous, but many ministers survived to fill Essex pulpits with calls for the election of godly men to the House of Commons in 1640. Their survival is testimony to the ineffectiveness of Bishop Juxon's administration, but also to the skill and ingenuity of Puritan ministers in their evasion of ecclesiastical justice. We may take a little space to examine the ways that were considered licit to defend the persecuted godly. For some, there was no just cause to evade trouble: Daniel Rogers, discussing the case of Rahab, the harlot who protected Joshua's spies (Joshua 2), claimed that she had sinned in lying, although he prayed 'the Lord keepe us from straits and from horned occasions'. He claimed that such 'Iesuiticall evasion' was to be abhorred and went on to explain that

in Queen Maries time, many would goe to Masse with their bodies, pretending to keep their consciences entire and undefiled: Sutable thereto is the practice of our Jesuits in their equivocations, whether in their oathes or other actions, when they swear in word, but say they reserve themselves mentally unsworne and meant it not, or by some trick of exception which they suggest to themselves, viz. That such a one went not this way, pointing to their sleeve; or that they were not in such a place of company meaning [they were not there] to betray it to others, &c.[20]

The brief mention of a man pointing to his sleeve comes from a commonplace in Roman Catholic casuistry, most notably in the work of Martin de

[19] GL 9539A/1 f. 22; J. F., *The Dead yet Speaking* (1679) p. 14; *VCH Essex* vol. II p. 51; A. G. H. Hollingsworth, *The History of Stowmarket* (Ipswich, 1844) pp. 145–6 shows Newcomen preaching in Young's pulpit at the combination lecture. When Newcomen preached in late 1641 more food was required, 'being abundance of ministers when Mr Newcomen, and a quart of wine they sent for'. I owe this reference to the kindness of John Walter; Simeon Ashe, *Grey Hayres Crowned with Grace* (1654) p. 54; for the meetings at the home of Calamy, see below, pp. 318, 330–1.

[20] Daniel Rogers, *Naaman the Syrian, his Disease and Cure* (1642) pp. 239–40.

Azpilcueta, known as Dr Navarrus. The story is from the life of St Francis; he was said to have seen a man fleeing from a murderer, who then asked Francis if the man had passed that way. Francis replied, 'He did not pass this way', pointing to his sleeve, thus deceiving the murderer and saving a life without telling a lie. His second example is something more like the full concept of mental reservation, where, in some circumstances, it was considered lawful to make a false statement, with an unexpressed addition in the mind which would make the statement true. Thus the confidential information was kept secret and, as God had access to the whole statement, uttered and reserved, He could see that no sin had been committed. For most of the godly ministers, mental reservation and the more sophisticated forms of equivocation were tainted by their Jesuitical associations.[21] Occasionally, one meets with situations where something similar seems to be practised; for instance, when Thomas Hooker returned to England in 1633, he travelled to Towcester to meet Samuel Stone, and when the two divines returned to Stone's house, they had scarcely arrived when the pursuivants of the High Commission knocked on the door. Stone answered, and when they asked for Hooker, apparently drawing courage from his pipe, he asked, 'What Hooker? Do you mean Hooker that liv'd once at Chelmsford?' The pursuivant replied, 'Yes, He!' and, in Mather's phrase, 'with a Diversion like that which once helped Athanastus, made this true Answer, "If it be he you look for, I saw him about an hour ago, at such an house in the Town; you had best hasten thither after him."' Thus Stone had not told a lie, for he had met Hooker in another house an hour earlier, but he certainly told less than the full truth.[22] Most evasion, however, came while ministers still held their preaching posts, in interviews during visitations. Puritans might reject equivocation and mental reservation, but

---

[21] On Navarrus, equivocation, mental reservation and the ideas in an English context, see P. Zagorin, *Ways of Lying: Dissimulation, Persecution and Conformity in Early Modern Europe* (London, 1990) chs. 8 and 9; the story of St Francis is discussed on p. 168; Puritan casuistry is discussed on pp. 221–42, 251–4. Zagorin discusses only the literature, and not really the practice, focusing very tightly on William Perkins, William Ames, whom he shows to have been extremely strict on the question of equivocation, and Richard Baxter. He almost certainly underestimates Puritan interest in casuistry; for a broader discussion of the literature, see N. Clifford, 'Casuistical Divinity in English Puritanism during the Seventeenth Century: its Origins, Development and Significance', University of London PhD (1957), J. P. Somerville, 'The "New Art of Lying": Equivocation, Mental Reservation, and Casuistry', in E. Leites (ed.), *Conscience and Casuistry in Early Modern Europe* (Cambridge, 1988) pp. 159–84, E. Rose, *Cases of Conscience: the Alternatives Open to Puritans and Recusants under Elizabeth I and James I* (Cambridge, 1974) and K. Thomas, 'Cases of Conscience in Seventeenth-Century England', in J. Morrill, P. Slack and D. Woolf (eds.), *Public Duty and Private Conscience in Seventeenth Century England: Essays Presented to G. E. Aylmer* (Oxford, 1993) pp. 29–56.

[22] Mather, III p. 62. Hooker had been reproving Stone for his smoking habits when the pursuivants arrived.

Clement Corbett felt that after the 1636 Norwich visitation, 'I dare confidently say, I can now teach a Jesuit to equivocate. If Hoc sunt, quod docentur; as the practice is ungodly, so I am sure the Doctrine is desperate: tis but this, They take oaths according to their fancie, and not the judges meaning', a practice that sounds like mental reservation. As he had told Wren in an earlier letter,

your Lo[rdship] will know how ordinarily they practice the trick and your lord have formerly & will heere find, although they let their tongues speake & traduce ye Jesuits, yet their practices in many things have Identity & equypage.[23]

When one encounters ministers usually considered early radicals subscribing in the 1630s, it is possible to speculate, albeit inconclusively, that the act was performed with some form of mental reservation: in the diocese of London, we find Edmund Calamy, Thomas Gouge, Obediah Sedgewick and John Goodwin all subscribing late in the decade. Understandably, it was not a subject of much discussion in the following decade, so we can take these speculations no further, although it is worth noting that Robert Cawdrey claimed, in a letter to Lord Burghley during the Whitgiftian drive for subscription, that many Northamptonshire ministers had subscribed despite their belief that 'some parts [of the Book of Common Prayer] are unlawful and others inconvenient'.[24] With more confidence, we can discuss more practical forms of evasion. Through the decade 1628–38, many godly ministers developed ways of limiting the worst effects of Laudian policy. As the authorities tried to reform the Jacobean preaching culture by regulating weekly lectures, some ministers took every opportunity the new emphasis on holy days gave them. Stephen Marshall, for instance, chose not to risk ecclesiastical censure by using the legacy of a friend and Wethersfield parishioner, Walter Wiltshire, to erect a lecture after Daniel Rogers was suspended. By observing all the feasts of the liturgical year, Marshall could preach on at least twenty-seven days, in addition to the fifty-two sabbaths and anniversaries such as 5 and 17 November.[25] This expedient was also followed by, for instance, Samuel Wharton, William Leigh of Groton, Richard Mather in Toxteth and Thomas Pierson in Herefordshire. Increase Mather explained his father's practice, making it clear that, 'this he did, not

---

[23] BodL Tanner MS 68 ff. 8, 1. It is indicative of the breadth of the divide that had opened up between Independents and Presbyterians that John Vicars made similar accusations of Jesuitical equivocation and mental reservation against the Dissenting Brethren in the mid-1640s: John Vicars, *The Schismatick Sifted* (1646) p. 32.

[24] GL 9539A/2 ff. 27, 33, 38v, 12; A. Peel (ed.), *The Seconde Parte of a Register* (Cambridge, 1915) ii. p. 92.

[25] SP 16/339/53; for Wiltshire: ERO D/P 119/25/195, GL 9531/15 f. 25 and T. Webster, *Stephen Marshall and Finchingfield* (Chelmsford, 1994) pp. 3, 11; D. Cressy, 'The Protestant Calendar and the Vocabulary of Celebration in Early Modern England', *JBS* 29 (1990) p. 34.

thinking that there was any Holiness in those times (or in any other day besides the Lords-day) beyond what belongs to every day; but because then there would be an opportunity of great Assemblies, and it is good casting the Net where there is much fish'.[26]

Other devices sought to evade the controverted ceremonies; Marshall was only one of the ministers who omitted the word 'Jesus' from the blessing in order to avoid bowing or being seen not to bow at the name; similar tactics were adopted by William Price, the vicar of Brigstock, for instance.[27] John Borodale's evasion, however, was more complicated, an attempt to follow the letter of the canon minutely, to the point of absurdity.[28] For the surplice, there was a tradition of evasion, which ministers drew upon and developed in the 1630s. Nathaniel Ward's churchwardens claimed that their surplice was 'old and not fit to be used'; Israel Hewitt of Maldon claimed that he only preached without the surplice when it 'was a washing'. The evasion of Thomas Witham of Mistley was more sophisticated: claimed that the chapel-of-ease in Manningtree, where he preached, was not consecrated and therefore had not acquired a surplice.[29]

Evasions multiplied when the Laudian altar policy was pressed. Other ministers tried John Carter's argument that their church was too large for them to read the second service in the chancel. John Stalham avoided high ceremonial by removing the table from within the rails when he came to administer the sacrament, a practice we have encountered in Northamptonshire. Many ministers and churchwardens attempted to prevaricate when they received orders to rail in their communion tables. At Kelvedon, the churchwardens initially seem to have provided rails around the table in its traditional position so close as to make the railing-in almost meaningless, a tactic also employed by Charles Chauncy. At Great Sampford, the churchwardens purchased the materials for the rails as ordered and then simply retained them in their homes. The most elaborate attempt to prevent the eastern placing of the table must belong to

---

[26] ERO D/ABA 5 f. 135v; BodL Tanner MS 68 f. 212; *MHSC* 5th ser. 1 (1871) p. 229; [Increase Mather], *The Life and Death of Richard Mather* (1670) pp. 8–9; BL Harl MS 7517 f. 29.

[27] SP 16/280/54.

[28] John Newton of Little Baddow also omitted the crucial word: SP 16/339/53; cf. SP 16/286/86; ERO D/ALV 2 f. 247v; BodL Tanner MS 68 f. 8.

[29] GLRO DL/C 319 f. 67; H. Smith, *The Ecclesiastical History of Essex under the Long Parliament and Commonwealth* (Colchester, 1933) p. 59; SP 16/218/43. For comparable excuses, see the case of Richard Parker, secretary of the Dedham *classis*, who claimed that his surplice had been burnt; when pressed, his wife produced the mutilated garment: F. G. Emmisson, *Elizabethan Life: Morals and the Church Courts* (Chelmsford, 1973) p. 195, cf. p. 237, and W. J. Pressey, 'The Surplice in Essex', *ER* 45 (1936) pp. 36–45.

Braintree, where an eastern gallery was erected at the expense of Mark Mott, a godly man of the town, in order to prevent the table being placed against the eastern wall.[30]

Faced with questions about their personal conduct, ministers would commonly admit to former nonconformist practices but claim that a former visitation had achieved complete reformation. This strategy met with some success when communications between the various jurisdictions worsened after Laud's departure, especially as his second visitation retained a reputation for effectiveness. Six years after Laud's last appearance, Brent reported: 'It is generally believed in the Diocese by the better sort that by your Graces strong persuasion and rigor mixed with mildness much reformation hath been wrought.'[31] More generally, the strategy of those godly ministers who made any attempt to mitigate the effects of their offence was to strive to appear conformable; we have already encountered this in many cases, from Thomas Shepard, Thomas Weld, Nathaniel Ward and even from Thomas Hooker, among many others.[32] This strategy was open to misunderstanding; the charitable construction was expressed by Henry Jessey, when he wrote:

These good men cannot abide these ceremonies, and if they might they would never use them. But to avoid the persecutions of these bishops, that would fetch them up to the High Commission, therefore these good men are fain to stoop to them sometimes.

The alternative conception of these strategies has been seen in the case of William Leigh; generally, Muriel Gurdon was sorry to see that 'many that seemed to be zealous doe yeld obedience to the inventions of men'.[33]

Beyond the variety of practice and the risk of misunderstanding, what is striking about these expedients is their lack of success. Ward, Weld, Brewer and Stansby, for instance, all won no more than a little time by presenting

---

[30] BodL Tanner MS 68 f. 4; ERO D/ACA 51 f. 157; D/ACA 52 ff. 226v, 227; D/ACA 53 f. 195v; Smith, pp. 60–2; ERO D/ACV 5 f. 37v; D/ACA 51 ff. 8v, 42v; D/ABA 6 ff. 133r, 143v, 147v. Joseph Downing, the rector of Layer Marney, used the same evasion as John Stalham: ERO D/ACA 52 f. 169. This peripatetic approach was, of course, in line with the Elizabethan injunctions ordering the position of the table: C. Durston and S. Doran, *Princes, Pastors and People: the Church and Religion in England, 1529–1689* (London, 1991) p. 41. The churchwardens at Braintree were ordered to pull the gallery down, and by the end of the decade the church certainly had an altar rail: Smith, p. 69. The arrangements initially adopted at Kelvedon would be acceptable to most of the godly: this was the form suggested by the moderate Ephraim Udall in his *Communion Comlinesse* (1641).

[31] E.g. SP 16/351/100 for John Newton, John Morse and Samuel Wharton; Smith, p. 59, for Israel Hewitt; ERO D/ALV 2 f. 247v, for Edmund Brewer; Brent quoted from SP 16/351/100.

[32] The same strategy was followed by Jeremiah Burroughes and Robert Stansby: BodL Tanner MS 68 ff. 204, 134.

[33] *Winthrop Papers* (Boston, Mass., 1929–43) vol. III pp. 59, 243.

themselves in a moderate light. Marshall, Wharton and John Carter were among the few ministers encountered so far who managed to convince the authorities that they were conformable, and Marshall, at least, suffered the censures of the godly for his compromises.[34] Marshall was an unusually adroit and flexible minister, as reflected in Thomas Fuller's assessment that he 'was so supple a soul that he brake not a joint, yea, sprained not a Sinew, in all the alterations of times'.[35] Many ministers owed their survival more to administrative failure than skilful practice. We may suggest that the failure of the godly ministers lies in an incomprehension of Laudian policy; while the ministers were striving to present themselves as 'conformable', committed Laudians were looking for conformity without exception: it was no longer sufficient to show willing by using sections of the liturgy, or wearing the surplice occasionally.

As members of the godly community came to realise, by experience or anecdote, this was the cumulative effect of the 1630s: the common ground of the Jacobean church was eroded on every front. Shared doctrinal concerns were perceived by the godly to be a thing of the past; the indifferent ceremonies were seen to be pressed to a greater degree, and new forms, increasingly offensive to the godly, introduced and eventually, the personnel of the episcopate of the 1630s was seen to be so vile as to invalidate the office. One poet of the early 1640s was so disenchanted that he pointed out that if one added up the Roman numerals of 'Will Laud' the result was 666, the number of the beast.[36] The assault on episcopacy will form part of the subject of the next section, but we may end here with the perception of Samuel Rogers, a product of the godly society of the 1630s. In October 1638, he spent a rare day of rest sightseeing in London. In his diary, he noted:

This day, I goe to westminster, to the Hall; to the Minster to see the monuments; was refused of the popish clerke to go to the sword &c: bec[ause] I would not pull of[f] my hat before the Altar; and there to a place called Hell, and thence to Ciaphas Hall [Lambeth Palace] (out of the frying pan into the fire) where sat those 2. cursed traitors to X [Christ]; W. L. and M Wren with the hang byes; I look about them, and have ioy in G[od]. and I shall dye better than they; I come home, and my mind hurrys over these th[ing]s strangelye.[37]

A decade of a policy that had produced antipathies such as these had removed every last sod of common ground. To change the metaphor, this

[34] Anon., *Godly Mans Legacy*, p. 7.
[35] Thomas Fuller, *The History of the Worthies of England* (1662) 'Huntingdonshire', pp. 52–3.
[36] Anon., *The Coppy of a Letter Sent to William Laud Late Archbishop of Canterbury, now Prisoner in the Tower* (1641) n.p.
[37] QUB Percy MS 7 f. 355.

was the end result of a process of evolution that had taken two related dialects, a godly and a 'mere Protestant' accent, within the rhetoric of unity available to all Jacobean Protestants, divided them and produced, by the end of the 1630s, two mutually incomprehensible languages.

Part IV

'THESE DANGEROUS TIMES': THE PURITAN DIASPORA 1631–1643

In the course of the last section we encountered ministers who received a new, or renewed, sense of the sinfulness of the controverted ceremonies as a result of the changed ecclesiastical climate. Some space was given to the strategies adopted to evade the ceremonies and the censure of the ecclesiastical courts, but the response of the godly ministers in this account, it must be said, seems rather passive and a little negative. As the authors of the *Apologeticall Narration* admitted, 'Neither at the first did we see or look further than the *dark part*, the evill of those superstitions adjoyned to the worship of God'. Like Goodwin and his associates, we are 'cast upon a further necessity of inquiring into and viewing the *light part*'.[1] For those writers, the 'light part' was a new model of church government and worship, and a consideration of some strands of the debate on church government will indeed be one of the tasks of this section. Firstly, however, we may discuss some other responses and draw out themes relating to the continuing patterns of association and to the eventual diaspora of the ministers.

The first chapter of this section discusses an element of the schemes of John Dury, the son of a Scots exile who had been working with Lutheran statesmen and divines in pursuit of a pan-Protestant union. His work in England brought him into the circles of godly ministers as he endeavoured to compile a work of practical divinity for European consumption, and an examination of his efforts reveals the networks and continuing patterns of association among the godly. It is also possible to consider the motives of those ministers who assisted Dury and to place their activities in the context of perceived changes in the English church. It becomes clear that, for some of the English divines, support for Dury's work rested upon interests at variance with Dury's own and that there are perspectives from which their work may be seen as subversive.

---

[1] Thomas Goodwin, Philip Nye, Sidrach Simpson, Jeremiah Burroughes and William Bridge, *An Apologeticall Narration, Humbly Submitted to the Honourable Houses of Parliament* (1643) pp. 2–3.

Having established that there were activist options available to ministers out of sympathy with the perceived changes of the 1630s, we can go further and consider what other choices were open to such men. This is the task of the second chapter, which focuses initially upon the situation of deprived ministers and considers how far a stinted ministry was a possibility for a resident suspended preacher. A second option, and one that has received much more attention, is that of emigration, and the remainder of this chapter is taken up with a discussion of why ministers emigrated and, equally important, why others did not. The sense of debate that emerges necessitates a re-evaluation of the so-called 'errand into the wilderness' as an ecclesiological mission, and finds a social dynamic behind some decisions to go or stay.

As New England moves up the agenda it becomes necessary to consider ecclesiology as a further element in the Puritan diaspora. To a degree this requires a longer perspective than most of this work and, accordingly I will trace some of the strands of debate leading into the new, and renewed, debates of the 1630s. The third chapter examines the tradition of ecclesiological thought in England and among ministers in exile and shows how these works were adapted by the first ministers settling in Massachusetts. Although there were strategies to obviate the necessity of ecclesiological martyrdom, there proves to have been a live constituency of ministers debating issues of church government.

This sketches in the background for a discussion of Thomas Hooker's ecclesiology, which can then be placed in the context of the native English ecclesiological tradition. This native tradition engaged with the Massachusetts adaptations and also became involved in early arguments with ministers who were to be among the authors of the *Apologeticall Narration*. What emerges is a stream of thought, most heavily influenced by William Ames, which saw developments in Massachusetts and at home tending toward sectarianism.

One of the consequences of these findings is a new context for the ecclesiological debates of the early 1640s. It becomes necessary to renew the search for the English Presbyterian tradition, as the mainstream English position is best described as 'Amesian'. After consideration of some of the possible sources for a renewed commitment to Presbyterianism, a re-examination of the Smectymnuan tracts suggests that the coalition that advanced this cause in the mid-1640s seems to consist of a number of ministers with an interest in forms of reduced episcopacy and former Amesians. Tracing these transitions is one of the tasks of the fifth chapter, along with an account of how the community of godly ministers fragmented over these issues.

13

John Dury and the godly ministers

I

The first activity to receive our attention is something of a footnote to the monumental labours of John Dury. His design was among the grandest: from 1628 to the year of his death, 1680, he strived in the cause of 'ecclesiastical pacification' between the disparate branches of the Lutheran and Calvinist churches, initially in the context of the Thirty Years War, but struggling on in the changed conditions of Europe after the Treaty of Westphalia. In the main, his projects have been regarded as a curious sideline to the period, the activities of an eccentric idealist, working against the grain of his times. While his reputation is now being rescued from whiggish ecumenical historians,[1] what is of present interest is his relationship with the godly ministers of England. Dury's activities brought him into the Puritan milieu twice; once in the 1640s, when he was a member of the Westminster Assembly and preached to Parliament: Hugh Trevor-Roper identified him, perhaps a little portentously, as one of 'the philosophers of the country party', showing John Gauden summoning the triumvirate of Samuel Hartlib, John Dury and Jan Amos Comenius in his sermon to both Houses of Parliament in late 1640.[2] However, Dury's arrival in the 1640s was by no means his first visit to England, or his first contact with prominent godly divines.

[1] For the former, see, for instance, J. M. Batten, *John Dury: Advocate of Christian Reunion* (Chicago, Ill., 1944); C. A. Briggs, *General Introduction to the Study of Holy Scripture* (Edinburgh, 1879). For the rescue from the whigs, see A. Milton, '"The Unchanged Peacemaker"? John Dury and the Politics of Irenicism in England, 1628–1643', in M. Greengrass, M. Leslie and T. Raylor (eds.), *Samuel Hartlib and the Universal Reformation* (Sheffield, 1994) pp. 95–117. I am grateful to Anthony for being the first to draw the Hartlib MS to my attention. For an overview of Dury's work in the 1630s: G. H. Turnbull, *Hartlib, Dury and Comenius: Gleanings from Hartlib's Papers* (Liverpool, 1947) pp. 132–222.

[2] H. Trevor-Roper, 'Three Foreigners: the Philosophers of the Puritan Revolution', in *Religion, Reformation and Social Change* (London, 1967) pp. 237–93. He deals almost exclusively with the late 1630s and 1640s.

Dury arrived in London in mid-1630, furnished with letters from Sir Thomas Roe, the English Ambassador to Sweden, and recommendations from Prussian divines. From the first, he sought official sanction for his negotiations, as he had in Sweden; although he gained an audience with Charles, he found the English king even less enthusiastic than Gustavus Adolphus, and was referred to Archbishop Abbot and Bishop Laud. Abbot offered him cordial, if impotent, support, and Laud suggested he should use his continental contacts simply to 'inhibit railing disputes in the Pulpit, and put down the names of partiality, so farre as could be done, and not suffer any debatements to be taken up or fomented about matters of Ceremony in the forme of publike worship'. Despite this effective rebuff, Dury courted Laud's approval through the decade, only nearing despair when he feared that the new archbishop would come to associate him with subversive elements in the church.[3] Even before his interviews with Charles and Laud, Dury had begun to build alternative contacts. From Chichester, Samuel Hartlib had been publicising Dury's scheme, and his friend and neighbour William Speed had helped to spread his ideas. As early as October 1628, John Davenport had expressed interest based on information from Hartlib and John Bastwick, and once Dury arrived in England, Speed provided him with a list of ministers 'able and sufficient for all manner of controversies besides very stirring and wondrous active to promote any cause that tends for the advancement of the kingdome of Christ'. He recommended William Twisse and John Cotton, John White of Dorchester and William Sedgewick of Farnham, among others. However, Dury's intention to seek common ground between Lutherans and Calvinists through a cumulative exposition of practical divinity was canvassed much more widely than this suggests. Speed had spoken to sympathetic divines in Sussex and reported that 'they are resolved . . . to appoint a day of meeting at Arundel'. Walter Welles, another friend of Hartlib and lecturer at Stephen Marshall's birthplace, Godmanchester, conferred with friends across his home county, and also in Northamptonshire, Oxfordshire, Warwickshire and Buckinghamshire. A week later, on 20 September 1630, he wrote to Dury, introducing himself and pledging his support. His discussions had stimulated some interest, for he added: 'I undertake for all Huntingdonshire wherein I dwell, for Bedfordshire, & also for Mr Harris of Hanwell, Mr Whately of Banbury & all their friendes whether [*sic*: whither] I am sending an expresse messenger upon another occasion.' Dury himself left London slightly earlier and spent

---

[3] Turnbull, pp. 129–32 for Sweden; John Dury, *A Briefe Relation of that which Hath Been Lately Attempted to Procure Ecclesiastical Peace among Protestants* (1641) p. 3, for his initial reception by Laud; cf. his indefatigable, if rather one-sided, correspondence with Laud through the 1630s: *HMC, Fourth Report* (London, 1876) pt. I pp. 159–63; SP 16/302/63.

six weeks travelling through Lincolnshire, Huntingdonshire, Cambridge-shire and Essex.[4]

By May 1631, these labours seemed to be bearing fruit. Archbishop Abbot had given Dury permission to collect signatures to his *Instrumentum Theologorum Anglorum,* a document which declared goodwill towards his schemes for reconciliation and called for prayers for peace among Protes-tants. Accordingly, when Dury left England in June 1631 he took a testimony from 'certaine divines . . . subscribed by their hands to witness for them in private that they desired not onely for their own parte to further so good and holie a purpose; but also intreated others to joyne with them in it'.[5] It is not clear when or where the testimony was signed, but it seems to have been collated on one occasion, probably in London. Fortunately, a copy has survived and so the network can be reconstructed. Essex is represented by Stephen Marshall, John Rogers, John Sym of Little Leighs, and Henry Burton of Maldon; Cambridge by Samuel Ward of Sidney Sussex College, and Thomas Goodwin of Trinity College; Norfolk by John Brinsley; Northamptonshire by Thomas Ball and Edward Rey-nolds; the West Country by John White; and Surrey by Henry Whitfield. Most of the ministers were from London and the Home Counties, including most of those involved in the Feoffees for Impropriations: Richard Sibbes, John Davenport and William Gouge, as well as Cornelius Burges, Henry and Philip Nye, Sidrach Simpson, Thomas Taylor, Thomas Edwards, Richard Holdsworth, George Walker and Walter Welles. The list of thirty-eight divines was headed by Archbishop Abbot's chaplain, Daniel Featley.[6] They were committing themselves to the preparation of a manual of practical divinity to be translated for European consumption. Dury was engaged in the project for thirty years afterwards, with some initial success, defeated by the outbreak of war and never really recovered after the Restoration. For the present a 'steering committee' of London ministers including Gouge, Downham, Burton and Sedgewick, with George Walker, John Stoughton and Joseph Symonds was appointed in answer to the request of a conference of eminent continental divines at Hanau, in February 1633. The steering committee persuaded James Ussher, now

---

[4] Turnbull, pp. 128, 132–6, 140; SU Hartlib MS 29/2/11b; 33/3/1b; 33/3/3a; cf. 23/47/25; 25/50/37. For Welles, see J. Morrill, 'The Making of Oliver Cromwell', in J. Morrill (ed.), *Oliver Cromwell and the English Revolution* (London, 1990) pp. 38–41.

[5] John Dury, *A Summary Relation of that which John Durie Hath Prosecuted in the Work of Ecclesiastical Pacification in Germanie since ye Latter Ende of Julie 1633 till 26 September 1633,* reprinted in C. A. Briggs, 'The Work of John Durie in behalf of Christian Union in the Seventeenth Century', *Presbyterian Review* 8 (1897) pp. 301–9, quoted at p. 301. I am grateful to Roger Staff of Aberdeen University for sending me a photocopy of this paper.

[6] BL Sloane MS 1465 f. 2. Abbot had given his permission for the signing of the *Instrumentum*: Turnbull, p. 141.

Archbishop of Armagh, to undertake the task. In 1654, Dury repeated the request, stressing its importance and the preparation disrupted by the war:

To procure the Compliment of the Body of Practical Divinity, the way is already chalked out unto us, and was agreed upon by some of our most able and godly ministers, who before these Troubles, did offere themselves unto the Work, and engaged to take their tasks to be elaborated under the direction of Doctor Usher, the primate of Armach.[7]

However, the work had not become the exclusive preserve of Ussher and the London ministers. Dury maintained his contacts in the provinces, using Hartlib and Philip Nye as go-betweens. In particular, he looked to Thomas Goodwin, Joseph Caryl, Thomas Ball and Stephen Marshall as representatives of Cambridge, London, Northamptonshire and Essex respectively.[8] In the first half of 1635, he wrote a joint letter to Ball and Marshall, regretting that they had left London before he had had a chance to confer with them regarding his work and explaining what he hoped of them. Dury was shortly to return to the continent to whip up support in Holland, and then to proceed to Germany where he intended to convene a conference

for the advancement of the Gospell of Christ in peace & truth against the Comon adversaries therof the Papists and Socinians who in a different way & in some sort opposite to each other both labour to subvert the Foundation of Christian Religion.

To combat this subversion, the English divines were to provide a spiritual foundation for his political negotiations. As Dury told them, 'my cheife labour is to have the meanes of setling mens Consciences in the life of God set awake by the rules of Practicall divinity contrived into a Compleate body that it may be Comunicated from hence unto forraine Churches which if it were done I hope needelesse contentions would soone fall to the ground of themselves'.[9] Some months later, having been unable to visit the divines of these two counties, he wrote to Marshall and Ball again, explaining his intentions in more detail for the ministers to pass on to their colleagues. He had hoped to address interested clergy together but had been prevented by 'the uncertaintie of your occasions and the shortnesse of my time'. He hoped his letter would 'contract the labour of many visits' and clearly saw the two ministers as being in a position to spread his ideas in conferences of sympathetic divines, asking them to 'communicate and conferre together upon the matter' with clergymen within their respective counties. As before, they were asked to help in the compilation of 'the principles and Doctrines of Practical Divinities which were more distinctly and plainly delivered in these Churches of Great Brittaine, than in all the rest of the Christian world besides'. By this means, the feuding continental

7 John Dury, *An earnest plea for Gospel Communion* (1654) pp. 79, 81–3.
8 SU Hartlib MS 4/3/79b.   9 SU Hartlib MS 17/2/1a–6b.

divines may escape the 'endlesse maze of controversies and debates' which was 'Polemicall Divinities . . . for as long as men know not what the State of Regeneration is, & how they ought to work out their salvation, in mortifying all earthly desires, & applying their knowledge to the direction of their own life and the amiable care of edifying others', then they will never overcome their differences.[10] Accordingly, Dury maintained his correspondence with Ball through the 1630s, personally and through Hartlib, who reported early in 1640 that 'Worthy Mr Marshall wrote lately that it was one of the highest and goodliest undertaking that could bee set upon in this Age'. Dury sought the advice of the Northamptonshire minister regarding the best ways to make peace with the Lutherans, although by the end of the decade he was very concerned about the perception of his work by Ball and others, attempting to 'cleere his secret suspicions'.[11]

Clearly, Dury was looking for the sort of devotional material that we saw earlier in chapters 5 and 6 as the bread and butter of the godly ministry. Both men were admirably fitted for the work: Ball was cooperating with Twisse on such themes, and was trying 'by his preaching to contrive a compleat body of divin[ity] and is gone over a great part of it. Hee writes all his sermons and has promised to communicate all', as Hartlib reported. He does seem to have acted upon this promise, for Robert Woodford noted in February 1639 that he preached 'very profitably in his former manner to set forth a body of religion'. Similarly, Marshall had been working on a piece about free grace the previous year; significantly, in reporting his work, Philip Nye noted that 'the Point of free grace was never m[ore] cleared than since those Armin[ian] Controv[ersies] about it were mooved'.[12] The eminence of the Essex divines in practical divinity made them particularly useful to Dury; Hartlib noted that Marshall and Nathaniel Rogers were his chief activists in the area, with Nathaniel Ward another useful source of ideas. Nye agreed that 'one of the best meanes to conveigh Practical Religion to the Church beyond Seas is a genuine and true translation of the best books in Practical Divin[ity]', and went on,

But to translate aright is a very hard matter, for first hee must bee a Godly man else hee wil never expresse the spirit of the Man et 2dly a Man of large abilities that hase a full compasse of the language. The Germans have notions enough but they doe not know how to apply them et to set them upon the Conscience. Also the preaching eloquence of English divines is very hard to be exprest. For they have made a new

[10] BL Sloane MS 654 f. 349.
[11] SU Hartlib MS 48/3/1a; 30/4/9b; 6/4/52a, 36a; 2/2/27a, 13a, 21a; 7/41/1a. The quotes are from 7/41/1a and 2/2/21a; cf. Milton, '"Unchanged Peacemaker",' pp. 100–4, 110–11; Turnbull, pp. 133, 205, 212.
[12] SU Hartlib MS 29/3/20a; NCO MS 9502 24 February 1639 (p. 332); SU Hartlib MS 29/3/21b; 29/2/49b.

language as it were, using new Termes et a new phraseology et therefore it were requisite one should make a new Lexicon for it, or Cause some English godly divine et able withal to translate some, such a one as Harris Sibs [*sic*: Sibbes] or Cotton their or other Treatises [Nathaniel] Rogers of S[uffolk] hase few new notions but several turnings et expressions to apply it . . . One of the hardest to translate were also Hooker of the preparation etc. which hase as many turnings and windings in his spirit as any whatsoever.[13]

The widely accepted expertise of the Essex ministers in these areas encouraged Hartlib to pursue Dury's initiatives among them. His surviving *Ephemerides* show that he solicited assessments of the work of Thomas Hooker, Nathaniel Ward, John Rogers and Jeremiah Dyke of Epping[14] and kept himself informed of the work of deprived ministers like Daniel Rogers. By the end of 1634, Rogers had completed the study, which was eventually published as *Matrimoniall Honour* in 1642, and was working on 'the Sinnes of the Times Here et Abroad'.[15]

The ministerial network could offer more than intellectual labours. A number of divines contributed financial support from their own pockets and were instrumental in encouraging sympathetic patrons to contribute. Martin Holbeach, Samuel Wharton, Herbert Palmer, Simeon Ashe, John Sedgewick, Edmund Calamy, William Greenhill, William Carter, Jeremiah Whitaker, William Price, Joseph Caryl, William Spurstow, John Ley, Daniel Cawdrey, Thomas Hill, William Gouge, Thomas Valentine, George Walker, Anthony Tuckney and Daniel Rogers all appear in Hartlib's accounts, as do Thomas Barrington, the Earl of Warwick, Sir Richard Knightley and Sir Nathaniel Rich.[16] In both aspects of support for Dury's schemes, the main Essex activist was Stephen Marshall, who put Hartlib in touch with his liberal parishioner, Edward Benlowes, as a possible source of money. In March 1633, Katherine Barnardiston of Witham, a daughter of the famous Suffolk family, died and left provision in her will to give 'two hundred pounds to be bestowed uppon such religious good and charitable worke as my Executors shall by and with the advice of the aforenamed Mr Marshall the minister thinke the same best to be bestowed uppon as may be most fitt for the glory of God'. Marshall did not immediately turn to Dury, who left England shortly after the will was proved, but he corresponded with John White of Dorchester and John Stoughton of St Mary Aldermanbury concerning the legacy, and Samuel Hartlib was informed that an unspecified sum was in Marshall's gift. In the event, 150 pounds was given to

---

[13] SU Hartlib MS 29/2/24a, 20b–21a.
[14] SU Hartlib MS 29/2/10a, 20b, 24a, 25a, 45a, 48a, 49b, 55b–56b; 29/3/12b.
[15] SU Hartlib MS 29/2/7, 51a.
[16] SU Hartlib MS 23/10/1–3a; 23/11/2b; 23/18/1; Turnbull, *Hartlib, Dury and Comenius*, p. 27.

support the cause of ecclesiastical pacification.[17] Later in the decade Marshall seems to have been pressing Katherine's relative, Nathaniel Barnardiston, for financial support of Hartlib's work.[18]

II

Despite these activities, the 'Body of Divinity' never appeared, unless Ussher's short catechetical work of this title was the fruit of these labours. Some works of practical divinity were translated for European consumption, including works by Hooker, Ames, Whately and Goodwin, but these enterprises seem to have owed little to Dury's efforts.[19] This leads us to ask two questions: why was so little achieved, and why did the godly ministers lend their assistance? For the first question, logistical difficulties may account for many of Dury's failures. He was constantly short of money, despite the fund-raising efforts of so many, and failed to build up sufficient momentum behind the English aspects of his work: he was rarely in England himself, and Hartlib had too many competing interests. As Dury complained to Marshall and Ball, 'there is want of order, want of communication, want of conjunction'.[20] There was an element of inadequate diligence in the work of the godly ministers; for instance, Speed complained that John Davenport was 'exceeding slow to Action'.[21] Moreover, Dury's energies in England were divided between the godly ministers, the universities, moderate Calvinist bishops and the Laudian hierarchy. Although it is dangerous to assume that these activities were necessarily incompatible, it does seem that nonconformist ministers feared that Dury's schemes might involve the countenancing of unlawful ceremonies, and indeed, in 1636, Dury reported that some divines had complained that the very notion of union between Lutheran and Calvinist theologies was 'a reconcilement of

---

[17] On Benlowes, SU Hartlib MS 29/2/64b; on his relations with Marshall, who rented a house from him, administered his charitable projects and worked closely with him in town government: ERO D/P 14/8/7; 14/18/1a; 14/25/3; H. Jenkins, *Edward Benlowes (1602–1676) Biography of a Minor Poet* (London, 1952) pp. 11–12, 134, 142; Benlowes was later noted as a recipient of a new work by Comenius: SU Hartlib MS 23/13/1a; on Barnardiston: PRO PROB 11/163/211; SP 16/310/93; CO 1/8/79; SP 16/351/100. Marshall was to preach Lady Barnardiston's funeral sermon at St Michael's, Cornhill, in London. He had formerly been chaplain to Sir Thomas Barnardiston and his son Giles, on the Suffolk/ Essex border: ERO D/DMs C2; K. W. Barnardiston, *Clare Priory* (Cambridge, 1962) p. 30; Anon., *The Godly Mans Legacy* (1681) p. 3.

[18] SU Hartlib MS 7/40/1a.

[19] James Ussher, *A Body of Divinity* (1653); M. A. Shaaber, *Check List of Works of British Authors Printed Abroad, in Languages other than English, to 1641* (New York, 1975); cf. K. L. Sprunger, *Dutch Puritanism: A History of English and Scottish Churches of the Netherlands in the Sixteenth and Seventeenth Centuries, Studies in the History of Christian Thought* XXXI (Leiden, 1982) pp. 359–61.

[20] SU Hartlib MS 17/2/4a.   [21] SU Hartlib MS 46/6/15a

truth and of errour'. William Prynne was among those who later referred to Dury as 'a time-serving Proteus', and his single-minded pursuit of reconciliation made him increasingly open to such accusations.[22]

Why, then, should any ministers have spent their energy and their own and their patrons' money in Dury's cause? Perhaps part of the reason can be found in the opportunities offered to deprived ministers. Daniel Rogers, as we have seen, turned to writing after his suspension, and similarly, Thomas Hooker considered a literary career before his exile in the Netherlands; Thomas Goodwin was resolved to live in college and 'to perfect a book in Pr[actical] Divin[ity]' after he resigned his place.[23] Clearly, such considerations are not sufficient to explain the interest of a busy man like Marshall. Perhaps some further light can be gained from these early enthusiasts for his scheme. A common element seems to be a pre-existing hostility to Arminianism: as was seen earlier, John Davenport's lack of interest in the ceremonial controversies stemmed from a perception that it was more important to join together to oppose Arminianism; William Twisse had written a book against the Arminians which he could not get published; William Sedgewick told Samuel Rogers in 1636 that 'idolatrous, superstitious Arminians carry the ball before them, they have prevailed lamentably these 7 yeares'.[24] Stephen Marshall made the connection explicitly when he explained to Hartlib that he saw the scheme as

The only way to crush the Armin[ians] or to bring them in to renounce their Tenants. Now they curry favour almost with every sect to make or to joine thems[elves] to a party. So they curry now favour with the Lutherans, Socin[ians], Anabap[tists], being but shut out by the Calvinists. Much m[ore] when from all Protestancy they are so solemly excluded they will be made m[ore] odious, or bee brought to renounce their fundamental untruths and to come at least to our fundamental Truths . . . Dur[y] promised according to law not to goe about to bring reconcil[iation with] the Armin faction . . . The thoughts of G[od]s heart they shall stand fore[ver], et in this worke there was much of the thoughts of G[od] in it.[25]

This preoccupation was some distance from Dury's main intention, which was to advance a pan-Protestant league against Rome. While the destruction of the Papacy would appeal to a broad range of English Protestants, the godly ministers would be less willing to work with those they saw as Arminians, or as advancers of ceremonial conformity and innovation. To some extent, Dury learnt this lesson and tendered

[22] Turnbull, pp. 132–222 esp. pp. 136, 178; William Prynne, *The Time Serving Proteus, and Ambidexter Divine, Uncased to the World* (1650) pp. 1–2; cf. Milton, *passim*.
[23] *MHSC* 4th ser. 6 (1863) p. 31; SU Hartlib MS 29/2/6a.
[24] I. M. Calder (ed.), *Letters of John Davenport* (New Haven, Conn., 1937) pp. 23–4; Turnbull, pp. 133–4; QUB Percy MS 7 f. 146.
[25] SU Hartlib MS 29/3/15b–16a.

alternative reports of his work in Germany, one tailored for the consumption of the divines who signed the *Instrumentum*, and another for the hierarchy. In both his extant letters to Marshall and Ball he suggested that the fundamental reformed doctrines would not only end the schism between Lutherans and Calvinists, but also show their agreement 'so far as they ought to be distinguished from Papists and Socinians; (who both alike though in a different way subvert the fundamentalls)'.[26] These themes were drawn together in great detail in a finely judged set of propositions in June 1635. Carefully designed to appeal to the strengths and interests of the godly ministers, the document proposed to answer the following question:

How the true ministers of the Gospell ought (in these dangerous tymes wherein Carnell and Politicke men oppose the power of godliness.) to ioyne together openly and profesedly in spirituall endeavours; to uphold the truth and advance the meanes of the state of regeneration in a christian life; by the care of mutuall edification through the Communion of Saints?

The paper names the church in France, and not England, although it is plain that the subject is the English Church. The first task is to make clear what the dangers of the times were. In general, the Antichrist is seen to be working through worldly policy and on the infirmities of the professors. The 'persons in cheife authority' are opposing 'such as endeavour to walke most conscionably & strictly in the wayes of God', partly as a consequence of the antipathy 'betwixt the true and formall professors'; partly to maintain a 'lordly hierarchie' and to advance 'plots of state' in the cause of the 'Roman and Spanish partie'. The course taken by the hierarchy is as follows:

1. they make use of their owne backed with civill authoritie to be an absolute law in matters of religion.
2. by this authoritie they impose new injunctions whereby they intend to discover the inclynation of men, to know those that will serve their ends from others that preferre conscience before worldly respects.
3. they undermine the principles and helpes to conscionable knowledge in suppressing bookes of practical divinitie, & oppose the meanes of powerfull preaching by setting up an idoll ministery when they have by subtill trickes gotten advantages against such as they intend to silence and cast out of their places.
4. They urge the outward formalitie more than the true worshipp.
5. they enlarge the liberty of papists and of loose livers to curry favour with the multitude, and become popular.
6. they interpret favourable the superstitious tenets of the Church of Rome and possesse the minds of men with an indifferencie of opinion towards the state thereof in respect of salvation.

---

[26] Turnbull, p. 146n.; BL Sloane MS 654 f. 349; cf. SU Hartlib MS 17/2/2b. In contemporary polemics Arminians were commonly called Socinians.

7. And by all this they make a way to exalt the temporall authoritie of the Clergie above all other power, & to exempt it from under the royall iuisdiccion in outward government, or Parliamentall statutes by which it hath beene curbed & kept in lyne.

The second section states the proper aims of a true minister of the gospel, very much in terms of the model discussed earlier: a man spiritually fit to preach, preaching plainly and active pastorally to apply his preaching and to act as an exemplar in his life. However, the sins of the times have brought new aims, 'requisite in the tymes of danger & opposition'. Among these, the minister is 'to draw nearer in a special manner to god to consult with him in the word & to strive with him by prayer and fastinge to obtain more graces to be able to encourter [*sic*] with the oppositions & dangers'. He is 'to walke more circumspectly in his owne wayes . . . than ever he did in former tymes', and lastly, 'to arm himself with strong resolutions to give up his life for the flocke rather than to fall backe & loose ground in any thinge that is materiall to salvation'. To advance the aims of the godly ministry, the preacher must lay special emphasis on a number of doctrines. He must stress, for instance, 'that it is vaine to worship god by the precepts of man' and 'that the Church of Rome is not onely superstitious in the worship of God but Idolotrous in the point of the masses & the worshipping of the saints'. The traditional precepts of practical divinity are to be pressed with renewed vigour, making it clear 'that to rely upon the outward civilitie of life & upon the outward formalitie of the worshipp is no wayes safe; but rather is a meanes to loose all sense of true religion & at last become a meare hipocrite & atheist'. Only by urging these doctrines will 'the corruptions of the puritie of the gospell in mixing with formalityes & doctrynes' be combated. Every true professor must play his part in this, for they 'are bound at all times as members of the same body one to another to entertaine spirituall Communion, which consisteth in a mutuall care that one should have for another to consider, exalt and provoke one another dayly to love and good workes'. Thus the individual minister is to draw strength from 'joint endeavours'. The godly ministers are to meet together

1. to consult upon cases of conscience one with another according as occasion shall require.
2. to elaborate joyntly some materiall treaties fit for the sinnes of the tymes.
3. to perfit the worke of practicall divinity in takeinge tasks and performing them.

Lastly, the ministers are to work for a conscionable peace by collecting the fruits of their labours 'into one common stocke from whence every particular member of the body may receive intelligence and have communication with other thoughts as from a store house of spirituall talents'. More than anything, this sounds like Dury's 'Body of Divinity', particularly with the mention of 'an Agency of sollicitation' appointed to gather the work, the role he wished for Hartlib. In the main he sees these positive actions as the preserve of preaching ministers; the silenced ministers are to make another contribution. They 'should relate the truth of the proceedings of their adversaries against them, and lay open to the world their shameful practises; that they may fear to attempt the like against others'. They should refute and reprove the sins of the times and warn others, and 'collect the strange practises which they have observed contrary to Christianitie in their government, and shew the opposition which it hath with the gospell and spirit of Christ'. Thus, the paper concludes, the positive truths working, on the one hand, and the 'discovery of wickedness', on the other, 'will make a complete worke of defence and offence in this warre fare'.[27]

Clearly, this paper is a strikingly explicit exposition of the fears and grievances of the godly ministry. It is in Dury's hand and among his papers, but I think we must entertain the notion that it is not by him. He was in England at the time of its composition, or at the time he copied it. It seems unusually concise and direct for Dury, and shows a detailed knowledge of, and preoccupation with, English affairs. Clearly, the appointment of an agent to collect the body of divinity suggests it is linked to his schemes: either it is tailored for the consumption of the alienated godly ministry or it is by such a minister with knowledge of Dury's project. There is a possibility, no more, that it is the work of Daniel Rogers, who, as we have seen, had been working on the 'Sines of the Times Here et Abroad'. The resolution to sacrifice himself before compromising with formality resembles the position Rogers took in his own ministry,[28] and the different roles assigned to preaching and silenced divines has a certain similarity to his own activities and those of his neighbour, Stephen Marshall. However, I would not want any weight to be attached to this suggestion; in itself, the paper advanced Dury's scheme in a way that would appeal to those godly ministers alienated by the Laudian regime. In this context, it is perhaps salutary to see that there is a perspective from which the compilation of a Body of Divinity is an act of opposition, a work of 'offence in this warre fare'. While no Protestant would oppose such a work on principle, and we might note that King Charles 'recommended that confession of faith might be composed, drawn from the fundamentall tenets on which both parties agree',[29] this line of argument adopts a rhetoric of 'opposition' and 'warfare' to resist the 'dangers of the times' that admits of no interpretation other than one rooted in a view of the work as subversive and reactive to Laudian changes.

[27] SU Hartlib MS 9/1/121a–26a. This paper is discussed very briefly in Turnbull, p. 170. Turnbull sees it as referring to France.

[28] SU Hartlib MS 29/2/7b; see above pp. 172–3.

[29] *HMC Fourth Report* (London, 1876) p. 160.

Here we may leave Dury's schemes: however appealing to the godly ministers, he never cultivated enough trust to move in their inner circles and spent too much of his energy on the pursuit of an official approval he was never likely to get. Consideration of his relations with the spiritual brotherhood has opened up questions regarding the positive options open to ministers in the new circumstances of deprivation and pressure. These questions can be pursued among the godly clergy.

Firstly, however, we may briefly examine a project that used the same networks for a purpose that can be seen as unambiguously subversive. We know that godly ministers used their wealthy friends and their fund-raising skills to raise money to support deprived ministers and their dependants in the aftermath of the Bancroftian disciplinary purges.[30] In the mid-1630s, the Laudian authorities suspected that something similar was in the air. One of the accusations voiced by Peter Heylin in his sermon in Oxford in July 1630 denouncing the Feoffees for Impropriations was 'whether they doe not keepe a common purse to susteine their partie, to relive silenced brethren; and cherish such, as are convicted by autoritie'.[31] The rumours implicated John White of Dorchester, encountered earlier, and John Stoughton, one of the London steering committee for the Body of Divinity, who was preaching in favour of ecclesiastical peace with the Lutherans as late as 1638.[32] In October 1635, Sir John Lambe reported his suspicions regarding money channelled out of Dorset into London, which he described as 'Treasure that is said to be here, kept for the Childrens portion'. Lambe hoped to 'discover a great matter', and asked Laud to dispatch a messenger to Dorset to raid White's study before he made his move on Stoughton, aware that if precipitate actions were taken in London, intelligence would be relayed to White and he would be able to cover his tracks.[33] Laud obliged and both studies were sealed and a number of documents seized. The two men were kept busy in the High Commission from November 1635 until early 1636, but nothing could be proved.[34] There were records of money passing between Richard Bernard of Batcombe and White and evidence emerged of money going on to Stoughton, who had certainly received petitions from poverty-stricken ministers.[35] A number of letters

---

[30] N. Tyacke, *The Fortunes of Puritanism, 1603–1640, Friends of Doctor Williams's Library Lecture 1990* (London, 1991) pp. 5–7.

[31] Cited by G. E. Gorman, 'A Laudian Attempt to "Tune the Pulpit": Peter Heylin and his Sermon against the Feoffees for the Purchase of Impropriations', *JRH* 8 (1974–5) p. 343.

[32] QUB Percy MS 7 f. 326.   [33] SP 16/300/2.

[34] SP 16/261 ff. 285, 286b, 300, 316b; 16/324 ff. 13, 19b; 16/301/4; D. Underdown, *Fire from Heaven: Life in an English Town in the Seventeenth Century* (London, 1992) p. 174.

[35] SP 16/278/51; 16/290/15.

and papers connected the two ministers with clergymen, lay people and opinions suspected to be hostile to the establishment. Correspondence connected James Forbes in the Netherlands and various people in New England and also implicated Stephen Marshall, Henry Whitfield, Sir Nathaniel Rich, John Goodwin and others, including, to his dismay, John Dury.[36] However, nothing more definite could be brought against the two ministers; men such as White were involved in many charitable schemes[37] and anything subversive could, with a little prudence, be concealed. Perhaps the authorities would have been more successful if they had searched Richard Bernard's study: White had a cryptic note from his carrier with some equally cryptic accounts. As there is an ever-present danger of succumbing to the attractions of Laud's own paranoia, in the absence of further evidence the matter is perhaps best left unresolved.

[36] SP 16/222/28; 16/258/62; 16/265/35; 16/284/6; 16/280/65; 16/308/33; 16/310/93; CO 6/63, 64; 8/15, 39; cf. the accusations in *Persecution Undecima: the Churches Eleventh Persecution* (1648) p. 55.

[37] Underdown, *Fire from Heaven*, pp. 44–5, 109, 112, 116, 119, 125–6, 227; F. Rose-Troup, *John White: the Patriarch of Dorchester* (London, 1930) pp. 294–304.

14

Choices of suffering and flight

I

It will become clear that in some respects the practices of the godly ministry in the 1630s exhibit a large degree of continuity with former times. In the course of answering the question of how true ministers should behave in such dangerous times, many of the proposals among Dury's papers[1] were for a renewed commitment to the patterns of sociability and religiosity already discussed. Many of these patterns were not susceptible to ecclesiastical censure and could not be legislated out of existence. Bishop Juxon made some attempts to limit the activities of silenced ministers, mainly to ensure that they could not preach, which was a public act and so possible for the ecclesiastical courts, if sufficiently well informed, to prevent. He also aimed to stop silenced ministers from holding conventicles, a more difficult area of activity to regulate, particularly on the household level, with all the ambiguities inherent in such meetings.[2]

This becomes plain if we examine the experience of a silenced minister such as Daniel Rogers. Rogers remained under suspension from 1631 until the 1640s, but in some respects his ministry continued. At the lowest level, he could continue the private devotional practices of fasting, prayer and meditation, the daily discipline he had learnt from his father and passed on to his children. Time seems to have been set aside in the early evening for each member of the household to perform their private devotions, although when Samuel Rogers returned to the household he found there was too little room to accommodate everyone in sufficient privacy.[3] After a period of private prayer, the whole household would meet, and Daniel Rogers would catechise the younger members of the family and then perform the family exercises, with preaching, admonition and extended *extempore*

---

[1] See above, pp. 263–5.
[2] STC 10265.5, Articles concerning the Clergy no. 19; cf. above, chs. 10 and 12; P. Collinson, 'The English Conventicle', in *SCH* 23 (1986) pp. 223–61.
[3] QUB Percy MS 7 ff. 182, 328.

prayer.[4] Beyond the household, Rogers could continue to minister to the parish in his pastoral capacity, and to organise and lead fasting and prayer among the Wethersfield godly. In this his household could assist; it seems that divinity students from the Rogers' extended clerical cousinage would cut their teeth in these meetings, and that such meetings were split along gender lines; Rogers' daughter, Mary, was prominent in these. After her death in June 1638, her brother mourned her as one 'much acquainted with self triall; and the life of faith in the parish which was her soules delight . . . A most publique sp[irit] shee had for the Church of g[od] and tenderly affected with the evell of the times.' She was, he continued, 'eminently gifted', as was evinced by the days of humiliation she led with a Mrs Clench, where prayers would continue for three or four hours. The male meetings were held in various houses in the parish; at the home of Goodman Wiggs, or at the lodgings of John Hubbart or Daniel Sutton, both relations and among Daniel's divinity students.[5] Rogers seems to have been fairly successful in ensuring that the pulpit at Wethersfield was never empty. From his initial suspension he began to bring in preachers from among his friends. After a little early trouble, there seems to have been regular preaching at Wethersfield, by his students, by his sons, and by such visitors as John Carter and Anthony Tuckney.[6] Rogers also led groups on regular trips, gadding to hear other preachers. Of these the most common was Stephen Marshall at neighbouring Finchingfield, where they also heard John Borodale,[7] but there were also excursions to Castle Hedingham and Stansted to hear Edmund Brewer, to Felsted and elsewhere to hear Samuel Wharton, to Barnston to hear John Beadle, and to Colchester to hear John Knowles.[8] In addition, he led expeditions to join with similarly godly groups in Earls Colne, Sudbury and Dunmow.[9] The journeys themselves formed part of the pastoral ministry: Samuel Rogers often found himself 'refreshed with the society of the faithful', 'delivered in journeye', or noted that 'our sweet discourse in the ioirney was that which most refreshed mee'.[10] It seems that a deprived minister (or in Rogers' case, a suspended one) could play an active part in the religious life of his parish. It must be noted that in all these practices there must have been an element of

---

[4] Ibid., f. 2 (catechising); f. 11 (Samuel admonished for being 'too effuse in laughter . . . and lavishe in words'); ff. 2, 25, 28, 110, etc. (exercises).

[5] Ibid., ff. 23, 26, 49, 352; for Hubbart, cf. f. 55; H. F. Waters, *Genealogical Gleanings in England* (Boston, Mass., 1901) vol. I pp. 228–9; T. W. Davids, *Annals of Evangelical Nonconformity in the County of Essex* (London, 1863) pp. 443–4; for Sutton, QUB Percy MS 7 ff. 23, 25, 345, 352; SP 16/351/100.

[6] GLRO DL/C 319 f. 77; QUB Percy MS 7 ff. 23, 48, 260, 345, 351.

[7] Ibid., ff. 23, 25, 30, 51, 52, 220, 234.

[8] Ibid., ff. 29, 52, 54, 61, 220, 274.

[9] Ibid., ff. 8, 24, 28, 29, 53, 173, 192, 222, 234, 260, 261, 275, 286, 352.

[10] E.g. ibid., ff. 220, 192, 48.

continuity: they are all the settled practices of voluntary religion. There is no sense in which these activities are necessarily to be seen as a withdrawal or a separation from the established church; indeed, many of them focused upon the ordinances of the parish church, albeit not exclusively on Wethersfield parish church.[11]

A similar continuity is seen in what we can recover of Daniel Rogers' social life among his ministerial colleagues. He could still receive visitors, such as Martin Holbeach, Anthony Tuckney and John Wilson, attend gatherings of ministers and noble professors at the Barrington seat at Hatfield Broad Oak, and travel to Cambridge for the Commencement.[12] It is not clear how maintenance was provided for him, and this may prove to be a crucial question, but the point must be made that a silenced minister was not one without work. Having said this, public preaching and the administration of the sacraments were also central to a minster's vocation, and the psychological impact of removing the right to play his full role in the parish and abroad must not be underestimated.

II

The practice of a stinted ministry was not the only option open to those ministers who would not compromise with the authorities or failed to present a sufficiently convincing conformable façade. For many ministers relations with the noble professors were sufficiently close for them to provide a haven from the storm. Ezekiel Rogers had spent the early part of his career in the Barrington household, until an opportunity arose for him to exercise his ministry without compromising his scruples regarding subscription and the ceremonies, and we have seen protection and employment given by gentle and noble professors to Thomas Shepard, Thomas Hooker and Jeremiah Burroughes.[13] There was, however, an additional

---

[11] This continuity in the case of a lecturer is partly dependent upon the nature of the incumbent. If the living was held by an unsympathetic minister these activities could be reported to the authorities; if the holder of the vicarage or rectory was sympathetic, a suspended lecturer could more easily play a supporting role. In Daniel Rogers' case, the rector was Trinity Hall, Cambridge, and the vicar, William Pasfield, was also rector of Chelmsford and seems to have been an absentee, although he was actually born in Wethersfield, around 1561. That he was educated at Peterhouse, and not Christ's College, suggests that he was not a protégé of Richard Rogers: R. Newcourt, *Repertorium Ecclesiasticum Parochiale Londinense* (1710) vol. II pp. 654, 129; Venn, s.v.

[12] QUB Percy MS 7 ff. 26, 48, 54, 182, 267.

[13] Waters, *Genealogical Gleanings*, vol. I p. 267: in his will, Rogers observed that 'being inlightened concerning the evell and snare of subscription and Cerimonies . . . I therefore chose rather to lye hide about a dozen yeares in an honerable famelly exerciseing my selfe in ministeriall dutyes . . . Then the lord Gave me a Call to a Publique charge at Rowley in Yorke shire [a Barrington living] whereby the Gentlenesse of Toby Matthewe I was favoured both for subscription and Cerimonies.' until the advent of Archbishop Neile; cf.

option of emigration, either to the Netherlands or New England. The debate on the motives for migration was joined as early as the 1630s and by the time of the trial of Bishop Wren had assumed a polarity of religious and economic explanation that has become familiar in twentieth-century historiography of the emigration to New England. Despite Wren's suggestion that most of those who had left the diocese of Norwich were economic migrants,[14] conventional accounts followed the explanations of the first two generations and saw the peopling of the colonies as a movement for religious liberty. This interpretation has survived the recasting of the debate by James Truslow Adams in 1921, once the New England patriot Samuel Eliot Morison had added his authority to the religious explanation, against Adams' economic emphasis.[15] Despite occasional works giving full weight to economic and social factors, including N. C. P. Tyack's well-balanced thesis,[16] the migration remained in most accounts very much a Puritan affair or even, in Bridenbaugh's much-imitated phrase, 'a Puritan hegira'.[17] Breen and Foster's seminal 1973 article criticised previous work for perpetuating the dichotomy of religion and economics, suggesting that the debate was hampered by a 'question badly posed,'[18] but it is not yet apparent that their recommendations have been adopted in the ways they might have hoped. The work which followed has taken their point on the complexity of the issues, but perhaps as a stick with which to beat those who adhere to religious explanations as much as a way to a new synthesis. The most recent exchange seems to have left the issue in a rather surprising state of hotly disputed agreement.[19]

J. T. Cliffe, *The Puritan Gentry: the Great Puritan Families of Early Stuart England* (London, 1984) ch. 9.

[14] BodL Tanner MS 314 f. 192.

[15] For this exchange, which still shapes the continuing debate, see J. Truslow Adams, *The Founding of New England* (Boston, Mass., 1921); S. E. Morison, *Builders of the Bay Colony* (Boston, Mass., 1930). C. E. Banks, of the Massachusetts Historical Society, effectively changed sides during the 1920s: 'English Sources of Emigration to the New England Colonies in the Seventeenth Century', *MHSP* 60 (1927) pp. 366–72; *The Planters of the Commonwealth* (Boston, Mass., 1930).

[16] N. C. P. Tyack, 'Migration from East Anglia to New England before 1660', University of London PhD (1951). His recent article retains this balance, perhaps with more emphasis on religious motives: 'The Humbler Puritans of East Anglia and the New England Movement: Evidence from the Court Records of the 1630s', *NEHGR* 138 (1984) pp. 79–106.

[17] C. Bridenbaugh, *Vexed and Troubled Englishmen, 1590–1642* (New York, 1963) pp. 434–73.

[18] T. H. Breen and S. Foster, 'Moving to the New World: the Character of Early Massachusetts Migration', *WMQ* 3rd ser. 30 (1973) pp. 189–222.

[19] There is a good survey in D. Cressy, *Coming Over: Migration and Communication between England and New England in the Seventeenth Century* (Cambridge, 1987) ch. 3 and esp. pp. 74–83. Cressy recognises the importance of religion, or at least of internalised religious rhetoric, but hopes to remove the appellation 'Puritan' from the migration: pp. 83–106. The most important recent works are D. G. Allen, *In English Ways: the Movement of Societies and the Transferral of English Local Law and Custom to Massachusetts Bay in*

The emphasis has, quite properly, moved from the lay and clerical elites, who formed the most outspoken explanations of the migration, in all of their polemical variations, to the individuals, families and servants who formed the less frequently vocal majority.[20] Here, however, we are mainly concerned with clerical migration, and in this context it seems worthwhile to ask a series of questions which may also cast some light upon the wider debate. Firstly, it has been too infrequently asked why people did *not* migrate. If ministers can be found with many factors in common with those who did migrate and yet chose to remain in England, can we find explanations for this behaviour? Secondly, of those who chose to migrate, which factors determined their choice of destination? The main choice was between the Netherlands and New England, and the competing claims of each might be discussed.[21] Thirdly, what does it mean to suggest that people emigrated for religion's sake? If we may assume, as we may for the ministry, that religion, to say the least, played an important part in the decision to emigrate, can we leave it there? Although we have a sense of what New England was, or became, that may not be the same as that held by the migrants when they came to make decisions. More specifically, we can ask of the ministers, did they migrate to avoid ceremonial conformity? Were their objections to the old or to the new conformity, as already discussed?[22] Was this a migration of silenced ministers, escaping to enjoy the chance to exercise their preaching vocations? Were these ministers men with a firm conception of the proper form of church government, which they were eager enough to see implemented to cross the Atlantic? Or were there other factors that made the colonies attractive?

We may begin by examining one case in detail and open up a discussion along broader lines. We saw earlier how Thomas Shepard was moved to consider ceremonial issues after he came up against accusations of non-conformity, and became convinced that the surplice, the cross in baptism,

---

the *Seventeenth Century* (Chapel Hill, N. C., 1981); V. DeJohn Anderson, 'Migrants and Motives: Religion and the Settlement of New England, 1630–1640', *NEQ* 58 (1985) pp. 339–83; *New England's Generation: the Great Migration and the Formation of Society and Culture in the Seventeenth Century* (Cambridge 1993), and the exchange between the two: Allen, 'The Matrix of Motivation', and Anderson, 'Religion, the Common Thread', *NEQ* 59 (1986) pp. 408–24.

[20] R. Thompson, *Mobility and Migration: East Anglian Founders of New England, 1629–1640* (Amherst, Mass., 1994).

[21] That many migrants moved to the Netherlands and that the vast majority stayed is noted by Breen and Foster, 'Moving to the New England', pp. 206–7; there is also a brief discussion of those who stayed, who had similar motivation to the emigrants, in Allen, 'The Matrix of Motivation,' pp. 415–16, which is answered in Anderson, 'Religion, the Common Thread,' p. 422n.3. To my knowledge, only David Cressy discusses reasons to stay: *Coming Over*, pp. 87–98, esp. p. 93.

[22] Above, chs. 7 to 8.

and kneeling for communion were all sinful, around July 1631. Much later, in the preface to his *Defence of the Answer*, he wrote of the 1630s:

Was it not a time when human worship and inventions were grown to such an intolerable height, that the consciences of gods people, enlightened in the truth, could no longer bear them? Was not the power of the tyrannical prelates so great, that, like a strong current, it carried everything down stream before it? Did not the hearts of men generally fail them?[23]

This much would have earned the assent of many ministers living through these times. A relatively small number, though, emigrated and only some of them chose New England. As he rode to the visitation at Dunmow in early September 1631, Shepard discussed the options with Thomas Weld, who had just been excommunicated. Their conclusion was not to take ship at the earliest possible opportunity, but to go to Scotland and then to try to preach in Ireland, where the episcopate was of a different character. In the event, by mid-September Shepard had received a letter from Ezekiel Rogers, encouraging him to take up a post as chaplain to the Darley family in Buttercrambe, near York. He accepted and stayed with the family for a year or more. Although he felt himself 'far from all friends', Shepard's labours met with some success, and he also met his first wife. After marrying Margaret Touteville, a relation of the Darleys, in July 1632, his fear of Bishop Neile combined with his wife's unwillingness to stay at Buttercrambe and he accepted a call to Heddon, near Newcastle.[24]

In his eighteen months in the north-east, he 'came to read and know more of the ceremonies, church government and estate, and the unlawful standing of bishops than in any other place'. As we will see, this does not necessarily make Shepard a Congregationalist, and, indeed, he was still not looking to emigrate. Even after 'the Bishop put in a priest [at Heddon] who would not suffer me to preach publicly anymore', his first response was to appeal to Bishop Morton, who declared himself afraid 'to give me liberty because Laud had taken notice of me'. After this he preached where he could around the county and eventually in the houses of friends, 'and there I stayed until Mr Cotton, Mr Hooker, Stone, Weld went to New England'. Over the next months, he began to regard a call he had received from New England more favourably, and by the middle of 1634 had decided to respond positively. He was aware that his decision was complex and he tried to sift out the various elements for his son:

1. I saw no call to any other place in old England nor way of subsistence in peace

---

[23] Thomas Shepard and John Allin, *A Defence of the Answer Made unto the Nine Questions . . . Against the Reply thereto By . . . John Ball* (1648) pp. 3–4.
[24] M. McGiffert (ed.), *God's Plot: the Paradoxes of Puritan Piety Being the Autobiography and Journal of Thomas Shepard* (Amherst, Mass., 1972) pp. 50–5.

and comfort to me and my family. 2. Divers people in old England of my dear friends desired me to go to New England, there to live together, and some went before and writ to me of providing a place for a company of us . . . 3. I saw the Lord departing from England when Mr Hooker and Mr Cotton were gone, and I saw the hearts of most of the godly set and bent that way, and I did think I should feel many miseries if I stayed behind. 4. My judgement was then convinced not only of the evil of ceremonies but of mixed communion and joining with such in sacraments, though I ever judged it lawful to join them in preaching. 5. I saw it my duty to desire the fruition of all Gods ordinances which I could not enjoy in old England. 6. My dear wife did much long to see me settled there in peace and so put me on to it. 7. Although it was true I should stay and suffer for Christ, yet I saw no rule for it now the Lord had opened a door of escape. Otherwise I did incline much to stay and suffer, especially after our sea storms.

Shepard went on to stress his desire 'to live among Gods people as one come out from the dead'. Although friends asked him to stay and preach privately in the north, Shepard 'saw that the time could not be long without trouble from King Charles'; he considered it better to emigrate where he could exercise his vocation publicly and hoped his friends would follow him over; finally, he thought it an awful prospect to die in Heddon and leave his wife and young child 'in that rude place of the north where was nothing but barbarous wickedness generally', and felt himself to be in danger from the High Commission.[25]

We may note that three-and-a-half years elapsed between Shepard's silencing and his decision to emigrate, and three years between his rejection of the ceremonies and that decision. Even while he was considering some fifteen reasons to set sail, he 'did incline much to stay and suffer'. Secondly, we may note that his ideas on church government scarcely seem to amount to a systematic position. We know that he was convinced of 'the unlawful standing of bishops', and was now against mixed communion and joining in the sacraments with the profane.[26] This could mean that he rejected prelacy, the high state and pomp of the English episcopacy, or that he found diocesan episcopacy unscriptural and preferred a reduced form, or, of course, that he was committed to some form recognisably Presbyterian or Congregational. His commitment to preaching to the mixed multitude without sharing in

---

[25] Ibid., pp. 55–6. As ever, there is a danger in accepting such retrospective accounts. Shepard may have been writing in good faith but this does not necessarily make changes of emphasis between 1634 and 1644, when this account was written, less likely. If anything, we might expect to find evidence of a greater ecclesiological commitment, so it may be that my impression of Shepard's pre-emigration ecclesiological vagueness is actually understated.

[26] This mention of 'sacraments' in the plural is perhaps the most intriguing part of his testimony. Does he mean that he is no longer willing to join in either the Eucharist or baptism with the profane, or merely intends to indicate communions in the plural? If the former, then this makes Shepard more radical than the tenor of his other remarks suggests. If the latter, or if Shepard is simply careless here, then he could have been in favour of nothing more extreme than a more rigorous application of discipline.

communion tends to make an adherence to a gathered church form less likely, but, without reading back later positions, it is difficult to say more about Shepard's ecclesiology before emigration than that he wanted reform and an element of spiritual discipline. Thirdly, it is clear that there was a social dimension to his decision. While at Buttercrambe, he was 'never so low sunk in my spirit as about this time', principally because he 'was now far from all friends', and dated his decision to the period after the emigration of Hooker, Cotton, Stone and Weld.[27] This may be part of the reason that he chose New England without, apparently, considering the Netherlands. Fourthly, there was a desire to exercise his preaching vocation and enjoy worship undefiled by the evil ceremonies, linked with a perception of persecution, and, finally, this links to an element which may be considered economic. Since his marriage, he had been seeking a more stable professional standing than the twenty pounds plus board available at Buttercrambe, and while his financial situation at Heddon may have been somewhat improved, Shepard, and possibly also his wife, must have had greater expectations of New England. Emigration could also therefore, in part, have been a response to career stagnation.

III

Although few ministers left such a full and frank account of the decision-making process, similar patterns can be discerned among other ministers who ended up in New England. The delay between silencing and setting sail for New England can, for instance, be seen in the experience of Samuel Newman, a product of William Whately's Banbury: after his initial silencing he moved seven times within England before emigrating in 1636.[28] While Thomas Goodwin and Philip Nye voluntarily resigned their livings in 1633, neither left the country until 1639, Nye possibly later.[29] While others left shortly after silencing, there is little sense of a stampede to New England: Hooker has been noted as spending eighteen months in the Netherlands; Cotton intended to go there before he was dissuaded; Thomas Weld left the country between his deprivation in September and his High Commission appearance in October 1631. He was certainly in the Netherlands by the end of November, sailing to New England the following year, after his candidacy for a ministerial post at Amsterdam had been resisted by John Paget.[30] Some of this pattern could be linked to the changing pace

---

[27] Ibid., pp. 52, 54–5.   [28] Mather, III pp. 113–24.
[29] K. L. Sprunger, *Dutch Puritanism: a History of English and Scottish Churches of the Netherlands in the Sixteenth and Seventeenth Centuries, Studies in the History of Christian Thought* XXXI (Leiden, 1982) p. 227.
[30] Ibid., p. 103; see above, ch. 9.

of emigration to the two locations. Robert Charles Anderson has pointed out that the pace of general emigration to New England might be described in terms of a small number of migrants in the years 1628 to *c.*1633, which he terms 'the Winthrop migration', followed by a rapid increase from 1634 to 1640, which he calls 'the Laudian migration'.[31] Something of the same pattern applies to ministerial emigration: the first period shows a slow and reluctant flow of ministers mainly, though not exclusively, among those with close associations with the colonising movement. In the mid-1630s, the flow increases, with fewer ministers choosing the Netherlands when Laudian pressures were increasing on the English congregations abroad, with John Forbes deprived and William Ames dead, and New England becoming more attractive once ministers of the stature of Hooker and Cotton had settled there. There was, however, a late revival of ministerial emigration to the Netherlands, including Goodwin, Nye, Jeremiah Burroughes and Samuel Ward, although Thomas Edwards suggested that some of these ministers were intending to move on to New England.[32] This may, in part, reflect a response to reports of the dissensions within Massachusetts and the manuscript debates over ecclesiology.

Other themes which appeared in Shepard's case might be extended. The question of the migrants' ecclesiology will be a concern of the following chapters, but Shepard is far from unique in holding relatively unformed views on church government upon emigration. Here we may simply note that whatever Thomas Weld's views were in 1631–3, his later defence of the New England way was heavily dependent upon the later work of John Cotton, citing and quoting extensively from Cotton's tracts.[33] It seems more than likely that Weld's ecclesiology came more from association than independent study. For such men, the social dimension of motivation looms larger. Recently, this element has received more sophisticated attention: not only was the bare fact of friendship important, but New England was seen to offer spiritual comforts that seemed less available in England, the forms of support and guidance discussed earlier in the context of the godly

---

[31] R. C. Anderson, 'A Note on the Changing Pace of the Great Migration', *NEQ* 59 (1986) pp. 406–7. As J. T. Horton, 'Two Bishops and the Holy Brood: a Fresh Look at a Familiar Fact', *NEQ* 40 (1967) pp. 339–63, points out, there is a diocesan element in the timing, with the activity of a bishop such as Wren precipitating a surge of emigrations; cf. above, ch. 10.

[32] Thomas Edwards, *Antapologia: or, a Full Answer to the Apologeticall Narration* (1644) pp. 16–18.

[33] Thomas Weld, *A Brief Narration of the Practices of the Churches in New England Written in Private to One that Desired Information therein; by an Inhabitant there, a Friend to Truth and Peace* (1645) pp. 2, 9, 10, 14, 16–18. It is difficult to date this tract closely: it is likely to have been written before 1641, when Weld was an inhabitant of New England, and after 1634, as his only other citation is Willet's *Synopsis* in the edition of that year.

ministry.[34] It may prove pertinent, however, that not every member of a group of friends fled, though equally subject to Laudian policy. Neither was this division a function of prior involvement with New England colonial ventures. Although Cotton, Hooker, Weld and Nathaniel Ward were variously involved in the Massachusetts Bay Company, so too was Philip Nye, who emigrated briefly to the Netherlands, and John Rogers' connection was at least as strong as Weld's, and his approval of emigration was somewhat qualified, as we will see.[35]

The theme of liberty to preach and minister in New England in contrast to the perceived persecution in old England is a large one in the stated motives and polemics of the settlers, notwithstanding the fact that more than a third of the emigrant ministers were not subject to any ecclesiastical censure at the time of leaving. Shepard explained

we might easily have found the way to have filled the prisons; and some had their share in those sufferings. But whether we were called to this when a wide door of liberty was set open, and our witnesses to the truth, through the malignant policy of those times, could not testify openly before the world, but were smothered in close prisons, we leave to be considered.[36]

This question of persecution and the lawfulness of flight became important in the light of later accusations from those who stayed and suffered, but it was debated at the time, too. John Cotton wrote from New England in 1634 to explain why he and Thomas Hooker had fled rather than suffer. He said they had 'conferred with the chief of our people', and in particular with John Dod, John Ball, Robert Cleaver, Nathaniel Cotton and John Winston, men we will encounter again. They had offered to stay, but Dod made the point that it was licit to escape: 'When Peter was young he might gird himself and go whither he would; but when he was old and unfit for travel, then indeed God called him rather than to suffer himself to be girt of others, and lead along to prison and death.' For the younger generation (and to the nonagenarian Dod, that must have meant most) it was lawful to flee, while the older, and perhaps the stronger, ministers should stay and witness.[37]

[34] Cf. C. E. Park, 'Friendship as a Factor in the Settlement of Massachusetts', *Proceedings of the American Antiquarian Society* n.s. 28 (1918) pp. 51–62; A. Zakai, 'The Gospel of Reformation: the Origins of the Great Puritan Migration', *JEH* 37 (1986) pp. 584–602.

[35] See above: N. B. Shurtleff (ed.), *Records of the Governor and Company of the Massachusetts Bay in New England* (Boston, Mass., 1853) vol. I pp. 1–76; *MHSC* 4th ser. 6 (1863) p. 472; ibid., 5th ser. 1 (1871) p. 197.

[36] Shepard and Allin, *Defence of the Answer*, pp. 5–6; R. Waterhouse, 'Reluctant Emigrants: the English Background of the First Generation of New England Puritan Clergy', *Historical Magazine of the Protestant Episcopal Church* 44 (1975) pp. 473–88, esp. 483–8.

[37] 'Cotton's Reasons for his Removal to New England', a letter of December 1634, in A. Young (ed.), *Chronicles of the First Planters of the Colony of Massachusetts Bay 1623–1636* (Boston, Mass., 1846) pp. 438–44; cf. John Norton, *Abel Being Dead yet Speaketh* (1658).

George Hughes was one such: considering emigration in 1633 he was dissuaded by Dod, as was John Ball.[38] A similar position seems to have been taken by Arthur Hildersham when Francis Higginson received his call to New England, although in Mather's account it is not clear, understandably, whether he was putting the case for remaining in England. Hildersham said: 'That were he himself a younger Man, and under his Case and Call, he should think he had a plain Invitation of Heaven unto the Voyage; and so he [Higginson] came unto a Resolution to comply therewithal.'[39] The same figure appears in the work of John Rogers, with the differential of strength made clearer:

> If God make us a way, we may [flee], as who haply are not as yet so fully fitted and resolved to suffer, as were meet, or who know not whether God would have us scatter his truth further, or remain to be as seeds thereof for afterwards, but if we see that its Gods minde we shall . . . suffer, then its our dutie willingly and cheerfully to put forth ourselves.[40]

If this sense that those that flee are the weaker brethren informs the ideas of one such as John Rogers, acquainted with the leaders of the enterprise and sympathetic to their projects, it is much more vehemently present in those who actively opposed the migration. This becomes plain if we return to Daniel Rogers. Not only was he silenced, and intimate with many emigrants, but he was actually to receive a visit from John Wilson, recruiting ministers for New England, in early March 1634.[41] Wilson was welcomed and stayed overnight, but he stood little chance of recruiting Rogers, who had already made his feeling plain in one of his last lectures before silencing. Rogers saw emigration as an abdication of spiritual duties, a cowardly evasion of God's trials, and placed it in the context of the general failure of godliness:

> Trash and drosse of mens profits, pleasures, ease, forme of religion, and such other scurfe, as is not fit to be named, hath eaten up all, as one said, The usury of the New hath eaten up the gaine of our Old University. So may we say, the spirit of our new hath eaten up the power of our old dayes, in point of edge, affection, earnestnesse and zeale. All is growne to discourse, contemplation, and empty shadowes of sincerity. Not to speake of many, who formally have stood for diligent preaching, and for the power of it, and are now gone aside, and slinke their neckes out of the Collar. Alas! brethren, it is not your going into new England, which will deliver you from the spirit of your old death and sloth, except the Spirit of Grace conduct you

---

[38] Anthony Wood, *Athenae Oxonienses* (London, 1813–20) vol. III p. 778; Clarke (1677) pp. 150–2.

[39] Mather, III p. 74.

[40] John Rogers, *A Godly and Fruitful Exposition of the First Epistle of Peter* (1650) p. 461; cf. pp. 79, 7.

[41] QUB Percy MS 7 ff. 26–7.

thither. All cannot goe, what will become of such as must stay, except God revive us at home?[42]

It seems clear that Rogers' principal objections were not ecclesiological, but moral. He condemned Separatists in the strongest terms, without identifying them with the colonists, although there was perhaps continuity with them in his complaint that the Separatists rail against abuses in the church without paying attention to 'the abuses of their own soules'. This was not to suggest that the English church was not in serious need of reformation; but, he asked, how do the Separatists speak of church abuses?

[Not] (as becomes them) in patience, and innocencie, to wait for a blessed redresse, but to overthrow the church quite, and pull downe the very frame and foundations of it, yea to raze it to the ground: which never did any (of those who were ten times more judicious than the best of them) attempt or intend.[43]

He saw the migration as a vain outlet for zeal that would be better employed at home; not only were those who chose flight the weaker brethren, but they compounded their weakness with arrogance and a misplaced sense of righteousness. Of 'those who are going from us into New England', he wrote,

They will not endure you to speake one word amisse of it, but their hearts are at their mouthes presently; they magnifie and extoll it in all places, wherever they become: their very spirits are possessed and taken up with the longing for it, they stand upon thornes, till they be there where their treasure is, they are soone knockt off from hence, though their native soyle, where they have had all their conversation, yet as if they had not knowne it, so doe they renounce it, and all the contents of it.

The emigrants were filled with such zeal that they would abandon parents, neighbours, spouses and children; they could not be countered by stories of the hardships to be endured or the conditions across the Atlantic. 'Paines, cost, selling all, and packing up their fardels is nothing to them, for their desires sake. Oftentimes I have wish't the place good enough for such affections: But in this argument, touching the spirit of Conversion and Grace, for the embracing of which, no affections can be sufficient, how do we flagge? Where is the man who can doe thus much for God and his glory, from the experience of mercy?'[44] Clearly, there were ministers among the society of the godly who regarded the migration as anything but a 'hegira', a holy flight.

Ministers expressing, to say the least, reservations about the call to flight, were drawing upon a tradition of such positions. William Perkins was prepared to acknowledge the flight of Elias from Jezebel, of the apostles,

[42] Daniel Rogers, *Naaman the Syrian, his Disease and Cure* (1642) p. 885.
[43] Ibid., p. 882.   [44] Ibid., p. 889.

indeed of Christ from the Pharisees, as godly; such flight was licit 'if he be not hindred by the bond of private or publike calling'. Emigration was lawful in the face of persecution, but one had to be sure that one was fleeing from the right sort of persecution. Perkins distinguished between two types of persecution: the first was 'the hand of God'; the second 'the worke of the wicked enemies of Gods church'. The latter was not necessarily a licence to flee, for 'them God useth sometimes as instruments, in laying his hand upon his Church, either for chastisment, or for triall'. If one was on trial and had 'libertie to flie', one could leave, provided that it was not against God's command, as in the case of Jonah. Often God called upon the godly to show their faith in the face of their enemies and so flight was not always an option: 'but if God give him libertie, and opportunity to flie, then he will not have him, at that time, to iustifie his religion by that meanes'.[45] This tradition provides an explanatory context for William Ames' justifications for emigration. He was careful to make it clear that to leave the church in England was not an act of separation, that the Church of England was a true church. One could remain in a corrupt church provided that one did not do so 'with a minde, by our silence, to cherish any of its defects, but that . . . we may doe our endeavour to take them away'.[46] A member of a corrupt church should not separate for four reasons. Firstly, 'because it may be the error or infirmity of the Church'; secondly, because offences should be borne with 'patience and long-suffering'; thirdly, because such a departure would hinder, not help, reformation; fourthly, because it was possible to worship in a corrupt church without sinning against one's conscience.[47] In fact, one could stay in a church with not only unscriptural discipline but even one '*where some of the Ordinances of Christ are wanting*', provided that these corruptions and potentially idolatrous ceremonies were to be tolerated 'as Civill meanes used and applyed to spiritual ends'. Given these not inconsiderable reservations, Ames said that there were still circumstances in which it was licit to withdraw (but not separate) from a true church:

As First, if a man cannot continue his communion, without a communication of their sinnes. Secondly, if there be any eminent danger of being seduced. Thirdly, If by oppression or persecution, a man may be compelled to withdrawe himselfe.

Having granted these possibilities, Ames immediately reassured his reader that this was not a schism, was not separatism: 'a separation be made from

---

[45] William Perkins, *A Chord of Faithfull Witnesses, Leading to the Heavenly Canaan* in *Works* (1618) vol. III pp. 190–1.
[46] William Ames, *Conscience with the Power and Cases thereof* (1639) Book VI, p. 62.
[47] Ibid., Book VI, pp. 63–4.

some certaine Actions or Persons only, although that separation be Schismaticall, yet doth it not presently separate from the Church'.[48]

Once we know that Ames, hardly an enemy to New England, located the licence to emigrate within a well-established set of boundaries, the insistence of godly ministers on reminding their colleagues of their pre-emigration consultations becomes more comprehensible. This insistence survived three generations, for it is still present in Mather.[49] It was also present in his father and grandfather, for Richard Mather preserved his arguments, which Increase Mather provided space for in his father's biography. In 1634, Richard Mather was deprived and his thoughts turned to the possibility of migration. He drew up his 'Arguments tending to prove the Removing from *Old England* to *New*, or to some such like place, to be not onely lawful, but also necessary for them that are not otherwise tyed, but free'. The Arguments were presented to several meetings of godly ministers in Lancashire. The ministers were, Increase Mather makes clear, convinced that his father had an adequate and legitimate call to New England.[50] He opened with an argument that appeared in Ames' *Conscience*, that it was legitimate to remove oneself from a corrupt church to one that was purer.[51] He reproduced the Scriptural examples of Elias, the apostles and Christ that Perkins had used, adding Paul and Moses and the advice of Ridley and Bradford from John Foxe, limiting his reservations to a required freedom from public commitments. He rejected the Amesian argument that one could stay despite corrupt ordinances, stressing that it was licit to flee '*for the enjoyment of some of Gods Ordinances*', broadening this position to define '*the Discipline of Christ*' as an ordinance to make it licit to flee on ecclesiological grounds. Mather made this clearer in his final passage, an 'Argument concerning Ministers onely'. Good ministers could emigrate because 'they are commanded to fulfill their Ministry, and to perform all the parts of their Pastoral Office, *Collos*.4.17.2 *Tim*.4.5. And this of Administring the Keyes of Discipline is one, *Matth*.16.19.' In 1635, faced with these arguments, 'Nothing was satisfactorily said to take off the strength of these Reasons', and Mather left Lancashire in April.[52]

IV

Having made his position so clear in public, it must have been extremely galling for Daniel Rogers when his own son, Samuel, expressed a strong interest in taking to New England. Samuel had not been party to John

---

[48] Ibid., Book V, p. 141.   [49] Cf. above, p. 58.
[50] [Increase Mather], *The Life and Death of Richard Mather* (1670) pp. 11, 19–20.
[51] Ibid., p. 12; Ames, *Conscience*, Book VI, p. 62.
[52] [Mather], *Life and Death*, pp. 12–20.

Wilson's discussions with his father; Daniel sent his son to the house of Edward Adey, the local physician, apparently to get him out of the way. However, he could not keep Wilson from making a lasting impression upon the twenty-one-year-old student. They shared a bed, and Samuel was much impressed with Wilson's prayer before sleep and immediately upon rising. However cordial the discussion between the older ministers may have been, there is likely to have been fundamental disagreement, and Rogers was in a foul mood for a week afterwards. He turned on Samuel for no reason: 'my father strangely, and furiously fell out with mee, as though he would have run through with words, which so distressed mee, that I knew not what to doe, till I fell downe upon my knees'.[53] Two years later, in March 1637, having almost resolved to emigrate, Samuel broached the subject with his father. In his diary, he recorded:

N.E. [New England] N.E. is in my thoughts; my heart reioices to think of it; L[or]d show mee thy way in it and bow the head of my father.

Clearly, Daniel Rogers found his son to be the image of the emigrant suggested above: 'possessed and taken up with the longing for it'. The days after he recorded his father's disapproval are perhaps the high point of Samuel's interest in New England, but they illustrate how central it had become in his prayers.

April. 1. [1637] This day I set apart for fasting, and prayer in private in espec: meane ab: N:E: A: the Lord hath sweetly drawne neare to mee and given mee an heart to blesse his name for his goodnesse to mee the more of N:E: I have, the more of God I inioy; L[or]d yet farther shew me thy selfe thy loving K: the way is in I shall walke;
2. Saboath, comfort at Hatfield; my heart is above; reioicing in god, and his saints; these two dayes have bine sweet to mee; the more I have of god, the more I rise after N. E. and the more I think of that, I thinke I find the more of god; Ld find thou out my way thither if it be thy will;
3. strong for N:E: and my peace more in thee love, and smiles of g. upon mee; my hope is only in him. I will walke before him in a desert way till I come to sion.[54]

Ultimately, Samuel did not emigrate. His change of mind allows us to enter a little more deeply into the processes that worked against migration, as well as the conception of New England that made it attractive in the first place. Kenneth Shipps, who discovered and studied the diary, suggested that the initial decision to emigrate was the result of Rogers' contact with a series of enthusiasts for the project, along with anxieties about his ministry,

---

[53] QUB Percy MS 7 ff. 26–9. Rogers mentioned only being sent to 'Mr Adyes'. The identification with Edward, the physician, is from Venn: he was a graduate of Emmanuel College, who corresponded with John Bastwick: F. Condick, 'The Life and Works of Dr John Bastwick', University of London PhD (1983) pp. 54–5.
[54] QUB Percy MS 7 ff. 216–17.

which was not meeting with much success. Shipps attributed Rogers' final decision to stay to the opposition of his father and half-brother.[55] It is certainly true that Daniel Rogers' opinion carried a good deal of weight with his son: his father's *Treatise on the Two Sacraments* was Samuel's bed-time reading, and he claimed that he 'could misse any booke lesse except [the] bible'. He found his father a great spiritual counsellor and profes-sional adviser, taking his advice to stay silent on the subject of his employ-er's addiction to fashion and recording his assessments of other clergymen.[56] It is also the case that Samuel's painful awareness of the faults of the English church and his friendship with emigrants contributed to his decision to join them in New England. On 7 March 1636, he wrote:

> This day I part with honest G. How to N. E. Oh how sweet is the companye of the saints and the lord rends them from us, and gleans away the cheife and choise, and full eares; oh lord thy meaning is to defend them certainly; thou art theire god, and so hast hedged ab: them, and soe wilt doe; lord stay also with us; purge our decaying estate; Lord preserve thy church which is now tottering; Lord preserve, and convert our king.[57]

However, there is another context which more positively explains both his desire to emigrate and his final decision to stay. As elsewhere, these decisions can be seen in terms of the social dynamic of Puritan spirituality. I have already argued[58] that the devotional cycles of this form of religiosity depended very heavily upon a sociability that brought comfort, advice and admonition from the 'communion of saints', and that Rogers found himself most insecure in those periods of his life when he was removed from such society. So intense was his need for the communion of the saints that, as we have seen, such ideas shaped his notion of heaven itself. He looked forward to a time when he would 'sit downe in companye, with Abraham, Paul, my grandfather [Richard Rogers], and all other blessed saints, and angels'.[59]

Despite the interest aroused by John Wilson's visit in March 1635, New England did not loom large in Samuel's thoughts until the conformist vicar of Bishops Stortford, Richard Butler, raised the issue at a dinner after an ecclesiastical court day at Stortford. Butler 'plays his parts ag[ainst] N.E.', Rogers felt moved to reply, but decided to hold his tongue in the presence of the bishop's officers.[60] However, this was the start of an association forming in his mind between the spiritless ministry of Butler (as Rogers saw it) and opposition to New England. Over the following months the other

---

[55] K. W. Shipps, 'The Puritan Migration to New England: a New Source on Motivation', *NEHGR* 135 (1981) pp. 83–97, esp. 96–7. The only other discussion of Rogers is in Cressy, *Coming Over*, pp. 94–5, 216, but he is mistaken in suggesting that this is the Samuel Rogers who became vicar of Great Tey in January 1638 and that Nehemiah Rogers was his uncle.
[56] QUB Percy MS 7 ff. 60, 316, 347.   [57] Ibid., f. 99.
[58] Above, ch. 6.   [59] QUB Percy MS 7 f. 92.   [60] Ibid., f. 57.

side of the coin was to become more prominent: his contacts with people in favour of the colonial project, even to the extent of going there, became associated with the few occasions when he received any spiritual comfort. It is striking that his strongest feelings for emigration were expressed when these two feelings came together. This powerful association between spiritual comfort and New England on the one hand, and lifeless formalism and opposition to emigration on the other, helps to explain Samuel's utter bewilderment at his father's refusal to sanction his departure. Between September 1635, when he first made this association, and the middle of 1637, when his zeal for emigration began to cool, was the period when he felt most desolate in his religious life, when he lacked the spiritual support of godly society. His vision of heaven was a society similarly full of godly support, a heaven upon earth. To Rogers, New England resembled this vision. His desire for New England had little to do with persecution in any personal way, almost nothing to do with ecclesiology, and everything to do with what he saw as his own spiritual well-being. Similarly, the period in which his enthusiasm waned was the time when he began to find comfort in meetings at Hatfield Broad Oak and fasts with William Sedgewick and George Hughes at Farnham. The opposition of his father seems to have had little to do with ecclesiology and, if we may judge from his published views, more to do with concerns for inner sanctity. By the end of 1637, Samuel was moving to London where the household of Lady de Vere would bring him the comforts of John Goodwin, John Dod and a host of other godly ministers. His affection for emigrating friends did not decrease, but his own willingness to leave England disappeared.

Samuel Rogers' experience fits in well with the work of Avihu Zakai, who has sought to locate the emigration in a social world of covenanting saints, comforting each other in a separation from profane sociability.[61] For people whose spiritual well-being depended upon godly society, the possibility of a place where such society was the norm and not a rare spiritual oasis, a place where, as Thomas Weld put it, 'Here the greater part are the better part, here Mordicai speaketh kindly to the hearts of his people[.] Here are none of the men of Gibea the sonnes of Belial knocking at our doors disturbing our sweet peace or threatening violence',[62] must have exerted an enormous pull. Although we know that New England was far from this heavenly pattern, the perception was important for Rogers and may have been important for many others too. That he could find something of such society in England in the 1630s returns us to the point made with regard to his father: the Laudian reaction could not root out voluntary religion, however hard it worked to redefine it as sedition and

---

[61] Zakai, 'The Gospel of Reformation'.   [62] BL Sloane MS 922 ff. 90–3.

schism. For someone like Thomas Shepard, who found himself far from friends, with a call to minister overseas and newly found scruples about bishops, the pull was overwhelming. For someone like Daniel Rogers, among friends, with a strong godly group in his parish established over fifty years of preaching, to uproot and commit oneself to the vagaries of sea travel and to an uncertain future seemed an unnecessary vanity when there was so much work to be done.

$$\text{---} \ \text{\textrsh} \ 15 \ \text{\textrsh} \ \text{---}$$

The 'non-separating Congregationalists' and early Massachusetts

I

For those godly ministers who emigrated and for those who stayed, for those who were silenced and those who survived in their cures alike, we have seen the 1630s as a decade of challenge and trial, overturning settled practices and assumptions, and forcing fissures between apparently like-minded men on issues of ceremonial conformity and emigration. These fissures were not so deep as to prevent continued fellowship or to make less important the settled social patterns of godly religion. The harshest words of condemnation and the triumph of mutual incomprehension were reserved for the 1640s: this decade saw the godly scattered across the face of the world, speaking different languages. In this, the final act of the Puritan diaspora, ecclesiology was of paramount importance, the single issue upon which final agreement proved utterly unobtainable. We have become familiar with the debates over church government in the Westminster Assembly and with the parallel pamphlet warfare.[1] These events will receive little attention here, because the Tower of Babel was a long time falling; rather, I am concerned with the pre-history of these events, and with tracing some of the forces involved.

The divisions over ecclesiology of the 1640s were not simply the eruption of longstanding conflicts within the godly ministry, the final, public battle of a guerrilla war that had been fought throughout the century by proto-Congregationalists and proto-Presbyterians. If nothing else has been demonstrated in the preceding pages, it must be clear that those ministers identified, and identifying themselves, as godly formed a society in which

---

[1] See, for instance, R. S. Paul, *The Assembly of the Lord: Politics and Religion in the Westminster Assembly and the 'Grand Debate'* (Edinburgh, 1985) *passim*, and esp. pp. 249–537; J. R. DeWitt, *Jus Divinum: the Westminster Assembly and the Divine Right of Church Government* (Kampen, 1969); R. D. Bradley, 'Jacob and Esau Struggling in the Womb: a Study of Presbyterian and Independent Religious Conflicts, 1640–48', University of Kent PhD (1975).

men who would eventually express an allegiance to opposing extremes of polity would find a place. From Henry Jessey, the Separatist and Anabaptist, to Edward Symmons of Rayne, who reaffirmed his commitment to episcopacy in his labours for constitutional royalism, the sociable religiosity of the godly clergy joined men who were to find themselves miles apart in the revolutionary decades. In the heart of the conference which formed the point of entry to all these discussions, we find men like Thomas Hooker, one of the foremost defenders of the New England way, and Stephen Marshall, one of the most conspicuous promoters of Presbyterianism in the 1640s.

There are two strategies to explain this situation: first, to extend the confession of Richard Baxter who, in an over-cited passage, admitted that before 1641, 'I never thought what Presbytery or Independency was nor ever spake with a man who seemed to know it'.[2] Thus it might be argued that until root-and-branch reform articulated a disenchantment with episcopacy, most ministers had given little or no thought to ecclesiological issues and were left in the position of Oliver Cromwell, who is said to have remarked to colleagues in the Commons in 1641, 'I can tell you, Sirs, what I would not have; tho' I cannot what I would'.[3] In the 1640s, this argument would have it, such men were thrown into the Grand Debate anchorless and bewildered, turning to Elizabethan precedents without a continuous tradition, or led by the convinced Presbyterianism of the Scottish ministers. As George Yule put it thirty years ago, writing of the ministry in the thirty years before the Civil War, 'the question of Church government had apparently ceased to be a major preoccupation, and the situation of the 1640s took them unawares.'[4] However, the conditions that applied to Baxter in 1641, an assistant minister in Shropshire without a university education, or to Cromwell, a godly, never very bookish, man of the lesser gentry,[5] did not apply to all ministers and this argument leads to many dangers if it is extended too far. Uncertainty and ignorance there certainly was, but Baxter did not necessarily mean that he had heard nothing of alternative ecclesiologies: he may have meant that what were to become denominational labels were polemical weapons hammered out in the years after 1640 and that the situation before had been much more fluid, mutable and ambiguous. While fine-tuned ecclesiological debate may not have been a feature of Baxter's

---

[2] Richard Baxter, *A True History of the Councils Enlarged* (1682) p. 92.

[3] Cited in Paul, *Assembly of the Lord*, p. 3n.

[4] G. Yule, 'Some Problems in the History of the English Presbyterians in the Seventeenth Century', *JPHS* 13 (1964) p. 6.

[5] The best account of Cromwell's religion is J. C. Davis, 'Cromwell's Religion', in J. Morrill (ed.), *Oliver Cromwell and the English Revolution* (London, 1990) pp. 181–208.

locality, I will show that, elsewhere, the issue was very much a live one, although the lines of antagonism were not always the ones that opened wide in the 1640s. Moreover, these debates were not all simply a response to Laudianism, the process of radicalisation seen in the context of the ceremonies; there were 'new' and 'old' nonconformists in church government too. For some, alienation from the institution of episcopacy was both very late and reactive: Richard Baxter himself only came to question diocesan episcopacy in the context of the 'Etc oath' passed by the Convocation of 1640. For him, the oath 'was a chief means to alienate me, and many others' from prelacy, encouraging many who had never examined the questions 'to honour the Non-conformists more than they had done'.[6] However, even for these men, as Baxter's account makes clear, the form and content of the debate was influenced, and its outcome perhaps partly determined, by a continuous tradition of debate, theory and practice located in the Netherlands and in Scotland, in New England and, we must not forget, in the extra-parochial sociability of the godly ministers in England. For this reason, we have to take a longer perspective than that which has informed much of this work.

This second approach necessitates something of a 'genetic' or even a 'genealogical' account to locate the debates of the 1630s and 1640s. While this may raise fears of the distortions forced upon many denominational historians, I hope that the lateral approach followed to this point and an attempt to remain aware of what Patrick Collinson has referred to as 'certain dynamic, fluid and even paradoxical features of the religious situation' will help to illuminate the developments to be discussed.[7] What follows is an attempt to sketch some of the lines of descent within ecclesiological debates, linking them to the practices of the godly ministers discussed already and to consider how these twin elements of theory and practice shaped the debates of the 1640s. To provide a comprehensive account of the evolution of church theory would be overambitious in a work which has so far resisted the attractions of logic-chopping internecine pamphlet wars, so, in accord with my earlier interests, I will confine my discussion to questions of association and ministerial authority, touching upon, where necessary, other areas of ecclesiology.

---

[6] Matthew Sylvester (ed.), *Reliquiuae Baxterianae* (1696) vol. I i pp. 15–16.
[7] P. Collinson, 'A Comment: Concerning the Name Puritan', *JEH* 31 (1980) p. 486; cf. C. Hill, 'History and Denominational History', *BQ* 22 (1967–68) pp. 65–71. For what follows, my own thinking was immensely stimulated by P. Collinson, 'Towards a Broader Understanding of the Early Dissenting Tradition', in *Godly People: Essays on English Protestantism and Puritanism* (London, 1983) pp. 527–47, although this is not to say that Professor Collinson would endorse all that follows.

II

We may begin with the Elizabethans. Most of the practices with which we have been concerned had their roots in this reign, to go no further. The conference movement of the 1580s, to which Hooker's was an heir, was predicated upon 'natural' attractions of professional and spiritual identity, but also had an ecclesiological rationale in the work of Cartwright, Travers and Field, assumed by most writers to have been capitalised Presbyterians in a Scottish (or French or Dutch) sense. However, in the attempts to justify and set in place classical and synodical structures there was, from the first, something of an ambivalence and ambiguity, studied or otherwise. In 1572, *A Second Admonition to the Parliament* was published, calling for conferences of 'some certain ministers and other brethren', for edification, discipline and examination of candidates for ordination. These were to be supplemented with provincial and national synods. Authority for matters which could not be decided at a local level was to lie in the national synod, 'except there be a more general Synode of all churches' and even there authority was qualified if the question was 'a great matter expressly against the Scriptures'. Otherwise, 'they must stand to the determinations'. However, a general principle resembling that inelegant modern notion of 'subsidiarity' seems to have applied, with matters to be dealt with, as far as possible, at the lowest level.[8]

How far such assemblies had the right to overrule particular congregations in matters according to Scripture is not always so clear. Thomas Cartwright, whose *Directory* became a live battleground in the 1640s, attested that 'no particular church has power over another, yet every particular church of the same resort, meeting and counsel *ought* to obey the opinion of more churches with whom they communicate'.[9] The high assessment of the particular congregation is reflected in the fact that the congregational presbytery, the minister and elders, is considered to be *iure divino*, while the supra-congregational networks are not. A similar ambiguity is to be found even in the work of Walter Travers, S. J. Knox's 'Paragon of Elizabethan Puritanism', generally held to be as much of a Presbyterian as England ever produced.[10] Travers allowed conferences and synods wide powers to issue authoritative statements for the good of the church, but undermined this centralisation by making the decisions of

---

[8] W. H. Frere and C. E. Douglas (eds.), *Puritan Manifestoes: a Study of the Origin of the Puritan Revolt* (London, 1954) pp. 107–10. The authorship of the *Second Admonition* is discussed in P. Collinson, *The Elizabethan Puritan Movement* (London, 1967) pp. 139–40. On this issue generally, cf. ibid., pp. 318–29; S. Brachlow, *The Communion of Saints: Radical Puritan and Separatist Ecclesiology 1570–1625* (Oxford, 1988) pp. 203–29.
[9] Thomas Cartwright, *A Directory of Church Government* (1644) n.p.; emphasis mine.
[10] S. J. Knox, *Walter Travers: Paragon of Elizabethan Puritanism* (London, 1962) *passim*.

synods 'void and of no effect if they be not such as in the last resort wherein the people have to rule and govern', without, it must be admitted, making explicit who 'the people' were.[11] There was something of a move to a clearer and more authoritative Presbyterianism in the 1580s, driven by Scottish influence, but this was hardly the broad path of English reform.[12] The obvious correlative of the limitation (or at least ambiguity) of extra-congregational power is a relatively high estimation of congregational autonomy. This has some grounding in the realities of Elizabethan practice, as Patrick Collinson made clear: in the power relations of the Dedham *classis*, the strongest bond was between minister and congregation, followed by the ties of the local ministerial community, stubbornly independent of higher assemblies.[13]

Here, both theory and practice undermine the novelty of the following generation. The so-called 'non-separating Congregationalists', usually seen as the heirs of the quintumverate of Henry Jacob, Robert Parker, William Ames, William Bradshaw and Paul Baynes, are seen to make a significant shift from the Presbyterianism of Elizabethan Puritans to Congregationalism, with a consequent resistance to classical structures.[14] This thesis was particularly important to Perry Miller, who, drawing upon hints in the work of Champlin Burrage, rescued the promoters of the New England way from the aspersions of Separatism.[15] In his study of Henry Jacob, Stephen Brachlow stressed the continuity of the early Stuart reformers with their Elizabethan forebears and convincingly showed that the search for the roots of his polity, which had baffled Miller and Burrage and remained contentious for Robert S. Paul, John von Rohr and B. R. White, who assumed Separatist influence,[16] could be pursued within the ambiguities of Elizabethan church theory. In his revisionary zeal, Brachlow may have understated the extent to which the ambiguities of Elizabethan ecclesiology were adapted and clarified in the early years of

[11] Walter Travers, *A Full and Plaine Declaration of Ecclesiastical Discipline* (1574) p. 178.

[12] P. Collinson, 'John Field and Elizabethan Puritanism', in *Godly People*, pp. 335–70; J. Kirk, '"The Polities of the Best Reformed Kirks": Scottish Achievements and English Aspirations in Church Government at the Reformation', *SHR* 59 (1980) pp. 25–53.

[13] Collinson, 'Dissenting Tradition', pp. 540–1.

[14] A theory most recently restated in N. Tyacke, *The Fortunes of Puritanism, 1603–1640, Friends of Doctor Williams's Library Lecture 1990* (London, 1991) pp. 4–5.

[15] P. Miller, *Orthodoxy in Massachusetts 1630–1650: a Genetic Study* (Cambridge, Mass., 1930) *passim*, esp. xxix; C. Burrage, *The Early English Dissenters* (Cambridge, 1912).

[16] S. Brachlow, 'The Elizabethan Roots of Henry Jacob's Churchmanship: Refocussing the Historiographical Lens', *JEH* 36 (1985) pp. 228–54; R. S. Paul, 'Henry Jacob and Seventeenth Century Puritanism', *Hartford Quarterly* 7 (1967) pp. 95–113; J. von Rohr, 'The Congregationalism of Henry Jacob', *Transactions of the Congregational History Society* 19 (1962) pp. 107–17; von Rohr, '*Extra Ecclesiam Nulla Salus*: an Early Congregational Version', *CH* 36 (1967) pp. 107–21; B. R. White, *The English Separatist Tradition* (Oxford, 1971) pp. 91, 165–7.

the seventeenth century. Certainly, there is a greater willingness in the work of William Bradshaw to stress the power of the civil magistrate and a greater emphasis on the sufficiency of particular congregations than had previously been the case. It is possible to accept Brachlow's thesis of considerable continuity without denying the fact of development. The changes may be attributed to a re-examination of the issues in the light of the failure of the Hampton Court Conference, to a greater willingness to clarify positions deliberately left ambiguous in the past, as the prospect of immediate reformation receded, an attempt to palliate fears of a clerical invasion of the royal supremacy or a response to development in covenant theology.[17]

Whatever the cause, the works of these five men do register a change of emphasis, or at least a clarification. William Bradshaw's *English Puritanisme*, published in 1605, did not, *pace* Miller, seek to distance a new form from Elizabethan Presbyterianism.[18] It did, however, assert the autonomy of individual congregations:

No other churches or spiritual officers have, by any warrant from the Word of God, power to censure, punish, or control the same, but are only to counsel and advise.[19]

It must be noted, of course, that while denying conferences any coercive or judicial power, Bradshaw is not suggesting that they are not to exist, and indeed implies that counsel and advice would be an important source of support. This much is granted by Henry Jacob, who paid rather more attention to supra-congregational structures than Bradshaw. Jacob advocated, with what appears to have been a neologism, 'consociation' of congregations 'by way of synods'. These were to be 'meetings of choise men out of many churches', dependent upon the civil magistrate for their meetings. They were to offer deliberation, counsel and advice, and at most apply unspecified 'persuasive' pressures to recalcitrant congregations, but in no case was their power to be authoritative.[20] Robert Parker produced

---

[17] P. Lake, 'William Bradshaw, Anti-Christ and the Community of the Godly', *JEH* 36 (1985) pp. 570–89; D. A. Wier, *The Origins of the Federal Theology in Sixteenth Century Reformation Thought* (Oxford, 1990); cf. Brachlow, *Communion of Saints*, pp. 239–40; C. Haigh, 'The English Reformation: a Premature Birth, a Difficult Labour and a Sickly Child', *HJ* 33 (1990) pp. 457–8.

[18] Miller, *Orthodoxy in Massachusetts*, p. 78; Brachlow, *Communion*, pp. 208–10.

[19] William Bradshaw, *English Puritanisme, Containing the Main Opinions of the Rigidest Sort of those that are called Puritans* (1605) pp. 5–6; cf. Bradshaw, *Several Treatises of Worship and Ceremonies by the Reverend Mr William Bradshaw* (1660) pp. 37, 85.

[20] Henry Jacob, *A Confession and Protestation of the Faith of Certain Christians in England* (1616) Sig.B2; Jacob, *An Humble Supplication* (1609) p. 14. The unreconstructed Elizabethan reformer Robert Cawdray offered the verb 'to consociate' with a neutral definition of 'companie with, or ioyne a companion unto': *A Table Alphabeticall, Conteyning and Teaching the True Writing and Understanding of Hard Usuall English Words* (1604) n.p. In his parallel work, *A Treasurie or Storehouse of Similes* (1600), Cawdray offers a

the most extensive discussion of synodical theory of the five. He followed Jacob in terming such meetings 'consociations', which he defined as meetings of two or more particular congregations, mutually agreed to consider problems that could not be solved at a local level. Their authority derived from the particular congregations and ultimately stayed with them. A synod could not 'obtrude anything upon churches unwilling'. Parker's work is rather ambiguous and even more difficult to place within Presbyterian/ Congregational frameworks, perhaps partly due to the persuasions of John Paget in the Netherlands.[21]

In the posthumously published works of Paul Baynes, the positions of Jacob, Bradshaw and Parker received the imprimatur of a prominent Cambridge preacher, silenced in 1608. Baynes' major ecclesiological work, *The Diocesans Triall*, is rich in ambiguity, but does provide a fully congregational definition of a church: 'we affirme that no such head Church was ordained either virtually or actually, but that all Churches were singular Congregations, equall, independent of each other in regard of subjection'. Once again, this was not to deny that synods are useful. The individual congregations 'have power of governing themselves, but for greater edification, voluntarily confederate, not to use nor exercise their power, but with mutuall communication, one asking the counsell and consent of the other in that common Presbyterie'. He even allowed the possibility of synodical authority in some special cases: at least, while arguing that 'every Church by Christs institution hath power of government . . . in ordinarie matters', he admitted that the temple at Jerusalem, and by analogy the synod, held authority 'in some reserved causes'.[22]

Baynes' *Diocesans Triall* was given a polemical and biographical preface by William Ames, in whom this style of polity gained a theologian of international stature, who provided a complex and balanced account of the congregational *locus* of authority. A particular visible church, according to Ames, is 'a society of believers joined together by a special bond among themselves, for the constant exercise of the communion of saints'. This bond, he made clear, 'is a covenant, either express or implicit, whereby believers do particularly bind themselves to perform all these duties'. Such churches are neither national, provincial nor diocesan, but parochial. They are advised to enter into a synodical relationship: particular churches 'may and oftentimes ought to enter into a mutual confederacy and fellowship

distinctly Genevan definition of the necessity of Discipline, and asserts the right of ministers to excommunicate princes, pp. 270, 533–4.

21 Brachlow, *Communion of Saints*, p. 211; K. L. Sprunger, *Dutch Puritanism: a History of English and Scottish Churches of the Netherlands in the Sixteenth and Seventeenth Centuries*, Studies in the History of Christian Thought XXXI (Leiden, 1982) p. 344.

22 Paul Baynes, *The Diocesans Triall* (1621) pp. 13, 21, 8. For the publication of his works, see Tyacke, *Fortunes of Puritanism*, pp. 8–12.

amongst themselves in classes and synods' for mutual help in matters 'of great moment'. This did not constitute a new church and, Ames stressed, 'neither ought it to take away that liberty and power which Christ has left to his churches'.[23]

Ames was unique among these men in seeing something of this vision realised beyond a parochial level. In the English synod in the Netherlands which met between 1621 and the early 1630s, Amesian ecclesiology gained a foundation in practice that was denied even the most ideologically motivated English associations. The synod, under the practical leadership of John Forbes and the intellectual guidance of Ames, had two prominent foes. James I, having issued suspicious permission for a meeting to suppress unlicensed preachers and reform scandalous ministers, attempted to appoint a permanent moderator of his own choice. Forbes and his allies avoided this by claiming, with some reason, that the Dutch authorities would never assent. More significantly, the synod received the disapproval of John Paget, minister to the Amsterdam church and a member of the Dutch *classis*, a more authoritatively Presbyterian structure, in the same mould as the Scottish discipline. Among his objections submitted to the synod of South Holland, the last was perhaps the most important:

That there were some in this classis which held the opinion that our Lord Jesus Christe hath committed the power of ecclesiasticall discipline to everie particular Church; and for that reason the disposing and supervising or overseeing thereof belonges not to anie Classical or Synodall Assemblie.

Paget's hostility was such that he even assisted the Laudian agent William Boswell, the English ambassador, to crush the synod. Before he succeeded, by the end of 1633, aided by the removal of Forbes as minister to the Merchant Adventurers and the death of William Ames, the synod had welcomed a number of dissident clergy, including some whose departure for New England further weakened the beleaguered conference, among them Thomas Hooker, Hugh Peter and John Davenport.[24]

---

[23] William Ames, *The Marrow of Sacred Divinity* in *The Works of the Reverend and Faithful Minister of Christ William Ames* (1643) pp. 139–40, 179; cf. K. L. Sprunger, *The Learned Reverend Doctor Ames* (Urbana, Ill., 1972). Parker was alone among these authors in allowing that a synod was a form of church: Brachlow, *Communion*, p. 211.

[24] The best account of the English synod is K. L. Sprunger, *Dutch Puritanism: a History of English and Scottish Churches of the Netherlands in the Sixteenth and Seventeenth Centuries*, Studies in the History of Christian Thought (Leiden, 1982) pp. 289–306, supplanting the accounts in A. C. Carter, *The English Reformed Church in Amsterdam in the Seventeenth Century* (Amsterdam, 1964), and R. P. Stearns, *Congregationalism in the Dutch Netherlands* (London, 1940), although Sprunger lacks ecclesiological sensitivity.

III

This account has moved progressively further from the English context. Three of the five men just discussed spent time in exile, although Bradshaw and Baynes continued a shadowy ministry in England. Ames arrived in the Netherlands in 1611, and eventually settled into teaching at the University of Franeker. It seems, then, that this account of ecclesiology becomes a Dutch story, with little relevance to conditions in England. To a degree this is true: many godly ministers in England applied the same views to issues of ecclesiology that we met with regard to the ceremonies. Many felt that is was both prudent and licit to neglect such contentious questions, particularly after the failure of the Hampton Court Conference to secure reformation on such issues. John Rogers was quite explicit that it was wise and lawful to neglect these subjects.[25] This was made easier by adopting the pre-Bucerian doctrine of the church, which depended upon two marks, right doctrine and proper administration of the sacraments, as opposed to the 'three mark doctrine' that also required proper discipline. Here, too, John Rogers was quite explicit:

That company that hath the Doctrine of the Prophets and Apostles soundly preached in all substantiall Points, and the Sacraments for substance according to Christs institution, is a true church of God, though there be blemishes therein.[26]

A related view is that there was a Scripturally given form of church, but that it was not necessary for the being of a church, only for its well-being, that it was desirable, but not of the essence. Daniel Rogers broached this subject, aware that he was entering a controversial area:

A point which if it had been well observed, might have settled and calmed the spirits of many in our Church, who maintain that pure constitution and visibilenesse of a Church are so inseparable, that without the former, the latter cannot be. Which is false. For although we cannot deny but that defect of apostolicall constitution of particular Churches, in order and discipline makes to the beauty and visiblenesse, yet to affirme hence that the absence of such a constitution, doth inferre a nullity of visibleness wholy, is very audacious. The absence of that first native and lovely hiew of a young Virgin (being now grown to be a woman of yeares) to a more sad gravity, disanuls not her sex, no nor virginity, but onely the beauty of it. We must distinguish between the *Totum generis*, and the *Totum integri* . . . So may a Church be called truly (though weakly) visible, though maimed of her constitution, because shee holds in kind, that is, hath the essentials of Word, Sacraments, outward profession, yea perhaps also an implicite faithfull covenant of the members of Christ in such or such an assembly, I know, that I have said will be much cavilled at.[27]

[25] John Rogers, *A Godly and Fruitfull Exposition of the First Epistle of Peter* (1650) p. 240.
[26] Ibid., p. 237. On the 'three mark doctrine' see Brachlow, *Communion*, pp. 116–18.
[27] Daniel Rogers, *Two Treatises* (1640) pt. 2, pp. 182–3.

Ministers of such views could live and work in the Church of England, without approving of its government, or drawing their confidence that it was a true church from the two essential marks of doctrine and sacraments, and perhaps some comfort from the notion of a covenant, either implicit or explicit, binding the truly godly in the congregation. Such clerics are not likely to be conspicuous, but, occasionally, shadowy evidence of a continuum of thought on the best constitution of the church is available. For example, Daniel Rogers was prepared to put into print his view of a congregational definition of the visible church. Edmund Brewer had been working on ecclesiastical questions in the early 1630s. Shortly before, George Philips, the minister of Boxted in the Stour valley, had preached publicly on church government. His 'Acquaintance with the Writings and Persons of some Old Non Conformists' had shaped his views on these matters. In this case his auditors consulted John Rogers, who told them that he was sure his friend would have delivered nothing without the warrant of Scripture.[28]

One of the 'Old Nonconformists', who provided an element of continuity from the Elizabethan reformers into the generation which is my principal concern, was Arthur Hildersham. A contemporary of Laurence Chaderton at Christ's College, Hildersham had been an activist at the time of the Millenary Petition and a friend of John Preston, John Dod, William Gouge, William Bradshaw and John Cotton.[29] Although he dissented from the approval given by Walter Travers, John Dod, John Wing and others when Henry Jacob gathered a covenanting church in Southwark in 1616, Hildersham continued his commitment to a reformed church polity.[30] He maintained something resembling a *classis* in the Midlands and encouraged eminent preachers such as Julines Herring and another friend of Thomas Hooker's, Simeon Ashe, to join the ministry. More importantly in this context, he had strong Essex connections; he had family in the county and was a visitor at Hatfield Broad Oak as late as 1630. He received gifts from the Barrington family, having acted in a household capacity for them early in the century, and corresponded with Lady Joan Barrington. Hildersham was, as we have had occasion to note,

[28] Ibid., pt. 2, p. 182; SU Hartlib MS 29/2/25a; Mather, III p. 82. After his emigration, Philips was assisted in his ministry by John Sherman, a former pupil of John Rogers: ibid., III p. 162.

[29] W. Haller, *The Rise of Puritanism* (New York, 1938) pp. 55–6; Arthur Hildersham, *Lectures upon the Fourth of John* (1629) 'To the Godly Reader'.

[30] Brachlow, 'Refocussing the Historiographical Lens', pp. 237–8; N. Tyacke, 'The "Rise of Puritanism" and the Legalizing of Dissent, 1571–1719', in O. P. Grell, J. I. Israel and N. Tyacke (eds.), *From Persecution to Toleration: the Glorious Revolution and Religion in England* (Oxford, 1991) pp. 24, 25; Hildersham, *Lectures*, pp. 165–7.

credited, with his friend Thomas Hooker, with Francis Higginson's conversion to nonconformity.[31]

Other ministers among the early Stuart reformers already discussed had connections with the region. John Wilson, the disciple of Richard Rogers and lecturer at Sudbury, was a pupil of Baynes and a friend of William Ames.[32] Ames himself came from Suffolk stock and was educated with John Yates, Thomas Hooker and others at Alexander Richardson's seminary at Barking. After being encouraged to leave Christ's College, where he had been a friend of Daniel Rogers, Ames attempted to take a post as town lecturer in Colchester in 1610 before Archbishop Abbot moved him on to the Netherlands. Before his emigration, Ames had been a regular preacher in the Stour valley.[33] While it is a big step, too often taken, to conclude that all these contacts evince sympathy with a reformed ecclesiology, it does suggest the possibility of a continuing tradition of ecclesiological thought in England.

The nature and extent of such thought is rarely susceptible to analysis until the later 1630s, but some indications can be gained from the reformed polity that was established in New England as Ames' experiment in the Netherlands began to wane. The first ministers sent out by the Massachusetts Bay Company, Samuel Skelton of Lincolnshire and Francis Higginson were both committed to a reformed church government, yet despite the advice of Arthur Hildersham to agree in advance the form of polity, they sailed in 1628 without any set form. This was not because there was any disagreement with Hildersham or any other minister, but because 'they had not, as yet, waded so far into the controversy of church discipline as to be very positive in any of the points wherein the main hinge of the controversy lay between them and others'.[34] The form they established, of a gathered, covenanting church, was not settled in all details but their refusal of the sacraments to newly arrived colonists occasioned misgivings in England. When George Philips, the scholar of ecclesiology noted earlier, sailed with the Winthrop fleet in April 1630, he felt it necessary to reassure those who

---

[31] The Massachusetts Bay Company sought the permission of the Midlands *classis* for Francis Higginson to leave his post at Leicester: N. B. Shurtleff (ed.), *Records of the Governor and Company of Massachusetts Bay in New England* (Boston, Mass., 1853) vol. I p. 37; ERO D/DBa A15 f. 3b; BL Egerton MS 2645 ff. 156, 164; *DNB* s.v. 'Arthur Hildersham'; W. Hunt, *The Puritan Moment: the Coming of Revolution in an English County*, pp. 206–7; Mather, III p. 71.

[32] Mather, III p. 42.

[33] See above, chs. 1 and 2; S. A. Bondos-Greene, 'The End of an Era: Cambridge Puritanism and the Christ's College Election of 1609', *HJ* 25 (1982) p. 201; Sprunger, *Learned Reverend Doctor Ames*, pp. 13, 17, 25.

[34] William Hubbard, quoted in E. S. Morgan, *Visible Saints: the History of a Puritan Idea* (New York, 1963) p. 85; Morgan's judgement on the beginnings of New England church government remains authoritative: pp. 80–112.

remained that the colonists were not separating from the Church of England. He knew that the prayers of the godly had been discouraged 'through the misreport of our intentions', and called for the renewal of such support for the colonists, 'who esteeme it our honour, to call the Church of England, from whence we rise, our deare Mother'. Despite the imputation of Separatism, Philips stressed that

we leave it [i.e. the Church of England] not therefore, as loathing that milk wherewith we were nourished there, but blessing God for the parentage and education, as members of the same body shall always rejoyce in her good.[35]

For Philips, it was a theme he would reiterate over the next fifteen years: the Church of England was a true church, her ministers true ministers, even if the covenant bond of the congregations and the election of the ministers were rarely explicit. As he later wrote, 'things are done either explicitly and in expresse terms, or implicitly and by a tacit and virtuall consent'.[36]

In the winter of 1630, it was John Cotton who was accusing the Massachusetts Bay ministers of an inclination to sectarianism. Cotton's criticisms are instructive, both for what they criticise and for the common ground they assume. He judged the ministers to be mistaken in their denial of the sacrament to such as were not members of a particular reformed church, and secondly, that 'none of our congregations in England are particular reformed churches'. This second was, to Cotton, the more important error, one which 'requires a booke rather than a letter to answere it: you went hence of another judgement, & I am afraid your change hath sprung fro new-Plimouth men'. Laying aside the charge of Separatist influence, Cotton's response is not to deny the usefulness of a church covenant, which he sees as 'very requisite for the wel being & continuance of a church', although not of the essence, effectively the position of Daniel Rogers. Cotton saw something of such a covenant on a national scale in Parliamentary renunciations of Catholicism, and an implicit covenant in some congregations. Moreover, some of the colonists knew 'that in some congregations in England the ministers & all the professours among the people have entered into such a covenant to yeeld professed subjection to the gospell of Christ, so farre as they conceive Christ requireth of them in their places in these tymes'. In this period, settled in Lincolnshire, Cotton took as his measure of the visible church a

---

[35] George Philips, *The Humble Request of his Majesties Loyall Subjects, the Governor and Company Late Gone for New England* (1630) pp. 3–4.

[36] George Philips, *A Reply to a Confutation of some Grounds for Infants Baptisme: as also Concerning the Form of a Church* (1645) pp. 143–4, 152–3. Hubbard reported that Philips 'was, at the first, more acquainted with the way of church discipline, since owned by Congregational churches, but being then without any to stand by him . . . he met with much opposition from some of the magistrates', quoted in Morgan, *Visible Saints*, p. 95.

congregational definition that could usefully be supplemented by a covenant, either implicit or explicit.[37] His chief influences, as he told Robert
Harris, Dod's colleague, were Richard Greenham and William Perkins, the
Elizabethan practical divines, and Paul Baynes.[38] In later controversies, the
response was quickly to invoke the ancestry of 'Mr Parker, Mr Baynes and
Mr Ames'.[39] However, it is striking that in the winter of 1630, Cotton
could declare himself the disciple of Baynes without declaring himself
satisfied with the developments in New England. This is all the more
striking in the light of Cotton's subsequent retraction of his criticism, in a
public recantation before a sermon preached at the Salem church which
had been the target of his attack.[40] By the time of his arrival in New
England, Cotton had moved to what might be regarded as a more sectarian
position, and had, in fact, adopted more rigorous standards of visible
sanctity in church membership, with the use of the compulsory 'church
relation' required of each applicant for membership, an innovation not to
be found in Parker, Baynes or Ames.[41] Stephen Foster has described in
detail what he calls 'the process of secularization' in the churches of the
Massachusetts Bay, detecting in the 1630s 'a discernible drift – or rush –
toward purity, toward a definition of the church that gave first thought to
the calling of the saints and deduced the terms of the puritan mission from
their needs and privileges. As the enthusiasm for the pure church rose in
New England, the failings of the English churches seemed progressively
more serious.' He accounts for this process by the influx of ministers
radicalised by longer exposure to the evils of Laudianism, and in this there
seems some truth. Certainly, Cotton's change of heart cannot be detached
to his experience of persecution between 1630 and 1633. Foster sees this
process most clearly evident in those ministers who had furthest to move,
in the same ways we saw John Davenport and Thomas Shepard radicalised
over the ceremonies.[42] However, this cannot be the whole truth, for the
majority of members who stayed in England throughout the Laudian era
did not rush headlong into sectarianism, and Thomas Hooker had, as we
have seen, similar experiences to Cotton, and if we turn to his ecclesiology,
we find no such shift.

---

[37] D. D. Hall, 'John Cotton's Letter to Samuel Skelton', *WMQ* 3rd ser. 22 (1965) pp. 478–85;
cf. the covenant instigated by Richard Rogers at Wethersfield in 1588: Richard Rogers,
Seven Treatises (1605) pp. 389, 497–8.

[38] SU Hartlib MS 29/3/13b.

[39] John Cotton, *The Way of the Congregational Churches Cleared* (1648) pt. 1 p. 13.

[40] John Cotton, *A Sermon Preached by the Reverend Mr John Cotton at Salem, 1636, To
which is Prefaced a Retraction of his Former Opinion* (Boston, Mass., 1713).

[41] Morgan, *Visible Saints*, pp. 93–100.

[42] S. Foster, 'English Puritanism and the Progress of New England Institutions, 1630–1660',
in D. D. Hall, J. M. Murrin and T. W. Tate (eds.), *Saints and Revolutionaries: Essays on
Early American History* (London, 1984) pp. 3–37, quoted at p. 16; cf. above, chs. 7 and 8.

16

Thomas Hooker and the Amesians

I

The first clear exposition of Hooker's ecclesiology came when he arrived in the Netherlands, although he had a reputation as a scholar of such issues long before his flight. From his long-standing friendship with William Ames we need not be surprised that his ecclesiology was already highly developed. When he became a candidate for the post of assistant to John Paget in the Amsterdam church in July 1631, Paget submitted twenty propositions, indicating his position and asking Hooker to make his own clear. On questions relating to salvation, Hooker found agreement easy and referred Paget to John Rogers' work; on relations with Separatists and the conduct of services he proved moderate and willing to seek agreement. On some questions, notably that of the lawful baptism of children whose parents are not church members, a question with a great future in New England, he pronounced himself insufficiently well read, but on the central questions of classical authority, he was already convinced and willing to dissent. There were four such questions. The first asked whether a particular congregation could call a minister without the approbation of the *classis*. Hooker answered by discussing the origins of the *classis* in terms derived from Ames, concluding that 'particular congregations had power from Christ to call a minister and so did by that, their power choose and call their ministers fully and completely before there was a Classis, and therefore had their power not derived from a Classis', although he acknowledged 'that, if by mutual consent the congregation hath freely combined itself with the Classis, they shall do piously and expediently: freely to crave the approbation of the Classis, that they may be more confirmed or . . . better directed in their course'. This set the tone for his following answers, regarding synodical authority. He referred Paget to Ames' *Cases of Conscience*, Parker's *Ecclesiastical Polity* and Baynes' *Diocesans Triall*, concluding: 'Wherein how far they differ from you I doubt not but you fully know.' Significantly for the future of New England, when asked whether church relations were necessary, Hooker replied that

Some members may be received without public examination and yet the case may fall out that some cannot without public examination.[1]

Unlike Cotton, Hooker did not revise his views during the unsettled times between old and New England: it was not the church government of Connecticut that raised most doubts in England, but the practices of the larger colony, Massachusetts. According to Robert Stansby, Hooker had judged the Massachusetts standards too rigid and preached to that effect before he left the Bay colony in 1636.[2] Hooker declined to put his own views into print until the very end of his life. At the request of his fellow ministers he began working on a systematic ecclesiological treatise in 1643, which he had finished by 1645. This manuscript was lost when the ship carrying it to London for publication sank, and Hooker was only finishing a new version when he died. This was published as *A Survey of the Summe of Church Discipline* in 1648.[3] As a whole, it is a defence of Amesian ecclesiology admirably fitted for the polemical conditions of the 1640s. Here Hooker proved himself far more moderate on the issue of church relations than Cotton; in essence the position was unchanged from that which he had taken in Holland. He feared troubles during the work of admission, specifically disliking 'curious inquisitions and niceties, which the pride and wantonesse of mens spirits hath brought into the Church, to disturb the peace thereof, and to prejudice the progresse of Gods Ordinances'. He was mainly concerned about the questioning of candidates by the congregation. At Hartford, Hooker seems to have been able to keep admission a concern of the elders, and to have restricted questions mainly to matters of lifestyle and knowledge, operating a broad 'judgement of charity' to reflect a vision of the church that was inclusive, at least when compared with Massachusetts and New Haven.[4] Hooker's position was much more fully developed in the work of his pupil and assistant, Samuel Stone. Baird Tipson, who has studied Stone's work, came to the conclusion that, for the two men, the question came down to a choice between a fairly inclusive and a rigidly exclusive vision of the congregation: a choice

---

[1] G. H. Williams, N. Pettit, W. Herget and S. Bush (eds.), *Thomas Hooker: Writings in England and Holland* (Cambridge, Mass., 1975) pp. 271–91, quoted at pp. 284–5, 283. For the context, see K. L. Sprunger, 'The Dutch career of Thomas Hooker', *NEQ* 46 (1973) pp. 17–44.

[2] *MHSC* 4th ser. 7 (1864) pp. 10–11.

[3] There is an account of the background to the work in S. Bush, *The Writings of Thomas Hooker: Spiritual Adventures in Two Worlds* (London, 1980) pp. 102–9.

[4] Thomas Hooker, *A Survey of the Summe of Church Discipline* (1648) pt. 3 *passim* and esp. pp. 4–6.

between 'church-type' and 'sect-type.' Hooker never strayed from the church-type.[5] He remained, to the end of his life, a thoroughgoing Amesian.

II

These related perceptions, of church relations as sectarian and ministerial authority in need of defence, prove crucial to fears among the godly ministry in England. When Robert Stansby was reporting his misgivings to John Winthrop in April 1637, similar feelings were troubling a prominent group of divines in the Midlands and beyond, and they gave a more systematic voice to their concerns. In mid-1637, thirteen ministers subscribed nine questions to the clergy of New England. The ministers were probably led by John Dod and Robert Cleaver, his associate, both men of the older generation. Of the other signatories, a number had connections with these two: one was Timothy Dod, the son of John; John Winston and Nathaniel Cotton were also Northamptonshire clergymen and probably Cleaver's sons-in-law. They were joined by Simeon Ashe, who had been close to Hooker during his days at Emmanuel, Ephraim Huitt, like Ashe, preaching in Warwickshire, William Bourne and Thomas Paget of Lancashire, Julines Herring, a much-troubled minister in Shrewsbury, now in Cheshire, Thomas Langley, Ralph Shearard and John Ball of Staffordshire, who proved to be the group's major ecclesiological controversialist.[6]

The questions stimulated a major defence of New England's practices to

---

[5] Stone's manuscript work, a 'Body of Divinity', is in the possession of the Massachusetts Historical Society. Tipson has published the relevant section, with a perceptive discussion, in 'Samuel Stone's "Discourse" against Requiring Church Relations', *WMQ* 3rd ser. 46 (1989) pp. 786–99. On this issue as a crucial sectarian innovation, see also B. Tipson, 'Invisible Saints: the "Judgement of Charity" in the early New England Churches', *CH* 44 (1975) pp. 460–71; Morgan, *Visible Saints*, pp. 93–105; W. B. Stoever, 'Nature, Grace and John Cotton: the Theological Dimension in the New England Antinomian Controversy', *CH* 44 (1975) pp. 22–33. The opposite view is expressed in R. P. Stearns and D. Brawner, 'New England Church "Relations" and Continuity in Early Congregational history', *Proceedings of the American Antiquarian Society* 75 (1965) pp. 13–45. There is some dispute over Hooker's refusal to follow Massachusetts' practice, but Stone's evidence states specifically that Hooker himself never made a church relation. C. Cohen presents evidence for exclusive government in Connecticut which is, at best, ambiguous, and he did not know of Stone's evidence: C. Cohen, *God's Caress: the Psychology of Puritan Religious Experience* (Oxford, 1986) ch. 5 esp. pp. 137, 143.

[6] The names are not given in the published version. They are given, with some biographical information, in N. Tyacke, *The Fortunes of Puritanism, 1603–1640, Friends of Doctor Williams's Library Lecture 1990* (London, 1991) pp. 18–19, from the original in the Boston Public Library in Massachusetts. Additional information is from Mather, III p. 58; A. Hughes, *Politics, Society and Civil War in Warwickshire, 1620–1660* (Cambridge, 1987) pp. 76–7; P. Lake, 'Puritanism, Arminianism and a Shropshire Axe-Murder', *Midlands History* 15 (1990) p. 47.

which John Ball replied on behalf of his friends. The three elements were published in 1643 in the context of the controversies between Presbyterians and Congregationalists, by William Rathband and Simeon Ashe, which publication provoked a response from John Davenport and another by Thomas Shepard and John Allin. The context in which they became public had seriously distorted their original significance: in 1637, this was not a dispute between Presbyterians and Congregationalists. John Ball was the chosen controversialist of the English clergy and his contribution, taken with his slightly earlier work against the Separatists, and his 1639 re-examination of the New England way significantly change our view of the developing split.[7]

Through Ball's work it becomes very clear that William Ames, traditionally considered the father of the New England way and little else, had influenced a generation of ecclesiological thinking in England itself. Ball accepted Ames' conception of the visible church as a society worshipping together under ministers and elders, a 'true and compleat constituted Church of Jesus Christ' on the congregational model. He was convinced that such a congregational church could ordain ministers and could excommunicate, provided that it had a sufficient number of members. Such a church was at least implicitly in covenant with God, and Ball gave a qualified approval to explicit covenants.[8]

When Ball went on to discuss the ways in which church government was exercised, he seems to be writing in a vein that could be called 'Presbyterian'. Authority is given to 'that assembly of officers or governours in every church which the Apostle called a presbytery'. Such an assembly is necessary for a church to exercise power:

If a societie enjoy but one Pastour or Teacher for the time, the power of government doth not belong unto him. For Christ hath not committed this power unto one but unto many . . . But the power of guiding or governing is given to the College Ecclesiasticall, or company of Governours, and must not be executed by any others.

---

[7] Simeon Ashe and William Rathband, *A Letter of Many Ministers in old England Requesting the Judgement of their Reverend Brethren in New England concerning Nine Positions. Written Anno Dom 1637: Together with their Answer thereunto Returned. Anno 1639 and the Reply Made unto the Said Answer* (1643); republished as *A Tryall of the New-Church Way in New England and in Old* (1644); John Ball, *An Answer to Two Treatises of Mr John Can* (1642); Ball, *A Friendly Triall of the Grounds Tending to Separation* (1640); Thomas Shepard and John Allin, *A Defence of the Answer Made unto the Nine Questions* (1648); John Davenport, *An Answer of the Elders of the Severall Churches in New England unto 9 Positions* (1643). On Ball and his colleagues and on this exchange, see also C. G. Schneider, 'Roots and Branches: from Principled Nonconformity to the Emergence of Religious Parties', in F. J. Bremer (ed.), *Puritanism: Transatlantic Perspectives on a Seventeenth-Century Anglo-American Faith* (Boston, Mass., 1993) pp. 167–200.

[8] Ball, *Tryall of the New-Church way*, pp. 23–4; cf. Ball, *A Friendly Triall*, p. 265; Ball, *An Answer to . . . Mr John Can*, pt. 1 p. 135.

However, it becomes clear that the presbytery referred to here is the authority of ministry and ruling elders in the particular congregation. Ordinations can be conducted within the single congregation if it possesses the necessary officers. Otherwise the advice of the neighbouring churches should be sought: ordination was the task 'of the Presbyterie . . . and may and ought to be performed by the Presbyters of neighbouring Congregations if . . . [a church] has none of their owne, or not a competent number'.[9]

To recast Ball and those he spoke for as Amesians is to change the perspective of their questions to New England. The topics which were explored in this controversy were questions of the distribution of authority within a congregation: the ministers in England were primarily concerned that too much power was being given to the ordinary members. The fifth position attributed to New England was that 'the power of Excommunication, &c. is so in the body of the Church that what the major part shall allow, that must be done, through the pastors and Governors, and part of the assembly be of another minde, and peradventure upon more substantiall reasons'. Tellingly, when Ball received the answer of the Massachusetts ministers, he introduced a distinction between the power of excommunication and admission given to the church, and the execution and exercise of that power confined to the officers of the church, an opinion he attributed to Dudley Fenner, Robert Parker and John Davenport. The alternative was the opinion that the body of the church could actually exercise the power of the keys. For Ball, this was

the stone at which they of the Separation stumble, and which we conceive to be your judgement and practise, wherein we required your plaine answer, with your reasons, but have received no satisfactions. You referre us to Mr Parkers reasons to prove the power of the keys to belong to the whole Church, who are of farre different judgement from Mr Parker to the point itself. And if your judgement and practise be according to that of the Separation (which we feare) you dissent from him, and we cannot but dissent from you.[10]

Plainly, this was not a Presbyterian accusing a 'non-separating Congregationalist' of Separatism, but one non-separating Congregationalist (or, as I would prefer, one Amesian) accusing another of going beyond the standard set by Parker, Baynes and Ames.

This view gains credence from two related incidents. Firstly, it has always been regarded as anomalous that one of the Ball group, Ephraim Huitt, emigrated to New England. This becomes less curious when it is noted that

---

[9] Ball, *A Friendly Triall*, p. 265; Ball, *An Answer to . . . Mr Can*, pt. 1 pp. 24–5, pt. 2 p. 35.
[10] Ashe and Rathband, *A Letter of Many Ministers*, 'The Nine Positions', n.p., p. 71. Ball also cited Parker with approval on p. 72 and states his agreement with Ames on church relations and other issues, pp. 45, 48–9, 74.

Huitt chose Connecticut, where Hooker's Amesian government held the field without sectarian adaptations. Secondly, the peers who came into conflict with Massachusetts over religious and political liberty, including Lords Brooke and Saye and Sele, rejected Cotton's restrictive church membership but maintained an interest in Connecticut. Many of the Ball group had contact with these peers, and Hooker was referred to with approval by Saye and Sele in his *Vindiciae Veritas*. This debate was not even between godly men in old and New England, but between Amesians with differing views held on either side of the Atlantic.[11]

This perspective makes an aspect of the nine positions clearer, which would have been puzzling had this been a Presbyterian/Congregationalist exchange. There is no question about supra-congregational structures: the issue does appear in the later rounds of the debate, but by then the issues are those of the 1640s.[12] In the late 1630s, both the Ball group and their New England correspondents were operating with Amesian expectations on this issue. When the issue was raised by a group of Lancashire ministers writing to their former colleague, Richard Mather, at about the same time, Mather was able to reply quite unequivocally that 'consociation of Churches into *Classes* and Synods we hold to be lawfull and in some cases necessary'. The form and authority of the meetings was 'laid downe by Doctor Ames', although the word 'consociate' links back to Henry Jacob and Robert Parker.[13] Shepard and Allin also used the term: 'a fraternall consociation we acknowledge: consociation we say, for mutualle consente and helpe, to prevente or remove sinne and schisme; yet fraternall onely, to preserve each others power; consociation of churches we would have cumulative, . . . to strengthen the power of particular Churches, not privative, to take away any power which they had from the gift of Christ before'.[14] There is a wealth of evidence that such meetings were utilised in the colonies and, despite early complaints from Samuel Skelton and the radical Roger Williams, were not seen as a 'Presbyterianising' tendency

[11] D. D. Hall, *The Faithful Shepherd: a History of the New England Ministry in the Seventeenth Century* (New York, 1974) p. 98n; cf. N. Tyacke, *Fortunes of Puritanism*, p. 19, where he notes that Huitt 'somewhat ironically' emigrated to New England; K. O. Kupperman, 'Definitions of Liberty on the Eve of the Civil War: Lord Saye and Sele, Lord Brooke and the American Puritan Colonies', *HJ* 32 (1989) pp. 17–33, esp. 24–5. For some of the connections: J. T. Cliffe, *The Puritan Gentry: the Great Puritan Families of Early Stuart England* (London, 1984) pp. 179–84. I am grateful to Dr Kupperman for discussions on this issue.

[12] E.g. Shepard and Allin, *A Defence of the Answer*, pp. 113–14.

[13] Richard Mather, *Church-Government and Church-Covenant Discussed, in an Answer to the Elders of the Several Churches in New England to Two and Thirty Questions, Sent over to them by Divers Ministers in England* (1643) pp. 64–5.

[14] Shepard and Allin, *Defence*, p. 113.

until the 1640s.[15] From all the evidence already reviewed, it would have been astonishing if the settled patterns of sociability had been disrupted in the new circumstances, especially when the natural sources of support and advice were now, if anything, more desperately needed.

These exchanges provide some salutary lessons for the historian of the ecclesiology of the mid-century conflict. When we encounter later Presbyterians describing the visible church in terms of congregations of worshippers, joined under the ministry in an implicit or even explicit covenant, we should be more wary of calling such activities proto-Congregationalist, and when we encounter ministers willing to describe themselves as Congregationalists or (more rarely) Independents in the 1640s meeting in conferences, albeit for nothing more than counsel and advice, we should be more wary of calling such activities proto-Presbyterian. The polemical situation before the 1640s does not lend itself to such exclusive categories. It may be more useful to include the ministers already discussed in a generic term such as 'Amesian' or, more neutrally, 'Reformist'. Contemporary usage allows at least two options: Bradshaw famously wrote in terms of 'the rigidest sort of Puritans', although, as Bradshaw knew, 'Puritan' was a loaded term, and remains so. In his exchange with John Canne, John Ball was happy to adopt Canne's own usage, and referred to himself as a 'Nonconformist'. This term, too, is flawed: it had principally ceremonial connotations, and became something of a contested position in the 1640s, especially when combined with 'good', 'old' and 'English', perhaps in contrast to 'bad, new and Scottish'.[16]

III

About the time that John Dod and his associates were framing their questions to the Massachusetts clergy the same arguments were being joined with errant Amesians in England itself. One of the minsters later among the authors of the *Apologeticall Narration*, probably Thomas Goodwin or Philip Nye, expressed views against the use of liturgies and communicating in the corrupt English church, in sermons and conferences around Banbury. William Whately, who, as we have seen, counselled silence on such issues, was reportedly 'much grieved' by the consequent disturbance. A conference was arranged at the home of Richard Knightly,

---

[15] R. F. Scholz, 'Clerical Consocation in Massachusetts Bay: Reassessing the New England Way and its Origins', *WMQ* 3rd ser. 19 (1972) pp. 391–414.

[16] William Bradshaw, *English Puritanisme*; John Canne, *A Necessitie of Separation from the Church of England, Proved by the Nonconformists Principles. Specially opposed unto Dr Ames, also Dr Laiten, Mr Dayrel and Mr Bradshaw* (1634); Ball, *An Answer to Mr Can*, *passim*; cf. John Geree, *The Character of an Old English Puritan or Nonconformist* (1646).

at Fawsley in Northamptonshire. Knightly was John Dod's patron, and John Preston had travelled there to die in 1628. At the conference, at which Simeon Ashe, William Rathband and Thomas Langley were present, Ball opposed the views expressed and there may have been a manuscript account of the discussions, such as Nye's copy of the conference proceedings at Ockley in 1633.[17] This seems to undermine the Apologists' claim to have found their 'new light' in the Netherlands after their exile.[18]

Thomas Goodwin had told Thomas Edwards some months after the Ockley conference that 'he had nothing to say, but against the Ceremonies, the Liturgy offended him not, much less dreamed he of this Church way he since fell into'.[19] Although Thomas Hooker gave John Davenport a copy of his exchange with John Paget, ecclesiology does not seem to have been a subject under discussion at the Ockley conference. As Edwards understood it, Goodwin had been converted to Cotton's position by letter after Cotton was settled in Massachusetts.[20]

Although Edwards made it clear that he had manuscript sources for his account and was in a position to ask ministers who knew them himself, it would be dangerous to accept the uncorroborated evidence of such a hostile witness. Samuel Hartlib reported only that Goodwin had resigned his place at Cambridge because of his changed views on the ceremonies.[21] It is only later that ecclesiological speculations begin to appear. There is evidence of Philip Nye's concern with church government before Goodwin is reported on these issues. Nye commended Baynes' *Diocesans Triall* as 'a prime book in that subject', in 1635. A little earlier, he had observed,

Christ hase beene made very glorious in England in his Propheticall Office by mighty Preaching and truths which have beene cleared. But in his Priestly only in a private way, but for his kingly not at all. The divel had laid plots ag[ainst] all these.

The priestly office of Christ was hindered by the Book of Common Prayer. Hartlib's note is not clear on what plot the devil had laid against the kingly office, that is, church government, but it seems that it was hindered by the

---

[17] Thomas Edwards, *Antapologia: or, a Full Answer to the Apologeticall Narration* (1644) pp. 22, 232; M. Sylvester (ed.), *Reliquiae Baxterianae* (1693) pt. 3 p. 19; George Crosse of Staffordshire and Francis Woodcocke of London were also present: Ball, *An Answer to Mr Can*, preface. On Fawsley: Cliffe, *Puritan Gentry*, pp. 182–3.

[18] Thomas Goodwin, Philip Nye, Sidrach Simpson, Jeremiah Burroughes and William Bridge, *An Apologeticall Narration, Humbly Submitted to the Honourable Houses of Parliament* (1643) pp. 2–3.

[19] Edwards, *Antapologia*, p. 17.

[20] I. M. Calder (ed.), *Letters of John Davenport* (New Haven, Conn., 1937) p. 54; Edwards, *Antapologia*, p. 17; cf. Robert Baillie, *A Dissuasive from the Errours of the Times* (1645) p. 56.

[21] SU Hartlib MS 29/2/6a.

royal prerogative, which would certainly explain why Hartlib put this section in cryptic form.[22]

Goodwin's first statement on church government appeared early in 1635, when he suggested that

The great Worke that G[od] is conceaved now to be about for the good of his ch[urch] is the Ch[urch]-Policy or government. That of the Ceremonies is the last part of it. Pagit hase begun at the most ticklish point which cannot bee cleared except of world of other new truths be premised, et so happily it may prove a special Providence. These truths are very Spiritual in so much as divers here of the godly sort are not capable of them, yet it may be that it will be when greater light in the particulars shall be discovered unto them. All those other Ordinances have been hitherto Humane, so the Genevans had a mixture of them, and therf[ore] no marvile that they sped no better. This ordinance or Policy will bee one of the best Meanes for the advancing of Godlines that ever hase beene . . . This point a greater matter than wee are aware on't.[23]

These observations do not show that the later Apologists had reached their mature positions by the mid-1630s, but they do make it clear that they were reading and thinking on ecclesiological subjects within a Baynesian framework, and that Goodwin at least had gone beyond Genevan models. As had been the case for Thomas Shepard and Nathaniel Rogers, the revelation that the ceremonies were unlawful had opened up questions on more fundamental topics. On these questions they had the guidance of Scripture, 'to search out what were the first Apostolique directions, pattern and examples of those Primitive Churches recorded in the New Testament'. They also 'had the advantage of all that light which the conflicts of our owne Divines (the good old Nonconformists) had struck forth in their times; which we found not in all things the very same with the practices of the Reformed Churches', and 'the recent and later example of the wayes and practices (and those improved to a better edition and greater refinement, by all the aforementioned helps)' of the New England divines.[24]

It is not at present possible to go much beyond polemical, retrospective evidence to date the ecclesiological conversions of the other Apologists. Jeremiah Burroughes, we may recall, had been tutored by Thomas Hooker in the early years of his ministry, and as early as 1632 had consulted John Cotton on the proper form for leaving a ministerial post,[25] but, as we will see, the tutelage of such a convinced Amesian as Hooker did not necessarily produce pupils of his church discipline; he does not seem to have regarded

---

[22] SU Hartlib MS 29/2/46b; cf. Thomas Hooker, *Survey of the Summe of Church Discipline*, sigs. A2v–4v, for an exposition of Christ's three offices.
[23] SU Hartlib MS 29/3/12b.   [24] Goodwin *et al.*, *Apologeticall Narration*, pp. 3, 4, 5.
[25] K. Shipps, 'Lay Patronage of East Anglian Puritan Clerics in Pre-Revolutionary England', Yale PhD (1971) Appendix 13.

it as any part of his role in England to spread his ideas on such issues. Indeed, Hooker seems to have adopted an almost Muggletonian attitude to the question of church government: he played no part in the debate on the practice of Massachusetts and only entered the conflicts of the 1640s when prompted by his colleagues. Burroughes proved himself sufficiently in sympathy with the colonial venture in the mid-1630s to provide a haven for his friend Thomas Shepard and his family while they waited for a ship, but it seems more credible to date his conversion to that period between his new resolution on the ceremonies and his departure for the Netherlands. Burroughes spent this time in Essex and London; we cannot construct many of his clerical contacts at this time, but he had opportunities to preach in London and it would be less than surprising if he had been in contact with Nye. In any case, the ultimate source of his conversion is likely to have been Massachusetts practice. He later declared himself to be wholly in accord with them.[26]

Similar patterns seem to have been followed by William Bridge and Sidrach Simpson. Bridge had been a lecturer in Norwich after an attempt to install him as town lecturer in Colchester. He had been suspended and submitted in 1634, but, like Burroughes, could not conform to the new regime of Matthew Wren. His ecclesiological conversion may post-date his exile: this seems to have been the understanding of a group of his former parishioners who received letters from him upon his arrival in the Netherlands.[27] Simpson had longer between his troubles with the authorities and his emigration to find his new light. He was briefly suspended during the metropolitical visitation and, despite submitting, left his lectureship at St Margaret's, Fish Street, emigrating in 1638.[28]

If this sketchy account of the origins of the positions of the Apologists establishes the existence of one side of the ecclesiological debates of the 1640s as convinced reformers, heavily indebted to Massachusetts practices and hammering out their position before emigration in the late 1630s, a process which continued in the Netherlands, it clearly does not explain the content of those debates. The opposition encountered in England was from fellow Amesians, who saw them as tainted with the sectarian tendencies of

---

[26] M. McGiffert (ed.), *God's Plot: the Paradoxes of Puritan Piety Being the Autobiography and Journal of Thomas Shepard* (Amherst, Mass., 1972) pp. 34, 62–3; Edwards, *Antapologia*, p. 12; W. Orme (ed.), *Remarkable Passages in the Life of William Kiffen* (London, 1823) p. 14. It was after hearing Burroughes and Mr Glover, himself bound for New England, that Kiffen declared himself satisfied with the unlawfulness of the ceremonies, formed an independent church and resolved to emigrate.

[27] See above, pp. 40–1; William Laud, *The Works of William Laud, Anglo-Catholic Library* (ed. J. Bliss and W. Scott) (Oxford, 1847–60) vol. V pp. 328, 340; BodL Tanner MS 68 ff.123, 79, 167–70; Edwards, *Antapologia*, p. 18.

[28] *DNB* s.v. 'Sidrach Simpson'.

the Bay colony. This was true of John Ball, and equally so of John Goodwin, Davenport's successor at St Stephen's, Coleman Street, who sent Thomas Goodwin a fraternal rebuke in the Netherlands over the compulsory church relation and the location of the power of the keys in the body of the congregation rather than in the congregational presbytery.[29] The normative ecclesiology of those ministers who dissented from the *status quo* of the Church of England was, it seems, Amesian. We have seen little fertile ground for the Presbyterianism that was to become the orthodoxy of the Westminster Assembly.

[29] Thomas Goodwin, *Works* (Edinburgh, 1865) vol. XI pp. 526–40, esp. 528–9. Goodwin's letter was later printed to reveal his ecclesiological changes: [John Goodwin,] *A Quaere, Concerning the Church Covenant* (1643).

⸺⸻ ⸺ 17 ⸺ ⸺⸻

Alternative ecclesiologies to 1643

I

Accepting that the bedrock of alternative English ecclesiological thought among the godly ministers was Amesian in form, we are led to ask a question that would seem strange to those who have assumed the normative content of ecclesiological opposition to be Presbyterian:[1] where were the English Presbyterians before 1643? Here it is necessary to reiterate that, despite the individuals discussed in the previous two chapters, many godly ministers, and probably the majority, regarded church-government issues as superfluous, as a divisive waste of energy or as questions of a secondary nature. Indeed, one of the lessons of the 1640s was that episcopacy was not an institution unanimously reviled as Antichristian, and if the middling sorts who put their names to petitions in favour of the bishops could distinguish between the office and the incumbent, and between Laudian prelacy and old-fashioned preaching bishops, so too could their ministers, and many of those ministers would be regarded as godly.[2] Moreover, before the civil war many ministers who might have been sympathetic to questions of ecclesiology and the ceremonies were put off by the manner of these disputes. Thomas Goodwin admitted that

It is to bee observed generally that All Men writing upon Ceremonies they fal to bitterness wrangling et personalities and so the matter becomes never to bee fully searched et elaborated. So in Dr Ames in all his other writings moderate yet here delinquent.

This was a common viewpoint, as noted by Hartlib: Alexander Leighton

---

[1] Eg. J. R. DeWitt, *Jus Divinum: the Westminster Assembly and the Divine Right of Church Government* (Kempen, 1969), *passim*, and esp. p. 31; W. A. Shaw, *A History of the Church of England During the English Civil War and Under the Commonwealth* 2 vols. (London, 1900).

[2] See, for instance, A. Fletcher, *The Outbreak of the English Civil War* (London, 1981) pp. 108–24; J. Morrill, 'The Church in England, 1642–9', in J. Morrill (ed.), *Reactions to the English Civil War* (London, 1982) pp. 89–114.

had written against bishops, reported one minister, 'but very railingly', and Nye's approval of Baynes almost registers surprise that his work is 'written very solidly yet without any bitterness'. Similarly, William Whately regarded such disputes as normally generating more heat than light.[3] Nye made the fears of contention clearer in part of a speech aimed at the clerical members of his audience in the early 1640s:

I have not observed any disputes carried men with more bitterness in mens writings, and with a more unsanctified heat of spirit, yea and by godly men too, then in controversies about Discipline, Church government, Ceremonies, and the like. Surely to argue about Government with such ungoverned passions, to argue for Reformation with a spirit so unreformed, is very uncomely. Let us be zealous, as Christ was, to cast out all, to extirpate and root out every plant his heavenly Father hath not planted; and yet let us doe it in an orderly way, and with the spirit of Christ, whose servants we are *The servant of the Lord must not strive, but be gentle to all men, apt to teach, patient, in meeknesse instructing those that oppose*, 2, Tim. 2.24,25. We solemnly engage this day our utmost endeavours for Reformation; let us remember this, that too much heat, as well as to[o] much coldnesse, may harden men in their wayes, and hinder Reformation.[4]

Some among this constituency may have been sympathetic to reformist ecclesiologies in the 1630s, but for most the available ideas were one or other of the versions of the Amesian critique. The ambiguities of the Cartwrightian tradition were colonised by Presbyterians in the early 1640s, but a decade earlier this tradition seems to have been almost the exclusive property of the Amesians. Michael Watts describes the 'near extinction of English Presbyterianism between 1590 and 1640' and the lonely struggle of John Paget, minister of the English reformed church at Amsterdam, to keep the Presbyterian flame alive. Paget's dogged efforts to keep the Amesian ecclesiologies of John Forbes, Thomas Hooker and John Davenport at bay has distorted our view of orthodoxy; Paget is best understood as a member of the Dutch Reformed *classis*, of Scottish extraction, and should be seen as a dissenter from the mainstream of alternative English ecclesiologies.[5]

If Paget is rejected as the *locus* of continuous English Presbyterianism, perhaps a more fruitful source for rejuvenated authoritarian ecclesiologies might be the very public martyrs of the 1630s. The sufferings of Alexander Leighton, John Bastwick, Henry Burton and William Prynne helped foster godly hostility to prelacy and may have stimulated a revival of non-Amesian ecclesiologies. Some of this can be found in the experience of

[3] SU Hartlib MS 29/2/23a, 21a, 46b; William Whately, *A Sermon on Pride* (1602) pp. 16–17, 20, 47.
[4] [Philip Nye and Alexander Henderson], *Two Speeches Delivered before the Subscribing of the Covenant* (Edinburgh, 1643) p. 13.
[5] M. Watts, *The Dissenters from the Reformation to the English Revolution* (Oxford, 1978) pp. 56, 62–3.

Samuel Rogers: his low opinion of individual members of the hierarchy has been noted, and was shared by many among the godly. In early 1637, he noted that 'I have now read mr Burtons booke, and my heart and portion be with those that contend for the faith, whether in life or death'. It is not clear whether the book was *For God and the King* or *An Apology of an Appeal*, both of which had arrived in London three weeks earlier, but Rogers' interest continued and he mentions mourning the outcome of the Star Chamber trial in godly company. He expressed similar interest in the lesser-known martyr, Alexander Leighton, to the extent of visiting him in the Fleet. He found Leighton 'a scotch spirit right; but sure upright, and one that hath tasted of the spirit of X, even in this affliction'. These interests, however, do not make a Presbyterian; Leighton was reputed to be one, but more on account of his nationality than any ecclesiological programme that could be found in his bloodthirsty rant, *Sions Plea*.[6] A further explanation can be found for the relative silence of Presbyterians. The preface to the will of Humfrey Fen, the Northamptonshire minister prominent in the campaigns for reform at the turn of the century and later lecturer of Coventry, was sufficiently polemic in its ecclesiological views to draw the attention of the central authorities in the early 1630s. Fen stated that 'I hould yt [discipline] by Pastors, Doctors, ruling Elders, & Deacons . . . is to be held Apostolicall, universal, & unchangeable', and that the Church of England sinned against Christ 'for uphoulding an ambitious, pompous, wordly [*sic*] Prelacie' (although it is noteworthy that Fen made no mention of classical authority in his account of reformed government). However, Fen went on to make it clear that 'yet I not hould it lawfull for these corruptions, to separate from communion of ye Church of England, if therein a Christian may inioy true doctrine, with ye Sacraments from a Minister able to teach ye trueth; & where a worship of God, is not forced by a personnal acte to approve those corruptions', that is, despite his vilifications of the present form of government, Fen held on to a two-mark doctrine of ecclesiology, licensing him to retain his opportunity to preach within the inadequately reformed church.[7] In short, the various libels of the 1630s did not engender Presbyterianism *per se*, but fed a hostility to lordly

---

[6] QUB Percy MS 7 ff. 207, 244, 336; S. Foster, *Notes from the Caroline Underground: Alexander Leighton, the Puritan Triumvirate and the Laudian Reaction to Nonconformity* (Hamden, Conn., 1978) *passim* and pp. 51–2, 19–20. Similar emotions can be found in Robert Woodford's diary: NCO MS 9502 25 and 26 August 1637, 28 and 29 November 1640 (pp.9, 515–16).

[7] SP 16/260/83. This was later published as *The Last Will and Testament, with the Profession of the Faith of Humfrey Fen* (1641); see also J. Eales, 'A Road to Revolution: the Continuity of Puritanism, 1559–1642', in C. Durston and J. Eales (eds.), *The Culture of English Puritanism, 1560–1700* (London, 1996) pp. 194–5.

prelacy. Serious students of such issues up to the late 1630s were more likely to be Amesians.

There was, however, a second tradition to be drawn upon. If the primary bond for English ministers was always between pastor and congregation, a fact which tended to undermine authoritarian Presbyterian experiments, a second principle worked against them in another way. A society of orders would always find hierarchical thinking difficult to reject, and the parity of ministers that is the *sine qua non* of Presbyterianism sat uneasily with a church that included ministers of widely differing gifts. Even among the godly, patterns of education and advice ensured that the idea of parity remained at variance with reality. Within the household seminaries characteristic of godly practice, a Richard Blackerby, a John Dod or a Thomas Hooker was unlikely to possess no more than equal authority with his disciples. Indeed, this seems to have extended into conference situations; when Thomas Shepard's lecture seemed bound for Coggeshall, Hooker intervened and the gift was given to Earls Colne.[8] It may not be fruitful to look for formal arrangements here, so much as to acknowledge that the nature of the godly vision of the ministry admitted the possibility of greater godliness, greater preaching gifts and greater renown being associated with greater authority among the brethren. The hierarchical social reality of the profession, in a hierarchical society, admits the possibility that a reformed church order could embody these elements.

Another factor that makes the absence of an English Presbyterian tradition between 1590 and 1640 comprehensible is that the model that had driven the Cartwrightian reformers toward more authoritarian schemes in the 1590s was being substantially modified in Scotland. From 1597, when the representation of Scottish bishops in their Parliament was increased, James VI was grafting diocesan government on to the Presbyterian briar, a process that continued after he added the English crown to his title. In 1606, at the General Assembly of Linlithgow, bishops were appointed as permanent moderators of synods and, although the move from Presbyterianism to episcopacy was not uncontested, James' policy was successful in creating a certain affection for the office, which was only wrecked by his son's disastrous ecclesiastical policy.[9] It is too easy for

[8] M. McGiffert (ed.), *God's Plot: the Paradoxes of Puritan Piety Being the Autobiography and Journal of Thomas Shepard* (Amherst, Mass., 1972) pp. 46–7.
[9] P. Collinson, 'John Field and Elizabethan Puritanism', in *Godly People: Essays on English Protestantism and Puritanism* (London, 1983) pp. 335–70; D. G. Mullan, *Episcopacy in Scotland: the History of an Idea, 1560–1638* (Edinburgh, 1986); A. I. McInnes, *Charles I and the Making of the Covenanting Movement, 1625–1641* (Edinburgh, 1991) pp. 17–18; I. Dunlop, 'The Polity of the Scottish Church, 1600–1637', *Records of the Scottish Church History Society* 12 (1958) pp. 161–84; C. Russell, *The Causes of the English Civil War* (Oxford, 1990) pp. 48–53.

students of the English situation to forget that as late as 1638, Robert Baillie, known in England as the most active of the commissioners in the drive to presbyterianise England in the 1640s, was in favour of a moderate episcopacy.[10] In this context, the significant point is that those Englishmen who looked to the northern kingdom for a model of reform would find, not Presbyterianism, but a form of reduced episcopacy.

In England such notions had a very respectable pedigree. From the first appearance of plans for ecclesiastical reform, there had been an element occupying the part of the ecclesiastical spectrum from moderate Puritans to moderate bishops, the area in which such 'party' nomenclature meets with its most serious problems, that saw a form of moderate episcopacy as desirable, realisable and Scriptural. John Knox felt that some such scheme might be the most appropriate for English conditions.[11] The eminent continental divine, Martin Bucer, a great influence on men who were to become central figures in the early Elizabethan church, limited the Scriptural sources for lordly prelacy, stressing the rights of presbyters to counsel their bishops and drawing attention to the fact that the term 'bishop' was applied to both groups in Scripture.[12] The opportunities of the Grindalian church in the mid-1570s were such that the revival of the rural dean, the introduction and extension of exercises with permanent moderators or *chorepiscopi* seemed a real possibility. The Whitgiftian reaction crushed such hopes for a while, but they resurfaced at the beginning of the new reign in the Millenary Petition and in the person of John Reynolds. At the Hampton Court Conference, Reynolds, the main spokesman, looked for the involvement of parochial clergy in discipline and ordination, for the revival of resident, preaching rural deans and a greater synodical element in episcopal jurisdiction. This was the most moderate form of what was to be known as 'reduced episcopacy', but it was only a few degrees away from the proposals for the multiplication of dioceses that less cautious moderates had proposed. Patrick Collinson has suggested that it would 'probably prove possible to recover a succession of moderate and pragmatic proposals of this kind', stretching from the beginning of Elizabeth's reign to the Long Parliament.[13] The trail goes a

---

[10] D. Laing (ed.), *Letters and Journals of Robert Baillie* (Edinburgh, 1841–2) vol. I pp. 2–5, 52–4, 178; C. Russell, *The Fall of the British Monarchies* (Oxford, 1991) p. 45; D. Stevenson, 'The Radical Party in the Kirk, 1637–45', *JEH* 25 (1974) pp. 135–65, esp. p. 142.

[11] J. Kirk, '"The Polities of the Best Reformed Kirks": Scottish Achievements and English Aspirations in Church Government after the Reformation', *SHR* 59 (1980) pp. 29–30.

[12] P. Collinson, *Archbishop Grindal* (London, 1979) pp. 53–4, 56; Martin Bucer, *De Regno Christi* in W. Pauck (ed. and trans.), *Melancthon and Bucer, Library of Christian Classics*, vol. XIX (London, 1969) pp. 284–92.

[13] P. Collinson, *The Elizabethan Puritan Movement*, pp. 179–90, 451–52, 455–56, 460,

little cold after Hampton Court, but we have suggestive fragments. Thomas Taylor, who ran a ministerial seminary at Reading, seems to advocate something along these lines in a work of 1619. John Yates, who had benefited from the tutelage of Alexander Richardson and John Rogers, left a particularly opaque account in a work of the early 1620s. He granted pastors the power of the keys, looked for congregational election of ministers to be 'moderated by the discretion of the civill Magistrate, or faithfull Pastours', and gave no account of separate orders within the ministry, but granted Timothy and Titus, the crucial Scriptural figures, a superintendency 'as Bishops properly so called'. Similarly, William Gouge expressed editorial approval of such positions in an extended version of a work by Nathaniel Byfield, published posthumously in 1637.[14] John Hacket reported an attempt of John Preston, 'a good Crow to smell Carrion', to use the Duke of Buckingham to persuade James I of the attractions, not least the financial ones, of 'the Dissolution of Cathedral Churches', Deans and Chapters and the reduction of land belonging to the higher parts of the church hierarchy, combining to produce a form of limited episcopacy not dissimilar to that in Scotland. James apparently allowed Buckingham to hold forth on the matter, partly because he hoped that this might provide a distraction from his attempts to promote a military conflict with Spain.[15] How are we to understand the manuscript tract of Edmund Brewer of Castle Hedingham 'of the unlawfullness of diocesan Bishops', reported by Samuel Hartlib? It is at least as likely to have been a scheme in favour of reduced episcopacy as a Presbyterian programme. It is noteworthy that his near neighbours Stephen Marshall and Samuel Fairclough favoured such ideas, at least in the late 1630s, and Fairclough reportedly longed for such a policy long after it had ceased to be practical politics.[16] The close association of all three men with Clare, on the Suffolk/Essex border, encourages a specula-tion that such principles might have been learnt at Richard Blackerby's household seminary.

That support for reduced forms of episcopacy is even less visible than more radical alternative ecclesiologies need cause no surprise. If Amesians

quoted at p. 181; Collinson, 'Episcopacy and Reform in England in the Later Sixteenth Century', *SCH* 3 (1966) pp. 91–125.

[14] Thomas Taylor, *A Commentarie upon the Epistle of S. Paul to Titus* (1619) pp. 81–6; cf. Thomas Taylor, *Works* (1653) p. 209; John Yates, *A Modell of Divinitie* (1622) pp. 252–7, 270–1, cf. above, Chapter 1; Nathaniel Byfield, *A Commentary: or, a Sermon upon the Second Chapter of the First Epistle of Saint Peter* (1637) 'To the Christian Reader', and pp. 566–9.

[15] John Hacket, *Scrinia Reserata* (1683) pt. I p. 204. The matter of the possibility of war with Spain, of course, places this attempt in or around 1624.

[16] SU Hartlib MS 29/2/25a; DWL Baxter MS 59.3.80; Clarke (1683) p. 175.

like Ball could justify their continued ministry in the Church of England on the grounds of a limited visibility of true churches and only expose their ideals when forced by aberrant, more radical brethren to defend their view of Scriptural proprieties, ministers with a loyalty to reduced episcopacy had still less reason to reveal their hands and risk ecclesiastical censure. Cornelius Burges was one who did reveal himself, in a Latin sermon *ad clerum* in London in 1636, subsequently refusing to supply William Juxon with a copy of this sermon, for which he was called into the High Commission Court. He held this view so strongly that as late as 1643 he expressed reservations regarding the article of the Solemn League and Covenant calling for the extirpation of episcopacy, receiving support from William Price and William Gouge and apparently publishing his petition to Parliament on this matter.[17] A colleague of Burges in the London clerical brotherhood, Thomas Gataker, set out his views in the 1650s, claiming that his judgement regarding church government was 'the same stil that it ever was'. He had hoped for a 'dulie bounded and wel regulated *Prelacie* joined with a *Presbyterie*, wherein one as *President, Superintendent* or *Moderator* (term him what you please,) whether annual or occasional, or more constant and continual, either in regard or yeers, or parts, or both jointlie, hath some *preeminence* above the rest, yet so, as that he doth nothing without joint consent of the rest'. What Gataker found offensive was the delegation of episcopal authority to chancellors, officials and surrogates, frequently lay civil lawyers and often focused on the income of fines and on punishing nonconformists rather than the inadequacy of conformists. Given the growth of what he saw as the worst side of prelacy in the 1630s and his admiration for the ecclesiology of the reformed churches in France and Holland, Gataker became willing to vote in the Westminster Assembly for the abolition of episcopacy and the erection of Presbyterianism 'as divers others, if not the greater part, did; not as deeming it absolutelie necessarie, but as *agreeable to Gods Word*'.[18] In terms of their visibility before the 1640s, however, such men could make their peace even more easily with the establishment than the Amesians, regretting the excesses of bishops like Wren and Laud and looking to model bishops like Ussher and Bedell in Ireland or Morton in England as exemplars of a more satisfactory way forward.

---

[17] William Laud, *The Works of William Laud, Anglo-Catholic Library* (ed. J. Bliss and W. Scott) (Oxford, 1847–60) vol. V pp. 337–8; John Lightfoot, *The Whole Works* (ed. J. P. Pitman) (London, 1825) vol. XIII pp. 10–16. If the petition was published, it does not seem to have survived.

[18] Thomas Gataker, *Discours Apologetical; wherein Lilies Lewd and Lowd Lies in his Merlin or Pasquil for the Year 1654 are Cleerly Laid Open* (1654) pp. 24–8, quotes from pp. 24, 26.

II

Without further evidence, it is impossible to say much about the extent of such views before the end of the 1630s, but those who looked to Scottish models would, as we have seen, find as much to commend in moderate episcopacy as in working models of Presbyterianism. If the concerns of the Scottish ministers arriving in London after the calling of what was to become the Long Parliament are any measure, moderate episcopacy was a more widespread allegiance than the neo-Amesian form that was to prove a greater obstacle to the establishment of Presbyterianism over the next few years. In late 1640, Robert Baillie warned that Archbishop Ussher 'and a great faction with him, will be for a limited good and James Mitchell's calked episcopacy'.[19] The energies of the Scots were devoted almost exclusively to opposing such positions over the next few months.[20] The most detailed proposals in this direction came, as Baillie warned, from Archbishop Ussher. His *Reduction* scheme allowed that the Apostolic Church had been governed by presbyteries with bishops as 'chief presidents' over them. Such bishops were forbidden to judge without 'the clergy' being present. Parochial ministers could withhold the sacrament and present offenders to a monthly synod, or conference. The conference would include all ministers within a rural deanery under a sub-bishop or *chorepiscopus*, with decisions according to majority vote. Appeals from this level would be made to a biannual diocesan synod composed of all the *chorepiscopi* and all or some of the parochial clergy. With the consent of the diocesan synod, matters of 'greater moment' could 'be concluded by the bishop or superintendent (call him whether you will)'.[21] William M. Abbot has substantially revised our understanding of Ussher's manuscript, arguing that the proposals were seen by the King and few others before March 1641, and were thereafter suppressed by Ussher himself as more radical proposals made him fear that his scheme would be used as a stepping stone to the complete abolition of episcopacy. By late May 1641, he had retreated from this position to publicise John Reynold's affirmation of the Apostolic

[19] Baillie, *Letters and Journals*, vol. I pp. 313ff.

[20] Alexander Henderson, *The Unlawfulness and Danger of Limited Prelacy, or Perpetual Presidency in the Church Briefly Discovered* (January, 1641); George Gillespie, *Certain Reasons Tending to Prove the Unlawfulness and Inexpediency of all Diocesan Episcopacy (even the most Moderate)* (February, 1641); Robert Baillie, *The Unlawfulness and Danger of Limited Episcopacie* (February, 1641).

[21] James Ussher, *The Reduction of Episcopacy Unto the Form of Synodical Government* (1656) pp. 4–7. This was the first time it appeared in print, edited by Nicholas Barnard, Ussher's chaplain, who had added notes. The original, or a draft of it, can be found in CUL Add MSS 44(6).

origins of episcopacy, a change of emphasis rather than a recantation, but nevertheless a crucial difference.[22]

For the short time that Ussher had held to his scheme for a radical reduction he had been close to the Bedford group of reformers and owed his lectureship at Covent Garden, which he had held since the spring of 1640, to Bedford himself. His older connections with Essex have been noted: in the 1620s he preached on the weekdays at the request of the Essex clergy; he had been an admirer of Thomas Hooker and a close friend of Nathaniel Ward, as well as a preacher at Hatfield Broad Oak, possibly on the occasion when Hooker established his conference. His responsibilities as Archbishop of Armagh, however, had almost obliterated his chances to cross the Irish Sea in the 1630s and, although he maintained some of his contacts by correspondence, he can hardly have remained as central to godly society as he had been.[23] There is fragmentary evidence that Gataker had seen his scheme.[24] It is possible that ideas were tentatively exchanged between the ministers in Bedford's circle who were sympathetic to limited episcopal government. These ministers had been meeting regularly at the home of Edmund Calamy in Aldermanbury since the calling of the Parliament, and certainly included Cornelius Burges, John White and Stephen Marshall, and probably Matthew Newcomen, Thomas Young and William Spurstowe. It was from these circles that the 'Smectymnuan' tracts emerged, the first in February 1641.[25] The knowledge that Burges and

---

[22] James Ussher, *The Originall of Bishops and Metropolitans* (1641); W. M. Abbot, 'James Ussher and "Ussherian Episcopacy" 1640–1656: the Primate and his *Reduction* Manuscript', *Albion* 22 (1990) pp. 237–59; cf. J. C. Spalding and M. F. Brass, 'Reduction of Episcopacy as a Means to Unity in England, 1640–1662', *CH* 30 (1961) pp. 414–32; H. R. Trevor-Roper, *Catholics, Anglicans and Puritans* (Oxford, 1987) p. 151.

[23] For the possible links with the Bedford group, see C. Russell, *The Fall of the British Monarchies*, pp. 249–51. Russell is ambiguous on the crucial questions of how widely Ussher's *Reduction* manuscript was known in detail and when it was presented and withdrawn. I cannot agree with his suggestion that the line of descent of ideas of reduced episcopacy passes through Richard Hooker. (See M. R. Somerville, 'Richard Hooker and his Contemporaries on Episcopacy: an Elizabethan Consensus', *JEH* 35 (1984) pp. 177–87; P. Lake, *Anglicans and Puritans? Presbyterian and English Conformist Thought from Whitgift to Hooker* (London, 1988) pp. 215–22.) Russell suggests that Charles committed himself to Ussher's scheme in March 1641, in the context of Bishop Williams' committee, by appointing Richard Holdsworth and Ralph Brownrigg as royal chaplains: *Fall of the British Monarchies*, pp. 271–7. Charles may have been in favour of the committee but it is hard to see that this evinces an approval of Ussher's scheme. For Ussher's Essex links, Clarke (1662) pp. 213–14; Giles Firmin, *The Real Christian* (1670) p. 51; ERO D/DBa F5/1; for his career in the 1630s, A. L. Capern, 'The Caroline Church: James Ussher and the Irish Dimension', *HJ* 39 (1996) pp. 57–85, esp. 59–60.

[24] Gataker, *Discours Apologetical*, p. 24.

[25] Shaw, *A History of the English Church*, vol. I p. 81; DWL Baxter MS 59.3.80; *Persecutio Undecima, the Churches Eleventh Persecution* (1648) pp. 57–8. 'Smectymnuus', of course, was an acronym, drawing upon the initials of the five authors, Stephen Marshall, Edmund Calamy, Thomas Young, Matthew Newcomen and William Spurstowe.

Marshall were interested in a reduced episcopacy, that Ussher was moving in these circles when he wrote his reduction manuscript and that his ideas in this area were known even if his manuscript was not distributed, encourages a revised context for the early Smectymnuan tracts.

III

Almost by accident, the change of leadership forced on the clerical godly of Essex noted earlier[26] brought a change of ecclesiological emphasis: while Hooker was the leading figure, however little he spread his views, the dominant strain in the county was Amesian; with Marshall a more moderate line emerges more strongly. This becomes clear if we take a look at the tracts produced by these men in early 1641. The two Smectymnuan tracts were written in response to Bishop Joseph Hall's *An Humble Remonstrance to the High Court of Parliament*. The Remonstrant was anonymous, but the Smectymnuans seem to have suspected Hall of being the author. At the very least, they engage occasionally with his slightly earlier work, *Episcopacy by Divine Right Asserted*, a tract published in 1640 as a response to Scottish criticisms, with Laud and his associates as advisers and revisers.[27] The Smectymnuan response has its own important pre-history in Thomas Young's *Dies Dominica*, a sabbatarian tract which the author had been working on in 1635 and which was published in 1639. Most of this work was an entirely orthodox defence of the Sabbath, although Young allowed himself to voice moderate objections to praying to the east and to reiterate the necessity of voluntaristic practices of conference and sermon repetition on the Sabbath and to defend *extempore* prayer.[28] More importantly, he touched upon the ancient office of bishops, appropriating the term for all those who laboured in the Word of God with the cure of souls. However, while the term *Episcopi* comprehended both bishops and presbyters, he made it clear that he saw a valid distinction between the two, and that bishops existed as overseers, watchmen or, in a significant word, super-intendents.[29] Thus Thomas Young, identified by Robert Baillie as the

---

26 See above, pp. 244–5.
27 Joseph Hall, *An Humble Remonstrance to the High Court of Parliament* (1641); Hall, *Episcopacy by Divine Right Asserted* (1640); Laud, *Works* vol. VI ii pp. 572–6; William Prynne, *Canterburies Doom* (1648) pp. 231–5; SP 16/429/40; Smectymnuus, *An Answer to a Booke Entituled, An Humble Remonstrance* (1641) pp. 71–2.
28 SU Hartlib MS 29/3/63b; [Thomas Young], *Dies Dominica* (1639) pp. 114, 127–31, 111.
29 Ibid., pp. 90–1: 'Episcopi nomen est generalis appellatio ad omnes in Verbo Dei laborentes, & curce animarum intentos significandos . . . Sub Episcopi titulo cum Epsicopi, tum Presbyteri comprehenduntur. Et licit sint, qui Presbyteru ab Episcopo non distinguant, ego tamen cum August. orationis, precationis, & postulationis voces exponentur, eligo in his verbis hoc intelligere, quod omnis vel pene omnis frequentit ecclesia. ep.59.'

author of the greater part of the Smectymnuan tracts,[30] allowed primitive episcopacy, grounded in the bishops' faithful preaching.[31]

This is important, for, contrary to William Haller, who wrote of the *Answer* to Bishop Hall's *Humble Remonstrance* that 'if anyone demanded a clear statement of the preachers' conception of the church with an outline of the standing arguments for its acceptance, based upon scripture and recorded history, here it was',[32] the Smectymnuan works are masterpieces of ambiguity and opaqueness. In choosing the form of a point-by-point rebuttal of Hall's work, the Smectymnuans obviated the necessity of developing a systematic model of an alternative ecclesiology and such as is contained within the piece must be carefully reconstructed. They used a great deal of space on venting their spleen against the episcopal practice of the previous ten years. In allowing the lawfulness of a set liturgy, they bemoan the imposition of the Book of Common Prayer 'to the casting out of all that scruple it, or anything in it'. In discussing of the role of bishops, they allow themselves space to criticise the state employments of bishops, surely intending Juxon as a target, and criticise the *ex officio* oath. In discussing the episcopate of Timothy and Titus, they ask

> Did ever *Apostolique authority* delegate power to *Timothy* and *Titus*, to rebuke an *Elder*? no; *but to entreate him as a Father*: and doe not our *Bishops* challenge to themselves, and permit to their *Chancellours, Commissaries*, and *Officials* power not only to *rebuke an Elder*, but to *rayle upon an Elder*? to reproach him with the most opprobrious termes of *foole, knave, jack-sauce, & which our paper blushes to present to your Honours* view . . . Did ever *Apostolique authority* delegate power to *Timothy* and *Titus*, to reject any after twice admonition, but an *Heretick*? and doe not our *Bishops* challenge power to *reject* and *eject* the most *sound* and *orthodox* of our *Ministers*, for refusing the use of a Ceremony; as if *Non-conformity* were *Heresie*.

Further outbursts condemn forced subscription, the new ceremonies, the Etc. oath, altar rails and the countenancing of Arminianism. These are powerful echoes of the experience of the dioceses of London and Norwich during the 1630s.[33]

The *Answer* dismisses the Apostolic origins of diocesan episcopacy by showing that such government was not possible in an age when there were

---

[30] Baillie, *Letters and Journals*, vol. I p. 306.

[31] Apart from Young and Marshall, we have no clues regarding the pre-war ecclesiology of the Smectymnuans. There is a tiny hint in the note that Hartlib made in 1639, that Calamy 'holds that the Office of an Evangelist is not extinct', a belief reported by Thomas Ball: SU Hartlib MS 30/4/27b.

[32] W. Haller, *Liberty and Reformation in the Puritan Revolution* (London, 1958) pp. 38–9.

[33] Smectymnuus, *An Answer*, pp. 6, 43, 45–7, 52 (quote), 62, 83–4, 90–1. The official receiving the criticism seems to resemble Clement Corbet. For an explicit attack on Dr Duck, see p. 75.

no parishes.[34] At greater length, they show that presbyters and bishops shared a name (as Hall admitted) and were not distinct in their offices.[35] The distinct office of bishops was a response to diabolical schisms: 'the occasion of this Imparity and Superiority of Boshops above Elders, was the divisions through which the Devils instinct fell among the Churches; *Postquam verò Diaboli instincta*'.[36] This became clear 'because as Doctor Whitaker saith, the remedy devised hath proved worse then the disease, which doth never happen to that remedy whereof the holy Ghost is the author'.[37]

If this seems to be a foundation for a call for Presbyterianism, Smectymnuus leaves space for the possibility, without an unambiguous espousal of the form. Thus, when Hall

> scoffes at the *Antiprelaticall Church*, and the *Antiprelaticall Divisions*; for our parts we acknowledge no Antiprelaticall Church. But there are a company of men in *the Kingdome, of no meane ranke* or *quality, for Piety, Nobility, Learning*, that stand up to beare witnesse against the Hierarchie (as it now stands:) the usurpations over Gods Church and Ministers, their cruell using of Gods people by their tyrannicall Governement: this we acknowledge; and if he call these the *Antiprelaticall Church*, we doubt not but your Honours [Parliament] wil consider, that there are many Thousands in this Kingdome, and those pious and worthy persons, that thus doe, and upon most just cause.[38]

The more positive elements contest the understanding of a separate order of bishops that reserves to itself the sole right of ordination and discipline. Ordination was not solely an episcopal power but involved the 'presbyters or chorepiscopi' who actually had the joint power to ordain without him. This is not to demand the extirpation of episcopacy, for they immediately proclaim that the bishop is bound 'in all his Ordinations to consult with his Clergy'. The assumption is that a properly constituted church will include bishops but that they will be of the same order as their Presbyters or *Chorepiscopi*, and that they will join with them in administration.[39] There is the vaguest hint of an alternative order in their denial that anything other than episcopacy as it stands will lead to endless divisions 'to the very Atomes . . . of separated congregations', when Smectymnuus writes,

> we read in Scripture, of the Churches of *Iudea*, and the Churches of *Galatia*; and why not the Churches of *England*? not that we denie the *Consociation* or *Combination* into a Provinciall or Nationall Synod for the right ordering of them.[40]

This was not an espousal of Presbyterianism: Ussher's scheme had allowed this much a few months earlier. Elsewhere, they turn with approval to Beza's division of bishops into three types: *divinus, humanus* and *diabolicus*. The

---

[34] Ibid., pp. 15–16, 58.   [35] Ibid., pp. 19–24.   [36] Ibid., p. 29.
[37] Ibid., p. 30.   [38] Ibid., p. 81.   [39] Ibid., pp. 21–5, 36–7, 39, 58.
[40] Joseph Hall, *An Humble Remonstrance*, p. 40; Smectymnuus, *An Answer*, pp. 80–1.

episcopus divinus was 'one and the same with a Presbyter'; the *episcopus humanus* was 'chosen by the Presbyters to be President over them'; the *episcopus diabolicus* was 'a Bishop with sole power of Ordination and Jurisdiction, Lording it over Gods heritage, and governing by his owne will and authority'. Given the condemnation of sole ordination and jurisdiction, at first glance, the bishops of the Church of England appear to be *diabolicus*, but the conclusion is that by accumulating the forms of power, the human bishop is 'swelling into a Pope'. As the hierarchy of the Church of England is later seen to be *'the same as the Church of Rome'*, they may be included in this category, but the accusation is not made clear.[41] Neither does the Bezan division necessarily imply an advocacy of Presbyterianism. Sir Edward Dering used the division shortly after this exchange as part of his call for *episcopus humanus*.[42] The nearest Smectymnuus comes to calling for the abolition of episcopacy is in turning Hall's rhetoric against himself.

Suffer us therefore humbly to appeale to your Honours [i.e. Parliament], whether this Remonstrant [Hall] hath not given sentence against himself, who is so confident of the Evidence of his cause, that he doth not feare to say, if there can be better *Evidence under Heaven for any matter of fact than there* is for his Episcopacy: Let EPISCOPACY BE FOREVER ABANDONED OUT OF THE CHURCH OF GOD.[43]

This form is repeated when Smectymnuus concludes the argument: 'Whereas this remonstrant saith, *If there can be better evidence under Heaven for any matter of fact, Let Episcopacy be forever abandoned out of Gods Church*: We beseech you remember how weake we have discovered his Evidence to be; and then the Inference upon all these we *humbly* leave to your *Honours Wisdome and Iustice*.'[44]

These ambiguities allow for the possibility of primitive episcopacy without losing the powerful rhetoric of a call for abolition. In these circumstances the options are not limited to Presbyterianism. In the discussion of Titus in Acts 20.28, the Greek is translated 'in ordinary English, *Bishops*, though our Translation there, (we know not for what reason) reads it *Overseers*', as we have seen, a favourite term for advocates of primitive episcopacy.[45] Attention may also be turned to Smectymnuus' modern sources; especially noteworthy are two references to John Reynolds, the primitive episcopalian of the Hampton Court Conference. The first is on the question of the episcopacy of Timothy and Titus, limiting the title 'for the Overseer of a particular Church', drawing upon his *Contra Hart*. The second is regarding the angels of Revelation, ending with the

---

[41] Ibid., pp. 86–7, 90.   [42] Sir Edward Dering, *Collection of Speeches* (1642) p. 125.
[43] Smectymnuus, *An Answer*, p. 32.   [44] Ibid., p. 66; cf. p. 65.
[45] Ibid., p. 22.

note that 'it is evident that Doctor *Reynolds* was an utter enemy to the *Jus Divinum* of the Episcopall preheminency over Presbyters by his Letter to Sir *Francis Knolls*'.[46] Although this letter had not been in print since 1608, manuscript copies seem to have been circulating among the godly, at least in the early part of the century.[47] A second source, reproduced in forms of arguments although never cited, may be Martin Bucer. Smectymnuus draws attention to the account of Jerome and employs the same stance on the importance of Scriptural nomenclature. The relevant passages from Reynolds and Bucer appeared together in the press in 1641, although they were the product of the efforts of Bishop Hall and Archbishops Ussher and Laud.[48]

Without calling for it themselves, the Smectymnuans allowed for the possibility of the abolition of episcopacy as the natural outcome of this argument. It was this eventuality that persuaded Ussher to withdraw his scheme; the Smectymnuans, while calling for nothing more than the removal of an episcopacy with sole powers of ordination and jurisdiction, were not unwilling to see episcopacy fall. This was not the immediate outcome, and Marshall, Calamy and Young, with Burges and Thomas Hill, could still contribute to Bishop Williams' Committee on Innovations with moderate bishops and a number of divines destined to be bridge appointments to the episcopal bench, while it lasted.[49]

The committee was representative of those in favour of a reduced episcopacy, and held six meetings in Westminster Hall, at which, according to Hacket, 'all passages of discourse were very friendly between part and part', despite the presence of Bishop Hall and three of the Smectymnuans. However, by May, the fissures between those willing to reform and those eager for change became increasingly clear. Calamy later claimed that he 'was the first that openly before a Committee of Parliament did defend that our Bishops were not only not an order distinct from Presbyters, but that in Scripture a Bishop and Presbyter were all one'. On 12 May the committee

---

[46] Ibid., pp. 51, 60; John Reynolds, *The Summe of the Conference betwene J. Rainoldes and J. Hart: Touching the Head and the Faith of the Church* (1580) (the most recent edition in English was published in 1609); the latter appeared in *Informations, or a Protestation, and a Treatise from Scotland. Seconded with D. Reignolds his letter to Sir Francis Knollis. And Sir Francis Knollis his Speach in Parliament. All Suggesting the Usurpation of Papal Bishops* (1608) pp. 73–87.

[47] W. D. G. Cargill Thompson, *Studies in the Reformation: Luther to Hooker* (London, 1980) p. 240n.75.

[48] *Certain Briefe Treatises, Written by Learned Men, Concerning the Ancient and Moderne Government of the Church* (1641) pp. 45–51; Capern, 'The Caroline Church', p. 82. It is also noteworthy that *The Judgement of Martin Bucer, Touching the Originall of Bishops and Metropolitans* was republished in 1641.

[49] Shaw, *A History of the English Church*, vol. I pp. 64–6; Abbot, 'James Ussher', p. 241.

broke up over the Commons' proposal to abolish deaneries and chapters, of which Burges was an outspoken opponent.[50]

This was not the end of interest in modified episcopacy among the godly ministers, although the increasing conservatism of Ussher, Brownrigg, Holdsworth and their like must have helped to drive some supporters of such ideas into the arms of the Scots. On 10 June, Marshall was among those present when it was decided to introduce the Root and Branch bill, but the next Smectymnuan tract, which appeared at the end of the month, shows no development and certainly cannot be seen as a stampede toward Presbyterianism.[51]

The *Vindication* restates many of the arguments of the *Answer*. The delegation of the episcopal power to chancellors, commissaries and officials is condemned again; the *ex officio* oath receives more criticism; the differences between bishops of the seventeenth century and those of '*the Primitive times*' are stressed once more.[52] The Remonstrant is no more clearly identified as Bishop Hall. Hall is mentioned as 'the last defendent of Episcopacy before this Remonstrant'.[53] John Reynolds appears more often as a modern source; his *Censura liborum Apocryphorum* is cited to show that the angels of Revelation are all angels, not seven individuals.[54] The main work of Reynolds referred to is his letter to Sir Francis Knollys, which Smectymnuus notes is 'now in print'.[55] His letter is cited to provide further support for the Scriptural identity of the names of bishops and presbyters and to make it clear that this stance taken by Aërius was not part of his heresy.[56] Most importantly, he is cited with Beza regarding the angel, showing that 'he was *Angelus Præses*, not *Angelus Princeps*. And that he was *Præses mutabilis*, and *ambulatorius*, just as a *Moderator* in an

---

[50] Thomas Fuller, *The Church History of Britain* (1655) book XI p. 175; Fletcher, *Outbreak of the English Civil War*, p. 105; SP 16/482/1; Edmund Calamy, *A Just and Necessary Apology* (1646) p. 9; D. Underdown, 'A Case Concerning Bishops' Lands: Cornelius Burges and the Corporation of Wells', *EHR* 78 (1963) pp. 18–48.

[51] Russell, *Fall of the British Monarchies*, p. 344; Smectymnuus, *A Vindication of the Answer to the Humble Remonstrance* (1641).

[52] For examples, ibid., pp. 105–6, 109–10, 100.   [53] Ibid., p. 75.

[54] Ibid., p. 146 referring to John Reynolds, *Censura liborum Apocryphorum Veteris Testamenti, adversum Pontificios, imprimis R. Bellaminum* (1611).

[55] Ibid., p. 150. John Reynolds, *The Iudgement of Doctor Reignolds Concerning Episcopacy, Whether it be Gods Ordinance. Expressed in a Letter to Sir Francis Knowls, Concerning Doctor Bancrofts Sermon at Pauls-Crosse, the Ninth of February, 1588. In the Parliament Time* (1641). Another edition appeared at the same time, produced by a different printer. Neither edition shared printer or bookseller with Smectymnuus.

[56] Smectymnuus, *A Vindication*, pp. 58–9, 128. An alternative source (not cited) from the same debate could have been [John Penry], *A Briefe Discovery of the Untruths and Slanders (against the True Governement of the Church of Christ) Contained in a Sermon, Preached the 8. of Februarie 1588 by D. Bancroft* (Edinburgh, 1589) p. 28; see W. D. J. Cargill Thompson, 'A Reconsideration of Richard Bancroft's Paul's Cross Sermon of 9 February 1588/9', *JEH* 20 (1969) p. 259.

assembly, or as the *Speaker* in the *House of Commons*, which is onely during the Parliament.'[57] Clearly, this can be read as an argument for the most extreme form of primitive episcopacy.

Elsewhere, there are passages that seem to advocate something more recognizable as Presbyterianism. From the angels of Revelation, 'which is common name to all the Ministers and messengers, &c.', Smectymnuus observes that had Christ been addressing one individual, he would 'have used some distinguishing name to set him out by: he would have called him *Rector*, or *President*, or *Superintendent*'. But as he doesn't address an individual, the criticism is addressed to all ministers.[58] In another passage on Revelation, the parenthetical comment suggests rule by *classis*. 'We say each Starre had its Candlesticke, not one Starre over divers. And wee thinke that this Candlesticke was but one particular Church, or one set Congregation (though happily when they multiplyed, they might meete indistinctly in divers, under divers Angels equally governing.)'[59] In a section discussing the passage of cares and offices from the Apostles and Evangelists to 'ordinary Church-governours', the division between Episcopacy and Presbyterianism is sharper: 'all the question is, whether these Church-governours are by way of Aristocracy the common Councell of Presbyters, or by way of Monarchy Diocesan Bishops?' If Hall cannot prove that Timothy and Titus were diocesan bishops (and Smectymnuus has suggested he cannot), then they cannot be used to defend diocesan episcopacy. In these circumstances, 'onely the common Councel of Presbyters may charge any or many Presbyters, as occasion shall require'.[60]

These implications, that Hall has been argued into a corner, as it were, are the most explicit calls for a specific form of church government. Even these asides have to be measured against the possibilities of primitive episcopacy already encountered. Other passages may be cited to balance calls for Presbyterianism. In the discussion of contemporary Protestant church government, Smectymnuus makes a point in a marginal note relating to German churches. With some approval, Smectymnuus notes that 'the Superintendents are nothing like our bishops. They are of the same degree with other Ministers, they are onely Presidents while the Synod lasteth; when it is dissolved, their prerogative ceaseth: They have no prerogative over their fellow Ministers. They are subject to their Presbyters. The Synod ended, they returne to the care of their particular Churches.'[61] Returning to the angels of Revelation, Smectymnuus claims that the Remonstrant fails to prove that they are '*Hierarchicall Bishops*', that they

---

[57] Smectymnuus, *A Vindication*, pp. 150–1.   [58] Ibid., p. 143.
[59] Ibid., p. 153.   [60] Ibid., pp. 129–30.   [61] Ibid., p. 182.

are a distinct order from presbyters or that they have sole power of ordination and jurisdiction. 'For ought of any thing said by you in this large discourse, *This individuall Angell* may be nothing else then a *Moderator of a company of Presbyters*, having onely a superiority of order, and this also mutable and changeable, according as *Paræus* and *Beza* hold, whom you follow in this interpretation.'[62]

It would be unhelpful to suggest that the Smectymnuan tracts propose that diocesan episcopacy should be reduced to primitive episcopacy rather than that they are a Presbyterian manifesto. It is perhaps more helpful to conclude that they emerge from the school in favour of primitive episcopacy, a school that had been driven to a more radical position by the experience of the 1630s. At the same time, it is worth considering the target audience. Even the most optimistic of the Smectymnuans cannot have expected to have achieved the conversion of Joseph Hall; perhaps it might have been seen as a way to encourage the moderate godly to take the first step away from diocesan episcopacy. That such clerics existed is shown by a petition of ministers from London and its suburbs, addressed to Charles, expressing disapproval of the 'reproach and miserie' of the 1630s, worse than that of 'Monks, Fryars, and Nuns of former times have been' but without calling for any ecclesiological changes.[63] This approach is made explicit in the correspondence of Sir Robert Harley at the beginning of the Long Parliament. Stanley Gower hoped for the complete abolition of episcopacy, but was willing to live under bishops, provided there was, at least 'much alteration' of their powers. Similarly, his colleague, William Voyle, suggested in December 1640 that it was perhaps politic to 'yield (in part) to the bishops'. Such was the tone of a survey drawn up by Gower relating to the Herefordshire clergy, asking for the total abolition of episcopacy or at least limitations upon their power, requiring responsibilities to be shared with the presbyters.[64] There are hints of support for Presbyterianism in the tracts by Smectymnuus, but the possibility of reduced episcopacy is still present and may have been seen as something that was likely to prove more attractive to moderates. Once we bear in mind the presence of a constituency in favour of primitive episcopacy, in moderate and extreme forms, the retention of this possibility becomes more comprehensible.

---

[62] Ibid., pp. 158–9.

[63] NRO Isham (Lamport) MSS 3381. This petition is considerably mutilated and there are no signatures attached.

[64] BL Add MS 70002 f. 363; J. Eales, *Puritans and Roundheads: the Harleys of Brampton Bryan and the Outbreak of the English Civil War* (Cambridge, 1990) pp. 110–11.

IV

Where, then, are the Presbyterians to be found? R. S. Paul surveyed the question for the period before the Westminster Assembly and concluded that 'the best way to discover the early Presbyterians is to start with the Smectymnuans'. It will be clear that there is evidence to the contrary, at least for 1641. Alternatively, he suggested that 'we do get hints that there may have been a group of London ministers in and around London with whom the Scots had been collaborating for some time', and that among this group we may find 'committed Presbyterians'.[65] This proves difficult to sustain when it becomes clear that the most prominent men in these contacts were Burges, of whom Baillie complained that he was 'too much Episcopall', Calamy and Twisse, both inclined to reduced episcopacy, and John Goodwin, at this stage an Amesian of the stamp of John Ball.[66] Goodwin was to distinguish himself as a radical Congregationalist, but most of those who can be shown to have been moderate Amesians in the late 1630s became Presbyterians. Ball died in 1640, but his work was adopted by survivors of the 1637 exchange for the Presbyterian cause in 1643, edited by Simeon Ashe and William Rathband. Ball was to be hailed as 'the Presbyters' champion' by a group of ministers who published his *Treatise of the Covenant of Grace* in 1645.[67] Among these divines are ex-moderate episcopalians and ex-Amesians, the former including Calamy and Thomas Hill, the latter including Daniel Cawdrey.[68] What was to become English Presbyterianism was a fragile and fluid alliance of these two groups. The great divide in the English godly ministry did not simply split Presbyterians and Congregationalists along established lines that we might call 'proto-Presbyterian' and 'proto-Congregationalist'. Rather, there were two splits, one that divided those in favour of a reduced episcopacy between moderates with increasingly conservative fears, and slightly less moderate men who embraced change with rather more enthusiasm. This division straddled the greater gulf that made ministers choose sides

---

[65] R. S. Paul, *Assembly of the Lord*, pp. 111–21. Paul does acknowledge the difficulties involved.

[66] SP 16/463/54; 458/19; 467/92, 93, 96, 100. Twisse contributed Rivet's disapproval of *jure divino* episcopacy to the Smectymnuans: Smectymnuus, *A Vindication*, p. 219. In an undated letter, evidently of the late 1630s, briefing William Cunningham for his work in England, Baillie advised him to get in touch with Samuel Ward at Cambridge, John Prideaux in Oxford and Richard Holdsworth, Daniel Featley and Cornelius Burges in London, hardly a set of Presbyterian activists: Baillie, *Letters and Journals*, vol. I pp. 285–6.

[67] John Ball, *A Treatise of the Covenant of Grace* (1645) preface, n.p.

[68] Cawdrey had been trained with Hooker and Ames under Alexander Richardson: GLRO DL/C 340 f. 210; DL/C 324 f. 2 and above, p. 30. His arguments against Cotton are similar to Ball's: Daniel Cawdrey, *Vindicae Clavium* (1645) *passim*, and esp. p. 79.

between King and Parliament. The second split was between Amesians, and might cautiously be characterised as between church-type Amesians and sect-type Amesians, between the nonconformist tradition of Dod, Ball and Hooker and the 'sectarian' tendencies of Cotton and Thomas Goodwin.

Some of these painful divisions had taken place by the third quarter of 1641. We have already seen that divisions among Amesians were apparent in the late 1630s, and gaps were clearer between moderate episcopalians by the middle of the year. For those godly ministers who remained to debate ecclesiology within the parliamentarian pale, the argument was not yet cast as Presbyterian against Congregationalist, but there was evidence that it was coming to be so. The first published evidence of such a split comes from Henry Burton's *Protestation Protested* and the reply of Thomas Edwards. In Edwards we can see the transition of an Amesian into a Presbyterian. He had begun to study ecclesiology in the aftermath of the exchange between Ball and the Massachusetts ministers, and his answer to Burton shows that he was aware of the exchange. He stressed that

the greatest Non-conformists and most able in that way, have writ the most against you, and laboured upon all occasions to preserve people from falling to you, as Mr Cartwright, Mr Brightman, Mr Parker, Mr Hildersham, Dr Ames, Mr Bradshaw, Mr Ball, Mr Dod, Mr Baines, with many others.[69]

Edwards repeatedly cited Ames approvingly, on ordination, on non-separation and on the 'need of direction and helpe of Presbyters both of the same Church, and for the most part of the Neighbour Churches'.[70] In his discussion of 'consociation' of churches he notes that 'Amesius showes that the light of Nature requires, that particular Churches may and ought to continue in Synods, for things of greater moment', but also cites Scottish testimony and, in discussing Acts 15.1–2, asserts that consociations of ministers can determine matters according to the Word, 'to which all those Churches should submit'.[71] It may be the case that some of this citation comes from a competition between the protagonists over the place of Ames in the ecclesiological spectrum. We can see this at its most extreme in John Paget's claim that Ames was a Presbyterian; perhaps it also lies behind the attribution of William Bradshaw's *English Puritanisme* to Ames, his translator, in the 1641 edition.[72]

The new edition of *English Puritanisme*, it must be noted, was more than

---

[69] For his ecclesiological study, Thomas Edwards, *Antapologia: or, a Full Answer to the Apologeticall Narration* (1644) 'To the Tender Conscienced, Scrupulous, Doubting Christian', Sig. Av; Edwards, *Reasons against the Independent Government of Particular Churches* (1641) pp. 32, 51.

[70] Ibid., pp. 5–6, 46.   [71] Ibid., pp. 10–13, 15ff., quoted at p. 13.

[72] John Paget, *A Defence of Church Government in Presbyteriall, Classicall, and Synodall Assemblies* (1641) preface; William Ames [sic], *English Puritanisme* (1641).

a reprint of the original tract. There were some crucial modifications, taking it beyond the Amesian ecclesiology towards the New England order. Bradshaw had included a section which authorised kings and the nobility to decorate their churches, that their *'Chappells, and Seats may be gorgeously sett forth with rich Arrace and Tapestrie, Their Fonts may be of Silver'*. Communion vessels could be gilded and ministers could wear silk and velvet. This permission was omitted in 1640, perhaps as a response to the 'beauty of holiness'.[73] Ecclesiologically, ministers were to be more tightly bound to their congregations; in 1640, they could no longer 'Officially administer in another'.[74] The authority of the laity was enhanced, for where the first edition had mentioned *'Pastors of particular Congregations'* as *'the highest Spirituall Officers in the Church'*, 1640 included 'Pastors, Teachers and ruling Elders'.[75] A slight, but crucial, change of tone gave the new edition a more sectarian stance. In 1605, unrepentant sinners were to be excluded from the sacrament; in 1640, they were to be ejected from the congregation. For Bradshaw, the role of the Doctor was *'to instruct by way of Catechizing the Ignorant of the Congregation'*; in 1640, it was to 'instruct by opening the sense of Scripture [to] the Congregation (and that particularly) in the maine grounds and principles of Religion'. Finally, the definition of a true visible church in the 1605 edition was simply an *'Assemblie of men, ordinarilie ioyning together in the true worship of God'*; in 1640 they had become an 'Assemblie of true beleevers'.[76] Taken together, these changes imply that the congregation consisted of established confessing saints already understanding their faith and only requiring more advanced exegeses.

The flurry of pamphlets that followed Burton's publication was a great embarrassment to the godly ministers, especially as Thomas Goodwin and his colleagues were now in London and campaigning for their polity. In September, Hugh Peter and Thomas Weld returned from New England to raise money for Massachusetts and added their voices.[77] The fears of ecclesiological disagreements were not solely concerned with internal arguments among the godly. In a response to a petition in favour of episcopacy, published in June 1641, the authors responded at great length to the article, pointing out that those who were in favour of the abolition of bishops 'have not yet agreed, nor (as we are verily perswaded) ever will or can agree upon any other Common forme of government to suceed in the

---

[73] Bradshaw, pp. 9–10.   [74] Ibid., p. 7; Ames, p. 8.
[75] Bradshaw, p. 12; Ames, p. 11.
[76] Bradshaw, pp. 30–1, 21, 5; Ames, pp. 27–8, 19, 7.
[77] R. D. Bradley, '"Jacob and Esau Struggling in the Womb": a Study of Presbyterian and Independent Religious Conflicts, 1640–48', University of Kent PhD (1975) pp. 29–31; M. Watts, *The Dissenters*, pp. 83–9; R. P. Stearns, *The Strenuous Puritan: Hugh Peter 1598–1660* (Urbana, Ill., 1954) p. 153; Edwards, *Antapologia*, p. 242.

roome of it, as appeares by the many different and contrary draughts, and platformes they have made and published, according to the severall humours and sects of those that made them'.[78] The respondents, apparently including Thomas Goodwin and Jeremiah Burroughes, with the assistance of Alexander Henderson and the approval of Robert Baillie, repeated the arguments employed by Smectymnuus, drawing attention to the differences between Scriptural bishops and present ones, citing Bucer's *de Regno Christi* and Reynolds' letter.[79] They closed with a survey of the areas in which there was no dispute among the godly, taking a definition of a particular church which combined the forms laid down in Cartwright's *Directory* and in the new edition of Bradshaw's *English Puritanisme*. The helpful resource of a *classis* was recognised, albeit as a matter of *bene esse* rather than *esse*, and their decisions made dependent on the 'common advice and consent' of the particular churches.[80] In all, this was a superbly constructed presentation of unity, masking the issues that were to prove irreconcilable in the Westminster Assembly. However, this stance had to be extended to minimise the attraction of this line to ecclesiological conservatives. The possibility of division and its dangers became still more acute after news of the Irish Rebellion reached the capital, and at some stage in November 1641 a meeting was called at Edmund Calamy's house.

The meeting seems to have been open only to the English reformers; even the Massachusetts ministers were excluded, although their sermons were discussed, and the Scots commissioners do not seem to have been present. It is clear that a considerable number of ministers attended, for some of the business was handled by a smaller sub-committee; Edwards describes it as 'a full and great meeting'. Calamy, Thomas Goodwin, Nye, Burroughes, Simpson and Bridge were all there, as were Edwards, John Goodwin, John Vicars and William Rathband, and it would be very surprising if Marshall, Newcomen and the other ministers associated with Calamy had not been. All present were 'sensible how much our differences, and divisions might distract the Parliament, and hinder the taking away of Episcopall government'. They agreed to continue to use parts of the liturgy in order to disarm episcopal criticisms, and sent for some ministers who were resolved to abandon the Book of Common Prayer altogether and dissuaded them. Some ministers were delegated to try to persuade the sectaries to take a lower profile. Finally, an agreement was made for a general silence on

[78] *The Petition for the Prelates Briefly Examined* (1641) p. 5. The date is drawn from G. K. Fortescue (ed.), *Catalogue of . . . George Thomason* (London, 1908) vol. I p. 19.

[79] *The Petition*, pp. 8, 23–4; for the suggested authors, see F. Bremer, *Congregational Communion: Clerical Friendship in the Anglo-American Puritan Community, 1610–1692* (Boston, Mass., 1994) p. 132.

[80] *The Petition*, pp. 31–2.

positive issues of church government. All the ministers undertook to preach against Anabaptists and Brownists, and a sub-committee drew up a frame of agreement to this effect, which all present signed.[81]

However, the agreement became a bone of contention: there were arguments over who broke it first, and Philip Nye was accused of taking what seems to have been the only copy to Hull and leaving it there, when it had been agreed that it should remain in Calamy's hands. What is far more significant is that November 1641 brought a recognition, for the first time, that unity was no longer sustainable without a formal agreement and that the diaspora that had spread the godly ministers from the Netherlands to New England involved an ideological diaspora of no lesser magnitude.

In the time following the agreement the godly ministers fell silent on the specifics of governmental reform. The fast sermons delivered to Parliament were full of calls for an energetic approach to ecclesiological change but without setting out the results that the ministers desired. The vow of silence was evaded in the press in two ways. Firstly, a number of writings from former times were reissued or even published for the first time. We have already noted the new edition of Bradshaw's *English Puritanisme*, the publication of Bucer's opinions on bishops and Reynold's letter to Francis Knollys. These were joined by Baynes' *Diocesans Triall*, Martin Marprelate's attack on Bishop Cooper, speeches of Francis Knollys on the issue, the opinions of the English representatives at the Synod of Dort on government, a petition to the Privy Council of 1590 and by an account of the Presbyterianism established in the Channel Islands.[82] Secondly, each side could look to external sources to promote their views. The Congregationalists could look to New England and this proved a very productive source of tracts in favour of Congregationalism written by ministers free from the agreement. Works on practical divinity appeared from John Cotton, Thomas Shepard and Thomas Hooker, perhaps partly to remind the

---

[81] Thomas Goodwin, Philip Nye, Sidrach Simpson, Jeremiah Burroughes and William Bridge, *An Apologeticall Narration, Humbly Submitted to the Honourable Houses of Parliament* (1643) p. 3; Edwards, *Antapologia*, pp. 238–43; John Vicars, *The Schismatick Sifted* (1646) pp. 15–17; John Goodwin, *Anapologesiates Antapologias* (1646) p. 252; William Rathband, *A Briefe Narration of some Church Course* (1644) 'Preface to the Reader', Sig. A2.

[82] Paul Baynes, *Diocesans Triall* (1641); Martin Marprelate, *Hay any Worke for Cooper: or a Briefe Pistle Directed by Waye of an Hublication to the Reverend Byshopps* (1641); *Speeches Used in the Parliament by Sir F. Knowles, and Written to my Lord Treasurer Sir W. Cecill* (1642); *The Opinion of the Doctors and Divines at the Synod of Dort concerning Episcopacy and Lay-elders* (1642); *An Humble Motion Made in the Reigne of Queen Elizabeth to the Privy Councell, for the Reforming of Ecclesiasticall Discipline and Church Government Printed 1590* (1641); *The Orders for Ecclesiastical Discipline, according to that which Hath Been Practised since the Reformation of the Church in his Majesties Dominions, by the Ancient Ministers, Elders, and Deacons of the Isles of Garnsey, Gersey, Spark* (1642).

English readers of New England's soteriological orthodoxy. John Cotton was the most active speaker for the Congregationalists, although he was joined by John Davenport, Shepard and Richard Mather, and Thomas Hooker's *Survey of the Summe of Church Discipline* was a late contribution, engaging with Charles Herle's *Independency on Scriptures*, the first draft having been lost in manuscript in its voyage across the Atlantic.[83] The Presbyterians could turn to reformed churches in Europe. They seem to have been a little less well organised than the Congregationalists, although Robert Baillie was constantly writing to William Spang in the Netherlands to encourage him to work through the Walcheran *classis* to produce helpful publications and letters to the Westminster Assembly.[84] Although no positive evidence of any request for them seems to exist, there are a striking number of treatises from Presbyterian sympathisers such as John Paget in the Netherlands, the French theologians Louis Du Moulin and Denis Petau, and the Bohemian Abraham Scultetus.[85] In short, the battle lines of the Westminster Assembly were being drawn.

[83] F. Bremer, *Congregational Communion*, pp. 145–51.
[84] Baillie, *Letters and Journals*, vol. II, pp. 75, 143–4, 169–70, 179–80, 184, 253–4.
[85] John Paget, *A Defence of Church-Government in Presbyteriall, Classical, and Synodall Assemblies* (1641); Denis Petau, *D. Petavii . . . Dissertationum Ecclesiasticarum libri dou* (1641); Irenæus Philadelphus, *Vox Populi Expressed in XXXV. Motions to this Present Parliament . . . for Reforming the Present Corrupt State of the Church* (1641); *Motions for Reforming the Church of England: most Taken Out of Irenæus Philadelphus* (1641); Christianus Alethocritus, *Consilium de Reformanda ecclesia Anglicana* (1642) ('Philadelphus' and 'Alethocritus' were pseudonyms for Du Moulin); Abraham Scultetus, *The Determination of the Question, concerning the Divine Right of Episcopacie* (1641).

18

Conclusion

It would not be true to say that the details of the final shape of the Puritan diaspora were inherent in the failed agreement subscribed at Edmund Calamy's house, but the main lines of development had been laid down. The Presbyterian alliance was to remain an unstable amalgam, driven forward by the energy and purpose of the Scots, and efforts for brotherly accommodation were to remain part of the programme of the godly ministers and were to continue, one might say, into the era of the 'Free Churches'. In late 1641, some of the ministers who have been prominent in this account had some of the most active years of their ministry ahead of them, and some of the ministers had much further to travel ideologically, but if the 1630s, the years of persecution, had been divisive, the 1640s, the years of triumph, were to prove decisively so. Moreover, the divisive possibilities of the 1630s were matched by a strenuous effort to maintain the ideal of the godly community, prompted, ironically, by the common enemy of Laudianism. The need, outlined by Arthur Hildersham, that 'Though we differ in iudgement in these things, yet should we endeavour, that the people may discerne no difference, nor disagreements among us',[1] that is, to maintain the visible boundary between godly and ungodly, was more intense in a period of perceived persecution and, to some degree, was successfully met. What proved to be a fatal challenge to the boundaries of godly community was the starkly contrasting position of the 1640s. Persecution operated as a unifying influence; an element of freedom and power provided by the 1640s led to the potential divisions becoming actual divisions.[2]

We have touched upon the emerging disagreements on ecclesiological matters, but among the unforeseen consequences of the end of the personal

---

[1] A. P. Cohen, *The Symbolic Construction of Community* (Chichester, 1993) pp. 20, 74; Arthur Hildersham, *CVIII Lectures upon the Fourth of John* (1632) p. 301.

[2] For a stimulating discussion of the maintenance of boundaries of collective identity, see A. P. Cohen, 'Of symbols and Boundaries, or, Does Ertie's Greatcoat Hold the Key?', in A. P. Cohen (ed.), *Symbolising Boundaries: Identity and Diversity in British Cultures* (Manchester, 1986) pp. 1–19.

rule of Charles I were different tones in piety, theology and spiritual hermeneutics, with the godly spectrum of the post-Restoration ranging from Anglicans with reservations, through Presbyterians committed to an ideal of a national erastian church to Quakers and Unitarians, from Calvinists such as John Owen to Arminians and quasi-Arminians such as Richard Baxter and John Goodwin and from prophets at the centre like Hugh Peter to parochial ministers struggling to foster godly ideals at the parish level such as Ralph Josselin. The details of these diverging trails need to be more thoroughly investigated and located in the intellectual and moral trials of the years of ferment. At this point, however, it is more profitable to take a retrospective glance and to assess some of the grounds for the developments that we have tried to describe in this study.

It has proved possible to trace a network of godly divines in early Stuart England, similar to William Haller's 'spiritual brotherhood',[3] but going far beyond the great names of Sibbes, Gouge, Preston and Dod to draw in the humblest of the painful preachers and the most junior of the aspirant ministers coming out of Oxford and Cambridge. This network need not be seen as a seventeenth-century conspiracy meeting in dark corners to bring down the ecclesiastical establishment, so much as a profession in the process of defining its role and spiritually improving its members through endeavours that were neither wholly within the official life of the church nor wholly opposed to it. The model of 'natural' professional collegiality, however, is not quite adequate and entails a certain amount of violence to the ministers' conception of their task. As well as recreating the network, we must pay attention to the ways in which young divines were inducted into the spiritual brotherhood. Here the practices of fasting and prayer, days of humiliation, profitable conferences and exercises for the extended household force us to remember that this was always a religious enterprise. It was rooted in what Peter Lake has called a 'certain evangelical protestant world-view' predicated upon the 'potentially transforming effects of the gospel on both individuals and on the social order as a whole'. It is Lake's contention that if Puritanism is to be defined at all it must be in terms of this 'spiritual dynamic'.[4] This much is true, but the nature of that spiritual dynamic, a sense of communion with God, Scripturally informed, deeply emotional and yet aspiring to something beyond the subjective, brought insecurities that give us ways of linking that world view to the arena in which it was enacted. The collective insecurity of the godly ministers, a frailty that was itself necessary if a perceived Assurance was to be anything more than carnal security and formal hypocrisy, made necessary the forms

---

[3] W. Haller, *The Rise of Puritanism* (New York, 1938) ch. 1.
[4] P. Lake, *Moderate Puritans and the Elizabethan Church* (Cambridge, 1982) pp. 279, 282–3.

of the spiritual brotherhood. The days of fasting and prayer and all the other voluntary religious exercises were designed to service the lonely search for evidence of Election. These forms, rooted in Lake's spiritual dynamic, allow a definition of Puritanism that draws more fully upon a complementary *social* dynamic that may be helpful in understanding the social contexts in which terms of abuse such as 'Puritan' were current.

It has been something of a difficulty for the literature on this subject to find an understanding of the Puritans that does not either elide with 'mere' English Protestantism or equate the Puritans with nonconformity and use that to seek what was distinctive about them. This seems to me rather to put the cart before the horse: for those ministers who felt that the ceremonies were an unconscionable imposition, and it has become clear that this was not the conclusion of all ministers recognised as godly, this conviction grew out of, and was consequent upon, the search for a valid religious experience as the ceremonies were seen to be a stumbling block which made it more difficult to pursue that goal. Indeed, the debates and actions of the godly ministers in the 1630s have revealed that such convictions were not written in stone. On both sides, these matters were conditional, with ministers such as William Leigh prepared to assuage their scruples to preserve their opportunity to preach, and ministers such as Goodwin *et al.* driven to abandon their compromises with conformity in the light of the ecclesiastical changes of the decade. It is in the lessons we have learned from these men that I am proposing that we add the term 'conformable' to our vocabulary, the sense that those godly clergy who conformed did so conditionally, that they accepted the *status quo* provided that it was not pushed too hard.

Similar remarks may be made with respect to those ministers who made true discipline in church government a further goal. The difficulties encountered in characterising schemes such as Thomas Hooker's conference may in part follow from the difficulties of understanding the mind that makes what we see as secular, administrative decision-making as an essentially spiritual matter to be undertaken in days of fasting and prayer. The purpose of Scripturally ordained church government was equally important as an aid to the realisation and assurance of salvation.

The ways in which the network fragmented or actively tore itself apart similarly have to be approached through a social dynamic. Though neither so complete, nor so clear, as the inevitable schematic structure of concluding remarks might suggest, some of the forms of the diaspora resemble, in a demonic mirror-image, the forms of sociability that characterised earlier godly groups. One of the central battlefields was the role of the conference, the formalisation of the regular practices of voluntary religion. John Cotton asked his reader, perhaps a little disingenuously, to

Consider again what the great chasm . . . is which has separated the two groups as effectively as a party wall . . . Like you we recognise and honor synods when there may be need for them. What small thing is it that remains to keep us apart? The acts of government which you wish to have performed by synods, these we seek to have given over by the synods to the churches and performed by the churches with synodal correction.[5]

By the time Cotton wrote this, it had become a common theme in godly writings to decry the contrasting divisions of the 1640s, which had replaced a perceived pre-war unity. This theme appeared in the *Certaine Considerations*, signed by Congregationalists and Presbyterians to plead for an end to the foundation of Separatist churches: 'beside the raging of the sword devouring us every where, our miseries increased by the severall ways of Brethren, and that many of those we dearely love in the Lord, are at this time entring themselves into Church-societies'.[6] Simeon Ashe had a tone of desperation when he asked: 'What Factions and Fractions, what Schismes and Separations, what rents and divisions are in this poore, distracted, distressed Church of *England*!'[7] William Strong struck a telling, optimistic note in his eschatological vision of 1647 when he entered into a series of predictions about 'this last Church'. He claimed that, 'There shall be a perfect and sweet Communion one with another; as Communion with God growes; so doth the Communion of Saints grow; the neerer the lives are to the Center, the neerer they come one to another. All divisions shall be taken away about the ways of worship, *Jehovah shall be one, and his name one* . . .'.[8] Stephen Marshall's mournful voice of the same time was probably more representative, certainly of the Presbyterians:

Our times are times of Divisions; such Divisions, as (I thinke) were hardly ever knowne in the Christian World; Divisions every where, divisions in Parliament, divisions in the Assembly, divisions in the Citie, divisions in State affaires; but woe and alasse, most of all, and worst of all, divisions among Gods people, the Servants of God who heretofore prayed together, fasted together, could have been banished together.[9]

There is a striking resemblance between the arguments over synodical authority in the 1640s and earlier, continental disputes over the Eucharist,

---

[5] John Cotton, 'Foreword', in John Norton, *The Answer* (1652) (ed. and trans. D. Horton) (Cambridge, Mass., 1958).

[6] *Certaine Considerations to Diswade Men from Further Gathering of Churches in this Present Juncture of Time* (1643) p. 1. The plea was signed by William Twisse, Thomas Goodwin, John White, Oliver Bowles, Stephen Marshall, Philip Nye, Charles Herle, Anthony Tuckney, John Arrowsmith, William Bridge, Thomas Young, William Carter, Herbert Palmer, Sidrach Simpson, William Greenhill, Jeremiah Burroughes, Richard Heyrick, Joseph Caryl, Thomas Hill, Thomas Wilson and Jeremiah Whitaker.

[7] Simeon Ashe, *The Church Sinking* (1645) p. 32.

[8] William Strong, *The Trust and Account of a Steward* (1647) p. 29.

[9] Stephen Marshall, *The Right Understanding of the Times* (1647) p. 36.

particularly in Geneva, what John Bossy has identified as 'the seeming fatality whereby reformed rituals of society transformed themselves into rituals of exclusion'.[10] In the same way, the issue of the *classis*, of discipline, became the single issue which divided where it had formerly united. The earlier forms had brought together all the heterogeneous positions held among the godly ministry, but in the 1640s what had been, and should have been, a rite of communality became a rite of exclusion.

One question that has not been addressed in any detail is why individual ministers adopted the positions that divided them from erstwhile friends. One approach, which has dominated much of the work in this area, is the genetic, tracing lines of contact and exchange and following ideas, as if they were viruses, along these lines. This approach, attractive as it is, does not seem to me to be sufficient. It is evident that there was room in the sociable world of the godly ministry for clerics of many different inclinations, and the ambiguities of this world allowed contacts and exchanges between men of contrasting positions. It is not self-evident that acquaintance with, or even tutelage from, a minister of a particular position necessarily led to a similar position being adopted by the friend or pupil. John Beadle, for instance, benefited from the 'droppings of the Elijah', Thomas Hooker, but made his later commitment to Presbyterianism clear in his late published work. It seems that intellectual allegiances were not a function of prior social connections.[11] Neither have I found entirely convincing the suggestion, exemplified by Stanley Fienberg, that ecclesiological divisions may be traced to a Congregational concentration on Christological salvation, a Biblicist tendency and an enhanced Millenarianism held in contrast to Presbyterians.[12] Perhaps a rather more fruitful approach would be a more intense study of local conditions, combined with a more detailed diachronic approach that allowed for the interaction of local experience and the pressures of the 1640s.[13] This is not to deny the autonomy of the ideas involved, to assert some form of 'ecclesiological determinism', only to attempt a more comprehensive integration of the social and spiritual dynamics that generated and, to some degree, controlled Puritanism.

To avoid ending this study with a recognition of a question we have failed to answer, I want to close with a suggestion of our principal

---

[10] J. Bossy, *Christianity in the West 1400–1700* (Oxford, 1987) p. 141.

[11] I am particularly grateful to Frank Bremer for our lengthy discussions on this issue, although he would not agree with my conclusions.

[12] S. P. Fienberg, 'Thomas Goodwin's Scriptural Hermenuetics and the Dissolution of Puritan Unity,' *JRH* 10 (1978–79) pp. 32–49; cf. T. Liu, *Discord in Zion: the Puritan Divines and the Puritan Revolution 1640–1660* (The Hague, 1973).

[13] This will be among the subjects of a study of Wethersfield, Braintree and Finchingfield on which I am currently working.

conclusion from this study. While our understanding of the early Stuart church has benefited hugely from a greater apprehension of the areas of common ground throughout the Church of England, this is not the whole story. Given the active, carefully nurtured godly clerical society, rooted in spiritual needs, given the ability of this community to organise, communicate and to foster a sense of embattled minority with a mission to change the spiritual state of the country and given the collective consciousness evinced by the common sense of persecution of the 1630s, we have what can accurately be referred to as an early Stuart Puritan movement. The means of this movement were different those of their forebears, concentrating on the particular, both individual and parochial, on producing better ministers through colleges, seminaries and pastoral care, rather than delivering petitions and admonitions to monarch and Parliament, but a movement nonetheless. That this movement failed to transform England into a wholly godly society may come as no surprise; at the very least, we should recognise that the Stuart Puritans made a strenuous, determined and protracted effort to do so.

INDEX

Cambridge Studies in Early Modern History

*Also published as a paperback